TRANSLATING THE BIBLE

TRANSLATING THE BIBLE

Problems and Prospects

edited by

STANLEY E. PORTER & RICHARD S. HESS

T&T CLARK INTERNATIONAL
A Continuum imprint
LONDON • NEW YORK

Published by T&T Clark International
A Continuum imprint
The Tower Building, 11 York Road, London SE1 7NX
15 East 26th Street, Suite 1703, New York, NY 10010

www.tandtclark.com

British Library Cataloguing-in-Publication Data
A catalogue record for this book is available from the British Library

ISBN 0567042901 (paperback)

Typeset by Sheffield Academic Press
Printed on acid-free paper in Great Britain by Cromwell Press Ltd, Trowbridge,
Wilts

CONTENTS

Part III
NEW TESTAMENT

ABBREVIATIONS

AB	Anchor Bible
ABD	David Noel Freedman (ed.), *The Anchor Bible Dictionary* (New York: Doubleday, 1992)
ABS	American Bible Society
AnBib	Analecta biblica
ASV	American Standard Version
AV	Authorized Version
BA	*Biblical Archaeologist*
BAGD	Walter Bauer, William F. Arndt, F. William Gingrich and Frederick W. Danker, *A Greek–English Lexicon of the New Testament and Other Early Christian Literature* (Chicago: University of Chicago Press, 2nd edn, 1958)
BARev	*Biblical Archaeology Review*
BASOR	*Bulletin of the American Schools of Oriental Research*
BHS	*Biblia hebraica stuttgartensia*
Bib	*Biblica*
BibRev	*Biblical Review*
BibTrans	*The Bible Translator*
BJRL	*Bulletin of the John Rylands University Library of Manchester*
BLG	Biblical Languages: Greek
CBQ	*Catholic Biblical Quarterly*
CEV	Contemporary English Version
ConBOT	Coniectanea biblica, Old Testament
EFN	Estudios de Filología Neotestamentaria
ERT	*Evangelical Review of Theology*
EvQ	*Evangelical Quarterly*
ExpTim	*Expository Times*
FN	*Filología neotestamentaria*
GBS	Guides to Biblical Scholarship
GNB	*Good News Bible*
HAR	*Hebrew Annual Review*
HAT	Handbuch zum Alten Testament
HTR	*Harvard Theological Review*
HUCA	*Hebrew Union College Annual*
HUT	Hermeneutische Untersuchungen zur Theologie
ICC	International Critical Commentary
IDBSup	*IDB*, Supplementary Volume
Int	*Interpretation*

JAL	Jewish Apocryphal Literature
JB	*Jerusalem Bible*
JBL	*Journal of Biblical Literature*
JETS	*Journal of the Evangelical Theological Society*
JR	*Journal of Religion*
JSJ	*Journal for the Study of Judaism in the Persian, Hellenistic and Roman Period*
JSNT	*Journal for the Study of the New Testament*
JSNTSup	*Journal for the Study of the New Testament*, Supplement Series
JSOT	*Journal for the Study of the Old Testament*
JSOTSup	*Journal for the Study of the Old Testament*, Supplement Series
JTS	*Journal of Theological Studies*
KJV	King James Version
LCL	Loeb Classical Library
LSJ	H.G. Liddell, Robert Scott and H. Stuart Jones, *Greek–English Lexicon* (Oxford: Clarendon Press, 9th edn, 1968)
McCQ	*McCormick Quarterly*
NASB	*New American Standard Bible*
NCB	New Century Bible
NEB	*New English Bible*
NICNT	New International Commentary on the New Testament
NIGTC	The New International Greek Testament Commentary
NIV	New International Version
NJB	*New Jerusalem Bible*
NKJV	New King James Version
NovT	*Novum Testamentum*
NRSV	New Revised Standard Version
NTL	New Testament Library
NTS	*New Testament Studies*
NTTS	New Testament Tools and Studies
OBO	Orbis biblicus et orientalis
OTL	Old Testament Library
OTM	Oxford Theological Monographs
OTP	James Charlesworth (ed.), *Old Testament Pseudepigrapha*
PGM	K. Preisendanz (ed.), *Papyri graecae magicae*
REB	Revised English Bible
RILP	Roehampton Institute London Papers
RSV	Revised Standard Version
SBG	Studies in Biblical Greek
SBL	Society of Biblical Literature
SBLDS	SBL Dissertation Series
SBLMS	SBL Monograph Series
SBLSCS	SBL Septuagint and Cognate Studies
SD	Studies and Documents
SIL	Summer Institute of Linguistics
SJT	*Scottish Journal of Theology*
SNTSMS	Society for New Testament Studies Monograph Series
SPIB	Scripta Pontificii Instituti Biblici

StudEv	*Studia Evangelica*
StudPat	*Studia Patristica*
TEV	Today's English Version
TTod	*Theology Today*
TOTC	Tyndale Old Testament Commentaries
TU	Texte und Untersuchungen
TynBul	*Tyndale Bulletin*
UBSGNT	United Bible Societies' *Greek New Testament*
USQR	*Union Seminary Quarterly Review*
VT	*Vetus Testamentum*
VTSup	*Vetus Testamentum*, Supplements
WBC	Word Biblical Commentary
ZAW	*Zeitschrift für die alttestamentliche Wissenschaft*

CONTRIBUTORS

Craig D. Allert, University of Nottingham, England

Kent D. Clarke, University of Bristol, England

Thomas R. Hatina, Trinity Western University, Langley, BC, Canada

Richard S. Hess, Denver Seminary, Colorado, USA

Gustavo Martín-Asensio, Roehampton Institute London, England

Matthew Brook O'Donnell, Roehampton Institute London, England

Brook W.R. Pearson, Roehampton Institute London, England

Stanley E. Porter, Roehampton Institute London, England

J.W. Rogerson, University of Sheffield, England

Y.C. Whang, Roehampton Institute London, England

INTRODUCTION:
THE PROBLEMS AND PROSPECTS OF TRANSLATING THE BIBLE

Stanley E. Porter and Richard S. Hess

In September of 1995, Dr Eugene A. Nida visited the Centre for Advanced Theological Research of Roehampton Institute London, to address the Biblical Studies Research Cluster on a number of issues regarding translational theory and practice. His three days of lectures and discussion covered, at his own request, the following topics: Sociolinguistics and Translation, a New View of Grammar, and Lexicography and Semantics. At the time of the lectures, there was plenty of useful discussion of various issues raised by Dr Nida, especially as they had direct bearing on matters of biblical interpretation and translation.

The discussion generated by those three days of intensive lectures continued, however, in the form of a research project within the Centre. In the course of the next several years, many connected with the Biblical Studies Research Cluster wished further to address issues related to matters of translation in papers presented to the Cluster at its regular meetings. The result is this collection of essays, dealing with many of the problems and prospects of translating the Bible. As the essays reveal, one of the most exciting and challenging tasks that anyone who studies the Bible faces is the question of how the words and texts are to be understood. Not only is this an invigorating task, but it is one that must confront a number of controversial and unsettled issues, many of them addressed in the essays in this volume. The translation and understanding of the Bible, whether by rendering it in the vernacular or through careful study of the original languages in which it was written, is an essential step in study and interpretation of the text. For this reason, it is surprising that more studies are not devoted to the questions involved in the process and the final product. It is the purpose of this collection of essays to ask such questions, to examine conclusions that others have reached, and to propose new directions and ideas in the translation of both the Old and New Testaments.

The essays are divided into three sections. Part I is concerned with Translational Theory and Method. As soon becomes obvious when investigating the issue of translation, there is much more to it than simply rendering the words of one language into the words of another. For example, questions are raised such as, how does a translation relate to other translations? Do any models exist for how to do a translation? And if so, how are they applied to a text such as the Bible, which has been translated so many times already? How do modern linguistic methods enhance or hinder the translation of an ancient text? What are the translator's responsibilities? Are there ethical implications for translating the Bible, and how can they be respected? In the first essay, Stanley Porter addresses many of these issues by examining the claims and practices of the Contemporary English Version in relation to past and present translational theory and practice. Using this recent translation as a practical instance, he asks wider questions regarding ideologies that are connected to translations, whether implicit or explicit. Y.C. Whang, a professional translator, addresses the translator's greatest dilemma, that of being responsible to reader or author. He does so from the standpoint of not only the theoretical issues, but his own widespread experience, examining what, if anything, the two have in common. The Septuagint is, of course, one of the most important translations ever made, and arguably the single most important from the ancient world. In his essay in this first section, Brook Pearson examines the traditions regarding the Septuagint as a means of gaining insights into the concept of the 'remainderless translation', and whether this is an attainable goal in the light of Nida's functional equivalence translational theory. The section ends with a theological essay by Craig Allert on how the issue of inspiration has had an effect especially on conservative theories of biblical translation, offering some important definitional distinctions as well as a solution to the problem.

In Part II, three essays address issues specific to translation of the Old Testament. As noted above, the Old Testament has been the longstanding object of translation. This does not mean that one is any closer to resolving the many issues involved in its rendering, however. As a result, there have been attempts to aid translators in their task. One such project was the now abandoned Old Testament Translator's Translation. In the first essay of this section, John Rogerson recounts his personal involvement in the Old Testament Translator's Translation. This project was designed to provide a translation, with annotations, for use by field translators. As Rogerson relates, many of the fundamental issues of translational theory, as well as other issues, ultimately proved insuperable to this project getting off the ground. Approaching the issue of translation of the Old Testament from another perspective, Richard Hess draws upon his experience of recent intensive work on Joshua and Judges to provide discussion of specific translational difficulties within these books. These begin with establishing the text for translation, and end with the debating of particular wordings.

The largest section of this volume, Part III, includes essays on issues of translation in the New Testament. A variety of issues and approaches comes to the fore, each of them debating how translation is affected by larger interpretative decisions. It is simply not enough to know the rudiments of the grammar of the original language. One must be familiar with other exegetical issues, as wide-ranging as historical backgrounds, discourse analysis and functional linguistics. In the first essay of this section, Matthew Brook O'Donnell explores the difference between types of translations, arguing for the place of an interpretative translation that reflects the results of exegesis informed by linguistic theory. He takes the narrative episode in Mk 5.1-10 as a test case, due to its implications for translation. Further endorsing the importance of linguistic modeling for translation, Gustavo Martín-Asensio defines the linguistic concept of foregrounding, and then applies it to the episode of Paul's shipwreck in Acts 27. On the basis of the linguistic structure of this text, he makes some suggestions regarding Spanish translation of the New Testament. Thomas Hatina examines the concept of verbal aspect, one that has recently been discussed in great detail, and exegetes the use of the perfect tense-form in the book of Colossians. He tests various theories by means of context, and clarifies their implications for translation. Brook Pearson draws upon issues of historical reconstruction, challenging the traditional theories regarding the situation reflected in the book of Philemon. He shows the relevance of this area for translational work by illustrating how a competing historical reconstruction can lead to other textual renderings. In the last essay, one that arguably could go at the beginning of the volume, Kent Clarke discusses the question of textual criticism from the perspective of issues regarding the canonical formation and shape of the New Testament.

Even though many, if not most, of the essays in this volume make specific proposals regarding problems of translational theory and practice, there is no definitive answer for many of the questions posed. However, these essays consider their relevance for modern translational work and suggest possibilities for enriching our enjoyment and appreciation as modern readers confronting the ancient biblical text. Dr Eugene Nida has been instrumental in promoting this discussion. Even though it will be clear that many of the contributors do not see eye-to-eye with him, many of these issues could not be discussed in this way if it were not for his work.

Part I

TRANSLATIONAL THEORY AND METHOD

THE CONTEMPORARY ENGLISH VERSION
AND THE IDEOLOGY OF TRANSLATION

Stanley E. Porter

1. *Introduction*

The history of Bible translation is charged with ideological issues.[1] For example, one of the earliest and arguably the most significant ancient translations, the Septuagint, has an apologetic mythology designed to justify its very existence.[2] With each new translation there seems to be a need to explain and justify its appearance. The same is true of the Contemporary English Version (or CEV), released in 1995 in North America and in 1996 in Britain.[3] Despite the ideological issues raised by every new translation, and in the light of the many issues raised by Eugene Nida's theories of dynamic (and now formal) equivalence Bible

---

1. I use 'ideology' in the sense shared with modern critical discussion to refer to a complex of ideas presupposed by a given perspective. In a very real sense all academic disciplines have an ideology. Here, however, the word is used somewhat pejoratively to refer to ideas that in some sense impede attempts at objective understanding.

2. This mythology was perpetuated on the basis of stories told in Eusebius (*P.E.* 13.12.1-2), Philo (*Vit. Mos.* 2.26-44), Josephus (*Ant.* 12.11-118), and especially the *Letter of Aristeas* (published by H.St.J. Thackeray in H.B. Swete, *An Introduction to the Old Testament in Greek* [Cambridge: Cambridge University Press, 1902], pp. 519-74; with translation and commentary in H.G. Meecham, *The Oldest Version of the Bible: 'Aristeas' on its Traditional Origin* [London: Holborn, 1932], pp. 12-86). See Swete, *Introduction*, pp. 1-28; S. Jellicoe, *The Septuagint and Modern Study* (Oxford: Clarendon Press, 1968), pp. 30-58 (cf. p. 59, where he cites P. Kahle as regarding the *Letter of Aristeas* to be propaganda); and M. Müller, *The First Bible of the Church: A Plea for the Septuagint* (JSOTSup, 206; Sheffield: Sheffield Academic Press, 1996), pp. 46-67.

3. *The Contemporary English Version* (Nashville and London: Thomas Nelson, 1995). This volume is abbreviated as *CEV* in the notes that follow, while the translation is cited as CEV.

translation,[4] it is not surprising that the CEV has raised a whole host of questions for discussion, many if not most of them ultimately ideologically based.[5] In this paper, I wish first to analyze how the CEV sees itself in relation to the history of Bible translation and the ideological issues suggested by this positioning, and then analyze how others, especially in the British translational heritage, view the CEV and highlight the differences in ideology raised by such a comparison.

2. *How the Contemporary English Version Sees Itself:*
History and Ideology

The best way to determine the place of the CEV within the history of translation, and with it the ideological issues that its relationship to this tradition raises, is to begin with statements that the CEV makes about itself. These are contained in two places, a 'Welcome to the Contemporary English Version', which serves as a forward, and 'The Contemporary English Version', a preface to the translation. Although the bibliographical information page makes clear that not all of the material in the printed volume is by those responsible for the translation (e.g. subject headings and maps), these two portions are. Hence they are

---

4.   His major works on translation are E.A. Nida, *Toward a Science of Translating with Special Reference to Principles and Procedures involved in Bible Translating* (Leiden: E.J. Brill, 1964); E.A. Nida and C.R. Taber, *The Theory and Practice of Translation* (Leiden: E.J. Brill, 1969); and J. De Waard and E.A. Nida, *From One Language to Another: Functional Equivalence in Bible Translating* (Nashville: Thomas Nelson, 1986). A useful critique of Nida's perspective is found in D.A. Carson, 'The Limits of Dynamic Equivalence in Bible Translation', *ERT* 9 (1985), pp. 200-13.

5.   The publication of a translation is often accompanied or followed (even if later) by some form of explanation or apologetic for it. As a far from complete set of examples concerning major translations, see G.S. Paine, *The Men behind the King James Version* (Grand Rapids: Baker Book House, 1977) (belated, but an apologetic nonetheless); A.L. Farstad, *The New King James Version: In the Great Tradition* (Nashville: Thomas Nelson, 1989; 2nd edn, 1993); B.F. Westcott, *Some Lessons of the Revised Version of the New Testament* (London: Hodder & Stoughton, 1897); C.S. Mann, *The New English New Testament: An Introduction* (London: Faith Press, 1961); G. Hunt, *About the New English Bible* (Cambridge: Oxford University Press and Cambridge University Press, 1970); E.A. Nida, *Good News for Everyone: How to Use the Good News Bible (Today's English Version)* (Waco, TX: Word Books, 1977); K.L. Barker (ed.), *The NIV: The Making of a Contemporary Translation* (Grand Rapids: Zondervan, 1986).

referred to as written by the translators. In fact, it appears that at least 'The Contemporary English Version' has been written by Barclay Newman, Senior Translation Officer of the American Bible Society and long-time associate of Nida.[6] In these two prefatory pieces, two kinds of important issues regarding the translation are raised. The first is in relation to translation theory and the second in relation to the tradition of translation, both important for positioning this new translation in regard to other translations. In essence, the CEV is clearly consistent with the dynamic or functional translational perspective of Nida and very closely akin to the TEV, but it positions itself as the legitimate heir to the intentions of the translators of the King James, or Authorized, Version. This surprising juxtaposition of perspectives clearly highlights the ideologically minded approach of the translators of the CEV, and is worth exploring in more detail.

a. *The* CEV *and the* KJV/AV
In terms of establishing its place in the history of Bible translation, the CEV, in a surprising move for a dynamic equivalence translation, wishes to be seen in complementary relation to the KJV/AV. As 'The Contemporary English Version' acknowledges, in a show of gratitude untypical of many dynamic or modern translations, 'The most important document in the history of the English language is the King James Version of the Bible'.[7] After a hyperbolic statement in which determining its impact is equated with counting grains of sand on the shore, the preface continues: 'Historically, many Bible translators have attempted in some measure to *retain the form* of the King James Version' (emphasis in original). Here conscious allusion is apparently being made to such translations as the New King James Version (1979, 1982), the Revised Version (1881), the American Standard (1901) and New American Standard (1971) Versions, the Revised Standard (1946, 1952)

---

6.   Newman has been involved in projects with and organized by Nida since at least the early 1970s, such as *A Concise Greek–English Dictionary of the New Testament* (London: United Bible Societies, 1971), as well as co-authoring a number of books, such as United Bible Societies Handbooks to various biblical books. The reason for thinking that Newman is the author of 'The Contemporary English Version' is that its outline, as well as much of its wording, is also found in B.M. Newman, 'In the Spirit of the King James Version', *Bible Collectors' World* 12.1 (1996), pp. 5-10; 12.2 (1996), pp. 5-9. Cf. his 'A New Concept in Bible Translation', *Bible Collectors' World* 11.3 (1995), pp. 5-11.

7.   *CEV*, p. vii.

and New Revised Standard (1995) Versions, to name but a few, all formal equivalence translations utilizing traditional language institutionalized by the KJV/AV and seeing themselves as some form of revision of it.[8] It is these translations, following in the line of the KJV/AV, that are largely responsible for the maintenance of the traditional language that is still often associated today with how a Bible should sound.

The translators of the CEV, however, further positioning their translation in relation to the KJV/AV, contend that 'the translators of the Contemporary English Version of the Bible have diligently sought to *capture the spirit* of the King James Version' (emphasis in original).[9] The preface of the CEV then proceeds to excerpt selected phrases from the 'The Translators to the Reader' printed in the KJV/AV as a guide to explaining their translation.[10] This is a bold and unexpected move, since most translations that have rejected much of the traditional biblical language and see themselves as modern-language translations clearly distance themselves from the KJV/AV. For example, in his introduction to the TEV, Nida himself defines the TEV largely in terms of comparing it favourably to the obscure KJV.[11] This is similarly done at the beginning of the modern translations of Weymouth, Moffatt, Rieu and Philips.[12] The fact that the CEV wishes to align itself with the KJV/

8. See D. Ewert, *From Ancient Tablets to Modern Translations: A General Introduction to the Bible* (Grand Rapids: Zondervan, 1983), pp. 204-51, for an interesting history of translations in the twentieth century.

9. *CEV*, p. vii.

10. Not surprisingly perhaps, in the light of the lack of ready availability of this document, the ABS has reprinted 'The Translators to the Reader', in E.F. Rhodes and L. Lupas (eds.), *The Translators to the Reader: The Original Preface of the King James Version of 1611 Revisited* (New York: American Bible Society, 1997). This contains a facsimile, a transcription with notes, and a modern English rendition!

11. See Nida, *Good News for Everyone*, pp. 9-16, which defines the TEV largely in terms of comparing it favourably to the obscure KJV. The same is true in Nida and Taber, *Theory and Practice*, pp. 1-11; and De Waard and Nida, *From One Language to Another*, pp. 9-11.

12. See also, for example, R.F. Weymouth, 'Preface', in E. Hampden-Cook (ed.), *The New Testament in Modern Speech* (London: J. Clarke, 1905), pp. ix-xi; J. Moffatt, 'Preface', in *The New Testament: A New Translation* (London: Hodder and Stoughton, rev. edn, n.d.), pp. v-vii; E.V. Rieu, 'Introduction', in *The Four Gospels: A New Translation* (Harmondsworth: Penguin Books, 1952), pp. x-xiv; J.B. Philips, 'Translator's Preface', in *The Gospels Translated into Modern English*

AV is no accident, as its extended utilization of the comments to the readers of the KJV/AV shows. I cannot help but think that this is an attempt to forestall the kind of criticism that has often met new translations[13] that depart from traditional biblical language by trying to take the high translational ground—the CEV is intended as the fulfilment of what the KJV/AV really meant to be. Ideologically, therefore, the CEV attempts to position itself with the KJV/AV, and a host of traditional translations.

b. *The* CEV *and Translation Theory*
The translators of the CEV are almost as forthcoming in their statements regarding their translation theory as they are regarding their purported relationship to the KJV/AV. These statements are not clearly labelled as following a particular school of translational theory nor are they enumerated, but they are evident nonetheless. They include addressing such varied issues as the priority of speech over writing, the concept of meaning, the relation of their translation to the original Hebrew and Greek texts, possible uses for the translation, including its relation to evangelization, and the issue of gender-inclusive language. After examining this assortment of topics, it will, I think, become evident that the CEV begins from a set of premises that radically distinguish it from the KJV/AV.

1. *The Priority of Speech over Writing*. The 'Welcome to the Contemporary English Version' states: 'Languages are spoken before they are written. And far more communication is done through the spoken word than through the written word.'[14] The CEV clearly positions itself within the mainstream of modern linguistics with its assertion of the priority of the spoken over the written word.[15] This basic premise, however,

(New York: Macmillan, 1957), pp. vi-vii (but not present in *The New Testament in Modern English* [London: Bles, 1960], pp. vii-xi).

13. See Ewert, *From Ancient Tablets*, pp. 213-48, and below in section 3 of this article.

14. *CEV*, p. v.

15. The number of linguists who make this point is legion, so much so that it is a truism of modern linguistics, as distinct from traditional, philologically based language study. For examples of articulation of this premise, see Nida, *Science of Translating*, pp. 123-24; Nida and Taber, *Theory and Practice*, pp. 28-31; D. Crystal, *Linguistics* (Harmondsworth: Penguin Books, 1974), pp. 22-24, 58-75; J. Lyons, *Introduction to Theoretical Linguistics* (Cambridge: Cambridge University Press, 1968), pp. 38-42.

also departs significantly from the mainstream of pre-linguistic trans-lation theory.[16] As the CEV 'Welcome' states, accurately I believe, 'Traditional translations of the Bible [and surely the KJV/AV must be placed here] count on the *reader's* ability to understand a *written* text'.[17] So far, this attitude is what one might expect of a modern-language and linguistically informed translation. It would place the CEV in the company of a number of modern-language translations, especially the TEV.

The CEV tries to go further, however. The claim is made that 'the *Contemporary English Version* differs from all other English Bibles—past and present—in that it takes into consideration the needs of the *hearer*, as well as those of the reader, who may not be familiar with traditional biblical language'.[18] This claim is an odd one to make for several reasons. The first is that it immediately undermines what has been said about its relation to the translational principles of the KJV/AV. Whereas the claim was made that the CEV was the ideological ful-filment of the KJV/AV, now it wishes to be seen as unique, differing from all other English Bibles. The second oddity is that it is in fact not true. A number of translations, even among more traditional versions, have had the needs of hearers in mind. For example, the KJV/AV, it must be remembered, was written for use in churches, when a relatively small number of people were literate enough to read it for themselves or wealthy enough to be able to afford their own Bible. Most of the original users of the KJV/AV were hearers, not readers.[19] Although it does not use the word 'hearer', the Preface to the NEB New Testament speaks of it being a translation into the 'current speech of our own time'.[20] The RSV states that it is 'intended for use in public and private worship, not merely for reading and instruction',[21] implying that it is designed to function from the perspective of hearers as well as readers. And the NIV has the ambitious goal of being a translation that can be useful for 'public and private reading, teaching, preaching, memorizing

16. See Nida, *Science of Translating*, pp. 11-26.
17. *CEV*, p. v.
18. *CEV*, p. v.
19. Cf. the review by A. Massie, 'This Desecration of Our Language', *Daily Mail*, Wednesday 17 January 1996, p. 8.
20. *The New English Bible New Testament* (Oxford: Oxford University Press; Cambridge: Cambridge University Press, 1961), p. vii.
21. *The Holy Bible Revised Standard Version* (Cleveland: World Publishing, 1962 [1952]), p. vii.

and liturgical use', with liturgical use apparently implying its use by hearers.[22] Thirdly, one would not gather from the above statement that the CEV is directly related to the TEV, following the same school of translational theory and retaining much of the language and style of the TEV,[23] and hence ameliorating its claim to uniqueness.[24] The CEV, therefore, appears to have been caught in an ideological struggle for self-definition, trapped between the desire to be seen as ideologically unattached, even unique, and the hope to be accepted as the ideological heir of the KJV/AV. It is not readily apparent that this tension can be resolved.

2. *The* CEV *and Meaning.* A second principle of translation that the CEV claims to have followed is that 'Every attempt has been made to produce a text that is faithful to the *meaning* of the original' (emphasis in original).[25] It is not surprising in the light of this claim that the CEV also makes a claim regarding its ability not to be misunderstood: 'a contemporary translation must be a text that an inexperienced reader can *read aloud* without stumbling, that someone unfamiliar with traditional biblical terminology can *hear without misunderstanding*, and that everyone can *listen to with enjoyment* because the style is lucid and lyrical' (emphasis in original).[26] Several points need to be drawn out here. The first is that many translations have had the purported aim of producing a text faithful to the sense or meaning of the original, while at the same time being able to be understood by its users. It is hard to imagine a translation arguing otherwise. These include not only the

22. *The Holy Bible New International Version* (Grand Rapids: Zondervan, 1978), p. viii.

23. Examples include some key wording (noted by Ewert as distinguishing the TEV from the RSV in *From Ancient Tablets*, p. 245), such as the use of 'boat' in Gen. 6.14, 'basket made of reeds' in Exod. 2.3, 'God's power' in Lk. 11.20, 'opportunity' in 1 Cor. 16.9, 'crazy' in 1 Cor. 14.23, 'to ask for money' in Acts 3.3. Without a word-for-word comparison it is difficult to know the exact amount of overlap, but it is clear that they are closely related.

24. So-called 'reader [or hearer?] response' has been a hallmark of Nida's linguistic programme: Nida, *Science of Translating*, p. 164; Nida and Taber, *Theory and Practice*, pp. 31-32; De Waard and Nida, *From One Language*, pp. 33-34. See B. Hatim and I. Mason, *Discourse and the Translator* (London: Longman, 1990), pp. 16-18.

25. *CEV*, p. vii.

26. *CEV*, p. viii.

KJV/AV, but the NIV, NEB, and a number of personal translations. The wording of the CEV statement, with its emphasis upon meaning, is presumably designed to contrast this translation with formal equivalence translations, a hallmark strategy of dynamic or functional equivalence translation. As Nida says,

> Translating must aim primarily at 'reproducing the message'... The translator must strive for equivalence rather than identity. In a sense this is just another way of emphasizing the reproduction of the message rather than the conservation of the form of the utterance...[27]

This is in distinction to the KJV/AV, which adopted much from previous translations, including that of Coverdale and Tyndale, and its successors, virtually all of which consequently retained much archaic language in their various revisions and translations. The statement about the CEV, therefore, is ambiguous in several ways. On first reading, it is difficult to determine what the specific nature of the claim is, possibly aligning the translation with the best intentions of all Bible translations. On subsequent reading, however, one can see that the wording places the translation into a specific ideologically based translation theory that distances it from other translations. The further emphasis upon understanding—especially of traditional biblical concepts—is also a hallmark of dynamic or formal equivalence translations.[28] In his treatment of these issues in his writings, Nida recognizes the difficulties involved in pursuing such a goal, discussing such things as the capacity of the receptor and the issue of noise in the channel. There is no such caveat in the CEV, perhaps giving readers an unrealistic set of expectations regarding the attainment of what must be acknowledged as subjective goals, such as those of enjoyment and understanding.

A further difficulty is what it means even to make the claim that one unfamiliar with traditional biblical terms could hear them without misunderstanding, as well as listen with enjoyment. The translators of the CEV appear to define 'understanding' in terms of expressing 'mainstream interpretations of the text in current, everyday English'.[29]

---

27. Nida and Taber, *Theory and Practice*, p. 12. See also Nida, *Science of Translating*, pp. 22-26 and *passim*; De Waard and Nida, *From One Language*, p. 9 and *passim*.

28. See, for example, Nida, *Science of Translating*, pp. 120-44, who recognizes the difficulties involved in attaining such a goal; Nida and Taber, *Theory and Practice*, pp. 31-32; De Waard and Nida, *From One Language*, pp. 11-19.

29. *CEV*, p. xi.

Listening to the text, paying attention to contemporary English, noting reviewers' comments and the guidance of the Spirit of God are also noted as ways of how to do this, but there is no explicit mention of what constitutes mainstream interpretation. Three examples illustrate the difficulty at this point: Isa. 7.14, Jn 1.1-14 and Phil. 2.6-11. The rendering at Isa. 7.14 is with 'virgin', rather than 'young woman'. In a lengthy translational note, the editors admit that the

> difficult Hebrew word did not imply a virgin birth. However, in the Greek translation made about 200 BCE and used by the early Christians, the word *parthenos* had a double meaning. While the translator took it to mean 'young woman', Matthew understood it to mean 'virgin' and quoted the passage (Matthew 1.23) because it was the appropriate description of Mary, the mother of Jesus.[30]

In other words, clearly conservative leanings (and perhaps not good conservative scholarship), including placing determinative priority on the New Testament for rendering the Old Testament, have led to this translation.[31] Concerning Jn 1.1-14, the understanding of the opening of John's Gospel by the translators is that it was an early Christian hymn. This is made clear by an introductory comment to the Gospel, but more importantly by the way in which the text is laid out. Following statements in 'The Contemporary English Version' regarding the CEV being the 'first translation in the history of the English Bible to develop a text with measured poetry lines',[32] the opening is displayed poetically.[33] Mainstream interpretation is divided over whether this

---

30. *CEV*, p. 883.

31. One might note that according to the principles of the CEV the use of the word 'virgin' might not be readily understood by many today.

32. *CEV*, p. ix. See also B.M. Newman, 'Features of Poetry in the CEV', *BibTrans* 48 (1997), pp. 218-21.

33. There are a number of noteworthy translational features of this opening in the CEV. For example, Jn 1.1 is rendered 'in the beginning was the one who is called the Word'. The Greek text at this point simply uses the copulative verb of being. If the translators were content to allow 'the Word' to remain—a fairly literal rendering of ὁ λόγος (see Moffatt, 'Preface', p. v, who disputes the clarity of such a rendering)—one wonders what the justification is for rendering 'was' as 'was the one who is called'. A second example is in 1.5, where οὐ κατέλαβεν is rendered 'have never put out', with a note giving the alternative 'not understood'. Mainstream interpretation would seem to endorse 'have not overpowered' as the alternative to 'not understood' (note also the judgment regarding the simple negative οὐ as 'never').

passage was a Christian hymn, but, even for those who argue that it was, the original hymn is not to be equated with what is in the text of John now, there being a number of Johannine additions.[34] Concerning Phil. 2.6-11, the CEV, although it does not explicitly say so, apparently takes the passage as a three-part hymn (there are three stanzas in poetic form), clearly arguing by this poetic format and the opening words— 'Christ was truly God'—for the traditional three-stage Christology. There is no mention of any Adam Christology, a topic of consideration in much current scholarship.[35] This debate hinges around how the opening statement is rendered, a rendering presented in its boldest possible form in the CEV.[36] It is easy to overlook such passages, especially when one is perhaps in agreement with the positions maintained (as I am with this one), but they reveal an ideological bias on the part of the translation that takes the translation out of the linguistic and into the theological realm.

The CEV's own example regarding misunderstanding concerns the use of 'and', and is perhaps even more revealing about the place of the CEV in the history of translation. The translators state that 'In the *hearing* of a translation, even the inclusion of a simple word like "and" can make a significant difference'.[37] They then cite the use of 'and' in Mt. 2.9: 'The wise men listened to what the king said, and then left. *And* the star they had seen in the east went on ahead of them...'[38] They then argue for the importance of 'and' at the beginning of the second sentence, showing how it assists the person who reads the text and those who hear it read, as opposed to a phrase without 'and' as in 'and then left the star they had seen'.[39] This example, however, does not support

---

34. For a summary of the positions, see R.E. Brown, *The Gospel According to John* (2 vols.; AB 29 and 29A; Garden City, NY: Doubleday, 1966, 1970), I, pp. 18-23.

35. See J.D.G. Dunn, *Christology in the Making: A New Testament Inquiry into the Origins of the Doctrine of the Incarnation* (Philadelphia: Westminster Press, 1980), pp. 98-128.

36. The boldness of the opening phrase might well be seen by its ambiguous tension with the following phrase, rendered 'but he did not try to remain equal with God', where a note by 'remain' gives 'become' as an alternative. How could Christ be 'truly God' and be in a position to try to 'become' equal with God?

37. *CEV*, p. viii.

38. *CEV*, p. viii (emphasis in original).

39. The quotation in the CEV preface stops with 'the star they had seen in the east'. Of course, if one were to hear the entire sentence, 'the star they had seen in

the unique contribution of the CEV to people being able to hear the Bible without misunderstanding. The word 'and' is found both in the *UBSGNT* third and fourth editions, and in many previous translations (including KJV/AV, NKJV, RSV, NIV, TEV, as well as Moffatt, Philips, Rieu and Lattimore). A second example is also instructive. The translators of the CEV cite Lk. 23.40, contending that, according to the rules of English grammar, in the statement 'Don't you fear *God*? You received the same sentence *he* did', the 'he' must refer back to God when it actually refers to Jesus. As a result, the translators of the CEV state, 'Traditional translations assume that the reader can study the printed text and finally figure out the meaning, but the Contemporary English Version is concerned equally with the reader and the *hearer*' (emphasis in original).[40] If I read the statement here correctly, the translators seem to be implying that traditional translations (which seems to be most, if not all, previous translations) have rendered Lk. 23.40 ambiguously. Such is not the case, however. The KJV/AV, NKJV, RSV and NIV all render the sentence in forms roughly equivalent to 'Don't you fear God, since you are under the same judgment?' One may dislike this rendering, but whatever problems it has are not because it has the ambiguous 'he' pronoun in it. In fact, it appears that it is some of the 'non-traditional' translations that have the problem that the editors of the CEV identify, not the traditional translations. Moffatt, Philips, Lattimore and the TEV have the ambiguous 'he' or something equivalent to it in Lk. 23.40.[41] The evidence here seems to point away from the unique contribution of the CEV, according to their own standards and examples, and toward support of the traditional translations that it purports to improve upon.[42]

3. *The* CEV *and the Original Text*. The translators of the CEV specify that they have used the Biblia Hebraica Stuttgartensia (*BHS*) fourth edition and Greek text of the United Bible Societies (*UBSGNT*) third

the east went on ahead of them until it stopped over the place where the child was', both reader and hearer should have realized the failure to pause appropriately.

40. CEV, p. ix.
41. Weymouth and Rieu do not.
42. Newman ('A New Concept', p. 8) cites the CEV's rendering of Lk. 11.38 as not having the difficulties of other translations (the issue here is an intervening participial construction). The CEV reads: 'The Pharisee was surprised that he did not wash his hands before eating'. The logic of those defending the CEV would seem to say that the pronoun 'he' should refer to the Pharisee, when it is, of course, Jesus.

edition corrected and compared with the fourth revised edition as their basis 'In order to assure the *accuracy* of the Contemporary English Version'.[43] Although these may arguably be the best editions to use for translation,[44] it is difficult to defend the proposition that, if one wishes to be faithful to the meaning of the original text, one can simply translate these editions. This is for at least two reasons. The first is that these two texts are of completely different sorts. The *BHS* is an edition of the Leningrad Codex, an eleventh-century Masoretic text,[45] while the *UBSGNT* third and fourth editions are eclectic texts based primarily upon the Alexandrian textual tradition followed by Westcott and Hort.[46] One is free to argue for a single text or an eclectic text as the basis of reconstructing the earliest version, but it is difficult to see how one can argue for both and claim to be translating the original. The second reason is that this begs the question of what it means to be translating the 'original' text. The Leningrad codex may be a good edition of the Masoretic tradition,[47] but the manuscript itself is removed by at least a millennium from the composition of the documents. The Qumran texts

43. *CEV*, p. vii.

44. The use of a specific text, especially one in the tradition of Westcott and Hort or Nestle and Aland, as the *UBSGNT* is, has been argued for by a number of scholars offering critiques of the NEB. See the articles by F.W. Beare, H.J. Cadbury and E.C. Colwell in D.E. Nineham (ed.), *The New English Bible Reviewed* (London: Epworth Press, 1965). The major criticism of the NEB New Testament is that it appeared to adjudicate textual decisions as they came along, without a consistent base (the edition is published in R.V. Tasker, *The Greek New Testament* [Oxford: Oxford University Press; Cambridge: Cambridge University Press, 1964]). This is not mitigated by the NIV claiming to use the *BHS* and an eclectic New Testament text, since virtually all modern New Testament texts are eclectic (NIV, pp. viii-ix).

45. See *Biblia Hebraica Stuttgartensia* (Stuttgart: Deutsche Bibelstiftung, 1977), p. xi, where K. Elliger and W. Rudolph write that 'There is no need to defend the use of the Leningrad Codex B19A (L) as the basis for an edition of the Hebrew Bible, whatever one may think of its relationship to the Ben Asher text'. This is only partly true. On the one hand, one may not need to defend the use of L for *an* edition, but, on the other, one certainly needs to defend it as the basis for *the* edition, as *BHS* has largely become.

46. See the 'Preface to the First Edition' of 1966, in K. Aland *et al.* (eds.), *The Greek New Testament* (Stuttgart: Deutsche Bibelgesellschaft and United Bible Societies, 1993), p. viii; cf. B.F. Westcott and F.J.A. Hort, *The New Testament in the Original Greek* (2 vols.; London: Macmillan, 1881), esp. II, pp. 191-94.

47. This might well be disputed by the undertaking by the UBS of a new edition of the Hebrew Old Testament based on the Aleppo Codex, a tenth-century text.

now confirm what has long been suspected, especially in the light of the Septuagint, and that is that there were many textual traditions of the Old Testament in the Judaisms of the turn of the eras.[48] The Masoretic tradition is one of these. One may wish to argue that it is the one that most accurately reflects the original, but it cannot simply be equated with it. The eclectic text of the New Testament is patently a reconstruction that does not conform to any single text of the New Testament. One could argue that individual readings may reflect the autograph (where such can be posited), but the text itself cannot be equated with the original. Whereas the CEV is wise to acknowledge the editions used for translation and hence avoid the criticism of other translations that have not done so, the use of these editions is not unique to the CEV (the TEV laid claim to using similar ones)[49] and does not necessarily guarantee what they claim that it does.

4. *The* CEV *and its Use*. The preface to the CEV states that the translators 'struggled to discover the best way to translate the text, so that it would be suitable both for *private* and *public* reading, and for *memorizing*' (emphasis in original).[50] Similar statements are again found in other translations (see, for example, the statements from the RSV, NIV and NEB mentioned above). However, this statement seems to be in some tension with the theory of dynamic equivalence translation, in which there is meant to be recognition of various audiences, varieties of language, sociological and situational factors, and levels of understanding.[51] Such a goal of one all-purpose Bible is perhaps understandable in a culture where there is only one Bible translation. For example, for a pre-literate culture getting its first Bible, and for which this may be their only Bible for a long period of time, it would of necessity be used for all biblical tasks.[52] However, this can hardly be said of the CEV in the English-speaking world, unless the editors of the CEV are making the claim that the translational procedure that they follow is the only legitimate one, thus rendering translations arrived at through other

48. See Müller, *First Bible*, pp. 41-45.

49. See *Good News Bible Today's English Version* (London: Bible Societies and Collins/Fontana, 1976 [1966]), p. vii, although the previous 1937 edition of the Hebrew text was used.

50. *CEV*, p. viii.

51. See, for example, Nida, *Science of Translating*, pp. 120-31.

52. See, for example, De Waard and Nida, *From One Language*, pp. 40-42.

means as insufficient (note the comments about the uniqueness of the CEV above).[53] This claim would be contradicted, however, by their own attempt to position the CEV as following the same translational agenda as the KJV/AV.

5. *The* CEV *and Evangelization.* In a surprising admission in the light of the above, the translators of the CEV as much as admit that the CEV is not the Bible for every purpose. Taking up statements from the translators of the KJV/AV, the translators of the CEV endorse the sentiment of having many versions, but primarily because each translation is seen to be the Word of God, and multiple translations are necessary to ensure that that Word is disseminated (and understood?). The translators admit that 'each translation serves to meet the needs of a different audience',[54] a statement that brings this explicit goal into apparent contradiction with the claim regarding the overall purpose of the CEV as the translation that is suitable in virtually all respects and not subject to misunderstanding. But here the editors of the CEV appear to have an even more specific purpose for their translation in mind. They wish for it to be seen as 'a *companion*—the *mission* arm—of traditional translations, because it takes seriously the words of the apostle Paul that "faith comes by hearing"' (emphasis in original).[55] Two points are being made here. The first is that the translation is seen to be an evangelistic tool. This has been a longstanding goal of the development of contemporary translations by those arguing for dynamic equivalence translations, including Nida himself.[56] However, it raises more than simply the issue of the interpretative element in translation. The equation here is apparently between the translation itself and proclamation. The second, and perhaps more troublesome, point, since it seems to contradict what has been outlined above, is that here the CEV sees itself, not as the clearly understood translation along unique lines, but as the translation that comes alongside and helps traditional translations. This would seem to acknowledge that the CEV is being used in a culture with an established history of Bible translation (and is not a 'first Bible' even

53. That this may well be what is being claimed can be seen in De Waard and Nida, *From One Language*, pp. 40-42, 182-85.
54. *CEV*, p. x.
55. *CEV*, p. xi.
56. See De Waard and Nida, *From One Language*, pp. 35-36. This is implied also for the TEV (p. iv).

for those who do not regularly read their Bibles), and it may well vitiate the claim that the CEV communicates without using traditional biblical language. It further calls into question the relationship of its theoretical underpinnings to other translational projects. How do other translations using dynamic or functional equivalence function in cultures where they are the first translation and there is no traditional or formal equivalence translation to aid them?

6. *The* CEV *and Gender-Inclusive Language.* The issue of what the translators of the CEV call 'gender generic' or 'inclusive' language must be raised as well. Their definition is that at the places where masculine nouns or pronouns in the original languages mean both men and women, the translation should reflect the meaning of the original even if the English form is different from that of the original.[57] I will return to this issue below, but this example clearly points out the interpretative nature of translation, including this translation. The claim is that the CEV is a faithful and accurate rendering of the meaning of the original biblical text, in the spirit of the KJV/AV, but this goal is not nearly as easy to accomplish as it is to make the claim, especially where gender-inclusive language is concerned. As an example of how to render gender-inclusive language, the translators of the CEV cite Mt. 16.24 (and following). Rather than 'if anyone wants to follow after me, let (him) deny himself and take up his cross and follow me', etc., the CEV utilizes the second-person singular pronoun. The result is

> If any of you want to be my followers, you must forget about yourself. You must take up your cross and follow me. If you want to save your life, you will destroy it. But if you give up your life for me, you will find it. What will you gain, if you own the whole world but destroy yourself? What would you give to get back your soul?

There is then a paragraph break in the CEV, and then it continues:

> The Son of Man will soon come in the glory of his Father and with his angels to reward all people for what they have done. I promise you that some of those standing here will not die before they see the Son of Man coming with his kingdom.

I would claim that at two points, at least, there have been arguably significant changes introduced into the text, which render the CEV at least as far from the original as the gender-exclusive language that it

---

57. CEV, p. x; cf. B.M. Newman, 'Guidelines and Quality Control for Gender Generic Language', *Bible Collectors' World* 13.4 (1997), pp. 8-13.

attempts to correct. The first is the specific focus of the admonition of Jesus upon the disciples with him by use of the second person pronoun, 'you'. The Greek text of v. 24 opens the protasis of the first class conditional with τις, the singular indefinite pronoun.[58] The verbs of the apodosis of the opening conditional structure, ἀπαρνησάσθω, ἀράτω and ἀκολουθείτω, do not in fact have explicitly stated subjects, something that typifies Greek syntax, unlike English. In v. 25, the masculine singular relative pronoun is used in the protasis of two conditional-like structures ('whoever...'). And v. 26 twice uses ἄνθρωπος as the subject of the verb. Verses 27 and 28 are connected to vv. 24-25 by γάρ, hence the lack of a paragraph break in the printed Greek text, as opposed to the CEV, which has a paragraph break and no transition word (the latter perhaps introducing the kind of ambiguity that the use of 'and' mentioned above was designed to alleviate). In other words, it appears that Jesus' words in vv. 24-26 are not addressed specifically or limited only to the disciples standing with him, but apply to any follower or potential follower. This is confirmed by the following words regarding the purpose of the coming of the son of man (on son of man, see below). This sense of wider application—something in other ways endorsed by the CEV—is lost in their translation, as well as making the son-of-man statement appear to be an independent or free-standing saying unconnected to what has preceded. In the son-of-man statement, the individualistic tone of the previous verses is maintained in Greek by reference to 'each' (ἑκάστω) receiving according to the actions of each (αὐτοῦ). This sense of individual recompense is lost in the CEV when it refers to 'all people' getting rewards for 'what they have done', something that takes on group proportions.[59] This illustration well exemplifies that at least some of the problems of translation may well be laid at the feet of the receptor language rather than the original language, and this needs to be squarely faced.[60] Nevertheless, at points the

---

58. One should note that τις is both the masculine and feminine singular form, even though the masculine singular pronouns are used after this, anaphorically referring to τις.

59. The best discussion of this passage I have found is in D.A. Carson, 'Matthew', in F.E. Gaebelein (ed.), *The Expositor's Bible Commentary* (Grand Rapids: Zondervan, 1984), VIII, pp. 378-82. The analysis I have offered is not compromised by reference to τινες τῶν ὧδε ἑστώτων οἵτινες, in the light of the notorious exegetical difficulties in defining this group.

60. As Nida does in other contexts. See Nida and Taber, *Theory and Practice*, pp. 3-6.

biblical text may well be considered hopelessly insensitive in matters of gender, but I am not convinced that it is in the best interests of making the meaning of the original text clear if the clear meaning that exists is in fact obscured. The attempt to be politically correct may not always be translationally correct.

In terms of the topic of this paper, one can conclude that the editors of the CEV wish to place the CEV in two apparently mutually exclusive positions. The attempt to do so, I believe, well illustrates the ideological motivation of much Bible translation, both in theory and in practice. On the one hand, the translators of the CEV wish to align themselves with the grand tradition of what they call traditional biblical translations, including pre-eminently the KJV/AV. The explicit appeal to the criteria for translation of the KJV/AV is an attempt to distinguish the CEV from a host of modern translations and paraphrases. One cannot but think that this is also an attempt not only to attract those who have long regarded the KJV/AV as the only Bible (some do not seem to think of it as a translation), but to stave off the kinds of criticisms that are often made of recent translations, including the TEV, the closely related forebear of the CEV (although this translation is never mentioned in relation to the CEV). Appeals to traditional tasks, such as reading the Bible, and to traditional interpretation are part of this. These appeals are made despite the evidence of the examples marshalled by the editors themselves. On the other hand, a competing ideological strategy is to claim virtually unparalleled uniqueness for the translation. The claim is made repeatedly that there are numerous features of the CEV that have never before been seen in a translation or that there are accomplishments of the CEV unattained by others. These all have the purpose of enabling the translation to fulfil the original agenda of the KJV/AV. Again, these claims are made, even if they do not appear to be borne out by the examples cited. The result is an apparently implicit claim that the CEV is the translation that the KJV/AV intended to be but never quite attained. In the CEV, we have the proper fulfilment of the translational task.

3. *How Others See the* CEV: *Ideology and Reception*

The ideological issues raised by the CEV itself, in terms of the claims made by the translators in relation to the translational tradition in which it falls, have implications regarding the wider issue of translation, especially as the translation is sold in the United Kingdom. The United

States is used to new translations appearing (not without controversy, however),[61] but Britain has been much more resistant to them. The priority of the RSV has been gradually usurped by the NIV, but the NRSV is attempting to reclaim some of the lost territory. There are even a few churches that use the TEV, but this has been slow in coming. Once having changed, many churches are hesitant to change again. Publication of the CEV, however, has raised a number of further ideological issues in relation to the use of the Bible in Britain. Three of these issues seem to be of greatest importance to those responding to the CEV. The first concerns the cultural ideologies reflected in translations, the second the ideology of translation theory, and the third the differences between meaning and translation. As will become apparent, the response to the CEV is at least as—if not more—instructive regarding the reviewers as it is regarding the translation itself.

a. *Cultural Ideologies of a Translation*
The first issue concerns the cultural ideologies reflected in translations. Two recent British reviews of the CEV each refer to the CEV as being 'American'.[62] There is longstanding cultural conflict between America and Britain, often focusing on the use of language,[63] and this translation

61. On the recent history of translations of the New Testament, see Ewert, *From Ancient Tablets*, pp. 217-19, 223-32, 237-48.

62. I base much of my analysis on these two reviews, since they were two of the first to appear and seem to represent two different kinds of review, each instructive in its own way. The first is by G. Smith, 'New English Bible Does away with the Manger', *Evening Standard*, Tuesday 16 January 1996, p. 15, and reflects popular-level journalism, which would be widely read. The second is by C. Rodd, 'Talking Points from Books', *ExpTim* 107.8 (1996), pp. 225-28, and reflects a mid-level scholarly response, such as clergy would turn to. The review in *The Times*, by contrast, was more descriptive than evaluative: R. Gledhill, 'New Simpler Bible Cuts out Grace in Search for Favour', *The Times*, Tuesday 16 January 1996, Home News, p. 6.

63. One is of course reminded of Churchill's remark (noting that Churchill was half American and half British) that the Americans and British were two peoples separated by a common language. On differences between American and British English, see T. Pyles, *The Origins and Development of the English Language* (New York: Harcourt Brace Jovanovich, 2nd edn, 1971), esp. pp. 229-74; M. Pei, *The Story of the English Language* (New York: Simon and Schuster, 1967), esp. pp. 166-73. More general sociolinguistic treatments that address issues of language varieties include P. Trudgill, *Sociolinguistics: An Introduction to Language and Society* (Harmondsworth: Penguin Books, 2nd edn, 1983), esp. pp. 141-68 on

brings much of it to a head. But calling the translation 'American' appears to mean slightly different things for the two reviewers. In considering these differences, one perhaps gets a sense of why the translators of the CEV approached their task of justification for their translation the way they did. One reviewer labels the translation 'American' in order to describe particular wordings. For example, the CEV uses 'Jordan River' when British English would use 'River Jordan', 'period' rather than 'full stop', 'cent' rather than 'penny', 'lumber' for 'timber', and 'rooster' for 'cockerel'.[64] These are perhaps fair criticisms. Even here, however, some of the corrections appear to be hypercorrections. For example, 'renters' seems perfectly acceptable to describe the tenants of Mk 12.3, and 'trash' seems understandable for 'rubbish' in 2 Sam. 13.7, 13.

More problematic is the use of 'American' as a purely pejorative term. For example, one review states that this new version is 'minus God's grace, Noah's Ark, Jesus in the manger and the Crucifixion, all swept away in a tide of linguistic "modernisation"'. This leads to characterization of the translation as, 'of course', American.[65] The evidence cited is, of course, highly misleading. The reviewer apparently has little inkling of (or at least little sympathy for) the translational theory followed by the CEV. It is not that the meaningful equivalents of these terms are gone, only that the enshrined language is no longer used. What is meant by these examples is that the CEV uses language of kindness rather than the word 'grace' (e.g. Rom. 5.15; Heb. 12.9; 2 Cor. 12.9), the word 'boat' for 'ark',[66] 'bed of hay' for 'manger', and 'nailed to the cross' for 'crucified'. These can hardly be characterized as Americanisms, or claimed as sufficient warrant for using 'American' as a pejorative term. In fact, I would contend that many of them are accurate, useful and meaningful translational equivalents. This disparaging reviewer uses the KJV/AV as the point of (for him) profitable comparison. The two major examples he cites, however, are ones that

---

'Language and Nation'; R.A. Hudson, *Sociolinguistics* (Cambridge: Cambridge University Press, 1980); and J.K. Chambers and P. Trudgill, *Dialectology* (Cambridge: Cambridge University Press, 1980).

64. Rodd, 'Talking Points', p. 225. One British native informant, however, tells me that even this list is perhaps too picky.

65. Smith, 'English Bible', p. 15.

66. Apart from losing the Bible school song about an 'arky arky', the use of 'boat' does not seem particularly troublesome.

illustrate the very problems that the CEV tries to address. The first example is a passage in the Song of Solomon, where the KJV/AV includes the word 'lo', a word that can hardly be claimed to have widespread currency in any language but that which is or is trying to be archaic English. The second example is Psalm 23. In dismissing comments by one of the translators of the CEV, who was explaining the use of 'lack' for 'want' in 'The Lord is my shepherd; I shall not want', the reviewer says that the translator was 'seemingly unaware that "to want" is synonymous with "to lack"'.[67] I do not know how aware or unaware the translator was, but the reviewer seems to be unaware that it is only in an excruciatingly small range of contexts that 'want' and 'lack' can be synonyms (Psalm 23 perhaps?). To say that one 'wants' money or one 'lacks' money is not to say the same thing in most English usage.[68] John D. Rockefeller purportedly always wanted more money, but was far from lacking in having it.[69]

This review makes plain that much of the concern of the CEV translators regarding its being evaluated in terms of the KJV/AV is legitimate. Their attempt to forestall this kind of criticism has not apparently worked, but has instead elicited rather sensational claims in response. This same reviewer states that the CEV 'is the first to use the words penis (for "flesh") and semen (for "issue of flesh") in translating Leviticus'.[70] This seems to be quite shocking to the reviewer, although I cannot understand why. The reviewer seems to be indicating that one of the distinctive Americanisms of the translation is the use of 'penis' and 'semen' (to my knowledge, neither is distinctively American). Although it is true that penis is not used widely in earlier translations, some editions of the KJV/AV, the RSV and the NIV use 'semen' at Lev. 15.16. The TEV uses 'penis' at Lev. 15.2. I am not sure where the reviewer got the idea that the CEV was the first to use these terms, but it plainly is not. The terms have been in use for at least 30 years, if not much longer. The place of cultural bias in translation is one that the translators of the CEV have apparently tried to address, but it is difficult to know how to do so when there seems to be a very firmly entrenched

---

67. Smith, 'English Bible', p. 15.
68. As of course recognized by De Waard and Nida, *From One Language*, p. 9.
69. The story is told that Rockefeller was asked how much was enough money, to which he replied, just a little bit more.
70. Smith, 'English Bible', p. 15.

bias against anything but a particular kind of language. So much so that the clear and plain facts are misrepresented or overlooked.

b. *The Ideology of Translation Theory*
The second issue concerns the ideology of translation theory. The CEV is a dynamic or functional equivalence translation, as noted above. This method of Bible translation runs contrary to the British tradition, inherited from the study of classical languages, with its emphasis upon translation as the sign of understanding. This tradition was apparently begun in the Renaissance, was firmly established in the nineteenth century by those with no formal rationale for its value, and appears to continue to this day.[71] For example, in a recent *Festschrift*, one of the contributors reminisces about the dedicatee's and his time together as classical scholars, where 'we learned together some of the art of translation',[72] apparently referring to the translational method of classical learning. It is significant that both of these men ended up devoting their professional lives to the study of the Bible, especially the New Testament. Other translations and translators have been aware of the fact that they are departing from the established translational tradition, even in devoting time and effort to translation of the New Testament. For example, Rieu in his Introduction to his translation of the Gospels for Penguin goes to significant lengths to argue that the Gospels are of literary merit not unlike classical texts.[73] As Bell states,

> It is easy to see how such a view could have held sway in the last century, when scholars—for the most part, dilettante translators engaging in translation as a pastime—were preoccupied with the translation of literary texts, and in particular, Classical authors; Latin and Greek... It is

71. See E.J. Kenney, 'A Theory of Classical Education II', *Didaskalos* 1.2 (1964), pp. 2-15, and M. and M. Thorpe, 'A Theory of Classical Education IV', *Didaskalos* 2.3 (1968), pp. 3-17, both reprinted in J. Mingay and J.S. Smith (eds.), *From Didaskalos: An Anthology* (Bristol: Bristol Classical Press, 1982), pp. 1-14 and 15-28 respectively; S. Morris, *Viae Novae: New Techniques in Latin Teaching* (London: Hulton, 1966), pp. 7-15, where he compares various methods; Ewert, *From Ancient Tablets*, pp. 183-209; and F.C. Grant, *Translating the Bible* (Edinburgh: Nelson, 1961), pp. 49-98.

72. H. Wansbrough, 'William Tyndale—A Martyr for the Bible?', in C. Rowland and C.H.T. Fletcher-Louis (eds.), *Understanding, Studying and Reading: New Testament Essays in Honour of John Ashton* (JSNTSup, 153; Sheffield: Sheffield Academic Press, 1998), p. 188. Note that Wansbrough was one of those involved in production of the New Jerusalem Bible.

73. See, for example, Rieu, 'Introduction', pp. ix-x.

also understandable that the attitude should have continued into the present century, during which both translation and translation theory have been dominated, at least until very recently, by Bible translators (especially Nida).[74]

Response to the CEV has generally identified wording that does not 'sound biblical', but the theoretical underpinnings of such translational choices have been largely overlooked in these responses. For example, the use of 'have sex', especially in such places as Leviticus 18, is cited under the category of an 'attempt to provide modern English' that has 'led to the introduction of colloquialisms that are sometimes coarse...' The reviewer asks the question: 'Why do the pages have to be spattered with "have sex"? Euphemism should be expressed by euphemism.'[75] The KJV/AV and RSV render the phrases as 'uncover nakedness'. It is true that this is euphemistic, but in this day and age, when there is plenty of nakedness that may not mean sexual intercourse, the euphemism is probably not a gentle way of phrasing the obvious, but simply unclear. The CEV is not alone in using the kind of wording that it does, since the NIV has 'have sexual relations'. The larger issue, however, is the attempt by the CEV to find the equivalent statement in the receptor language, and at this point it appears to have done so. These chapters of Leviticus are full of rather explicit regulations regarding the behaviour of the Israelites, and the CEV does capture them. But there are indeed places where the CEV fails to communicate the original meaning accurately. There is no hesitation, for example, to use the word 'testicle' in Lev. 21.20, as does the RSV, regarding regulations for those who may become priests (the KJV/AV uses 'eunuch'), but at Mt. 19.12 the CEV translates 'eunuch' with 'stay single', which misses the point completely. Is it possible, in the light of the overtly evangelistic purpose of the CEV, that the New Testament has been toned down in some places so that it does not scare off those attracted to Christianity?

Although in recent translational theorizing the issue of dynamic equivalence is addressed,[76] such theorizing does not seem to have made

74. See R.T. Bell, *Translation and Translating: Theory and Practice* (London: Longman, 1991), pp. 4-5. Note that he puts Nida in the category of almost prelinguistic translators!

75. Rodd, 'Talking Points', p. 226.

76. See, for example, Hatim and Mason, *Discourse and the Translator*, pp. 7-9, where in fact dynamic equivalence seems a bit old fashioned in the light of recent discussion; Bell, *Translation*, p. 5. However, its acceptance as an established theory is often in terms of moving well beyond that theory.

significant inroads in much discussion of Bible translations in Britain, apart from places devoted to such work, such as SIL and Wycliffe.[77] This is a shame, since in the last century there was significant work in this area that might have had an influence on the current situation. Although Benjamin Jowett is cited by Nida as an example of a formal equivalence translator,[78] the evidence from the response to his translation is that many in his day thought of him as quite free with the Greek text. Jowett, in the preface to his translation of Plato's dialogues, describes the task of the translator. The translator, he says,

> must carry in his mind a comprehensive view of the whole work, of what has preceded and what is to follow—as well as of the meaning of particular passages. His version should be based, in the first instance, on an intimate knowledge of the text; but the precise order and arrangement of the words may be left to fade out of sight, when the translation begins to take shape. He must form a general idea of the two languages, and reduce the one to the terms of the other... The translation should retain as far as possible the characteristic qualities of the ancient writer...or the best part of him will be lost to the English reader. It should be read as an original work, and should also be the most faithful transcript which can be made of the language from which the translation is taken, consistently with the first requirement of all, that it be English. Further the translation being English, it should also be perfectly intelligible in itself without reference to the Greek, the English being really the more lucid and exact of the two languages.[79]

Two points can be drawn from this extended quotation. The first is that there is already a precedent among respected translators in Britain of paying attention to the major issues raised by the CEV. No less a Greek scholar than Jowett laid down a number of important standards for his own translation that are reflected in more recent theorizing regarding the translational process. Thus the kinds of dismissive comments that are often found regarding the CEV and other translations are unwarranted on theoretical grounds, although of course individual problems in translation must still be addressed. The second point to

---

77. See, for example, E.R. Wendland, *The Cultural Factor in Bible Translation* (UBS Monograph Series, 2; London: United Bible Societies, 1987) and P.C. Stine (ed.), *Issues in Bible Translation* (UBS Monograph Series, 3; London: United Bible Societies, 1988). However, just because these works are published in Britain does not mean that they are widely read here.

78. See Nida, *Science of Translating*, pp. 164-65.

79. Cited in Grant, *Translating*, p. 136.

observe is that there is much in Jowett's description that needs to be reiterated and even expanded upon in contemporary translational theory. These can be listed briefly because of their apparent similarities to some dimensions of dynamic equivalence translation. (1) Jowett does not wish to establish one-to-one correlations between the two languages at any point, even around such things as basic structures transferred between source and receptor language. The translator, according to Jowett, is to master each language individually, and work in such a way that what is done in one is reproduced in the other. This seems to be similar to what dynamic equivalence theory means by reproducing the same effect or meaning in the receptor as in the source language.[80] (2) Jowett emphasizes that the translation must read as an original work. One of the major pitfalls in Bible translation has been the desire to retain the sound and feel of previous translations. Although Jowett does not dismiss the need for accuracy, an even higher priority must be that the translation read as an original work, without reference to the original from which it was taken. (3) This is compatible with a third emphasis of dynamic equivalence translation theory, that there needs to be sufficient material presented in the text that it can be understood without recourse to the kinds of supporting material that are often demanded of older translations. In that sense, the biblical text ends up being its own best commentary on itself.[81] (4) The fourth emphasis is Jowett's prescient emphasis upon discourse considerations in translation. Of course, Jowett knew nothing of what is now called discourse analysis (or, as it is sometimes called, textlinguistics),[82] although his opening statement contains the unrecognized essence of the modern linguistic discipline. Noticeably lacking in much of the CEV theory is an appropriate emphasis upon discourse features, reflecting the dynamic equivalence school of thought regarding translation, especially

80. See Nida and Taber, *Theory and Practice*, pp. 3-8; De Waard and Nida, *From One Language*, pp. 60-77. But cf. E.L. Keenan, 'Some Logical Problems in Translation', in F. Guenthner and M. Guenthner-Reuter (eds.), *Meaning and Translation: Philosophical and Linguistic Approaches* (London: Gerald Duckworth, 1978), pp. 157-89, who disputes the 'exact translation hypothesis'.

81. For suggestions on how this is to be done with dynamic equivalence translations, see Nida, *Science of Translating*, pp. 226-40.

82. For a brief history of discourse analysis in New Testament studies, see S.E. Porter, 'Discourse Analysis and New Testament Studies: An Introductory Survey', in S.E. Porter and D.A. Carson (eds.), *Discourse Analysis and Other Topics in Biblical Greek* (JSNTSup, 113; Sheffield: JSOT Press, 1995), pp. 24-34.

with its use of kernel transformations.[83] Discourse considerations seem to be the next major area of exploration for translational theorists.[84]

c. *Meaning and Translation*

The comments of Jowett provide a useful transition to the third issue to emerge in consideration of the CEV in a British context—the difference between meaning and translation. The traditional British focus is ambiguous at this point. On the one hand, there is in traditional translation an equation of meaning and translation, in the sense that it is supposed that a test of understanding of the original language is the ability to produce a glib and fluent rendition in the receptor language. This is the tradition widely followed in classical language instruction and studies, already addressed above. On the other hand, there is also a tradition in which there is a differentiation between meaning and translation, with the result that wording can be left ambiguous or non-committal as to meaning even though a translation is offered. An explanation of such practice might be that the original is unclear or shrouded in mystery, something that the translation cannot help but reflect. The result is often an analysis of the receptor language, rather than an understanding of the source language. For example, if two verb tense-forms are available in the receptor language, but one in the source, it is tempting to think that one must debate the merits of the two tense-forms on the basis of the original, when the relative merits of the forms apply only to the receptor. As Gleason says, 'Translation can obscure some features of meaning and falsify others'.[85]

The CEV, however, following the theories of dynamic or functional equivalence, treats the translated text as a vehicle for conveyance of meaning.[86] The difficulty with the idea of a translation conveying meaning is that it implies that a meaning of the original text must have

83.   See Nida and Taber, *Theory and Practice*, pp. 39-55.

84.   See, for example, Hatim and Mason, *Discourse and the Translator*, esp. chs. 3, 4, 5, and 10. But cf. Nida, *Science of Translating*, pp. 210-13; Nida and Taber, *Theory and Practice*, pp. 131-33, where discourse features are considered.

85.   H.A. Gleason, Jr, *An Introduction to Descriptive Linguistics* (New York: Holt, Rinehart and Winston, 2nd edn, 1961), p. 77. See also S.E. Porter, 'Studying Ancient Languages from a Modern Linguistic Perspective: Essential Terms and Terminology', *FN* 2 (1989), pp. 166-67.

86.   See T. Tymoczko, 'Translation and Meaning', in Guenthner and Guenthner-Reutter (eds.), *Meaning and Translation*, pp. 29-43.

been arrived at, and that one cannot hide behind non-expressive word-ing. This has the result of making others uncomfortable with the mean-ing advocated, or leaving oneself open to judgment whether the mean-ing conveyed is the best possible expression of meaning. Of course, the opposite approach—of leaving meaning undecided—runs the risk of having no meaning, an equally if not more detrimental problem. For example, the CEV often renders the Greek γέγραπται ('it stands writ-ten') as 'the Scriptures say' (e.g. Mt. 4.4; Rom. 1.17; 3.4). One reviewer objects to this 'part of [the] conservative stance' of the CEV.[87] It seems to me that such a rendering is entirely appropriate, especially in such places as Mk 1.2, Lk. 2.23, Jn 6.31, 12.14, Rom. 1.17, 2.24, 3.4, 3.10, 4.17, 8.36, 9.13, 9.33, 10.15, 11.8, and so on, where the phrase is used in conjunction with an Old Testament quotation. This is by far the most common use of the word in the New Testament. Thus, such a ren-dering may not be merely a reflection of a conservative stance, but a concise way of capturing the meaning when this term is used.

The area where the issue of translation versus meaning may be at its most acute is in terms of what have become known as technical terms.[88] The CEV has apparently handled these on three levels, introducing a number of intriguing relations between meaning and translation.[89] The first level is those instances where, as pointed out above, technical terms are rendered in the CEV into a more meaningful and generally more expressive form for modern readers. Hence 'grace' becomes 'kindness'. Other examples include words for justify and righteousness being rendered with words of 'accept', synagogue being rendered by 'meeting place', covenant becoming 'agreement', and 'story' used for parable. At the least, all of these are reasonable attempts to use contemporary language, although they will undoubtedly continue to be highly debated for their adequacy. I do not think that it is true, as one reviewer suggests, that there is nothing wrong with use of 'synagogue', since 'everyone knows that synagogues are the Jewish "churches"'.[90] I am not convinced that those for whom this Bible is addressed would know that, and I am equally unsure that thinking of the synagogue as a

---

87. Rodd, 'Talking Points', p. 225.
88. See Rodd, 'Talking Points', p. 226.
89. Cf. B.M. Newman, 'A Message in Terms that Most People Can Under-stand', *BibTrans* 47 (1996), pp. 201-207, where some of this kind of terminology is discussed.
90. Rodd, 'Talking Points', p. 226.

Jewish church conveys the right meaning at all, especially in terms of the history of their developments and what is typically thought of the church today. The second level of handling technical terms is where the CEV has used terminology that fails to convey the right meaning. For example, 'the festival of thin bread' may convey the sense of what the bread looked like, but it does not get at the reasons for its thinness, more important than its final shape. Perhaps 'the festival of bread made without yeast' would have been better. It is at least no more awkward than 'festival of thin bread'.

The third category is where the CEV has not altered the traditional language but rather retained it. In the light of what has been said above, it may come as a surprise that there is any traditional language retained, especially a number of these technical terms. They include 'son of man', 'kingdom of God', 'disciples', 'sinners', 'glory', and 'holy'. Some of these seem easier to translate than others ('follower' is used for disciple in some places), and the failure to do so is surprising. For example, 'sinner' could become 'breaker of God's law' or 'divine-law breaker'. Others, however, are not so easy, especially if there is dispute over their meaning. For example, 'kingdom of God' could be rendered 'the rule of God as king'. Although for many the concept of a king is foreign to their first-hand experience, the concept seems current enough for continued use. It is certainly not any more difficult than 'kingdom of God'. Nevertheless, there are those who would disagree that this is the meaning. As one reviewer rightly asks, 'what can [son of man] possibly mean to the uninstructed today for whom the translation is intended?'[91] The apparent problem for the CEV, like most other translations, is not necessarily its theory at this point but its execution. 'Son of man' is a classic example. All of the other translations that I have consulted in writing this article have 'son of man'. The scholarly community is divided on what the son of man means, and hence any attempt to translate the meaning as opposed to the wording[92] is sure to be less than satisfactory to a large number, and hence arguably fail to accomplish its purpose of conveying meaning accurately. For example, with 'son of

---

91. Rodd, 'Talking Points', p. 226.

92. It must be noted, however, that the translation is not word for word, since the Greek is ὁ υἱὸς τοῦ ἀνθρώπου, literalistically 'the son of the man'. See C.F.D. Moule, *The Origin of Christology* (Cambridge: Cambridge University Press, 1977), pp. 11-22.

man' does one eliminate the gender reference, and use 'son of humanity' or even 'offspring of humanity'? These attempts are even less clear than 'son of man', and fail completely to come to terms with the meaning of the phrase. They end up being simply non-gendered word substitutions. An attempt to capture what many see as the generic use—'one like me' or 'any human'—loses track of the fact that the term is a technical one in the New Testament. One could attempt to decipher the phrase in terms of its Old Testament background. This would require a clear understanding of, for example, Daniel 7, again something not shared by all scholars. Thus as Tymoczko argues, 'Knowing the semantic structure of a language, I have argued, depends upon knowing about the speakers, their environment, their society and their beliefs'.[93] This is a very tall order for any translation project.

4. *Conclusion*

Although on the surface the CEV may appear to be just another translation, its publication, especially in Britain, but elsewhere as well, raises important issues regarding how any Bible positions itself in relation to other previous translations. The CEV, it seems to me, is ambiguous regarding itself. On the one hand, it wishes to be identified with the grand tradition of traditional Bible translation, especially as marked by the continuing recognition of the place of the KJV/AV. On the other hand, the CEV wishes to be seen as a product of modern biblical (and linguistic?) translation theory, exemplifying a number of unique features as it seeks to communicate to its hearers and readers. In assessing these dimensions of its self-conception, a number of strengths and limitations have come to the fore. Nevertheless, none of these shortcomings—no matter how much they may appear to depart from the traditional verities—justifies an uncritical response to the translation, ignoring the many important issues debated in the arenas of translational theory. And certainly nothing with regard to the CEV justifies apparent misinformation and misrepresentation of the evidence. Although the CEV is the newest and latest Bible translation, it is certainly not going to be the last. An assessment of its ideological basis and its ideologically based responses clearly illustrates potential future directions for translational theory.

93. Tymoczko, 'Meaning and Translation', p. 43.

To Whom Is a Translator Responsible— Reader or Author?

Y.C. Whang

1. *Retrospect*

I was most astonished to be asked to write a paper about translation, because for the last almost fifteen years during which I have engaged in translation as my profession I have almost never thought theoretically about translation itself.[1] This does not mean that I have been unconscious of my job. It simply means that I have been one of those who are so busy undertaking their work as to be unable to spare time to contemplate the theoretical nature of it. It is common for practitioners not to contemplate the nature of their own work; instead, it is done by those who are not engaged in the work. For example, critics are generally not writers.[2]

Even though I have not studied the theoretical nature of translation, it would not be true to say that I have not reflected at all on the nature of translation. The topic is, however, very much a practical one for me. There are, for example, such considerations as the necessity of education for the improvement of the translator's ability, social concern for translation work, the need of a certificate for translators and so on, which I have thought to be so urgently needed for a better translational culture in Korea.

This will explain why personal experience and introspective comments are introduced in this essay. In a sense, it would be unavoidable for this essay to be a sort of personal recollection of my profession,

---

1. I have translated more than 30 English books into Korean, all of which were Christian books. They cover a broad range of books from academic to devotional, and commentaries.

2. J. De Waard and E.A. Nida, *From One Language to Another: Functional Equivalence in Bible Translating* (Nashville: Thomas Nelson, 1986), p. 185.

which has become more and more difficult ever since I first translated a small booklet.

2. The Complexity of Translation

Translation is such a complex work, involving many factors, that it seems almost impossible to approach the subject of translation as a whole. The first factor is a personal one.[3] It is unnecessary to point out that the most important factor in translation is the competence of translators. They have to be competent not only in the source language, but also in the receptor language. However competent they may be in the source language, if they are not good writers of the receptor language, they are far from being good translators. Many publishers have learnt this truth by trial and error.[4] The other important personal factor is the professionalism of a translator. Translation is such an energy-consuming intellectual work that the translator may always be tempted to finish the work roughly and quickly. If the translator spends more time reading and analyzing the *Vorlage*, the possibility of mistranslating will be reduced. Also, almost all translated sentences have room for improvement. If a translator spends more time reviewing the translation, the sentences can be made smoother and more readable. These factors are mainly related to the professionalism of the translator. Even though these are very important factors in translation, which should be dealt with in the study of translation, it is not my aim to deal with them here.[5]

3.   For more detailed treatment of this subject, see E.A. Nida and C.R. Taber, *The Theory and Practice of Translation* (Leiden: E.J. Brill, 1982), pp. 99-102. They enumerate as personal problems 'too much knowledge of the subject matter', 'taking translationese for granted', 'insecurity about one's own language', 'a desire to preserve the mystery of language', 'wrong theological presuppositions, ignorance of the nature of translations'.

4.   Korean publishing companies that ask persons who have recently come back from the English-speaking world to translate English books are almost invariably disappointed with their translations. It is not because they do not read the English, but because they do not know how to express their thought in the Korean. Characteristic of their work is that the translated sentences are unintelligible to readers, even though they are not to themselves.

5.   Those who have English as their own language might not feel the importance of translation as keenly as those for whom English is a foreign language. At least in the Korean Christian book market, translated books (mainly from English) far exceed Korean books in their number and influence. In this situation, the Christian publishers are in a position easily to be dominated by commercialism, the

However, it will be necessary to be reminded of the fact that, whenever the translation is approached in a theoretical manner, a type of perfectly competent translator, who does not exist in reality, is presupposed.

The second factor is the cultural gap that has to be surmounted by the translator. The cultural gap is not only spatial, but historical. It can be said that a linguistic gap is a kind of cultural gap. Translators have frequently felt the utter insurmountability of some cultural gaps. A simple example will serve to clarify the point. Let us imagine a Korean who is reading a paragraph such as the following:

> Two men stand before a restaurant. They are friends. One man searches his pocket to find money in vain. He forgot to bring his wallet. He asks his friend to lend him money for lunch. His friend tells him that he has sufficient money to lend him and lends him money for lunch. They have lunch and chat.

This kind of thing is not unfamiliar to westerners. Any Korean who reads this story translated into Korean, however, would either think that they are not friends ('chin-ku' in Korean), or think the man who lends money rather than pays the price for his friend's lunch is unqualified to be a friend of the other man. In a Korean cultural background, 'to be a friend' means setting up a relationship in which one can share one's money (though not all of one's money). So, in such a situation, there could be no question but that a person who has money will pay for a friend. This example shows that the English term 'friend' is not equivalent to the Korean word 'chin-ku'. But there is no other Korean word than 'chin-ku' for the English word 'friend'. Even a very simple story like this raises all kinds of difficulties when a language is translated into one of totally different cultural background. This aspect is well summarized by Tymoczko when he says,

> The subject of translation is an interdisciplinary topic. Naturally, in the investigation of translations one utilizes such linguistic theories as phonology (or graphology), syntax, semantics and pragmatics. However, there are also extralinguistic factors involved in translation and to accommodate these factors, the translation theorist must draw on additional theories of the language speakers, their environment, culture and beliefs. The point that translation involves such extralinguistic factors

result of which is books poorly translated by the unqualified.

has been made in different ways by Nida (1945) and Quine (1960). Yet
it is a point not always appreciated.[6]

According to Tymoczko, translation is not simply changing a sentence in one language into the equivalent in the second language by
using the semantic devices of the second language. If it were, translation would simply be a form of applied semantics. But in reality semantics itself is a high-level interdisciplinary subject. This means that
translation is interdisciplinary, also. Thus he concludes that 'Knowing
the semantic structure of a language depends upon knowing about the
speakers, their environment, their society and their beliefs'.[7] If this
insight is applied to translation theory, it can be said that the semantic
procedure of translation is at the same time sociological and cultural.

This idea is also expressed in Korean in a somewhat exaggerated
expression among professional translators as, 'Translation is a creation', or 'Translation is a rebellion' (against the author, maybe).

3. *What is the Aim of Translation?*

In my experience, almost all of the publishing companies that ask translators to translate English books provide them with their basic guidance
for translation, in which it is asked that the translation should meet two
conditions: one is to follow strictly the author's intent and style, and the
other is to make the sentences smooth and readable. But every translator knows that the two requests are almost incompatible, even though it
is the ideal of good translation. It is inevitable that translators take a
position on a scale of style of translation, at one end of which is wholly
literal translation and at the other end wholly free translation. The position one takes is dependent upon how one understands what translation
is. Is the translation to be faithful to the author so as to transfer even
style as well as intent into the receptor language, or to change the

6.   T. Tymoczko, 'Translation and Meaning', in F. Guenthner and M. Guenthner-Reutter (eds.), *Meaning and Translation: Philosophical and Linguistic
Approaches* (London: Gerald Duckworth, 1978), p. 29.
7.   Tymoczko, 'Translation and Meaning', p. 43. He argues, using the concept
of the meaning assignment, that the meaning of a sentence is dependent upon the
social and cultural environment of the speaker/writer. Cf. also Nida and Taber, *The
Theory and Practice of Translation*, p. vii. De Waard and Nida, in *From One Language to Another*, p. 184, express the latest approach to translation as socio-
semiotic.

source language drastically so as to be readable for those who do not know the source language? This has a far-reaching effect on the way in which a translator translates the source text.

Nida's approach can serve as a point of departure, because he addresses this problem as he makes a contrast between the 'traditional' way and the 'new' way of translation. He calls the traditional method 'formal equivalence' or 'formal correspondence', and the new one 'dynamic equivalence' or later 'functional equivalence'. What does he mean by these terms?

a. *Formal Equivalence/Correspondence*
In his book *Toward a Science of Translating*, published in 1964, Nida defined 'formal equivalence' as a method which 'focuses attention on the message itself, in both form and content'.[8] This translation

> is concerned with such correspondences as poetry to poetry, sentence to sentence, and concept to concept. Viewed from this formal orientation, one is concerned that the message in the receptor language should match as closely as possible the different elements in the source language.

He calls this kind of structural equivalence 'a "gloss translation", in which the translator attempts to reproduce as literally and meaningfully as possible the form and content of the original'.[9] To clarify his idea he adds that

> a gloss translation of this type is designed to permit the reader to identify himself as fully as possible with a person in the source-language context, and to understand as much as he can of the customs, manner of thought, and means of expression.[10]

He relates this emphasis on source to a philological approach in his other book, *From One Language to Another*.[11]

However, in his book, *The Theory and Practice of Translation*, published five years after his first, Nida's position on formal equivalence becomes more critical. In this book, he uses the term 'formal correspondence' rather than 'formal equivalence'. In the glossary, he describes the term as follows:

8.   Nida, *Toward a Science of Translating with Special Reference to Principles and Procedures involved in Bible Translating* (Leiden: E.J. Brill, 1964), p. 159.

9.   Nida, *Toward a Science of Translating*, p. 159.

10.   Nida, *Toward a Science of Translating*, p. 159.

11.   De Waard and Nida, *From One Language to Another*, p. 182.

> Quality of a translation in which the features of the form of the source text have been mechanically reproduced in the receptor language. Typically, formal correspondence *distorts* the grammatical and stylistic patterns of the receptor language, and hence distorts the message, so as to cause the receptor to misunderstand or to labor unduly hard; opposed to DYNAMIC EQUIVALENCE.[12] (Italics mine)

This method focuses, according to Nida and Taber, on the 'form of the message, and translators took particular delight in being able to reproduce stylistic specialties, e.g., rhythms, rhymes, plays on word, chiasmus, parallelism, and unusual grammatical structure'.[13] It is noticed that Nida's understanding of 'formal equivalence' has been changed, and he has become tougher and more critical of it, using the term 'distort'. In his first book, 'formal equivalence' is related to 'the message itself, in both form and content'. But in his second book, 'formal correspondence' is related only to form, not to content. In his first book, 'formal equivalence' does not necessarily lead to misunderstanding. It just asks for more footnotes in the translation, and more effort on the part of the reader. But in the second book, it leads to misunderstanding, and presumably should never be allowed in translation.

b. *Dynamic/Functional Equivalence*
As the opposite of formal equivalence, Nida puts dynamic equivalence. Later he uses the term 'functional equivalence' in place of dynamic equivalence to avoid possible misunderstanding.[14] He shows a consistent understanding in terms of functional equivalence. In *Toward a Science of Translating*, he declares that this method

> is based upon 'the principle of equivalent effect'. In such a translation one is not so concerned with matching the receptor-language message with the source-language message, but with the dynamic relationship, *that the relationship between receptor and message should be substantially the same as that which existed between the original receptors and the message.*[15]

This same idea is expressed in his second book, *The Theory and Practice of Translation*:

12. Nida and Taber, *The Theory and Practice of Translation*, p. 201.
13. Nida and Taber, *The Theory and Practice of Translation*, p. 1.
14. De Waard and Nida, *From One Language to Another*, p. vii.
15. Nida, *Toward a Science of Translating*, p. 159 (italics mine).

Dynamic equivalence is therefore to be defined in terms of the degree to which *the receptors of the message in the receptor language respond to it in substantially the same manner as the receptors in the source language.* This response can never be identical, for the cultural and historical settings are too different, but there should be a high degree of equivalence of response, or the translation will have failed to accomplish its purpose.[16]

In the glossary of the same book, he describes functional equivalence in the same vein as the 'quality of a translation in which the message of the original text has been so transported into the receptor language that the response of the receptor is essentially like that of the original receptors'.[17]

c. *Some Questions*

As the italicized portions in the above paragraphs show, the key issue of the new approach to translation is the equivalence of response between receptors of the source language and receptors of the second language. This raises several questions, not only in terms of semantics, but in terms of the possibility of actually undertaking such a translation.

First, if the aim of translation is to induce a response from the receptors of the second language which is identical to that of the receptors of the first language, how can a translator confirm whether the response of the former induced by the translation is identical to that of the latter? This problem makes functional equivalence so much more complicated than formal equivalence, that transition from the latter to the former seems not a wise option. In a sense, functional equivalence appears smart in theory, but it seems impracticable in reality.

Secondly, to achieve functional equivalence, a translator must first imagine the dialogue between the *Vorlage* and the original receptors, and then should try to find the translation which will best build the functionally identical dialogue between the translation and the present receptors. Now, how can a translator identify the dialogue between the *Vorlage* and the numerous readers? This is practically impossible.

In terms of quantity, there is a good example to illustrate the point. Recently I received from my linguist friend an e-mail invented by Deborah and Loren Haarsma as a Christian joke:

---

16. Nida and Taber, *The Theory and Practice of Translation*, p. 24 (italics mine).

17. Nida and Taber, *The Theory and Practice of Translation*, p. 200.

Parables for Modern Academia: New Revised Academic Version (NRAV)

- By Deborah and Loren Haarsma

If Jesus taught on the campus today, what might His parables say?

When you are writing a paper about exciting new data, do not overstate the impact of your result. Someone else may come along later with better data and prove you wrong, and then you will be humiliated and your colleagues will not respect your work. But when you have an exciting new result, be modest about its implications. Then when the review paper comes out, it will say, 'This is an important piece of work', and you will be honored in the presence of all your colleagues. For everyone who exalts himself will be humbled, and he who humbles himself will be exalted (See: Luke Chapter 14, verses 7-11).

No one runs untested code on a network server, for the code may crash and take down the server. Likewise, no one puts old format data files into new databases. The new database will be corrupted, and the data will be lost. No, you put new-format data into new databases (See: Matthew Chapter 9, verses 14-17)

The kingdom of heaven is like an original manuscript in a used book store. When a historian found it, she sold all her other books to buy the manuscript. Again, the kingdom of heaven is like a scientist looking for new projects. When he found one theory of great promise, he joyfully gave up all his other projects to focus on it (See: Matthew Chapter 13, verses 44-46).

I cannot imagine a better example of a perfect functional equivalence than this modern version of Jesus' parables. But the point which this example raises is that an infinite number of different translations is needed to meet the requirement of functional equivalence. The number of responses of persons affected by the *Vorlage* is innumerable. If this is the case, whose response is the one which a translator should take into account in a translation? This difficulty, together with the difficulty of confirming the identicalness of the original receptors and the present receptors, renders functional equivalence untenable.

Thirdly, if the burden of translation is moved from the author's meaning to the receptor's response, where does the translator search for the meaning of the text? It is true that the author would not have written in a vacuum, and the existence and situation of the receptors would have had an important effect on his writing. But in the case of ancient books like the Bible, it is easy to get into wild speculation about the receptor's response due to the lack of background knowledge about the situation. Rather, it seems safer to put the author's text in the center, and use the provable data about the receptor as a subsidiary means of support. This means that concentrating on the text itself rather than on a vague response of the receptor is a more realistic approach to translation.

Fourthly, in the appendix of the book, *From One Language to Another*, the authors admit the difficulties involved in Bible translating:

> In the first place, there are difficulties posed by the cultural and temporal distance between the source texts and the present day... In the second place, the translation of the Scriptures differs from the translation of present-day documents because one cannot consult an author of any biblical book, and there are no informants who can provide insight on linguistic usage based on their own native use of such languages... In the third place, for any one writer in the Old Testament or New Testament there is a very limited corpus, so it is difficult to test for most stylistic patterns.[18]

If this is true, it is difficult to see why De Waard and Nida should have put forward the response of the receptor as the better approach to translation. It would have been sufficient for them to point out the problem of too literal translation, and show ways of dealing with that problem.

Fifthly, even though Nida and Taber declare the comparison of the responses of the receptors then and now as the new and better approach to translation, it is not possible to find the concrete method of comparison in their books. All they have done is to show the better way of understanding the source language and translating it into the receptor language. It seems that in this work they have achieved remarkable results. In terms of methodology, they provide plenty of examples and a concrete way of improving translation. It seems, however, that some of their understanding of translation as communication[19] needs to be scrutinized, which will be done in the next section.

Sixthly, in terms of my own experience, I put myself psychologically in the position of authors, not readers. This is a shared experience of almost all translators. They unconsciously identify themselves as a mouthpiece of the authors. Their sole aim is to speak as exactly as possible what the authors speak in their books. I do not try to speak what the original or present readers would understand from the texts, but

18. De Waard and Nida, *From One Language to Another*, pp. 185, 186.
19. De Waard and Nida, *From One Language to Another*, pp. 185, 186.

what the authors speak. It means that I have presupposed that translators are responsible to authors, not readers. The role of the translator is to convey the idea of the author, and to understand the idea is the role of the reader. In this respect Nida's suggestion is opposed to my practice. According to him, translators should put themselves not in the position of the author but in that of readers then and now. They should identify themselves with the readers, not the author. However, Nida does not state this plainly, but presupposes it. Thus, because the concrete way of achieving the suggested goal is not provided, I cannot find the applicability of his suggestions. As pointed out earlier, although his books are useful for improving one's translating skill, his suggestions of the new criteria for translation are, it seems to me, untenable, even though they should continue to be discussed by professional translators.

4. *Ambiguity versus Clarity*

Why do people translate one language into another? Why has translation become so necessary? The simple answer is that it is to overcome the barrier of language. But it was only during the days of confusion of the language at Babel when translation could simply be an 'overcoming of the barrier of language'. At the moment of the confusion of language, to translate one language into another would not have been as difficult as today, because at that moment the social and historical background would have been the same. As the years have passed and cultures diversified according to the places they occupy, however, translations have become the way of overcoming the barrier of language, culture, time, space, and so on—in summary, all the barriers to communication.

But in terms of the Bible, translation does not always achieve the overcoming of the barrier to communication. In many cases, even though there is not a barrier of language, meaningful communication does not occur. For example, the fact that there is no barrier of language does not guarantee that there is no problem of communication or understanding. The New Testament itself is a good example. One of the most conspicuous examples would be the parable of the sower in Mt. 13.1-9 (Mk 4.1-9; Lk. 8.4-8). Whether it was originally told in Aramaic or Greek, even though the sentences would have conveyed some meaning to the original hearers, had it not been for the interpretation by Jesus, there would have been no way to grasp fully the

intended teaching of the parable.[20] However, the fact that the interpreted part is still to be interpreted should not escape our attention.[21]

In these cases, the real issue is not translation but exegesis. Much of
Scripture remains to be interpreted by later readers. Even those passages that were interpreted are still in need of later re- interpretation.[22]
It seems that in such a case the best way to translate is to leave ambiguity as it is. The translation of the word σάρξ is a good example. The
meaning and usage of this word is so complex that it is difficult to
translate this into any one single word. But the difficulty is that the
translator must choose an equivalent word as a result of his interpretation of it. Should this word be translated into a somewhat ambiguous
word like 'flesh' whenever it appears, or into a clearer word like
'human being' according to context?[23]

The difficulties of communication in Paul's writings had already
been recognized in the New Testament period (2 Pet. 3.16). A similar
problem is found in many parts of the New Testament writings (Jn 6.1-
71; Acts 8.30-31). It means that many parts of the New Testament must
be studied carefully to be understood. Or it means that the New Testament is a book, much of which must be taught by qualified teachers.
Focusing on communication in translation without taking this fact into
consideration can be misleading. The translator of Scripture should be
reminded that the text they are translating is not the sort of text which

20. It is interesting to note how Richard B. Gaffin Jr connects this aspect with
the gift of tongues in the New Testament period. See his *Perspectives on Pentecost*
(Phillipsburg, PA: Presbyterian and Reformed Publishing, 1979), esp. p. 80. He
suggests that 'tongues' could not have been a sort of meaningless sound, as being
proposed by some today. Rather, he thinks that 'tongues' in the New Testament
period could have been like the parable in the New Testament. As the parable has
to be interpreted before it becomes a meaningful message, so also 'tongues'. This
could have some implications for translation of the New Testament.

21. The fact that the Bible is a book to be interpreted has to be taken seriously
into consideration. It means that the more a translator's interpretation is eliminated,
the more room is given to readers to interpret. Even if it is true that how a translator's interpretation can be eliminated in the process of translation is an ongoing
question, it does not allow unbridled or subjective opinion to be incorporated into
the translation.

22. For example, the parable of the sower was interpreted by Jesus. But the
interpreted part is still to be interpreted.

23. TEV translates the σάρξ in Jn 1.4 as 'human being'. This problem was discussed in the seminars with Eugene A. Nida at the Centre for Advanced Theological Research, Biblical Studies Research Cluster, of Roehampton Institute London.

can easily be understood by every one. Translators might be translating a text, the real meaning of which they themselves do not know. Sometimes it might be more important and require more effort for the translator to maintain the ambiguity of the text than to make the text easier to understand. It is true that some expressions of the Bible can be translated into more updated and readable ones. But this is sacrificing the original ambiguity to make the expression easier to read.

One of the problems which an easy-to-read translation might cause is well exemplified by the translation of the term 'these last days' in Heb. 1.2. NEB translates this term into 'this the final age'.[24] But this translation raises two questions. First, is 'this the final age' easier to understand than 'these last days' for ordinary readers? Secondly, and more importantly, is 'this the final age' the right translation of the original Greek ἐσχάτου τῶν ἡμερῶν τούτων and its Semitic background?[25] The answers to both of these questions, it seems, should be negative. Especially in terms of the second question, the NEB translation sacrifices the technical term, burdened with heavy theological implications. Then why should the more literal translation 'these last days' be changed into 'this the final age'? No matter which translation is chosen, the real meaning of the term can be known only by studying the issue.

There is one more case in which the principle of ambiguity should be kept. In some cases, words of a writer or a speaker can be misunderstood by the original readers or hearers for some reason, but are rightly understood after many years. In this situation, translators have the vantage point of history. They have an understanding of the text which the original reader or hearer did not have. In this case, the translator should try not to incorporate later knowledge into the translation. Nevertheless, the translator and contemporary reader can be said to have a built-in problem; they cannot go back to the state of ignorance of the original readers or hearers. They cannot read the text without the knowledge they obtained through the development of history. Because of this, the fact that the original reader did not understand the meaning can be overlooked. A total misunderstanding of the text, or at least a weakening of the meaning of the text, can result.[26]

---

24. Nida and Taber, *The Theory and Practice of Translation*, p. 142.

25. See G. Vos, *The Pauline Eschatology* (Grand Rapids: Baker Book House, 1982), pp. 1-42. Vos prefers the expression 'the latter days' to 'the last days'.

26. A good example is the term Messiah. In the New Testament period the term is hardly applied to Jesus Christ as it is applied to him today. If this is not taken into

For example, let us imagine a sentence uttered by a scientist. He says 'Apparently the earth is round' at a time when people still do not know the fact that the earth is round. The problem is that the word 'apparently' can be interpreted differently according to the context. If the translator is not cautious enough to discern which meaning was used by the scientist, he can easily translate it as 'certainly', when the scientist actually meant 'seemingly' because he had not been sure of the fact.

5. *Multiple Translations*

I expect that objections will be raised against the idea of maintaining ambiguity in the translation of Scripture. The main objection would possibly be that, because the Scriptures of the Old and New Testament are intended to be understood, every effort should be made to make the book easily readable.[27] But, as noted above, the fact that the Bible is intended to be understood does not necessarily mean that all of it can be understood without studying or instruction.

However, some complex aspects are involved in the method of translation of the Bible. They are related to the unique position which Christianity and its canon have come to occupy in the thousands of years that have passed since its inception. At first, Christianity started as a small religious movement in Palestine. The New Testament was at first a sort of recollection of their master and encouragement to be faithful to their common faith in times of difficulties. To the Christians of the first few generations, what became the New Testament were exclusive writings which could be received and understood by their own small group. It was strictly a 'religious' book for a small group. And they felt not only that their principle of life was different from that of the rest of the world, but that there was a deep gulf between them and the rest of the world (e.g. 1 Cor. 6.1-6; 2 Cor. 6.14-18). It seems

account, the episodes in which Jesus was called Messiah could easily be misconceived. A.C. Thiselton provides a good opposite example. It is related to the situation in which contemporary readers lose the dynamic meaning the original hearers could get from the discourse. See *The Two Horizons* (Grand Rapids: Eerdmans, 1984), pp. 12-14.

27. It seems that Nida accepts the 'exact translation hypothesis'. See *The Theory and Practice of Translation*, p. 4. But this view is refuted by Edward L. Keenan in his article 'Some Logical Problems in Translation', in Guenthner and Guenthner-Reutter (eds.), *Meaning and Translation*, p. 189.

that sometimes they did not expect their faith to be received and understood by the world (1 Cor. 1.18-25). The only way by which their faith could be understood and received was to be enlightened by supernatural intervention. They would never have dreamt that the writings they had used for religious purposes would become part of the most popular book in the world. This can be illustrated by the fact that a large part of the New Testament is letters.

But the picture has changed drastically since then. That small religion has become a world religion, and their religious writings a permanent best-seller. Now the Bible is not a book of a small group of people who believe that they are different from the rest of the world. The Bible is literally the property of humanity and its history. When we think of this situation, it is natural that the use of the Bible is so diverse.

To some the Bible is a book of historical data. It contains valuable historical data of the ancient Near East. To those who study the history of the ancient Near East, the Bible is an indispensable source of data to be consulted. To some the Bible is the source of inspiration of their literary imagination. To many people the Bible is an essential book for reading for refinement. To some the Bible is purely the source of their theology. They erect their building of theology on the basis of the Bible in a purely external way—without any internal relationship between their thought and the teaching of the Bible. To some the Bible is the authoritative and infallible divine book. If all of this is true, it can be seen that multiple translations of the Bible is not baseless.[28]

The translation for those who read the Bible as a book for culture and for those who study the Bible to prepare sermons is not necessarily the same. Rather, the two kinds of translations should be different. Even though it is not possible to translate the Bible for all conceivable purposes, it seems necessary to distinguish a translation for the Church from that for the general reader.

---

28. The need for different types of translation is pointed out in *The Theory and Practice of Translation*, p. 31. The authors enumerate three types of scriptural translation: (1) a translation which will reflect the traditional usage and be used in the Church, largely for liturgical purposes (this may be called an 'ecclesiastical translation'), (2) a translation in the present-day literary language, so as to communicate to the well-educated constituency, and (3) a translation in the 'common' or 'popular' language, which is known to and used by the common people, and which is at the same time acceptable as a standard for published materials. But in my view, it is difficult to see how (2) and (3) should be different.

It seems that the principle of ambiguity and more literal translation could be kept for those who read and study the Bible throughout their lives, possibly in the context of attending Church services and hearing sermons. It seems that the more accurate rather than easy-to-read translation is appropriate for them. But for those for whom reading is the primary way to understand the Bible, a more paraphrased version could be prepared. But even in this case, the translators would have to decide carefully how much they would run the risk of misrepresentation for the easier and more readable text.

APPENDIX

The following is the result of double translation. The purpose of this survey is to test whether translated sentences are correctly transferred to second-language readers. Five sentences, listed below, were chosen and translated into Korean. And the translated Korean sentences were sent to six Koreans who are studying in the U.K. to be translated into English again. The analysis of the result is left to readers. The five sentences are listed below. The results are as follows:

1. We need to be wary of our technology too. We stand on the threshold of what Marshall McCluhan has called the electric era.

2. In the present case the gang has not been apprehended although arrests are believed to be imminent.

3. As she waited in the crowd of people who were all waiting for the train, she had the feeling that she was being watched. A few feet away from her a tall man in a dark coat had his eyes fixed on her. As she looked up, he turned his head away.

4. We found that the law of causality, as usually stated by philosophers, is false, and is not employed in science.

5. In order to justify the claim that a sentence S in language L cannot be adequately translated into e.g. English we must be able to explain (in English) what properties S has which fail to be captured in English. This explanation itself provides the basic translation of the original sentence!

1. We need to be wary of our technology too. We stand on the threshold of what Marshall McCluhan has called the electric era.

1-1. We need to be careful with our technology. We are now on the threshold of 'electricity generation' as Marshall McCluhan termed it.

1-2. We should be careful about our technology. We are faced at the threshold of the age which is called as 'Electrical generation' by Marshall McCluhan.

1-3. It is necessary to be cautious for our technology. We are standing at the threshold of the era which Marshall McCluhan calls the electricity era.

1-4. It is necessary for us to be cautious about our technology. We are now standing on the threshold of Electric period named by M. McCluhan.

1-5. We are care about our technics. We stand on the verge of the period which Marshall McCluhan calls it an election age.

1-6. We also need to be careful in using our technology. We are at the threshold of the 'electric age' named by Marshall McCluhan.

2. In the present case the gang has not been apprehended although arrests are believed to be imminent.

2-1. The gang is believed to be on the verge of being arrested this time, but he is still at large.

2-2. It is believed that the arrest has drawn near at this time, but a gang has not still arrested.

2-3. It is believed that the gangsters will be nearly arrested, but they weren't yet.

2-4. It is believed that the arrest is imminent, but still the gang has not been caught yet.

2-5. In this case, though it seems to believe that the arrest would be reached, the gang still is free on the arrest.

2-6. In this case, the arrest of the gang is expected to be near at hand, but he is still at large.

3. As she waited in the crowd of people who were all waiting for the train, she had the feeling that she was being watched. A few feet away from her a tall man in a dark coat had his eyes fixed on her. As she looked up, he turned his head away.

3-1. As she, too, was among the crowd who waited for a train, she felt someone's eye on herself. A tall man in a dark coat standing a few feet away from where she was, fixed his eye on her. Once she raised her eyes to him, he turned his head away.

3-2. She was waiting in the crowd who all were waiting a train, but she felt that she was observed closely by someone. A tall man who wore a dark coat was standing at gaze into her in the apart only some feet from her. He turned as his head as she looked up.

3-3. She was waiting for the train in a crowd with the same aim. She realized that someone observed her. A tall man wearing a dark coat at a few feet distance from her fixed his eyes on her. When she looked up him, he turned his head.

3-4. When she was waiting for the train within the crowds, she noticed that someone was staring her. From a few feet away, a tall guy putting dark coat on was fixing his eyes on her. As soon as she stared him back, he turned his eyes to the other side.

3-5. She felt herself that somebody was watching her in the people who were waiting for the train like she did. The tall man with the dark jumper distant some feet from her kept his eyes on her. He turn aside as soon as she looked at him.

3-6. When she was waiting for a train in a crowd, she felt herself looked on by somebody. At a few yards away from her, a man wearing a dark jacket was looking at her. On meeting her eyes, he turned away his eyes.

4. We found that the law of causality, as usually stated by philosophers, is false, and is not employed in science.

4-1. We came to realize that the law of causality set forth by philosophers is not true and adopted by science.

4-2. The Law of Cause and Effect almost stated by philosophers is not true and we discovered this has not been adopted from the Science.

4-3. We found that the laws of cause and effect explained usually by philosophers were not true and not accepted in science.

4-4. According to the theory described by most philosophers, the law of causality is not true, and we found that these theories were not accepted by science.

4-5. We found out that the rule of cause and effect argued by most philosophers is not true, and does not adopt in the science.

4-6. We found that the law of cause and effect generally mentioned by philosophers was not the truth and could not be adopted in the field of science.

5. In order to justify the claim that a sentence S in language L cannot be adequately translated into e.g. English we must be able to explain (in English) what properties S has which fail to be captured in English. This explanation itself provides the basic translation of the original sentence!

5-1. In order to justify the claim that the sentence S composed of language L cannot be properly translated in English, we must be able to explain what property of S cannot be grasped in English. The very explanation becomes the basic translation of the original sentence.

5-2. I don't understand the meaning its question into Korean.

5-3. It must be able to explain why some aspects in sentence 'S' can't be translated into English in order to justify an opinion that sentence 'S' in language 'L' can't be translated into English properly. The very explanation will be a basic translation of the original sentence.

5-4. A sentence 'S' of language 'L' cannot be properly interpreted in perfection. To justify this theorem, it is needed to explain why a certain attribute of 'S' cannot be recognized in English. Thus, this explanation becomes original basic interpretation of this sentence.

5-5. It should be explained that the justification of the argument that L, the sentence of 'S', could be translated in English exactly should need the explanation what characteristics of 'S' are. It is the basic translation of the original sentence.

5-6. In order to justify that sentence S written in language L cannot be properly put into English, you should be able to explain why certain character of S cannot be rendered into English. That explanation itself becomes basic translation of the original sentence.

REMAINDERLESS TRANSLATIONS? IMPLICATIONS OF THE
TRADITION CONCERNING THE TRANSLATION OF THE LXX
FOR MODERN TRANSLATIONAL THEORY

Brook W.R. Pearson

1. The Tradition Concerning the Translation of the LXX

The study of the LXX translation is a most fascinating area in biblical studies. For this paper, however, the LXX itself is not the primary focus. I am not concerned here with the characteristics of the translation, the *Vorlage*, or the recensions. As instructive as all of these may be, for modern translational theory, it is the tradition *about* the origin and purpose of the LXX and its translation process that has the most potential pay-off. A careful examination of the orientations of the different ancient writers towards this tradition, in the light of philosophical hermeneutics, shows striking similarities between the modern orientation of translational theorists and the need ancient Jews and Christians seemed to feel concerning the defense of their access to the very words of God.

a. *The Chronological Development of the Tradition Concerning the Translation of the LXX*
One issue that has been standard in the discussion of the LXX is that of origin. In part, this has meant a lengthy discussion of a piece of literature known as the *Letter of Aristeas*—a document purporting to be contemporary to the translation of the LXX, telling the story of its origins. The tradition that the LXX (as its Latin name and the Roman numerals typically used as an abbreviation for that name imply) was translated in seventy or seventy-two days by seventy or seventy-two Jewish elders almost surely has its beginnings in this pseudepigraphical document.

There are many excellent summaries available of this fascinating document, but here we will concern ourselves mainly with those features of *Aristeas*'s story that relate directly to our topic. According to

Aristeas, the translation of the LXX was undertaken at the request of the second of the Ptolemaic kings, Philadelphus, as part of the continuing library project at Alexandria.[1] *Aristeas*, the *Letter*'s purported author, is supposed to have been a Greek courtier at the court of Philadelphus. The *Letter*, supposedly addressed to Aristeas's brother, Philocrates, begins with a vignette where Demetrius of Phalerum, who is, according to the *Letter*, the head librarian under Philadelphus,[2] reported to the king that the Law of the Jews would be a worthwhile inclusion in the library. The king, wanting to know what is hindering their inclusion, is informed that the problem is one of translation.[3] The king then immediately orders a letter written to the 'high priest of the Jews' (*Letter of Aristeas* 11) to request that arrangements be made to effect such a work. Aristeas, being present while this exchange takes place, takes the opportunity to point out to Philadelphus that there are a great number of Jewish captives in Egypt as a result of Ptolemy I Soter's (his father's) campaigns in Palestine and neighbouring areas. Aristeas had apparently been lobbying for their release with the heads of the king's bodyguard for quite some time, and this request for a translation of the Jewish Law seemed like the perfect time to have his case heard by the king himself. From this point on, Aristeas becomes the king's advisor and envoy in the whole process of requesting from the high priest in Jerusalem both the Hebrew texts of the Law and the translators required to make a Greek translation thereof.

What follows this introductory section is essentially a treatise on, and apologetic for, Judaism. The king, deciding to emancipate the Hebrew slaves, pays a sum of money to all their owners[4] (the content of the

---

1. A project actually started by his father, Ptolemy I Soter.

2. There is some question as to whether or not Demetrius ever actually held this post, although *Aristeas* is backed up by the fragment of Aristobulus preserved by Eusebius in *Prep. Evang.* 13.12. On this see H. Meecham, *The Oldest Version of the Bible* (London: Holborn, 1932), pp. 120-21, 140-41, and C.R. Holladay, 'Aristobulus (OT Pseudepigrapha)', *ABD* 1 (1992), pp. 383-84.

3. At this point in the narrative, there is a most interesting characterization of the Hebrew language: 'There is a need further of translation. For in the Jews' country they use peculiar marks (just as Egyptians use their system of letters), as also they have a peculiar speech. They are supposed to use the Syrian [Aramaic] language. But that is not the case. It is another dialect' (*Letter of Aristeas* 11) (all quotations taken from the ET in Meecham, *The Oldest Version*).

4. The sum, twenty drachmas, is apparently far below the market value of such slaves, but see Meecham, *The Oldest Version*, pp. 175-76 for the suggestion

decree is given in §§22–25). We are then shown the contents of the official report made by Demetrius to Philadelphus regarding the books of the Jewish Law:

> To the Great King from Demetrius... [The books of the Jewish Law] happen to be written in Hebrew characters and in the Hebrew tongue, and have been interpreted somewhat carelessly[5] and are not as in the original, according to a report submitted by the experts; for the books have never chanced upon the forethought of a king. It is necessary that these also should in an emended form be in thy possession, because this code of laws, since it is divine, is somewhat philosophic in character and unimpaired... (*Letter of Aristeas* 30–31).

It is interesting to note that, given that it is commonly understood that *Aristeas* is pseudepigraphical, and that most (if not all) scholars are quick to point out that the author was not merely not Aristeas, but that he was also likely not Greek, there seems to be very little understanding of the significance that this pseudepigraphy must have had for the writer of the document itself. Although it is often viewed as an apologetic document, aimed at one of several groups (Palestinian Jews, Alexandrian Jews, Greeks), it has never been examined from the standpoint of the orientation the author must have had towards his own tradition to write such material.[6] A good example of where such a discussion would prove helpful to the topic is in a recent paper by Sebastian Brock, concerned with the significance of the existence of 8HevXIIgr, the scroll of the Twelve Prophets in Greek that was found in the Naḥal Ḥever, for the study of LXX recensions and revisions. He undertakes a study of the tradition concerning the translation of the LXX much like the present one, but from the standpoint that each writer

---

(following Westermann) that this is not a purchase price, but rather a token compensation for the loss that the slave owners underwent.

5.   There is a great deal of discussion over the exact meaning of the term σεσήμανται, translated here 'interpreted'. Although this translation seems to make it look as if there have been earlier translation attempts (something which *Aristeas* itself intimates [312–13]), another way of understanding this word is with the translation, 'written', that is, the manuscripts which were available *in Hebrew* were faulty. For a thorough discussion of this issue, see G. Howard, 'The Letter of *Aristeas* and Diaspora Judaism', *JTS* 22 (1971), pp. 337-48, and the sources listed there.

6.   Howard does, however, come closer to the mark than most when he suggests that, evidently, 'enough had been said by those who regularly used the original Hebrew to create a problem in the minds of Egyptian Jewry about their Greek translation' ('*Aristeas* and Diaspora Judaism', p. 342).

is actually talking about the concept of revising the LXX. It is interesting to note that Brock, in his discussion of the *Letter of Aristeas*, assumes that the whole purpose of the document is 'aimed at undermining the position of would-be revisers of the original translation'.[7] After this statement, he goes on to summarise what he sees as the salient portions of the letter. It is somewhat damaging to his argument to note that, in his summary, he ignores the prelude to the document, then jumps from §32 to §§46–47, and then, with only two references to the body of the document (§§121 and 176), to the conclusion at §§310–311. Of course, at some level, the author of *Aristeas* may be polemicizing against the possibility of revising the LXX, but such a scanty group of references to the document itself to support such a claim does not make it a convincing one. Perhaps we would do better, along with Sidney Jellicoe, to 'regard it basically as an apology for Judaism...'[8]

This being said, the document, whatever its intended purpose or purposes, has as its expressed *raison d'être* the story of the LXX translation. What it has to say on the topic is important, being one of the very earliest accounts of the LXX and its origins (if not the earliest). Some elements in particular regarding the translation itself must be noticed, specifically those that show development later on in references to the tradition:

1. The *Letter of Aristeas* presents the LXX translation as something that came about as the result of a request from the pagan king Philadelphus. It shows Philadelphus in a very humble role vis-à-vis the High Priest in Palestine, but in a way that makes him seem very astute in terms of the proper way of approaching the Jews.[9]

---

7.   S. Brock, 'To Revise or Not to Revise: Attitudes to Jewish Biblical Translation', in G. Brooke and B. Lindars (eds.), *Septuagint, Scrolls and Cognate Writings* (SBLSCS, 33; Atlanta: Scholars Press, 1992), p. 306. Brock claims support for this 'Correctly understood' viewpoint from Klijn, Barthélemy, and Orlinsky (p. 334, n. 11). However, Orlinsky never actually talks about the question of revision in the essay cited by Brock (H. Orlinsky, 'The Septuagint as Holy Writ and the Philosophy of the Translators', *HUCA* 46 [1975], pp. 89-114), and Klijn and Barthélemy (along with Pelletier) are in the small minority with this viewpoint (see S. Jellicoe, *The Septuagint in Modern Study* [Oxford: Clarendon Press, 1968], p. 49).

8.   Jellicoe, *Septuagint in Modern Study*, p. 49.

9.   See, for instance, the non-offensive design of the gifts intended for temple

2. The number and constitution of the body of the translators is portrayed as representative of the entire nation of Israel—six from each tribe.[10]

3. The bulk of the document is taken up with an account of a series of seven banquets where the king puts seventy-two (rather difficult) questions to the translators, which each of them manages to answer with consummate wisdom and diplomacy. The prime significance, for this discussion, of this lengthy section is that the answers are *never* given on the basis of an appeal to authority (such as the Old Testament texts), but wholly and consistently reflect the Hellenistic ideals of natural law and logic.

4. The translation project, undertaken after this series of banquets, happens on the isle of Pharos, which was connected to the city by a breakwater, but remote enough that their work would go undisturbed. This work takes place in seventy two days, *by means of consultation between the translators* (§302).

5. Once the translation is finished, Demetrius accepts the final version from the hands of the translators, then he

> assembled the Jewish people in the place where the translation had been made and read it over to all in the presence of the translators, who received another great ovation from the people, inasmuch as they had been the agents of great blessings. And they accorded a like welcome to Demetrius as well and requested him to have the whole Law transcribed and to present it to their rulers (*Letter of Aristeas* 308–309).

usage discussed in §§51–82, and the way that the king is portrayed as being personally responsible for their oversight.

10. Several authors have noticed that this is somewhat of an impossibility at this point in the history of the nation (e.g. Orlinsky, 'The Septuagint as Holy Writ'), but it is significant that the author (who was probably more aware of that fact than we) nevertheless makes it a key point in his portrayal of the whole process. M. Hadas points out that the 'basis of the tradition is doubtless the body of seventy elders which Moses set up. At Exodus 24.11 where the elders are spoken of and where the Hebrew gives, "And upon the nobles of the children of Israel He laid not his hand", the LXX gives, "And of the chosen ones of Israel not one perished". The verb used is [διαφόνειν], of which the common meaning is "disagreed". Such a homonym is ideal material for midrashic ingenuity' (*Aristeas to Philocrates* [JAL; New York: Harper and Brothers, 1951], p. 71).

6.   This is followed by a section where

> some members of the Jewish community and the rulers of the
> people stood up and said, 'Since the translation has been
> effected in so excellent and pious a fashion and with entire
> accuracy, it is right that it should remain in its present state
> and that there should be no revision' (*Letter of Aristeas* 310).

A curse is then pronounced on those who would do so.

7.   Here, at the close of the letter, one more thing should be
noted: When the King receives the translation and has it read
to him, he marvels,

> 'How is it that none of the historians or poets has thought to
> mention the accomplishment of matters of so great an impor-
> tance?' And [Demetrius] said, 'Because the Law is holy and
> has come into being by God. And certain men taking in hand
> to [mention it] were stricken by God and desisted from the
> attempt' (*Letter of Aristeas* 312–13).

Demetrius then goes on to give two examples where such did,
indeed, take place, both with fourth-century BCE Greek
authors.

These features form the basic skeleton of a story that became more and
more embellished in certain respects as the years passed, and the story
was used to serve other purposes, perhaps, than it had originally.

The writers who refer to the tradition up to the beginning of the
Common Era are few, but are particularly interesting in their variation:
While the *Letter of Aristeas* is likely either the earliest witness to the
tradition[11] or its inventor, Aristobulus, a Jewish philosopher of the
middle of the second century, either formed a source for or used a
common source of the tradition as *Aristeas* presents it, or is influenced
by either *Aristeas* or a common source. We have only fragments of
Aristobulus, but that which is preserved in Eusebius, *Prep. Evang.*
13.12.1-2 is relevant to our discussion here. In this passage, Aristobulus
argues that Plato and Pythagoras were influenced by the Jewish Law—
having at least part of all five books of the Pentateuch, although

---

11.   Probably dated most safely to the period c. 170 BCE. (So Jellicoe, *Septuagint and Modern Study*, pp. 49-50, on the basis of a variety of indicators placing it
in the early second century, argues convincingly that, 'a *terminus ante quem* of c.
170 BC would best meet the circumstances'.)

the entire translation of all the (books) of the Law (was made) in the time of the king called Philadelphus... He brought greater zeal (to the task than his predecessors) [who had had the portions of the law translated to which Aristobulus posits Plato and Pythagoras had access], while Demetrius of Phalerum managed the undertaking.[12]

The next mention we have of the LXX is in the prologue to Ben Sira's translation of his grandfather's book of wisdom now commonly known as Ecclesiasticus or Sirach (132 BCE). He is interested in the LXX, naturally, from a translator's point of view. In the prologue to the book, he briefly discusses the whole idea of translation, specifically from Hebrew into Greek:

> You are urged...to read with good will and attention, and to be indulgent in cases where, despite our diligent labor in translating, we may seem to have rendered some phrases imperfectly. For, what was originally expressed in Hebrew does not have exactly the same sense when translated into another language. Not only this work, but even the law itself, the prophecies, and the rest of the books differ not a little as originally expressed (Sirach, prologue RSV).

The next, and perhaps most interesting, writer on the topic is Philo (fl. c. 10 BCE–45 CE). His work, *On the Life of Moses*, naturally brings him to discuss the version of Moses' Law which was in common usage in his day, the LXX. Apparently the tradition that we see begun in the *Letter of Aristeas* had either developed during the interim time, or, equally possibly, there was a parallel tradition from which Philo draws:

> Sitting here in seclusion with none present save the elements of nature, earth, water, air, heaven, the genesis of which was to be the first theme of their sacred revelation, for the laws begin with the story of the world's creation, they became as it were possessed, and, under inspiration, wrote, not each several scribe something different, but the same word for word, as though dictated to each by an invisible prompter. Yet who does not know that every language, and Greek especially, abounds in terms, and that the same thought can be put in many shapes by changing single words and whole phrases and suiting the expression to the occasion? This was not the case, we are told, with this law of ours, but the Greek

---

12. *OTP* translation. The theme of the Jewish Law having been available to or responsible for the tradition of Greek philosophy and wisdom, was, apparently, a widespread one during the Hellenistic period. The most popular version has to do with the relationship between the Jews and the Spartans. See M. Hengel, *Judaism and Hellenism: Studies in their Encounter in Palestine during the Early Hellenistic Period* (trans. J. Bowden; 2 vols.; Philadelphia: Fortress Press, 1974), I, p. 26.

words used corresponded literally with the Chaldean [Hebrew], exactly suited to the things they indicated (*On the Life of Moses* 2.7.37-38 LCL).

He goes on to compare the translation to geometrical terms—essentially a remainderless translation. He then adds that,

> The clearest proof of this is that, if Chaldeans [Hebrews] have learned Greek, or Greeks Chaldean [Hebrew], and read both versions, the Chaldean [Hebrew] and the translation, they regard them with awe and reverence as sisters, or rather one and the same, both in matter and words, and speak of the authors not as translators but as prophets and priests[13] of the mysteries, whose sincerity and singleness of thought has enabled them to go hand in hand with the purest of spirits, the spirit of Moses (*On the Life of Moses* 2.7.39-40 LCL).

Added to this is, if the story given in the *Letter of Aristeas* and here in Philo is completely legendary, the rather odd story that every year a public assembly and festival was held on the isle of Pharos, celebrating the translation (and, apparently, the fact that it made the Law accessible to those who, possibly, may have never had the chance to learn to speak or understand Hebrew) (Philo, *On the Life of Moses* 2.7.41-43).

The final early writer of any note in this regard is Josephus (37–100+ CE). Josephus writes in a completely different time and setting than any of the previous writers. His position vis-à-vis the Roman empire naturally adds a dimension not felt in any of the previous authors. His three references to the tradition of the LXX translation dwell mainly on the status that the Jews were accorded in the Ptolemaic kingdom. Meecham, following Stählin, notes:

> His primary aim is to show that the Jews were treated with great honour by heathen kings. In this regard the story of Aristeas was much to the point. Hence Josephus has turned it to account three times. In *Con. Apion.* [2.44–47] its apologetic value predominates; in *Antiq.* [1.10] it furnishes for Josephus a sort of literary model [for his own action]. In both passages the story of the LXX translation is only briefly mentioned. In *Antiq.* [12.11–118], however, it is set forth in generous measure.[14]

The one point in all of Josephus's use of the tradition that is salient to the question at hand, namely the orientation that the various preservers

---

13. Jellicoe (*Septuagint and Modern Study*, p. 40 n. 1) notes that this word, translated as 'priests', is actually ἱεροφάντης, which actually brings out more the sense of 'one who teaches the rites of sacrifice and worship'. This word does not occur in either the LXX or the New Testament.

14. Meecham, *The Oldest Version*, p. 336.

of the tradition had towards the LXX translation, is found at the end of his final reference to it in *Ant.* 12.108–109. He changes the imprecation against alteration and revision that, as we mentioned above, forms part of the epilogue, into a somewhat confused command to leave the work as it is, along with an invitation to revise and complete it:

> all of them, including the priest and the eldest of the translators and the chief officers of the community, requested that, since the translation had been so successfully completed, it should remain as it was and not be altered. Accordingly, when all had approved this idea, they ordered that, if anyone saw any further addition made to the text of the Law or anything omitted from it, he should examine it and make it known and correct it; in this they acted wisely, that what had once been judged good might remain forever (*Ant.* 12.108–109 LCL).

Perhaps Josephus was aware of some of the revision which had already gone on in Jewish circles, and was loathe to leave under a curse those who sought to improve the translation's relation to the Hebrew original (which, for an apologetic historian, would be somewhat of an inconsistency).

b. *Disagreement among the Earliest Writers Regarding the Nature of the Translation*
As the concept of divine inspiration is perhaps the most well-known feature of the tradition concerning the translation of the LXX, it is interesting to note that it is a relatively late development. Neither Ben Sira, Aristobulus nor the *Letter of Aristeas* refers to the translation process as a divinely inspired one.[15] However, even without any question of

15. Orlinsky has tried to make a case that the *Letter of Aristeas*, with its passage regarding the reading of the Law after the translation had been completed, actually has as its primary purpose the proclamation that the translation was inspired. He does so by a rather spurious equation of the Hebrew phrase קרא...באזני העם (read aloud...in the hearing of the people) with the concept of canonization: '[this phrase], usually followed by an expression of consent by the assembly, describes the biblical procedure in designating a document official and binding, in other words, as divinely inspired, as Sacred Scripture'. While it is obvious that this kind of ceremony in the Hebrew Bible is covenantal in nature, it is equally clear to Orlinsky that the idea of 'divine inspiration' and even that of 'Sacred Scripture' are somewhat later developments. To go on and assert that this expression is equivalent to 'canonize' as Orlinsky does, then to jump from this equation to the further equation that the *Letter of Aristeas*, using similar language as the LXX does in translating this Biblical Hebrew, is asserting that the LXX is divinely inspired, leaves one somewhat breathless (see Orlinsky, 'The Septuagint as Sacred Writ', pp. 94-96).

inspiration, they display vastly differing regard for the translation itself. *Aristeas* is in favour of the translation. While he does not actually ascribe the translation to divine inspiration, there is definitely an element of the miraculous in the fact that the translators finish their task in seventy two days. It is also significant that the translation, as noted above, is done by a body that represents, both symbolically and physically, the historical nation of Israel. This gives the translation something of an authority that, if not divine, nevertheless purports to carry the same weight as the elders who judged the nation of Israel under the authority of Moses.[16]

Aristobulus does not specifically mention the status of the translation being either inspired or not, but it does not seem that the tradition had developed by his time to include the idea of overt divine inspiration.[17] His orientation towards the LXX itself seems to be positive, but again, this does not seem to be the primary focus of his discussion.

Ben Sira's brief comment is the first dissenting voice in what, for various reasons, became an ongoing dialogue. Quite apart from *Aristeas*'s assertion that the translation was effected 'with entire accuracy',[18] Ben Sira states that the two languages of Greek and Hebrew simply do not match up 'with entire accuracy'. It is important to note that, of the two dissenting voices regarding both the status of the LXX as an inspired document (or documents), and its status as a correct translation, both come from translators. Both Ben Sira and Jerome, as we shall see later, speak from experience, and with a critical point of view towards the LXX. In some ways, this same bifurcation is present in modern translational theory, except that now, it is theory based on and aimed at the translation of the biblical texts that has taken on the stance that was formerly occupied by those uninvolved in translation work (see the discussion below).

c. *The Development of the Idea of a Divinely Inspired Translation*
By Philo's time, the tradition had apparently undergone a great deal of lively development. There are several points in his discussion of the matter worth noticing:

16. Hadas, *Aristeas to Philocrates*, pp. 71-73. See also Howard, '*Aristeas* and Diaspora Judaism', pp. 337-40, concerning the significance of the Palestinian provenance of both the translators and the manuscripts which they translate.
17. Whether Aristobulus depends on Aristeas or vice versa does not affect this discussion, but it seems that the former is more likely.
18. *Letter of Aristeas* 310.

1. He talks of a festival that has grown up celebrating the translation, and is held on the very site where the translation is supposed to have taken place. The existence of such a celebration is something that Philo would certainly not have made up (if he expected his audience to take him seriously), and it points to, at least on some level, a popular regard for the LXX amongst Egyptian Jewry.

2. Philo describes the process of translating, as the translators understood it, as 'giving an oracular interpretation of divinely inspired laws' (*On the Life of Moses* 2.6.34),[19] and adds that the translators were, from the beginning (rather than after the translation process was completed), required to 'not add or take away or transfer anything, but must keep the original form and shape' (*On the Life of Moses* 2.6.34). These two elements in Philo's version of the tradition are highly significant. The first assumes that the translators were in some way inspired (and then, apparently, their work was also inspired, a point which Philo drives home a little later). The second then goes on to show that, from the outset, the translators were under constraint to produce a certain *kind* of translation—namely one that stuck *very* closely to the original. It may be possible to see this, in the light of the dissenting voices in the dialogue concerning the tradition about the LXX translation, as answering the criticism that the LXX was not actually a good approximation of the original. Philo nips this question in the bud by placing the criteria for the manner in which the translators were to respect the original Hebrew text in their translation *before* the inspiration takes place. Thus, the inspired nature of the translation (if one believes the story, as most of the sympathetic ancient world seems to have) a priori answers the question as to whether or not the translation is an accurate one.

3. Philo's account of the translation process itself is fairly straightforward. The translators are obviously inspired, and,

19. This is the translation offered by H.St.J. Thackeray (*The Letter of Aristeas* [London: SPCK, 1917]), and seems to make much better sense of θεσπισθέντας νόμους χρησμοῖς διερμηνεύειν than 'to make a full version of the laws given by the Voice of God', given by F.H. Colson in the LCL version.

from the way he talks about it, this seems to have been a popularly held idea at the time he writes. Where Philo's most significant contribution in this story can be seen is his equation of the LXX translation with geometry—which does 'not admit of variety in the expression which remains unchanged in its original form' (*On the Life of Moses* 2.7.39). This idea of a remainderless translation is intriguing, in that it is very similar to the aims of Eugene Nida's functional equivalence, as we will discuss more fully below.

It is plain to see that, as the tradition developed, the idea of divine inspiration became more and more central to the story. The reasons for this, as hinted at above, are complex. However, at the heart of it, it seems that the idea of the inspiration of the LXX came about primarily to provide those who depended on the LXX as their primary source for truth and practice with an unassailable argument against those who would suggest that it possibly did not completely convey the ideational thrust of the original.

d. *Early Christian and Rabbinic Usage of the Tradition*

The tradition branches into two distinct veins after the inception of Christianity: one Jewish, one Christian. That the LXX came to enjoy a fairly high status in all of the Jewish Diaspora, and likely even in Palestine, can be inferred by the references to it in rabbinic literature, which Hadas has helpfully collected and chronologically arranged.[20] The earliest of these is of specific interest. *b. Meg.* 9a repeats the idea that the translators were placed in separate rooms and produced seventy two identical translations, then adds that they managed to all alter the same thirteen or fourteen passages, all of which prevent one from getting an impression of polytheism from the translation. *y. Meg.* 1.71d also has the tradition concerning the alterations, but does not mention anything else about the tradition.

Early Christian usage, when it specifically refers to the translation process, seems largely to accept the fairly fantastic version of LXX

---

20. Hadas, *Aristeas to Philocrates*, pp. 80-83. Quotations and references taken from rabbinic literature are gathered from this source. See also E. Tov, 'The Rabbinic Tradition Concerning the "Alterations" Inserted into the Greek Pentateuch and Their Relation to the Original Text of the LXX', *JSJ* 15 (1984), pp. 65-89.

origins. The earliest Christian writing on the subject is arguably 2 Tim. 3.16 (RSV): 'Every Scripture is inspired by God and profitable for teaching' and so on. Although it does not explicitly state that it is speaking of the LXX, it is very unlikely that it could be referring to any other tradition—even if it had come to mean, by whatever time this document was written or forged, the inspiration of Christian documents as well, the idea of inspiration still had its genesis in the tradition concerning the translation of the LXX. Justin Martyr mentions the process, but does not say one way or the other as to whether or not the translations were inspired, or whether the seventy[21] were separated or worked together (*Apology* 1.31). In short, Justin refers to the tradition concerning the LXX translation as a historical fact,[22] rather than with any concern for its status as a translation. The earliest Christian document that preserves (and somewhat embellishes) the fully fantastic version of the tradition is Pseudo-Justin, *Exhortation to the Greeks* (c. mid-second century?). He names two sources for his story: Philo and Josephus, and adds a few details that he claims he received from the natives of the isle of Pharos. Irenaeus (c. 175 CE), Clement of Alexandria (150–212 CE), Tertullian (b. c. 160 CE), and Chrysostom (344–407 CE) all take for granted the inspiration of the LXX. Of the early Christian writers after Justin Martyr, the only one to refer to the translation process of the LXX without making specific reference to its inspired nature is Eusebius.[23] He 'presents an unadorned and generally reliable epitome of about a fourth of Aristeas [*Prep. Evang.* 8.2-5, 9; 9.38], accurate enough to be of use in textual criticism of that book'.[24]

---

21. Confusion regarding the number of translators is not uncommon—seventy and seventy two are the most common numbers, but one rabbinic passage (*Massakhet Sop.* 1.7-10) seems to say that there were five who did the work. Hadas gives a fairly convincing argument (*Aristeas to Philocrates*, p. 81 n. 109) that this number is the result of a scribal error. Of course, this scribal error, giving the idea of five elders doing the translation, would have been very natural to retain, given that the original translation project consisted of only the Pentateuch.

22. Unfortunately for Justin, his history is slightly skewed—he has the time frame somewhat confused, and places it in the time of Herod. Whether this two-and-a-half-century blunder is the result of a faulty source or a faulty memory, is unknown. At another place (*Dialogue* 68), he does refer to the time of Ptolemy, but without specifying *which* Ptolemy.

23. By this time the whole of the Old Testament had now taken on this inspired status, rather than just the Pentateuch.

24. Hadas, *Aristeas to Philocrates*, p. 76. See H.St.J. Thackeray, 'Introduction

e. *A Shift in Both Later Jewish and Later Christian Usage of the Tradition*

1. *The LXX's Loss of Status in Jewish Circles.* By this time, the LXX had ceased to be highly regarded in Jewish circles, probably largely because of its status as the official version of the Old Testament Scriptures for Christianity, and, more specifically, because of the Christological proof-texts taken by Christians from the LXX, not clear from the Hebrew.[25] The rabbinic literature preserves this distaste in two passages, *Massakhet Sop.* 1.7-10 and the Gaonic addition to the *Megillat Taanit*. The former compares the day that the translation was completed to that on which the nation of Israel made the golden calf, while the latter asserts that the world grew dark for three days when the Law was translated.

All in all, this would seem to be a wholly negative view of the translation. One specific point must be highlighted, however. The *Massakhet Sop.* passage records that the reason this translation was so bad for Israel was that 'the Law was not capable of being interpreted according to all its requirements'. This is extremely interesting in the light of the way that it seems to portray a prevailing attitude towards the idea of the translation of the Scriptures. If indeed this is what 'interpreted' means in this passage, it would stand to reason that the concept of translation underwent considerable scrutiny in the light of events in the first two centuries of the Common Era. In contrast to a time of relative prosperity for the Jews in terms of proselytization, the first and second centuries saw the complete defeat of all Jewish nationalistic hopes, and a much decreased position in the Roman world. Coupled with this political defeat was the religious problem of Christianity, which claimed a common ancestry with Judaism, but radically reinterpreted the very documents upon which Judaism was grounded. Naturally, this did not make the rabbis look back with longing towards the time when Judaism attempted to assert itself in terms of other traditions (i.e. Greek), of which process the translation of the LXX was a part. This was even less attractive when it was, in many cases, specifically the differences between the Hebrew Bible and the LXX that were giving, as it were, comfort to the enemy.

to the Letter of Aristeas', in H.B. Swete, *An Introduction to the Old Testament in Greek* (Cambridge: Cambridge University Press, 2nd edn, 1914), pp. 516-18.

25. See Tov, 'Rabbinic Tradition Concerning the "Alterations"'.

2. *A Split in Later Christian Tradition Regarding the LXX.* Later Christian reference to the tradition greatly emphasized the inspiration, even to the point of re-embellishment in Epiphanius (c. 315–403) in *On Weights and Measures* 3–11, where he essentially records the fantastic version of the tradition, but changes the seventy two individual translations into thirty six, each prepared by a pair of the translators (still with the miraculous agreement), who each slept in the same room with their partner and crossed over to the island each day on one of thirty six skiffs, again with their partner. He adds a variety of other detail to flesh out the account, but essentially just preserves the miraculous Philonic version of the story.

The first dissenting voice concerning the quality of the LXX translation, since Ben Sira in the second century BCE, was Jerome in the late fourth to early fifth centuries CE. He writes,

> I know not who was the first lying author to construct the seventy cells at Alexandria, in which they were separated and yet all wrote the same words, whereas Aristeas, one of the bodyguard of the said Ptolemy, and long after him Josephus have said nothing of the sort, but write that they were assembled in a single hall and conferred together, not that they prophesied. For it is one thing to be a prophet, another to be an interpreter (*Preface to the Pentateuch*).

As damning as this criticism appears to be, it did not apparently influence too wide of an audience, as his contemporary, Augustine, saw fit to perpetuate the more fantastic version of the tradition in the *City of God* 18.42. In fact, there was a long, drawn out disagreement between Augustine and Jerome, precipitated by Jerome's translation work.[26] The fact that the first reading of Jerome's new, non-LXX, translation of Jonah in Carthage caused a riot shows that this disagreement occurred at more than just a leadership level, however.

f. *A Consistent Bipolar Tension regarding the LXX*
It is easy to see how the inspiration tradition concerning the LXX gained such a wide following. When groups rely on texts for their identity—'faith and practice' as it is often put—the texts themselves often become sacred, inviolate, holy. This is the case for much more

---

26. The first chapter in W. Schwarz, *Principles and Problems of Biblical Translation: Some Reformation Controversies and their Background* (Cambridge: Cambridge University Press, 1955), tracing the development of both writers' viewpoints and of the disagreement between them, is standard reading in this matter.

than religious texts, however—any area of human understanding where new ideas challenge traditionally held ones is prone to the same tendency to enshrine the traditional idea. Consider the history of science, and Thomas Kuhn's now famous analysis of the 'paradigm shift', or even, on a less grand scale, the ongoing argument between PC and Apple Macintosh users—whichever one the individual has used will typically be the one they staunchly defend, and go on buying. Typically, this opposition breeds a kind of apologetic argumentation in which the loudest voices usually know the least, and are most likely to display faulty logic in their argumentation. This has certainly been true in such popular and long-standing arguments such as the creation–evolution debate, or the infamous 'Battle for the Bible' in the United States. We should therefore not be surprised to see a similar trend with the tradition concerning the LXX translation, and as we have seen, the tension is amply clear.

Any group that not only finds its existence based on texts, but also cannot actually apprehend those texts in their original form or language, finds itself on some psychologically shaky ground. When one is forced to appeal to an authority that may or may not mean what it *seems* to mean in translation, the implications are unsettling. When one goes even further back to the original languages and discovers that there is a great difficulty in actually determining what the original *form* of the text is, the ground gets even shakier. In biblical studies, just the disparity between the theory of textual criticism in Old and New Testament study points to the fact that, as a discipline, textual criticism will never be able to *definitely* decide the question as to the original form of the documents that make up the Bible. The student of either Greek or Hebrew hoping to finally 'find out exactly what it says' will discover very early on that both text-critical and just plain grammatical questions are not so easily solved as one might hope. However, for the student of these texts who is unable to study them in their original language, it is not surprising that an idea such as the 'illumination of the Spirit' should grow up. In its own way, it answers the same need that the tradition concerning the LXX translation did for those who depended on the LXX.

In fact, it is possible to trace the development of the more fantastic tradition concerning the LXX translation in direct proportion to two elements. Both elements are internal to the group using the LXX. One is dissension from those who would criticise the quality of the translation, the other, often from the same quarter, concerns the validity of using a translated text at all. Ben Sira's criticism, Jerome's comments on and practice of translation, and even the existence of various recensions of the LXX, many of them apparently striving for greater faithfulness to the original, all point to a dissenting voice in the tradition that parallels the affirming one. It is most interesting to note that, by the time of Jerome and Augustine, the translation that was originally defended on the basis that it was faithful to the original by right of divine inspiration has become, in Augustine's thinking (which reflects the more popular position in the Church at the time), a *supplanter* of that original by right of divine inspiration! It is also quite interesting to note the different offices held by the dissenting voices in this dialogue. As noted above, the opposition party in this debate is seemingly entirely made up of translators.

2. The Tradition Concerning the Translation of the LXX, Hermeneutical Tension and Modern Translational Theory

a. *The Ancient Debate Surrounding the Translation of the LXX and Insights from Philosophical Hermeneutics Concerning Translation*
The tradition concerning the LXX translation, being, as it is, a dead issue, except to those who are interested in it for historical or scholarly reasons,[27] provides us with a unique glimpse into some of the philosophical/theological assumptions and motivations which underlie the translation process in modern times. It is an excellent example of how different orientations towards texts can have a drastic effect on one's interpretation of and work with those texts. It can be argued that a 'good translation', that is, one most clearly understood by the receptor in the receptor language, is perhaps the most interpretative activity in which one can engage. As Hans-Georg Gadamer says, 'Having to depend on an interpreter's translation is an extreme case that doubles the hermeneutical process, namely the conversation: there is one conversation between the interpreter and the other, and a second between the interpreter and oneself'.[28] There is no getting past the fact that, in order to make sense, a translation must be a radical interpretation of

27. Or perhaps for the Greek Orthodox Church, which still uses the LXX.
28. H.-G. Gadamer, *Truth and Method* (trans. J.C. Weinsheimer and D.G. Marshall; London: Sheed and Ward, 2nd edn, 1989), p. 385.

tradition. It must make the Different into the Same. The LXX was certainly a good example of this. It was effected in Alexandria, the most Hellenistic of Hellenistic cities, and it was made, as all translations are, for practical reasons—the most important of which was to make the tradition contained in the Hebrew Bible accessible to those who, while having their faith and practice rooted in that tradition, were unable to apprehend it in its original form. Over time, as we have seen, the translation became viewed as an inspired document. This rather radical step sought to eliminate the middle-man—to make the doubling of the hermeneutical process null and void. When the translation became inspired, it was no longer the *interpretation* of the original, but rather became *the original itself*. The factor of uncertainty regarding the status of the translation as being an accurate conveyer of the original texts was eliminated.

One need go no further to explain the ongoing embellishment of the tradition than to note the unwillingness on the part of those who depended on the LXX to accept, following Gadamer's description, the doubling of the hermeneutical process. By eliminating this, they did not have to settle for the solution of the translator—'a solution that can never be more than a compromise'[29]—but rather went directly, as it were, to the original. As was mentioned above, the fact that those who criticize the LXX translation are themselves translators is significant. Those who are closest to the texts, those who are actually engaged in the work of translation are, in this tradition, the ones who are the quickest to acknowledge the difficulties in both the process of translation itself and the difficulties with the finished product that is the LXX.

Almost all who read this article will likely be scholars and/or translators. In part, this is unfortunate, in that the largest part of the problem concerning translation is not in the translation process, and not (usually) with the actual translations. The largest problem is with the receptors of the translation. The tradition concerning the LXX translation did not happen within a vacuum—it seems most likely, given the evidence, that the support of and perceived need for the 'inspired' view of the LXX came from the popular level and was then used by theologians and apologists. Philo quotes a tradition that had developed on a popular level, the rabbis quote the tradition in a similar manner, and by the end of a long line of Christian apologetics, Augustine's opposition to

---

29. Gadamer, *Truth and Method*, p. 386.

Jerome is based largely on the concern for how the masses will react to a new translation that disagrees with the LXX.

b. *Implications for the Modern Field of Translation Theory*
As far as the implications of this tradition for modern translational theory are concerned, the question thus becomes, 'What part should the translator play in this process?' This is, however, a very difficult topic to discuss, as little to none of the literature available on the theory of biblical translation actually addresses it.

In so far as biblical translation is concerned, the overwhelming bulk of a rather underwhelming corpus of literature in terms of its size is either authored by or co-authored by Eugene Nida. Even in the books he has co-authored, it is admitted that he is largely responsible for the theoretical portions.

It is perhaps understandable that much of the concern with translation, both its theory and practice, has typically come from translators of the Bible. Translation undertaken under conditions of *necessity* or perceived necessity is something altogether different than translation undertaken simply as the result of a desire to read what has been written in another language. The actual process of transferring texts from one language into another may be the same, but the conditions under which it occurs are vastly different. For most, biblical translation carries the burden of this necessity, even a certain urgency—the large majority of biblical translators do not undertake their tasks to simply allow different language groups to read a nice book called the Bible, but rather because they believe that it is, for religious reasons, imperative that the content and message be communicated to these different language groups.

The religious groups that are based on these texts that we call the Bible are not, however, merely separated by language and culture from the original documents. They are separated by a large amount of time, and by the fact that the understanding of the languages and cultures that spawned these documents has been filtered through that same gap of time, and, over that time, several different cultural groups as well. If this was a problem in the time of the LXX translation, we should not be surprised to see that, the longer the time gap, the worse the problem.

It is, certainly, an interesting and somewhat daunting idea that this uncertainty exists concerning the meaning (and, in the case of textual criticism, content) of the documents upon which Christian (and, for the Hebrew Bible, Jewish) faith and practice are based, and with which

Christians (and Jews) call others to do the same. Is it any wonder that translators of the Bible are loathe to publicize this uncertainty?

Unfortunately, this unwillingness feeds the same sort of process by which the LXX became an inspired, remainderless, translation in the minds first of popular Judaism and Jewish theologians, then of popular Christianity and Christian theologians. A modern example of this, although its following is certainly proportionately smaller, is the King James Version of 1611—the so-called Authorized Version.[30] In fact, it could be posited that there is a tendency for those who are unable to read the original languages of any texts to assume, whether consciously or not, that the translations they read tell them the whole story, much as the original would. That this is present in the reading of all translated texts is arguably doubly true of the reading of translated sacred texts.

It is the contention of this paper, and its final point, that the translational theory advocated by Nida and his cohorts fosters an atmosphere in which such an understanding concerning translations can occur. This is not to say that Nida's idea of 'functional equivalence'[31] (developed from his earliest writing [where it was known as 'dynamic equivalence'] onwards) is not extremely helpful for the practice of translation. Indeed, it can be very convincingly argued that this method of translation, along with many of the warnings that go with it concerning how to handle style and idiom that exist in the source language, is the best way to translate the most meaning to the largest possible audience.

What needs to be examined, however, are the assumptions made concerning the possibility of a seemingly remainderless, or almost so, translation. It was pointed out above that Philo's appeal to geometry resembled this tendency in Nida's work. In the light of this, it is perhaps significant that Nida chooses, as an introductory illustration concerning the need to translate meaning rather than just form, an example from avionics:

30. The similarities between the translation of the KJV (effected under a king's command and sponsorship in a relatively short period of time by a relatively small group of scholars) and the story with which the *Letter of Aristeas* presents us make for an interesting comparison.

31. See esp. E.A. Nida, *Toward a Science of Translating with Special Reference to Principles and Procedures Involved in Bible Translating* (Leiden: E.J. Brill, 1964), E.A. Nida and C.R. Taber, *The Theory and Practice of Translation: Helps for Translators* (Leiden: E.J. Brill, 1969), and J. De Waard and E.A. Nida, *From One Language to Another: Functional Equivalence in Bible Translating* (Nashville: Thomas Nelson, 1986).

One specialist in translating and interpreting for the aviation industry commented that in his work he did not dare to employ the principles often followed by translators of the Bible: 'With us', he said, 'complete intelligibility is a matter of life and death'. Unfortunately, translators of religious materials have sometimes not been prompted by the same feeling of urgency to make sense.[32]

It should be obvious to even the casual reader that there are at least two points at which this comparison breaks down. First, a document explaining anything about the operation of a machine can be re-written from experience. The translator of such a document is, at no point, under the kind of constraints as the translator of a biblical (or any literary) document—he will have access to experiment and (likely) experience, and even possibly the author of the original to test the translation. Secondly, the kind of communication in a manual is vastly different than the kind of communication found in the biblical documents. Indeed, it is closer to the mathematical, geometrical examples to which Philo appeals than to the literary nature of the biblical documents.

This kind of thinking regarding Nida's concept of 'functional equivalence' calls for serious re-examination of the theory, to which I will, in conclusion, offer some thoughts.

Nida's theory of functional equivalence is essentially fourfold:[33]

1. A translation cannot be said to be a good translation unless it communicates the meaning *as understood by the original author* to the receptor in his own language, and does it well.

2. The original meaning *as understood by the original author* is apprehendable and communicable by the translator.[34]

3. 'Anything that can be said in one language can be said in another, unless the form is an essential element of the language.'[35]

---

32. Nida and Taber, *Theory and Practice of Translation*, p. 1.

33. What follows is a synthesis of the key ideas from the first two chapters of *The Theory and Practice of Translation* and *From One Language to Another*.

34. While Nida (*From One Language to Another*, pp. 32-33) does admit to the problematic nature of this point (a point which he does not explicitly state, although without this assumption his theory seems to fall apart), he does not resolve the difficulty, and leaves the reader feeling as though the problem is minor.

35. Nida and Taber, *Theory and Practice of Translation*, p. 4.

4.   'To preserve the content of the message the form [of the
      source language] must be changed.'[36]

As assumptive underpinnings of a theory of translation, these do not
inspire confidence. The most troubling element is, perhaps, dependence
on what seems to be a version of Romantic hermeneutics, where the
interpreter needs to get into the head, as it were, of the original author,
recreating the document in the process of interpretation. This approach
to hermeneutics is, first, outmoded, and secondly, demonstrably impossible. Positing some sort of spiritual communion between interpreter
and author seems to be an easy way out of a very difficult problem, but,
in reality, solves nothing.

This does not necessarily mean that Nida's theory should be abandoned. However, unless this theory of translation can deal with the
multitude of difficulties that stand in the face of its most basic assumptions, the atmosphere of (over-) confidence fostered by such a theory
will be harmful to the communities who rely upon the texts that are
translated by such a theory. In no way does this mean that translation
should not go on—this article, and the project of which it is a part,
assume at the outset that translation is a necessary undertaking—but it
does mean that this dominant theory of translation needs to undergo a
major overhaul. Otherwise, the climate produced both by the theory
and by the translations themselves will begin to (if it has not already)
assume many of the negative aspects of the LXX translation, and the
traditions which grew up around it. We would do well to remember and
learn from those who have gone before, through much the same process, and with many similar results.

---

36. Nida and Taber, *Theory and Practice of Translation*, p. 5.

IS A TRANSLATION INSPIRED? THE PROBLEMS OF VERBAL INSPIRATION FOR TRANSLATION AND A PROPOSED SOLUTION

Craig D. Allert

Most works on translation are concerned with the act of translation—the rules a translator should follow, the goals of a translator, certain difficulties a translator faces, or the quality of a translation. These are all valuable and necessary concerns which, indeed, should be addressed. The purpose of this essay, however, is to address a much less prominent, and even conveniently ignored, theological implication of translation—inspiration.

There exists, within the theological implications of translation, a gap that appears unbridgeable by the conservative evangelical, or verbal plenary, theory of inspiration. This *theory*, however, has largely been elevated to the status of essential Christian belief. I believe that by elevating this theory to such heights, its adherents have not adequately answered (and in most cases not even attempted to answer) the theological question posed in this essay—Is a Translation Inspired?

The structure of the essay is contained under three main headings. In the first section I discuss the problems of verbal inspiration as it relates to the finished product of translation. This section concludes that the verbal theory cannot view any translation as inspired. The second section presents a case for moving away from the verbal theory and offers an optional theory of inspiration. The final section then examines the implications that this optional theory has for a translation and concludes that a translation can be viewed as inspired.

It is necessary, at the outset, to recognize the limitations of this essay. Because it is not an examination of the verbal plenary theory proper, space will not be given over to a full examination of all its presuppositions and beliefs.[1] I believe that the verbal theory is unacceptable on

---

1. For a full examination of the verbal theory from its adherents, see D.A. Carson and J.D. Woodbridge (eds.), *Hermeneutics, Authority, and Canon* (Grand

theological and historical grounds, but the question posed in this essay limits any extensive examination of the theological and historical issues except where they come into play with the issue of translation.[2]

1. *The Verbal Theory and Translation*

The translation of a biblical document presupposes its importance for the community of faith, for those who hold the canonical Old and New

Rapids: Academie/Zondervan, 1986); P.W. Comfort (ed.), *The Origin of the Bible* (Wheaton: Tyndale House, 1992); S. Custer, *Does Inspiration Demand Inerrancy?* (Ann Arbor: Craig, 1986); D.S. Dockery, *Christian Scripture: An Evangelical Perspective on Inspiration, Authority and Interpretation* (Nashville: Broadman & Holman, 1995); M.J. Erickson, *Christian Theology* (Grand Rapids: Baker Book House, 1985); R.T. France, 'Evangelical Disagreements About the Bible', *Churchman* 96 (1982), pp. 226-40; L. Gaussen, *'Theopneustia': The Plenary Inspiration of the Holy Scriptures* (London: Passmore and Alabaster, 1896); C.F.H. Henry, *God, Revelation, and Authority. IV. The God Who Speaks and Shows* (Waco, TX: Word Books, 1979); J.W. Montgomery (ed.), *God's Inerrant Word: An International Symposium on the Trustworthiness of Scripture* (Minneapolis: Bethany House, 1974); L. Morris, 'Biblical Authority and the Concept of Inerrancy', *Churchman* 81 (1967), pp. 22-38; R. Nicole, 'The Inspiration and Authority of Scripture: J.D.G. Dunn versus B.B. Warfield', *Churchman* 97 (1983), pp. 198-215; 98 (1983), pp. 7-27; 98 (1984), pp. 198-216; J.I. Packer, *'Fundamentalism' and the Word of God* (Grand Rapids: Eerdmans, 1958); B.B. Warfield, *Inspiration and the Authority of the Bible* (Phillipsburg, NJ: Presbyterian and Reformed, 1948).

2. For a full critique of the verbal theory, see W.J. Abraham, *The Divine Inspiration of Holy Scripture* (Oxford: Oxford University Press, 1981); P.J. Achtemeier, *The Inspiration of Scripture* (Philadelphia: Westminster Press, 1980); J. Barton, *People of the Book? The Authority of the Bible in Christianity* (London: SPCK, 2nd edn, 1993); G.C. Berkouwer, *Studies in Dogmatics: Holy Scripture* (Grand Rapids: Eerdmans, 1975); A. Dulles, 'Scripture: Recent Protestant and Catholic Views', *TTod* 37 (1980), pp. 7-27; J.D.G. Dunn, *The Living Word* (Philadelphia: Fortress Press, 1988); J.T. Forestell, 'The Limitation of Inerrancy', *CBQ* 20 (1958), pp. 9-18; J. Goldingay, *Models for Scripture* (Grand Rapids: Eerdmans; Carlisle: Paternoster, 1994); T.A. Hoffman, 'Inspiration, Normativeness, Canonicity, and the Unique Sacred Character of the Bible', *CBQ* 44 (1982), pp. 447-69; J.T. Lienhard, *The Bible, the Church, and Authority: The Canon of the Christian Bible in History and Theology* (Collegeville, MN: Liturgical Press, 1995); R.A.F. MacKenzie, 'Some Problems in the Field of Inspiration', *CBQ* 20 (1958), pp. 1-8; J.L. McKenzie, 'The Social Character of Inspiration', *CBQ* 24 (1962), pp. 115-24; D.A. Milavec, 'The Bible, the Holy Spirit and Human Powers', *SJT* 29 (1976), pp. 215-35; K.R. Trembath, *Evangelical Theories of Inspiration: A Review and Proposal* (Oxford: Oxford University Press, 1987).

Testaments as authoritative for faith and practice. To those who thus uphold the Bible there is some affirmation of inspiration. Broadly stated, an affirmation of the inspiration of the Bible means that in some way the Bible comes from God, that he has somehow had a part in its origin, that there is a linkage between the basic mode of thought through which he has communicated with humanity and the coming into existence of these canonical documents.[3]

The above definition of inspiration is broad. The adherents of the verbal theory would necessarily want to add certain limitations to it before it could be accepted. To state simply that God somehow had a part in the Bible's origin is not specific enough for some and must be qualified. Thus, D.S. Dockery defines inspiration as 'The superintending influence the Holy Spirit exerted on the biblical writers, so that the accent and interpretation of God's revelation have been recorded as God intended so that the Bible is actually the word of God'.[4] Likewise, M.J. Erickson defines inspiration as 'that supernatural influence of the Holy Spirit upon the Scripture writers which rendered their writings an accurate record of the revelation or which resulted in what they wrote actually being the Word of God'.[5]

Rather than accepting a somewhat vague statement about inspiration, the verbal theory posits the necessity of the Holy Spirit supernaturally influencing the biblical writers so that they wrote what God wanted written. The influence of the Spirit is so pervasive that even the choice of words was directed by the Spirit. The product is therefore the written word of God. This, in a nutshell, is the verbal plenary theory of inspiration.[6]

a. *The Autographa*
Any assertion of the verbal inspiration of the Bible is meant only to refer to the original manuscripts. This assertion is usually made under a discussion of inerrancy, which is claimed to be the natural outcome of inspiration. Since God is the author of inspired Scripture, and since

3. J. Barr, *The Bible in the Modern World* (London: SCM Press, 1973), p. 17.
4. Dockery, *Christian Scripture*, p. 240.
5. Erickson, *Christian Theology*, p. 199.
6. *Verbal* meaning that the very words were directed by the Spirit, therefore inspired. *Plenary* from the Latin *plenus* meaning full. When applied to the concept of inspiration, it means that the Bible is inspired in all its parts. See Dockery, *Christian Scripture*, p. 243.

God is the God of truth and not falsehood, then all of Scripture is inerrant in the original autographs. Since this is asserted for inerrancy, the conservative evangelical doctrine also asserts this of verbal inspiration, that is, only the original autographs are verbally inspired.

Since its appearance in 1978, 'The Chicago Statement on Biblical Inerrancy'[7] has become the working definition of verbal inspiration and inerrancy. It has become the 'official' stance of the conservative evangelical community in North America.[8] It can, therefore, be seen as an accurate representation of a large part of the conservative evangelical community's view of inspiration and inerrancy. Article X of the 'Statement' makes the following affirmation:

> We affirm that inspiration, strictly speaking, applies only to the autographic texts of Scripture which in the providence of God can be ascertained from available manuscripts with great accuracy. We further affirm that copies and translations of Scripture are the Word of God to the extent that they faithfully represent the original.

J.I. Packer reflects this 'official' stance when he states,

> Inspiredness is not a quality attaching to corruptions that intrude in the course of the transmission of the text, but only to the text as originally produced by the inspired writers. The acknowledgment of biblical inspiration thus makes more urgent the task of meticulous textual criticism, in order to eliminate such corruptions and ascertain what the original text was.[9]

Erickson makes the same claim with respect to inerrancy: 'The doctrine of inerrancy applies in the strict sense only to the originals, but in a derivative sense to copies and translations, that is, to the extent that they reflect the original'.[10] These types of statement are integral to every writer espousing a verbal theory of inspiration and can therefore be found in all their writings.[11]

An unfortunate fact with the biblical documents is that we possess no original manuscript of any Old or New Testament book. The fact that

---

7. 'The Chicago Statement on Biblical Inerrancy', *JETS* 21 (1978), pp. 289-96.

8. The framers of the statement did not propose creedal weight be given to the statement but do believe this to be the proper stance for the evangelical community.

9. J.I. Packer, 'The Inspiration of the Bible', in Comfort (ed.), *The Origin of the Bible*, p. 36.

10. Erickson, *Christian Theology*, p. 239.

11. See n. 1.

we do not possess the original manuscripts calls for the necessary human activity of textual criticism. Textual criticism, as any who have attempted its practice will know, is not simply a registration of words and phrases. It requires choices between textual recensions, and between textual variants.[12] These choices cannot be regarded as unimportant.

A high degree of confidence is placed in the results of textual criticism. It is generally accepted that we have a reliable Greek text from which to translate into other languages. By reliable is meant a text close to the original. For the devotee to the verbal inspiration theory, this means that we are very close to the actual inspired words. C.F.H. Henry thus states,

> The original manuscripts have a theopneustic quality because of their divinely given rational and verbal content and because of the Spirit's superintendence of the prophets and apostles in the process of writing; copies of the originals, and copies of the copies, on the other hand, share in the theopneustic quality of the originals to the extent that they faithfully reproduce the autographs.[13]

This poses a problem to the verbal theory of inspiration. The copies of the originals are said to share in the theopneustic quality to the extent that they faithfully represent the originals. The question is, from whom does the determination come that the copies faithfully represent the originals? The answer to the question is found in the necessary human activity of textual criticism.

Textual criticism does not claim to have an absolute degree of certainty in what variant or recension its practitioners choose. Because we do not possess the original manuscripts the textual critic has nothing with which to compare or refer his decisions. This lack of absolute certainty is reflected in the letter ratings of the United Bible Society's third edition (corrected) of the *Greek New Testament*.[14] The best that

---

12. The standard introductions to textual criticism are K. and B. Aland, *The Text of the New Testament: An Introduction to the Critical Editions and to the Theory and Practice of Modern Textual Criticism* (Grand Rapids: Eerdmans, 2nd edn, 1989); B.M. Metzger, *The Text of the New Testament: Its Transmission, Corruption, and Restoration* (Oxford: Oxford University Press, 3rd edn, 1992); E. Würthwein, *The Text of the Old Testament* (Grand Rapids: Eerdmans, 4th edn, 1979).

13. Henry, *God, Revelation, and Authority*, p. 233.

14. K. Aland, M. Black, C. Martini, B.M. Metzger and A. Wikgren, *The Greek*

can be said concerning any choice of variant is that it is the virtually certain reading.

It is granted that the 'greatest proportion of the text represents what may be called an A degree of certainty'.[15] But aside from the lack of absolute certainty, we must ask about those variants which have some degree of doubt, considerable degree of doubt, and a very high degree of doubt.[16] This has direct relevance to the verbal theory of inspiration.

The theory of verbal inspiration places a great deal of importance on the actual words because they were chosen by the Holy Spirit. The theory is apparent in B.B. Warfield,[17] but it receives a clear explanation in Erickson.[18]

In explaining the verbal inspiration of Scripture, Erickson bases his argument on the nature of God. He states,

> It is our suggestion here that what the Spirit may do is to direct the thoughts of the Scripture writer. The direction effected by the Spirit, however, is quite precise. God, being omniscient, it is not gratuitous to assume that his thoughts are precise, more so than ours. This being the case, there will be, within the vocabulary of the writer, one word that will most aptly communicate the thought God is conveying (although

New Testament (Stuttgart: United Bible Societies, 3rd edn corr., 1983): 'By means of the letters A, B, C, and D, enclosed within 'braces' {} at the beginning of each set of textual variants, the Committee has sought to indicate the relative degree of certainty, arrived at on the basis of internal considerations as well as of external evidence, for the reading adopted as the text. The letter A signifies that the text is *virtually* certain, while B indicates that there is *some degree of doubt*. The letter C means that there is *a considerable degree of doubt* whether the text or the apparatus contains the superior reading, while D shows that there is a *very high degree of doubt* concerning the reading selected for the text' (pp. xii-xiii, italics mine). It should be noted that the fourth edition of the United Bible Societies *Greek New Testament* has altered these letter ratings. For criticism of this alteration I defer to K.D. Clarke, *Textual Optimism: The United Bible Societies' Greek New Testament and its Evaluation of Evidence Letter Ratings* (JSNTSup, 138; Sheffield: Sheffield Academic Press, 1997).

15. Aland *et al.*, *The Greek New Testament*, p. xiii.

16. Of the total of 1,444 rated variants in the UBSGNT [3 corr.], 126 (9%) are A ratings, 475 (33%) are B ratings, 699 (48%) are C ratings, and 144 (10%) are D ratings. These figures are taken from Clarke, *Textual Optimism*.

17. Warfield, 'The Biblical Idea of Revelation', in his *Inspiration and the Authority of the Bible*, pp. 71-102.

18. Erickson, *Christian Theology*, pp. 214-20.

that word in itself may be inadequate). By creating the thought and stimulating the understanding of the Scripture writer, the Spirit will lead him in effect to use one particular word rather than another.[19]

To answer the charge that he is espousing a theory of dictation, Erickson claims that he is forced to 'theorize' regarding the process of inspiration. He uses the example of Luke's vocabulary resulting from his education and his lifetime of experience, in which God was involved. The vocabulary was, therefore, that which God wanted him to have:

> Equipped with this pool of God-intended words the author then wrote. Thus, although inspiration in the strict sense applies to the influence of the Holy Spirit at the actual point of writing, it presupposes a long process of God's providential working with the author. Then at the actual point of writing, God directs the thinking of the author. Since God has access to the very thought process of the human, and, in the case of the believer, indwells the individual in the person of the Holy Spirit, this is no difficult matter, particularly when the individual is praying for enlightenment and displaying receptivity. The process is not greatly unlike mental telepathy, although more internalized and personalized.[20]

Many criticisms could be offered concerning Erickson's explanation but my concern here is with his insistence that God led the writers of Scripture to choose one particular word over another. Here is where that lack of absolute certainty in textual variants butts up against the theory of verbal inspiration. If the particular words are inspired, then it follows that these particular words are important. Yet textual criticism has shown us that many words and phrases chosen have some degree of doubt, a considerable degree of doubt, and a very high degree of doubt. If there is a certain degree of doubt about the variants chosen, then it is also uncertain whether a text can be regarded as verbally inspired.

In response to the charge that the variants cast doubt on the reliability of the text, the conservative evangelical generally counters that no essential element of the Christian faith is affected by the presence of variants.[21] For the conservative evangelical, the important thing in recognizing the reliability of the text is not the words, but the fact that no copy of the original will destroy the *meaning* of the text so as to render it unable to give its reader 'wisdom which leads to salvation through

19. Erickson, *Christian Theology*, p. 215.
20. Erickson, *Christian Theology*, p. 218.
21. Article X, 'The Chicago Statement on Biblical Inerrancy'.

faith in Christ Jesus' (2 Tim. 3.15). In so doing, the importance of the God-chosen words is overshadowed by the concept or meaning of the text because that is what makes the reader wise unto salvation.

The inconsistency is clear. Great emphasis is placed on the particular *words* in the original because they are, in effect, chosen by God himself. Through the transmission of the texts, however, the variants which came into existence matter little to the *meaning* of the text. The importance of verbal inspiration is thus lost to the practical value of the text. Even if verbal inspiration could be proven, it matters little to the community who hold the Bible as authoritative.

This has direct relevance to the translation of these documents. Translations are made from these copies. If it is the meanings that are important in these copies, this must also be the case for translations which are made from these copies. Thus, the translations cannot be *verbally* inspired.

b. *Interpretation*
We must also consider the issue of translation and interpretation. That is, we must ask the question of whether interpretation is in order only after the translation or whether it already plays an important role during translation.[22] This question is brought into focus by statements like the following:

> When the Bible is being translated, its own doctrine as to its verbal inspiration imposes limitations on the translators' function. The Scripture teaches us that, as God's word written, its form as well as its thought is inspired. The translator of Scripture has, therefore, above all else, to *follow* the text: it is not his business to interpret it or explain it.[23]

The above statement is quite naïve to anyone who has attempted translation. Translation is not simply a matter of finding equivalent words in two languages. It is the complicated task of transposing material from one world of thought and language to another.[24] The different

---

22. Berkouwer, *Holy Scripture*, p. 217.
23. I. Murray, 'Which Version? A Continuing Debate', in J.H. Skilton and C.A. Lacey (eds.), *The New Testament Student and Bible Translation* (Phillipsburg, NJ: Presbyterian and Reformed, 1978), p. 132.
24. For the task and goals of Bible translation, see J. De Waard and E.A. Nida, *From One Language to Another: Functional Equivalence in Bible Translating* (Nashville: Thomas Nelson, 1986); E.A Nida and C.R. Taber, *The Theory and Practice of Translation* (Leiden: E.J. Brill, 1969); E.A. Nida, *Toward a Science of*

worlds of thought necessitate that translators reproduce the message of the text. The literal translation of which Murray speaks means nothing; it is an unreachable and unrealistic goal, especially for the pragmatic outworkings of Scripture espoused by the above mentioned conservative evangelicals.

While this essay is not an examination of the problems, tasks and goals of a translator, it does recognize the fact that in translation the translator must make grammatical and lexical adjustments in order to allow the reader in the receptor language to understand the words of the text.[25] For example, the Semitic idiom expressed in the phrase, ἐνδύσασθε.... σπλάγχνα οἰκτιρμοῦ ('put on...bowels of mercies'), in Col. 3.12 can be literally rendered in English, but it would mean little to the reader. We have both words, 'bowels' and 'mercies', in English but we do not employ them together in this combination. Therefore the translators chose to interpret the idiom to mean 'put on a heart of compassion' (NASB) or 'clothe yourselves with compassion' (NIV) in order to make sense of it for the English reader.

Even words that are not that uncommon in the New Testament present certain challenges to the translator. Mk 12.6 states, ἔτι ἕνα εἶχεν υἱὸν ἀγαπητόν. The RSV translates the phrase, 'He still had one other, a beloved Son'. The NASB translates the phrase, 'He had one more *to send*, a beloved Son'. And the NIV translates it, 'He had one left to send, a son, whom he loved'. An examination of the term ἀγαπητός reveals that it has been used to express two basic meanings throughout pre-Christian literature, the Septuagint, the New Testament, Josephus and Philo. First, it is used in the sense of 'beloved'. This indicates no unique relationship, but simply a description. Secondly, it is used in the sense of a unique relationship between father and son. Of special significance is the use of ἀγαπητός modifying υἱός. When this sort of structure appears in the New Testament it always indicates a unique relationship between father and son.

Surely the translator must take these issues into account when attempting to convey the message. Is it not a matter of interpretation to decide which translation best fits the context of a passage? This is not to say that the choice of one or the other term drastically changes the

Translating with Special Reference to Principles and Procedures Involved in Bible Translating (Leiden: E.J. Brill, 1964).

25. The following example is taken from Nida and Taber, *The Theory and Practice of Translation*, p. 12.

doctrine of the passage. But it does say that one word may convey different meanings in different contexts.

There are also words in the New Testament which present a different sort of challenge. These are words where we are simply unsure of the correct translation. Consider Heb. 2.17 where Jesus is said to become man so that he could become a merciful high priest and ἱλάσκεσθαι τὰς ἁμαρτίας τοῦ λαοῦ. The word I am concerned with is the verb ἱλάσκομαι. It carries two meanings. Liddell and Scott give the meaning of the verb as to appease, propitiate, or expiate.[26] Likewise Bauer, Arndt, Gingrich, and Danker offer the same gloss.[27] The problem is that the meaning which is chosen by the translator affects the doctrine of the atonement. Expiation carries the idea of covering sin while propitiation carries the idea of appeasing God. So the question is—did Christ simply cover and cleanse the sin of the people or did he actually appease the wrath of God? The NASB makes the choice of propitiation over expiation. This is a clear interpretive choice. The NIV and RSV, however, attempt to avoid the confusion by translating the verb as 'make atonement for' (NIV) and 'make a sacrifice of atonement for' (RSV). Is this all that the writer of the book of Hebrews wanted to convey? Or did he want to be more specific by the sense of either expiation or propitiation? It is the translator's job to investigate this and to make interpretive choices based on contextual usage.

Expressions in the ancient world are far removed from our thought and mode of expression. This also poses problems for the translator requiring interpretive decisions. Consider the example of Amos 4.2-3 in the Authorized Version which reads,

> The Lord God hath sworn by his holiness that, lo, the days shall come upon you, that he will take you away by hooks, and your posterity with fish-hooks, and ye shall go out at the breaches, every cow at that which is before, and you shall cast them into the palace, saith the Lord.

This verse is not very intelligible to the English reader even though it may accurately portray what the Hebrew says. The fact is that for most readers of the Bible the translation is the text. They depend on it entirely—there is no appeal beyond the translation. Therefore the

26. R. Liddell and R. Scott, *An Intermediate Greek–English Lexicon* (Oxford: Clarendon Press, 1991), p. 379.

27. W. Bauer, W.F. Arndt, F.W. Gingrich, and F.W. Danker, *A Greek–English Lexicon of the New Testament and Other Early Christian Literature* (Chicago: University of Chicago Press, 2nd edn, 1979), p. 375.

translator's task is limited on two sides.[28] He must not violate the world of the text, but he must also make the text understandable to the reader. This requires an act of interpretation.

The issue of interpretation and translation has ramifications for the verbal inspiration of Scripture. The few problems presented above show that it is not possible to render a text in exactly the same words as the original or copy of the original. Interpretive and grammatical decisions render the text accessible for the reader to whom the translation is aimed. This is a necessary fact of translation. Understanding this in the light of the theory of verbal inspiration means that we cannot have an inspired translation. If the very words are inspired in the original, then changing the words and phrases to be understood in the receptor's mode of thought renders the inspired words uninspired. It is impossible to get the exact nuance of a word from one language to another. And, as has been shown with the Greek verb ἱλάσκομαι, in some cases we cannot even be sure what the meaning of the word is in every context.

If the exact words are inspired they must, therefore, be important. But the exact wording cannot be retained in translation. Changes inevitably occur in the switch from one thought-world to another. The verbal inspiration school should, logically, hold to translations with a rather high degree of doubt. But this is not the case. In discussing the value of translations the 'Chicago Statement' explains that,

> no translation is or can be perfect, and all translations are an additional step away from the *autographa*. Yet the verdict of linguistic science is that English-speaking Christians, at least, are exceedingly well-served in these days with a host of excellent translations and have no cause for hesitating to conclude that the true Word of God is within their reach. Indeed, in view of the frequent repetition in Scripture of the main matters with which it deals and also of the Holy Spirit's constant witness to and through the Word, no serious translation of Holy Scripture will so destroy its meaning as to render it unable to make its reader 'wise for salvation through faith in Christ Jesus' (2 Tim. 3.15).[29]

According to the 'Chicago Statement', the excellent translations of the Bible should cause us to conclude that the true Word of God is within our reach. This conclusion is based on the belief that translations do the job of bringing people to salvation. I cannot disagree with the

---

28. P. Ellingworth, 'Theory and Practice in Bible Translation', *EvQ* 55 (1983), p. 166.

29. 'Exposition', 'The Chicago Statement on Biblical Inerrancy', p. 296.

above statement. My point is that it is in paradox with the verbal inspiration theory of the Bible. If the very words, by their inspiration, are important then why is the stress on the meaning of the words and the fact that the repetition of the main matters gives us the overall message? The verbal inspiration school should logically argue that we should not translate because it distorts the originally inspired *words*.

The verbal plenary theory of inspiration has no real pragmatic value in the life of the Church. The Church has functioned without these verbally inspired documents for close to two thousand years. It has found salvific value in the copies, which are once removed from the originals. It has also found salvific value in the twice removed translations of these copies. The important point has not been the words which were contained in the Scriptures, but the message which the Scriptures conveyed. The copies and translations that are possessed by the Church function to make the reader 'wise unto salvation'. Verbal inspiration is, therefore, an irrelevant doctrine because the Church has functioned with non-inspired documents (in the verbal inspiration sense) for almost two thousand years. And, unless the highly unlikely event of a discovery of the original documents occurs, the Church will continue to function with these 'uninspired' documents.

2. Redefinition of Terms

In the light of the problems with verbal inspiration and translation outlined above,[30] I propose a fundamental redefinition of inspiration based on historical, theological, and exegetical grounds. The shift I propose allows the translations of the biblical documents to be viewed as inspired. The inspiration of which I speak, however, is not *verbal* inspiration. A proper theory of inspiration must take the phenomena and historical developments of the Bible (canon) seriously. It must be formed from the idea that biblical criticism can offer a better understanding of these foundational documents of the Christian faith.

One's conclusions concerning inspiration are, to a large degree, determined by the findings of biblical criticism. Sometimes the issue is presented as the difference between studying simply what Scripture says and studying the phenomena of Scripture. Some have even characterized the difference between the conservative and the liberal in this

---

30. The criticisms above are only a fraction of the whole. The whole lies outside the scope of this essay but can be gathered from the sources listed in n. 2.

way.[31] But to frame the critical study of the Bible in this way does not describe the true picture.

Certainly there are liberals who deny the inspiration of Scripture. But to characterize evangelicals as denying all the results of critical scholarship and refusing to employ it is false. This is not to deny a certain tendency among evangelicals to pay only lip service to critical study.[32] There are many evangelical scholars who have employed critical scholarship to frame their doctrine of inspiration.[33]

One evangelical scholar in particular has shown the importance of the critical study of Scripture. I.H. Marshall[34] believes that biblical criticism must itself be subjected to criticism: 'The moral of the story is that the answer to bad biblical criticism is better biblical criticism, and also that the theories of yesterday and today can be upset for good or ill by freshly discovered evidence tomorrow'.[35]

Throughout his book on inspiration, Marshall maintains belief in the trustworthiness and inspiration of the Bible. But he also maintains that it cannot be a blind trust or one that is not informed by the text and phenomena of Scripture:

> I have deliberately chosen an example which demonstrates how application of the grammatico-historical method can help to maintain the reliability of the New Testament account of things over against other theories which call the truth of the account into question. Yet it must be said that the use of this method will not remove or solve all the difficulties and problems that readers find in the text. One does not need to be a follower of the historical-critical method to discover apparent contradictions and errors in Scripture. The radical may look for them

31. See, e.g., Achtemeier, *The Inspiration of Scripture*, pp. 94-95. Although Achtemeier is not correct in his contention that all conservative scholars have denied the nature of Scripture as critical scholarship has revealed it, he is correct in his contention that we should critically use the results of the discipline.

32. See, e.g., Warfield, 'The Real Problem of Inspiration', in his *Inspiration and Authority of the Bible*, pp. 214-26.

33. See, e.g., Abraham, *The Divine Inspiration of Holy Scripture*; Berkouwer, *Holy Scripture*; D.A. Carson, 'Recent Developments in the Doctrine of Scripture', in Carson and Woodbridge (eds.), *Hermeneutics, Authority, and Canon*, pp. 5-48; Dunn, *The Living Word*; Goldingay, *Models for Scripture*.

34. I.H. Marshall, *Biblical Inspiration* (London: Hodder and Stoughton, 1982), pp. 74-93.

35. Marshall, *Biblical Inspiration*, p. 88.

with more zeal than the conservative, but even the latter can hardly avoid noticing, for example, that there are two rather different genealogies of Jesus in the Gospels. There is nothing wrong with discovering such things, and scholarly objectivity indeed compels us to take account of them...it may be necessary to ask how the existence of particular types of problems may affect one's understanding of the nature of Scripture. The scholar who believes in the entire trustworthiness of Scripture will regard his belief as a well-founded presupposition which is relevant to his treatment of critical problems, but at the same time he will be aware that his doctrine of the nature of Scripture must be consistent with the actual character of Scripture.[36]

Marshall recognizes the shortcomings of historical criticism, as evidenced by his assertion that it must be answered by better criticism. He is concerned not only with the content of Scripture but also with its phenomena. In attempting to understand these phenomena, biblical criticism has led the way. In this vein, Marshall lists three benefits that historical criticism has produced.[37] First, it continually reminds us of the historical setting of the Bible and thus the great acts of God to which it bears witness. Secondly, it widens our understanding of the Bible as a human book, and hence as God's book. Thirdly, it prevents us from understanding the Bible in a sort of vacuum, as a book written solely for us in our situation, as we may run the risk of trying to understand what it is saying to us without paying proper attention to what it was saying to the original readers. Biblical criticism forces us to understand the Bible in its original situation and so helps us not to read our own ideas into it. By forcing us to attend to the historical, human elements in the Bible, biblical criticism opens our eyes to a better and fuller appreciation of the divine revelation which it contains.

The point at emphasis in biblical criticism is the need not only to see Scripture as a divine book, but also to see its human aspect. A proper view of Scripture cannot view the Bible as a book written solely for us and our time. The importance of viewing the phenomena of biblical literature (its authorship and forms) is especially in need of attention. The attention is needed in refutation of the verbal theory which has thoroughly misrepresented what the biblical texts actually say about themselves.

36. Marshall, *Biblical Inspiration*, p. 89.
37. Marshall, *Biblical Inspiration*, pp. 92-93.

a. *What the Bible Says about Itself*

When the pertinent texts concerning inspiration are examined it is surprising how little the Bible actually says about its own inspiration. Upon examination one cannot help but be amazed at the liberties the verbal theory has taken with the key term θεόπνευστος. I am in fundamental disagreement over the definition that the theory of verbal inspiration has given this term, and I question whether such importance should be placed on this New Testament and LXX *hapax legomenon*. The verbal theory builds its definition of inspiration on three main texts, with only the first containing the key term θεόπνευστος: 2 Tim. 3.16; 2 Pet. 1.20-21; Jn 10.35. A cursory examination of these texts will show the unacceptability of the verbal theory's definition of θεόπνευστος.

2 Timothy 3.16 conjures up many ideas of inspiration for those raised in the conservative evangelical tradition. The influence of Warfield is felt when it is seen to prove that the Bible is a direct product of God. In commenting upon 2 Tim. 3.16 Warfield believes that 'these sacred Scriptures are declared to owe their value to divine origin...their divine origin is energetically asserted of their entire fabric'.[38] Erickson states that the verses give the impression that Scripture is divinely produced.[39] Likewise, Dockery vaguely claims that Scripture is a product of God.[40] He goes on to confirm that the New Testament emphasis on inspiration is that God 'breathed out' what the sacred writers communicated in their writings.[41]

The point that is manifestly affirmed by the verbal theory is that Scripture is the *product* of God. It assumes that in some way God is the author of Scripture. The question this raises is whether the text will support what these three representatives have claimed for it. Six observations warrant attention here. First, Dockery states that the New Testament emphasis on inspiration is that God breathed out what the writers communicated. Interestingly, immediately before this statement Dockery correctly affirms that this is the only occurrence in the New Testament and the LXX of θεόπνευστος. If this is the only occurrence of 'inspiration' in the entire Bible, how can Dockery claim what the

38. Warfield, 'The Biblical Idea of Inspiration', p. 134.
39. Erickson, *Christian Theology*, p. 202.
40. Dockery, *Christian Scripture*, p. 38.
41. Dockery, *Christian Scripture*, p. 41.

New Testament emphasis is? The best he can do is state that this is 2 Timothy's emphasis.

Secondly, because θεόπνευστος is a *hapax legomenon* it is very difficult to discover what the author meant in that particular situation. We can be informed by extra-biblical and secular literature, but that is also sketchy. To claim that we know the definition of θεόπνευστος from the biblical material alone runs the risk of misrepresenting the evidence and allows it to say more than it actually does.

Thirdly, the text of 2 Timothy 3 gives no detailed theory of inspiration. It only claims that all (every) Scripture is inspired by God. The emphasis does not rest solely on the inspiration, but also on the didactic nature of Scripture.

Fourthly, there is no mention of the popular model of God speaking or the prophetic model. That link is made by those trying to understand what inspiration is, but it is not warranted in the text.

Fifthly, the relationship between the human and divine elements in Scripture is not defined here. What we have is an affirmation, not an explanation.

Sixthly, what is actually meant in vv. 15 and 16 by ἱερὰ γράμματα and πᾶσα γραφή is not entirely clear. They do not necessarily mean the Jewish canon. Further, even if they can be understood to refer to the Old Testament canon, this begs the question of the standing of the New Testament canon.

The second text is 2 Pet. 1.20-21. Warfield explains that 'Scripture' in this text means the whole of Scripture because the entirety of Scripture is elsewhere conceived and spoken of as prophetic.[42] He goes on to state that the claim here is the exact equivalent to the passage in 2 Timothy, which is as much as to say that it is a divine gift.

Warfield believes that the 'singularly precise and pregnant' statement in 2 Peter shows three important things. First, there is the emphatic denial that prophecy (Scripture) owes its genesis to human initiative. Secondly, there is the equally emphatic assertion that its source lies in God. Thirdly, the prophets spoke things not from themselves, but from

---

42. Warfield, 'The Biblical Idea of Inspiration', p. 137. Claims such as this point out a certain inconsistency with another article by Warfield ('The Nature of Revelation', in his *Inspiration and Authority of the Bible*). He states, 'We are warned, however, against pressing this distinction [revelation and prophecy] too far by the inclusion of the whole body of Scripture in such passages as 2 Pet. 1.20-21 in the category of prophecy' (p. 95).

God. Through this understanding of 2 Pet. 1.20-21 our understanding of inspiration is therefore seen to be advanced. Both Dockery and Erickson make similar assertions concerning this text.[43]

The glaring question in this understanding of the text is the ascription of all Scripture to 'prophecy'. I affirm that elsewhere in the New Testament prophecy can mean all of Scripture, but what about the mention of prophets and prophecy which are strict delineations? The context of 2 Peter may argue for this kind of strict delineation.

The third text is Jn 10.35. This verse is generally presented as representative of Jesus' own view toward Scripture. The important phrase here is καὶ οὐ δύναται λυθῆναι ἡ γραφή ('and Scripture cannot be broken').

Warfield states that the point to note is that Jesus' defense in this passage takes the form of an appeal to Scripture, and it is important to note how he makes this appeal.[44] In appealing to the Law and then quoting from the Psalms it is tantamount to calling Scripture and Law synonyms. Then, by stating that Scripture cannot be broken Jesus drives home the point of ultimate authority of the Scriptures.[45]

There is no doubt that Jesus is arguing from a common view of the authority of the Scriptures. The question that begs to be asked is what does the text say concerning inspiration. The primary concern of the passage is *not* to state a position on inspiration. It makes no mention of inspiration at all; Jesus is drawing upon a mutual respect for the authority of the Old Testament. Why that authority exists is not discussed.

These basic texts are made to say more than they actually do say. The verbal theory of inspiration claims that this definition of inspiration safeguards the authority of the Bible.[46] The problem that I see is that this unique authority was not given only to the biblical documents.[47] The lack of a clear definition of inspiration calls, at least, for a reassessment of the verbal definition of inspiration, if not a redefinition.

b. *The Phenomena of Scripture*

A redefinition of inspiration rests on the belief that biblical literature has been composed from earlier traditions, and is not the result of a

43. Dockery, *Christian Scripture*, pp. 7-8; Erickson, *Christian Theology*, p. 201.

44. Warfield, 'The Biblical Idea of Inspiration', pp. 138-40.

45. See also Dockery, *Christian Scripture*, p. 41; Erickson, *Christian Theology*, pp. 202-203.

46. Dockery, *Christian Scripture*, p. 11.

47. This point will be discussed in greater detail below in section c.

single 'inspired' author. Through the transmission and combination of these traditions, theological reflection and reappropriation occurred. Scripture therefore reflects a dynamic process at work in the community of Israel and the Church.

The belief that biblical books are formed and shaped from oral and written sources is well attested in all circles of biblical scholarship. Yet the adherents to verbal inspiration within conservative scholarship fail to see the problems that their view holds in regard to traditions and sources.

In identifying inspiration three different seats of inspiration have been offered: the author, the writing, and both the author and the writing. The problem with identifying inspiration with any of these is that when the author becomes the key, each position assumes individual authorship. Almost thirty years ago R.A.F. MacKenzie stated that

> New problems have been raised by the great advance in our understanding of the actual process of composition of ancient literature, particularly the sacred literature of the Jews. All the doctrinal affirmations concerning inspiration take the two concepts of 'Author' and 'Book' as simple univocal expressions, which there is no need to analyze. But we have come to realize now that in reality they are both extremely hard to define.[48]

Certain biblical books testify to the elusiveness of an inspired author. For example, the book of Judges has no clear evidence as to who the author was. Conservative scholars accept that the author of Judges 'seems to have made use of original sources... All the author's material has been arranged according to a unitary plan exhibiting a single dominant idea: Israel's welfare depends upon her spiritual relationship to Jehovah.'[49]

In reality, Judges is not the work of a single inspired author. It is a collection of sources or traditions. Where does one locate the author in all this? Is the author the final editor of the collection? Is the author the person(s) responsible for the earlier stages of the book's composition? At what stage does the composition of a book begin? If sources were collected they most likely started orally—can this in any sense be regarded as inspired?

---

48. MacKenzie, 'Some Problems in the Field of Inspiration', p. 2.

49. G.L. Archer, *A Survey of Old Testament Introduction* (Chicago: Moody, rev. edn, 1974), p. 282.

The problem of authorship can further be illustrated from the Penta-teuch. Consider the assertion of Mosaic authorship in the light of Deuteronomy 34 which records the death of Moses. This certainly shows that Moses did not write at least the final chapter of the Penta-teuch and suggests the possibility of a redactor for other parts of the first five books of the Old Testament. Further,[50] some conservative scholars are very willing to explain certain 'differences' in Genesis 1 and 2 on the basis of different sources. D. Kidner believes, however, that 'the mechanics of composition are small matters, since the parts of this whole are not competing for credence as rival traditions'.[51] If, therefore, the book of Genesis can be seen to be composed by a redac-tor using written and oral sources, we see the difficulty of locating the 'author'. One wonders why it has been so important in some conserva-tive introductions and commentaries to argue for the Mosaic authorship of an anonymous work.[52]

The Gospels are perhaps the best-known examples of authorial elusiveness. Not only are the Synoptic Gospels all anonymous, they are all considered to contain written and oral sources. Since these sources were involved in the composition of the Gospel by the redactor, how does inspiration account for this? Consider also instances when some material common to two Gospels has little verbal similarity, and others where the material is placed in different historical settings. For example, the healing of the centurion's servant (Mt. 8.5ff.; Lk. 7.1ff.) is not only placed in a different order in the two Gospels, but there are differences in their narration. The passion narratives of the Synoptic Gospels, while conforming fairly closely in sequence, contain many differences of detail and wording. Which form is then to be seen as inspired if they differ in any way? Further, there are also instances where Matthew and Luke appear to be in flat contradiction with Mark. In the narrative of the sending of the twelve disciples Mk 6.8 records Jesus as instructing the disciples to take nothing for their journey except a 'mere staff'. Both Mt. 10.10 and Lk. 9.3, however, record Jesus as telling the disciples *not* to take a staff. Which of these differing accounts is the inspired form?

50. This example is taken from C.A. Armerding, *The Old Testament and Criti-cism* (Grand Rapids: Eerdmans, 1983), pp. 23-28.

51. D. Kidner, *Genesis: An Introduction and Commentary* (Downers Grove, IL: Inter-Varsity Press, 1967), p. 22.

52. See, e.g., Archer, *A Survey of Old Testament Introduction*, pp. 109-23.

This is not to say that every book in the Bible is necessarily the product of a redactor. It does, however, show the inadequacy of the authorial models. The mental picture of a single author sitting down to 'write' certain books does not show the true picture of the composition of some biblical books. A definition of inspiration must allow for this.

Important in connection with this is the understanding that the Christian faith grew not as a response to a book, but as a response to God's interaction with the community of faith:

> Scripture not only reflects God's word to the community but also that community's response, both positive and negative, to that word. Scripture did not drop as a stone from heaven. It grew out of the life of a community chosen by a God it barely understood and often did not want to follow, yet who would not release his people to their own devices. On the other hand, if the community produced Scripture out of its struggle to shape its life to the will of God, that Scripture also sustained the community in times of severe crisis. If one cannot imagine the Bible without the community whose life and struggle of faith it records, one cannot imagine the community without the traditions that helped it understand and sustain itself. The Christian faith, therefore, is not a response to a holy book. Church and Scripture grew up alongside each other—the traditions shaping the life of the church, and the church interpreting and reshaping the traditions in light of its own proclamation of those traditions.[53]

There exists a necessity of viewing Scripture as a product of the community because traditions of the community provide the context in which Scripture was produced. These traditions were shaped and reshaped to be used in different ways. Evidence of this is manifest and will not be presented save for the mention of two general examples.[54] First, traditions were sometimes made to say things that were in opposition to the original intent. This can be seen in the way the Prophets use the tradition of the selection and blessing of Abraham originally found in Gen. 12.1-3 and 17.1-8. The tradition that Abraham's progeny became great and possessed the land of Canaan is cited in Ezek. 33.23-29 and Isa. 51.1-3. Upon examination of these citations it becomes

---

53. Achtemeier, *The Inspiration of Scripture*, pp. 90-91.

54. For a fuller treatment and examples of the reappropriation of these traditions, see Achtemeier, *The Inspiration of Scripture*; W. Brueggeman and H.W. Wolff, *The Vitality of Old Testament Traditions* (Atlanta: John Knox Press, 1975); G.W. Coats and B.O. Long (eds.), *Canon and Authority* (Philadelphia: Fortress Press, 1977); J.A. Sanders, *Torah and Canon* (Philadelphia: Fortress Press, 1975).

apparent that they are cited for different reasons. Isaiah uses the tradition to reaffirm the promise of restoration for Israel while Ezekiel uses it to announce that the tradition may not be used as a basis for hope and comfort. Further, the Prophets often use the traditions about God giving the promised land to Israel, not as a guarantee that the promise of God is sure, but as a threat to show that just as God gave the land, he can also take it away. The meaning of the tradition was given by the community which was reappropriating the tradition.

The second example of reappropriation of traditions can be seen in the Gospels. It is almost axiomatic that the Gospels are collections of oral and written traditions formed for a theological purpose. Thus, each Gospel was shaped for the community for which it was intended.

The point here is this—if inspiration is to be properly understood it must be seen within that community which produced those Scriptures. As Achtemeier states,

> If it is true, therefore, that the church, by its production of Scripture, created materials which stood over it in judgment and admonition, it is also true that Scripture would not have existed save for the community and its faith out of which Scripture grew. This means that the church and Scripture are joint effects of the working out of the event of Christ. The close tie between community and Scripture has a most important consequence for our thinking about the inspiration of that Scripture. It is this: if Scripture is to be understood as inspired, then that inspiration will have to be understood equally in terms of the community of faith, and must be located at least as much within that community as it is with an individual author.[55]

This importance of the community is affirmed when Paul states that the Spirit is given to the community for its common good (1 Cor. 12; cf. Acts 2.1-4). If it is the same Spirit which gives inspiration to Scripture then one cannot dispense with the community and still hope to understand the inspiration of Scripture.

c. *The Importance of Canon Formation*

The history of the formation of the canon is where the redefinition of inspiration comes together and is best understood. Included in the formation of the canon is the attitude that the pre-Chalcedonian Fathers had toward Scripture. In the examination of the key New Testament texts concerning inspiration it was shown that the verbal theory causes

---

55. Achtemeier, *The Inspiration of Scripture*, p. 116.

these texts to say more than they actually do. The verbal theory sees the canonical documents as inspired and therefore authoritative for the believing community. The problem this poses is that in the early Church inspiration was not ascribed only to the canonical documents. In an examination of the Apostolic Fathers for their views on authority, inspiration and Scripture in relation to the New Testament writings, one can conclude that they employ the concept of inspiration rather loosely.[56] Rather than claiming that inspiration places a work on a higher plane than any other writing, the Fathers reserve that claim for apostolicity. Clement of Rome claims inspiration for Paul's writings (*1 Clem.* 47), but he also claims inspiration for his own (*1 Clem.* 59.1; 63.2). For Clement the difference boils down to the separation of the age in which he lived from the apostolic age. Ignatius of Antioch backs this up with his belief that the Spirit is at work in every believer; every believer, therefore, is inspired, but not every believer can make a claim to apostolicity (*Trall.* 3.3; *Rom.* 4.3; cf. *Rom.* 7.3; *Philad.* 7.2)—this is the watershed issue.

Apparently the authority of the New Testament documents for certain Apostolic Fathers did not rest in inspiration. The authority is found in the fact that the gospel is reported in the apostolic age, an age that is seen as authoritatively separate from any age that follows. The close link with the actual events of the gospel and the truth of the gospel itself gives the texts authority, not their inspiration.

It is, in fact, difficult to show that the early Church understood inspiration in the same way that the verbal theory understands it. The inspiration that the pre-Chalcedonian Church ascribed to the Scriptures was only one facet of the inspiring activity of the Holy Spirit in many aspects of the Church's life.

Gregory of Nyssa (c. 330–c. 395) in the introduction to his *Hexaemeron* refers to his brother Basil's commentary on creation as an 'exposition given by inspiration [θεόπνευστος] of God…[admired] no less than the words composed by Moses himself'. In a letter written to Jerome (342–420), Augustine (354–430) states not only that Jerome has been favored by divine grace, but also that he writes under the dictation of the Holy Spirit (*Epist.* 82.2). The epitaph on the tomb of Abericus Marcellus (bishop of Rome d. c. 200) was called an 'inspired

---

56. It should be noted here that none of the Apostolic Fathers use the term θεόπνευστος. The terms used by the Apostolic Fathers are πνευματικῶς and ἐμπνέω.

inscription' (*vita Abercii*). *The Letter of the Synod to Pope Celestine* from the ecumenical council at Ephesus describes the council's condemnation of Nestorius as 'a decision given by the inspiration [θεόπνευστος] of God'.

The theory which I propose calls for a balanced understanding of the definition of inspiration based on the wider use of the concept. The *hapax legomenon* θεόπνευστος in 2 Tim. 3.16 is little warrant for the doctrine of verbal inspiration being raised to the level of essential Christian doctrine.

The redefinition of inspiration must also be concerned with specific issues in the canonization of the Bible. To neglect the historical issues in the forming of the biblical canon is to neglect an important aspect of inspiration.

J. Barr correctly points out that many traditional doctrines of Scripture assume a situation whereby the Bible is already 'complete, defined, known, and acknowledged. The Bible is understood to be already *there*, it is already demarcated from other writings.'[57] I view this as a major weakness in the traditional doctrines of Scripture. It contributes to a 'drop out of the sky' mentality that has little or no interest in the development of the canon for informing a doctrine of inspiration.

This shortcoming can be seen in the classic treatment on Scripture by Warfield, where he fails to discuss the historical issues, except to state that this is the historic position of the Church. In an appendix he does include a short study on the canon;[58] however, it is wholly inadequate and fails to discuss any issues of real historical importance. There is no discussion of either the development of the biblical writings or their acceptance by the local or universal Church. He takes the stance that the New Testament books were accepted as canonical as soon as they were available: 'They received new book after new book from the apostolical circle, as equally "Scripture" with the old books, and added them one by one to the collection of old books as additional Scriptures, until at length the new books thus added were numerous enough to be looked upon as another *section* of the Scriptures'.[59]

57. J. Barr, *Holy Scripture: Canon, Authority, and Criticism* (Philadelphia: Westminister Press, 1983), p. 2.

58. Warfield, 'The Formation of the Canon of the New Testament', in his *Inspiration and Authority of Scripture*, pp. 411-16.

59. Warfield, 'The Formation of the Canon of the New Testament', p. 413.

That the position taken blindly by Warfield continues right up to the present day is evident in Dockery's volume on the doctrine of Scripture. He introduces his short discussion on canonicity with the following paragraph:

> We must not think that the church determined or defined the books in the church's canon. In reality, the church did not create the canon, but received the canonical books as spiritually superlative writings by which all other books were measured and found to be of secondary value in general church use. The church then did not decide which books belonged in the canon, but only affirmed those books that God had inspired.[60]

Foundational to this understanding is the contention that the books were included in the canon because they were believed to be inspired.[61] However, the above discussion of the early Church Fathers has severely put this claim in doubt.

Much of the discussion of canonicity and inspiration seems somewhat misguided. Many do make inspiration a criterion for canonicity,[62] but they also correctly temper this criterion within the understanding of the early Church's concept of inspiration: 'The New Testament writings did not become canonical because they were believed to be uniquely inspired; rather they were judged to be inspired because they had previously commended themselves to the Church for other, more practical reasons'.[63] Inspiration, in the verbal sense, simply could not serve as a criterion for canonization. Inspiration in the early Church was too broad to be limited to the canon.

In his (unfortunately) unpublished Doctor of Theology thesis,[64] E.R. Kalin investigated the concept of inspiration in the writings of Irenaeus,

60. Dockery, *Christian Scripture*, p. 85.

61. See Dockery, *Christian Scripture*, p. 90; Erickson, *Christian Theology*, p. 219; E. Schnabel, 'History, Theology, and the Biblical Canon', *Themelios* 20 (1995), pp. 16-24.

62. F.F. Bruce, *The Canon of Scripture* (Downers Grove, IL: Inter-Varsity Press, 1988); H.Y. Gamble, *The New Testament Canon: Its Making and Meaning* (Philadelphia: Fortress Press, 1985); L.M. McDonald, *The Formation of the Christian Biblical Canon* (Peabody, MA: Hendrickson, rev. edn, 1995); B.M. Metzger, *The Canon of the New Testament: Its Origin, Development, and Significance* (Oxford: Clarendon Press, 1987).

63. Gamble, *New Testament Canon*, p. 72.

64. E.R. Kalin, 'Argument from Inspiration in the Canonization of the New Testament' (unpublished ThD thesis, Harvard University, 1967).

Origen, Eusebius, and other relevant texts, with a view to the relationship between inspiration and canonicity.[65] Through his research Kalin confirms the breadth with which inspiration was applied to orthodox writings:

> ...inspiration functions almost exclusively as a positive criterion. That is to say, whenever these authors consider a writing scripture, they invariably consider it to be inspired by God. Inspiration is one of the presuppositions for the status of scripture. But very rarely is the concept of inspiration employed as a negative criterion. A writing that is contrasted to the New Testament scriptures is almost never evaluated as 'non-inspired'. The reason for this is that these writers of the early church consider not only the scriptures and their authors to be inspired but also a number of other writings and their authors. Their concept of inspiration is much wider than their concept of scripture. The concept of inspiration is applied to many aspects of the church's life, including bishops, monks, interpreters of scripture, martyrs, councils, and a wide array of prophetic gifts.[66]

Generally speaking, discussion in the Fathers over the question of inspiration has to do with orthodoxy and heresy. If a writing was seen as orthodox, then inspiration was attached to that writing; if it was seen as heretical, it was not viewed as inspired.

The belief in inspiration as the criterion for canonicity has a further shortcoming. Christianity possessed many writings that were used by the Church but were ultimately not accepted as part of the canon. If only inspired writings were accepted into the canon it is only natural to ask what the criteria were for determining that inspiration. It seems that another inspired event would have to take place in order to determine which books were inspired. Erickson's belief that 'the sensitive reader will probably detect within the whole of the Bible a quality which unmistakably points to inspiration'[67] is not an acceptable explanation of the criteria.

---

65. The writings and writers included under these 'other texts' are: Dionysius of Alexandria, Clement of Alexandria, Gregory of Nyssa, *Vita Abercii*, Cyril of Scythopolis, Pseudo-Justin, Gregory of Nazianzus, Clement of Rome, *Epistle of Barnabas*, Ignatius, *Hermas*, Justin Martyr, Theophilus of Antioch, Basil, the *Muratorian Fragment*, Cyril of Jerusalem, Amphilochius of Iconium and Epiphanius.

66. Kalin, 'Argument from Inspiration in the Canonization of the New Testament', p. 1.

67. Erickson, *Christian Theology*, p. 219.

Further, how does the traditional doctrine explain the difficulty that some books encountered along the way to canonization? The hesitation to accept the Apocalypse in the East and the Epistle to the Hebrews in the West comes to mind here. Why was inspiration finally recognized in these documents even after certain doubts were entertained concerning the respective documents?[68]

Consideration must also be given to the books that have come to be regarded as fringe documents or works on the outside edges. This refers to documents that were used in certain communities as authoritative Scripture but for some reason were not included in the present day canon. That certain books were authoritative is clearly seen by their inclusion in two of the most important extant New Testament codexes. Sinaiticus contains *Barnabas* and *Shepherd of Hermas* while Alexandrinus contains *1 Clement* and *Pseudo-Clement*. Were these documents originally thought to be inspired and then realized not to be?

The unavoidable realization in any study of the formation of the canon is that the various biblical documents were collected into a canon because they were seen as useful to the Church. They were not collected into a canon because these and only these documents were inspired.

In the past ten years a number of important works on the formation of the canon have been produced that list certain extrinsic factors and intrinsic criteria for canonicity.[69] Each of these works testifies to the high probability that the ultimate criterion of whether a book was included in the canon appears to have been the use made of it in the early Church. Factors such as Marcion's canon, the threat of Gnosticism, and the threat of Montanism helped the Church to delineate which books they would view as best representing the beliefs of the community. McDonald is correct in stating that 'the writings that were

68. For discussions concerning the acceptance of the Apocalypse and Hebrews, see Bruce, *Canon of Scripture*; Gamble, *New Testament Canon*; E.J. Goodspeed, *The Formation of the New Testament* (Chicago: University of Chicago Press, 1926); R.M. Grant, *The Formation of the New Testament* (London: Hutchinson University Library, 1965); G.M. Hahneman, *The Muratorian Fragment and the Development of the Canon* (Oxford: Clarendon Press, 1992); E. Lohse, *The Formation of the New Testament* (Nashville: Abingdon Press, 1981); McDonald, *Formation of the Christian Biblical Canon*; Metzger, *Canon of the New Testament*.

69. See, e.g., Bruce, *Canon of Scripture*, pp. 117-269; Gamble, *New Testament Canon*, pp. 57-72; Metzger, *Canon of the New Testament*, pp. 75-112, 251-66; McDonald, *Formation of the Christian Biblical Canon*, pp. 99-119, 146-63.

believed to have best conveyed the earliest Christian proclamation and that also best met the needs of the local Churches in the third and fourth centuries were the writings they selected for their sacred scriptures'.[70]

In actuality, the evidence shows that the Church decided what books should belong in its canon. The canon was formed, therefore, in much the same way that a great deal of biblical literature was formed—as responses to new situations that represented threats to the community of faith. It was a living tradition that served to meet the contemporary needs of the community.

The theory of inspiration I propose, as seen from the three sections above, recognizes that somehow inspiration is related to the way the biblical material was, and is still, used in the community of faith. Inspiration cannot, therefore, be defined as being located in the individual 'author', the text, or the 'author' and the text. Inspiration is not seen as something that is inherent in a writing or a writer. It is best seen as applied to an orthodox writing by the community of faith.

What is proposed above is an understanding of inspiration that does not lie in the very words of the product. The authority of the biblical documents is not found in its inspiration—if this were the case then there are many documents which should therefore be authoritative for the Christian today because they were also viewed as inspired. The authority of the biblical documents is found in the fact that they witness to the gospel.

3. *Assessment: Inspiration and Translation*

In relating the redefinition of inspiration to the product of translation it is important to understand that inspiration is not necessarily a unique concept. It is very significant that the key verse for the inspiration of Scripture is 2 Tim. 3.16. Inspiration is there linked to specific functions of Scripture, such as catechetical, soteriological, and ethical ones.[71] This is where the focus of our understanding of inspiration should lie, not on other matters that are outside these legitimate functions.

In this respect, the inspiration of the Bible can be seen as a faith claim made by the community of faith as a result of the appropriation

70. McDonald, *Formation of the Christian Biblical Canon*, p. 162.
71. D.C. Arichea, 'Theology and Translation', in P.C. Stine (ed.), *Bible Translation and the Spread of the Church: The Last 200 Years* (Leiden: E.J. Brill, 1990), p. 60.

of those texts. In time some inspired documents came to be valued more than others and were canonized as an accurate representation of the community's faith. Inspiration, therefore, was attached to these writings, not as an a priori assumption, but as an a posteriori discovery.[72]

The effect that this has on how one views a translation of the Bible is really quite simple. Since inspiration was placed on a document because of its worth and function (its orthodoxy) in the community of faith, then that worth and function still continues to the present as it is encased in the canon. Inspiration must be seen as a functioning criterion.

It is beyond dispute that translations of biblical documents are used in the Church today for teaching, reproof, and soteriological reasons. The documents were seen in this light from their first appropriation in the ancient world and continue to be seen and used in this way—regardless of the language in which the Scriptures appear. It is this appropriation by the Church that gives the documents their inspiration. If the document does not promote heresy it is viewed as inspired.

Translations, therefore, can be viewed as inspired. Inspiration is not unique to the original biblical documents, or even solely to biblical documents. Translations provide the Church with a supremely important object of authority—the foundation documents of the Christian faith. From these documents the Church views the significance of the actions of God from the perspective of the community. They are inspired because the community views them as accurately reflecting what the community as a whole believes. This reflection is preserved in the canon and is authoritative for the historic orthodox community of faith today. Because the Church continues to use these documents—in translation, in day to day worship, and in instruction—they are deemed as inspired by the community that uses them.

Many may see the close relationship between the theory which I propose and the social theory of inspiration.[73] Indeed, I am indebted to the

72. Achtemeier, *The Inspiration of Scripture*, p. 135.

73. See, e.g., Forestell, 'The Limitation of Inerrancy'; MacKenzie, 'Some Problems in the Field of Inspiration'; McKenzie, 'The Social Character of Inspiration'; K. Rahner, *Inspiration in the Bible* (Freiburg: Herder; Edinburgh: Thomas Nelson, 1961); L.J. Topel, 'Rahner and McKenzie on the Social Theory of Inspiration', *CBQ* 16 (1964), pp. 33-44; B. Vawter, *Biblical Inspiration* (Philadelphia: Westminster Press; London: Hutchinson, 1972).

social theory for a considerable amount of thought-provoking material on the community aspect of Scripture. My theory, however, departs from the social theory at what I believe to be an important point—the uniqueness of inspiration. The major shortcoming that exists in the social theory is that it still attempts to place the authority of the Bible in its unique inspiration. But, as I have shown, inspiration is not best viewed as unique to the biblical documents.

I stress that the proposal I offer must be seen only as a theory. One of the foundational problems I have with the verbal theory is that it has been elevated to the status of essential Christian doctrine. The evidence upon which any theory of inspiration is based, however, is too inconclusive to form the basis of any essential doctrines. I believe that the fresh approaches to inspiration in the past decade can only serve to allow positive strides forward in its discussion. A high view of Scripture demands as much.

Part II

OLD TESTAMENT

THE OLD TESTAMENT TRANSLATOR'S TRANSLATION—
A PERSONAL REFLECTION

J.W. Rogerson

The Old Testament Translator's Translation (OTTT) was launched in Glasgow in September 1965 under the auspices of the British and Foreign Bible Society (BFBS). Those present at the inaugural meeting included Professor W.D. McHardy (Oxford, Chairman), Professor William Barclay (Glasgow, and representing the National Bible Society of Scotland), Professor G.W. Anderson (Edinburgh), Professor A.S. Herbert (Selly Oak), Dr William McKane (Glasgow), the Revd William Johnstone (Aberdeen), and the present writer (Durham). The project was introduced by Mr W.J. Bradnock, head of the Translations Department of BFBS.

Mr Bradnock explained that Bible translation was entering a new phase. In the indigenous churches there was a need for the revision of existing translations. The latter had been done by European and American missionaries with the help of 'native informers'; but they were not entirely satisfactory, having been done by translators who were translating into a language that was not their mother tongue. With the emergence of indigenous leaders in young churches, there now existed church leaders who could undertake, as native speakers of their languages, the necessary revisions of existing translations. The question was, on what would they base their work? Since indigenous leaders were not in a position to spend years acquiring sufficient Greek and Hebrew to translate the Bible from the original languages, BFBS was committed to providing translations for translators, and had already produced a series of Greek and English diglots of individual books of the New Testament for these purposes.[1] What was now needed was an

---

1. This work culminated in *The Translator's New Testament* (London: The British and Foreign Bible Society, 1973). (This was an English translation with translational notes.)

Old Testament equivalent: a translation into English from the Hebrew and Aramaic done with the special needs in mind of translators for whom English was a second language.

At the initial meeting a start was made on Genesis 1, and the panel soon encountered a problem, apart from the contentious issue of how to translate the opening sentence (see below). How was the Hebrew word *râqî'a*, rendered in traditional English translations as 'firmament', to be translated? Suggestions included 'dome', 'arch' and 'ceiling'; but the final decision was to stick with 'firmament', and to produce notes and a glossary that would accompany the translation and would set the term *râqî'a* in the context of the cosmology of Genesis 1 as a whole.[2] It was argued that, in the target languages, there might well be exact equivalents for *râqî'a*, whereas if the OTTT went for a word such as 'dome' and did not explain its position in the Genesis cosmology as a whole, the translators might introduce an alien concept. Thus, the principle was informally established that, in cases of doubt, it was better to use a word that was likely to be unfamiliar to translators and which they would have to look up in the glossary, than to provide a familiar English word which might produce a misleading translation. As will be related below, this principle brought undeserved criticism to the project.

Work on the OTTT continued in 1966 with the one panel working on Genesis; but at the end of that year the panel was divided, and I became a member of the Psalms panel chaired by George Anderson, meeting in Edinburgh, and with a core membership of Robert Davidson (then at St Andrews), John Sawyer (Newcastle) and myself. The Revd Brynmor Price of BFBS, and a former Baptist missionary to China, was the secretary. The Glasgow panel continued with Genesis. Other panels were established in Cambridge, Selly Oak and London. Thereafter, the Psalms panel met for several days two or three times a year during university vacations, until the project fizzled out in around 1974. the last meeting of the Psalms panel was during the Easter vacation of 1974.

---

2.   In fact, the final version of Genesis OTTT substituted 'dome' for 'firmament'. See *Translator's Old Testament. Genesis* (unpublished typescript, London: BFBS, no date), p. 1. Whether the substitution was made by the Genesis panel after I had left it, or whether it was done during the final revision at Bible House, I do not know. My discussions with E.A. Nida may throw some light on this, as may the fact that the Good News Bible used the word 'dome'.

A significant event, and one which indicates why the project was never completed, was a consultation on Bible translation held at Bernhäuser Forst near Stuttgart in September 1972, and convened by Eugene Nida on behalf of the United Bible Societies. William McKane, by now professor at St Andrews, and I represented the OTTT. I was glad to meet Nida, since I had studied linguistics under Chaim Rabin in Jerusalem in 1963–64, and although my research had moved via sociolinguistics to Social Anthropology, I still retained an interest in linguistics, especially because of my participation in the OTTT. I had read Nida's *Toward a Science of Translating* with much interest, as well as a number of his other books on the subject of Bible translation.[3]

In conversations at Bernhäuser Forst, Nida expressed strong criticism of the OTTT, and mentioned, as an example, the translation of *râqî'a* as 'firmament'. I countered by explaining the reasoning for this, but Nida did not seem to be convinced. It was clear that he regarded the whole concept of the OTTT as a mistake. He himself was pushing for the production of common-language translations, versions such as the Today's English Version which could be used not only in English-speaking countries, but in parts of the world where English was widely known and used as a second language. Other common-language translations would include those in Spanish, Portuguese, French and Mandarin Chinese. I could see the logic of this; but I had severe reservations about the notion of dynamic equivalence translation (the theory that a translation should try to reproduce in the target language the impact made upon original readers in the source language), which was part and parcel of the common-language translation programme. I made all of the following points to Nida.

First, there was the difficulty that, short of a time machine, there was no way of knowing what the original impact of a book of the Bible was on the original readers/hearers. Was there only *one* such impact? Secondly, it was arguable on the grounds of historical linguistics that, when the early Church read the Septuagint, it read a work that was

---

3.   E.A. Nida, *Toward a Science of Translating with Special Reference to Principles and Procedures involved in Bible Translating* (Leiden: E.J. Brill, 1964). The other works that I had read included E.A. Nida, *God's Word in Man's Language* (New York: Harper & Row, 1952) and *idem, Customs and Cultures* (New York: Harper & Row, 1954). I had not, at that stage, read Eugene A. Nida and Charles R. Taber, *The Theory and Practice of Translation* (Helps for Translators, 8; Leiden: E.J. Brill, 1969), but was to do so later.

written in Greek that then seemed archaic. Indeed, part of its aura as 'scripture' may well have depended upon its impact as slightly archaic. If this was a correct view, should not dynamic equivalence translation deliberately render the Old Testament into archaic English so that it would make upon Christians today the same impact that it was presumed to have made on readers in the early Church? Thirdly, by translating the Old Testament according to its supposed impact on Israelite readers/hearers, the Good News Bible (the embodiment of Nida's principles) closed off a whole dimension of interpretation. This could be illustrated from the GNB rendering of the opening of Psalm 110: 'The LORD said to my Lord, the king', where 'the king' is an interpretative gloss which closes off the possibility of Jewish or Christian messianic uses of the Psalm.

All this was said in 1972, when Old Testament studies knew nothing of reader-response criticism, or openness versus closure, or gender or class issues in biblical translation. All that has happened in biblical studies since 1972 has only served to increase my difficulties about the notion of dynamic equivalence translation. It is also arguable that common-language translations have adversely affected some aspects of Bible translation, in that there is evidence that translations into the languages of Indonesia have, under the guise of being dynamic equivalence translations, used not the Greek or Hebrew, but the English GNB as the basis for these translations. Since one of the principles of dynamic equivalence translation is that the culture of the target language should have preference over that of the source language, this use of the GNB as a basis of translation introduces the possibility that a translation that reflects the cultural needs of modern Western society is then imposed upon an Asiatic society.[4]

These reservations about dynamic equivalence do not detract from my admiration for Nida's work, from which I have learned much, and which has sought to introduce a linguistic professionalism into Bible translation that was hitherto lacking. Too often, there has been an assumption in Bible translation among academics that, as long as the translator is skilled in Greek or Hebrew, little else matters. No one who reads Nida's works can possibly go on thinking that, even though it

---

4. See further A.J. Nichols, 'Bible Translation: A Critical Analysis of E.A. Nida's Theory of Dynamic Equivalence and its Impact on recent Bible Translations' (PhD dissertation, University of Sheffield, 1997).

may be possible to place severe question marks against some aspects and outcomes of his work.

Nida's belief that the OTTT was a fundamentally flawed project reflected a power struggle that was going on behind the scenes between Bible House in London and the American Bible Society, with the latter tending to dominate the translations policy of the United Bible Societies. I was not party to this struggle and knew of it only because its apparent resolution in Nida's favour brought the OTTT to an end before it was completed. No doubt the details are minuted in the archives of the Bible Society, and it is not impossible that I have unintentionally misrepresented what happened. The outcome, however, was that the Psalms panel was disbanded, as, I presume, were also the other panels, and that its members were told that the OTTT would be completed by Bible House with the advice of experts such as Professors McHardy, Anderson and Herbert. To my knowledge, the OTTT was never formally published, but circulated in duplicated fascicles to members of panels. It was, however, used to some extent among translators in the field, and the Psalms panel certainly received feedback occasionally in general terms.

This is all that I intend to say about the project from my personal point of view. The remainder of the essay will examine several specific issues that arose from my membership of the Genesis panel before it was divided up.

The OTTT rendered Gen. 1.1 as follows:

> In the beginning God created the earth and the sky.

The notes (pp. 81-113) added the following information:

> *In the beginning, God created...* A possible alternative translation of vv. 1-3 would be: 'When God began to create...God said' etc., verse 2 being understood as a parenthesis.

> *the earth and the sky.* The reference here is to the upper part of the created world rather than to heaven as the dwelling place of God, or the spirit world. The sky, as indicated in v. 6 is thought of as a solid dome above the earth.

It has to be remembered that this translation was first proposed in 1965, which is a long time ago in terms of scholarship. I supported what went into the main text, whereas I would now support the alternative translation. There is no doubt that my own preference at the time was swayed by the theological consideration that I did not know what our constituency would make of the alternative translation if it appeared as the main text. The explanation in the notes, which was not done by the Genesis panel but in Bible House, seems to me now to give no help to the presumed translator, and seems to be more designed to reflect domestic scholarly opinion than to be a genuine help to translators. On the other hand, while I do not like the phrase 'spirit world', which arguably could suggest to indigenous translators in parts of Africa ideas far removed from what the Old Testament writers believed, the intention of the note is clearly to be helpful to the translators.

The same is true of the note on the word 'dome', which replaced 'firmament' in v. 6 of the final version of Genesis. The note read:

> a dome. In the ancient world it was believed that the earth was flat, and the sky was thought of as a solid hemisphere, standing upon and enclosing the flat surface of the earth as an upturned bowl might cover a plate. Verse 2 indicates that the earth itself was thought of as already existing, but as submerged in water. The act of creation envisaged here is therefore the provision of a solid dome to stand upon the submerged earth. Earth and sky are still completely submerged, so that there is water below and above the dome, but in v. 9 the water below or inside is partly removed, so that areas of dry land appear, surrounded by areas of sea.

This seems to me to express admirably what members of the Genesis panel hoped that the notes would achieve. It puts the word translated 'dome' into the perspective of Hebrew cosmology as a whole, enabling translators to decide whether, in their own cosmologies, there was a technical term with the same or similar function. Straightforward rendering of 'dome' as understood in English would not achieve this.

In translating Gen. 1.2 the panel opted for 'a mighty wind was moving on the water' with the following note:

> a mighty wind. The same Hebrew word is used for 'wind' and 'spirit'. The phrase here would mean 'the Spirit of God' or, 'a wind from God'. But the word God is sometimes used in the Old Testament in a superlative sense to indicate something of exceptional size or intensity, e.g. in Ps. 68.16 the Hebrew 'mountain of God' means 'a mighty mountain', and in Jonah 3.3 'a great city to God' means 'a very large city'. It is likely that the same idiom is used here, and that a 'wind of God' means 'a mighty wind'. (see also Glossary 'SPIRIT').

Translators who looked up 'SPIRIT' in the glossary would have found the following helpful account:

SPIRIT (Hebrew ruah)

The same Hebrew word means 'spirit', 'wind' and 'breath'. The 'spirit of Yahweh' is understood as an extension of his personality by which he is present among men to be the source of strength, skill, wisdom and the prophetic gift. In Genesis there are two references to the 'spirit' of God: 6.3 which regards God's spirit as the source of men's life, and 41.38 where Joseph's ability to interpret the will of God through dreams is attributed to the 'spirit of God'.

The glossary entry went on to distinguish more uses of *ruah*, such as wind (Gen. 3.8 'the evening breeze'), the living, breathing principle in humans and animals (Gen. 6.17 'the spirit of life') and spirit in the sense of disposition (Gen. 26.25 where the Hebrew 'bitterness of spirit' meant 'a source of sorrow').

I am now of the opinion that the panel was wrong to translate Gen. 1.2 as 'mighty wind', and that it was too much influenced by the work of the New English Bible Old Testament translation panel. That the Hebrew word for God can be used, with other words, to express a superlative is not in doubt, as pointed out, for example, in the mediaeval Jewish scholar Ibn Ezra's comment on Gen. 23.6, where the Hebrew 'prince of God' means 'mighty prince' (cf. the Authorized Version).[5] The question is how Hebrew speakers (and modern translators) knew when 'God' meant the supreme divine being, and when it indicated a superlative. Presumably the answer is that the matter was decided by context, so that in Jon. 3.3 it was unlikely that Nineveh was literally being called a city of God, and probable that the phrase indicated a superlative. Whether, however, the same would be true when 'God' was combined with either the word for mountain or that for spirit is another matter. It is true that most, if not all, modern translations render 'the mountain of God' (or gods) at Ps. 68.15 (the note in the OTT gives the reference to the Hebrew numbering) as something like 'mighty hill', but the verse presents problems of interpretation, and the Hebrew may connect the hill of Bashan (which is the subject) with polytheistic worship, or conceal a time when Bashan *was* the hill of God. At any rate, there is nothing in the context of Gen. 1.2 to indicate that the word 'God' does not have its usual meaning; and it is noteworthy that the Revised English Bible restored the rendering 'Spirit of God'.

---

5.   Abraham Ibn Ezra, *Pêrushê HaTorah* (Jerusalem: Mossad Harav Kook, 1976), I, p. 73.

It is, in fact, arguable that the OTTT missed an opportunity by not explaining in a note that the word translated 'was moving' by the OTTT is used at Deut. 32.11 of a bird hovering over its nest. This could imply a cosmic egg cosmology, to which there might have been parallels, and therefore appropriate terms, in some of the target cultures.

These few examples merely indicate what any Bible translator will acknowledge only too readily: that translation is a series of compromises, that it is provisional, that the line between translation and interpretation is not always easy to draw, and that translation will be affected by the linguistic theories or lack of them held by the translators, together with their awareness or lack of awareness of gender and class issues. While sharing most, if not all, of the above faults, the OTTT was nonetheless significant in being a translation that attempted to explain some, at least, of the difficulties to the target users. It also was carried out against the background of competing interests within the Bible Societies, and sharply differing estimates of what was needed in the areas traditionally targeted by them. It is important that a younger generation of scholars should be reminded that, thirty years ago, a considerable number of biblical scholars in Britain devoted time and energy to this project which, rightly or wrongly, turned out to be stillborn, but which gave those concerned an exposure to problems that can hardly be appreciated by those who have not attempted Bible translation themselves.

But there is one more issue that the OTTT seems to me to raise, and that is whether it is right to publish translations of the Bible that are not accompanied by notes such as those that were prepared for the OTTT. The older English tradition of producing Bibles was one of publishing Bibles with notes. It is true that these notes often had a strongly doctrinal flavour, but they did also explain things that were not necessarily clear in the translation themselves. In the eighteenth and early nineteenth centuries, for example, editions of the Authorized Version with notes by J.F. Ostervald (1783), John Brown (1778) and Thomas Scott (1788) were published, the latter appearing in weekly numbers. Between 1788 and 1812, twelve thousand copies of Scott's Bible were printed in Britain, while the number reached twenty-five thousand in America between 1809 and 1819. A popular nineteenth-century edition with extensive notes was that of Adam Clarke (1825). Ironically, it was the British and Foreign Bible Society that changed the reading habits of churchgoers in Britain and elsewhere by issuing Bibles without any notes at all. Partly, this was no doubt to reduce the cost of Bibles and to make them more widely available; but there were also doctrinal reasons, in that the alliance of Anglicans and Free Churches in the Bible Society did not want either party to gain a doctrinal advantage via explanatory notes. In a strange way, and certainly not deliberately, dynamic equivalence translation could be seen as a way of reintroducing commentary into biblical translation by way of the strict principles that are part of the theory and practice of dynamic equivalence.[6] It needs to be asked whether, at least in the affluent one-third world, there is any longer any justification for producing translations of the Bible without any translational notes; whether, in fact, something like the OTTT ought to be revised, completed and widely circulated.

---

6.   See Nida and Taber, *Theory and Practice, passim.*

REFLECTIONS ON TRANSLATING JOSHUA

Richard S. Hess

The book of Joshua presents an interesting case study in the translation of the Hebrew Bible. It is not an extremely difficult book with unusual vocabulary and syntax (such as Job). However, Joshua contains its share of problem texts. Again, it does not have the crucial doctrinal issues of a book like Genesis or Isaiah, where specific words must be translated in a specific fashion if one wishes to be doctrinally orthodox. However, it does include translation issues that can challenge cherished beliefs. In fact, these two areas—difficulties of translation and issues of orthodoxy—exemplify the two major areas of translation. When one translates one does so from one language into another. One takes a text in one language and creates a new one in another language that is related to the first text in certain important ways. In Bible translation, as in most other translations that are published, the person or people doing the translating do not do it for themselves alone. They have an audience in mind, an audience that has certain expectations regarding the original text and that new creation, the translated text.

In order to appreciate some of these problems, the text of Joshua was chosen as an example. Since this has been a text on which I have worked recently, it is one whose familiarity allows me to select some of the more interesting examples of problems and issues raised by the process of translation.

1. *The Original Text*

The issues raised in translation can be divided into two categories: those that concern the original text and those that concern the text that is the newly created translation. First, consideration will be given to the original text. This consideration itself includes at least two major areas: the choice of the text and the method used to undertake the translation.

Although the second is more commonly thought of as translation proper, the choice of the text forms a significant part of the translation process.

a. *The Choice of a Text*

For the Old Testament text selection has often been a debated issue. For many years Western Christianity assumed that the Latin Vulgate was the most important text just as Eastern Christianity referred to the Greek Septuagint. With the advent of the Reformation and Enlightenment, arguments were advanced to examine the Hebrew text, something that Judaism had long followed. Since the Masoretic Text was assumed to be the correct text, the issue was relatively simple—choose the earliest prototype as the basic text for translation. However, scholars soon recognized that even so carefully preserved a manuscript as the Masoretic Text contained copyists' errors. When the Septuagint was seen to correct these, it became a source for the establishment of the text for translation.[1] So did other ancient versions such as the Syriac Peshitta and the Vulgate. With the discovery of the Dead Sea Scrolls a new source for translating the Old Testament was recognized. Meanwhile, more authoritative sources for the Masoretic Text were located so that the present preparation of a new edition of the United Bible Societies' Biblia Hebraica will use the tenth century CE Aleppo Codex for the first time.[2]

1. *Canon*. There is, of course, a difference between Bible translation and textual criticism. However, the translator must choose which text to translate. They are not all alike. Nor is this choice a purely academic one. The community for whom the translation is prepared will have input to a greater or lesser extent. They may not wish to choose a text that is the oldest or most original. They may use other criteria for their choice of text. This is the case, for example, with the edition of the Biblia Hebraica upon which most modern translations of the Old

---

1.   E. Tov, *The Text-Critical Use of the Septuagint in Biblical Research* (Jerusalem Biblical Studies, 3; Jerusalem: Simor, 1981).

2.   E.R. Brotzman, *Old Testament Textual Criticism: A Practical Introduction* (Grand Rapids: Baker Book House, 1994); F.E. Deist, *Witnesses to the Old Testament: Introducing Old Testament Textual Criticism* (The Literature of the Old Testament, 5; Pretoria: NG Kerkboekhandel, 1988); E. Tov, *Textual Criticism of the Hebrew Bible* (Minneapolis: Fortress Press, 1992); E. Würthwein, *The Text of the Old Testament* (trans. E. F. Rhodes; Grand Rapids: Eerdmans, 1979).

Testament are based. The committee that chose this text was influenced by its religious commitment. Therefore, it chose to identify the text that it would use as the one that was first recognized as Scripture by the community of faith. This is, of course, not necessarily the same thing as the text that left the hand of the author. Furthermore, it stipulated that the Masoretic Text was an accurately preserved edition of this text.[3] Therefore, variant readings from other texts could not be considered on an equal basis with the Masoretic Text. Only when the latter was in clear error would an alternative textual reading or emendation be acceptable. It is important to be aware of the impact that this has had on biblical translation because it means that most readers of the Old Testament are in fact readers of the Masoretic Text's version of the Old Testament without knowing that variations exist. It is not necessarily wrong to give priority to the Masoretic Text but it is important to be aware that this is the textual tradition used in most translations.[4] It is, however, not agreed by all scholars that this preserves the oldest text of the traditions of Joshua. For example, Graeme Auld has argued that the Hebrew *Vorlage* behind the Septuagint consistently bears witness to an older text.[5] If he is correct, then the choice of the Masoretic Text renders a translation of a later text than would be possible by carefully using the Septuagint.

2. *Version.* What sort of difference would this make? One example suffices for the purposes here. In Josh. 15.20-63, there is a list of towns within the tribal allotment of Judah. This list divides into eleven

3.   D. Barthélemy, *Critique textuelle de l'Ancien Testament: Tome 3, Ézéchiel, Daniel et les 12 Prophètes* (OBO, 50.3; Fribourg, Switzerland: Editions Universitaires; Göttingen: Vandenhoeck & Ruprecht, 1992), pp. i-v, ccxxviii-ccxxxviii.

4.   For criticism of this approach, see B. Albrektson, 'Translation and Emendation', in S.E. Balentine and J. Barton (eds.), *Language, Theology, and the Bible: Essays in Honour of James Barr* (Oxford: Clarendon Press, 1994), pp. 27-39.

5.   A. Graeme Auld, *Joshua, Moses and the Land: Tetrateuch–Pentateuch–Hexateuch in a Generation of Study since 1938* (Edinburgh: T. & T. Clark, 1980); *idem*, 'Cities of Refuge in Israelite Tradition', *JSOT* 10 (1978), pp. 26-40; *idem*, 'Textual and Literary Studies in the Book of Joshua', *ZAW* 90 (1978), pp. 412-17; *idem*, 'The "Levitical Cities" Text and History', *ZAW* 91 (1979), pp. 194-206; *idem*, 'Joshua: The Hebrew and Greek Texts', in J.A. Emerton (ed.), *Studies in the Historical Books of the Old Testament* (VTSup, 30; Leiden: E.J. Brill, 1979), pp. 1-14; *idem*, 'The Cities in Joshua 21: The Contribution of Textual Criticism', *Textus* 15 (1990), pp. 141-50.

segments, each concluding with a summary of the total number of
towns listed in that segment. The Masoretic Text's list does not
mention Bethlehem. However, in the Septuagint v. 59 continues with a
district that does mention Bethlehem Ephratah as well as ten other
towns. It might be expected that Judah would have twelve districts. The
omission of Bethlehem is inexplicable from the town list of the
Masoretic Text. Has the Septuagint preserved the missing twelfth
district or has it attempted to fill in a list that was already lost to its
Vorlage or never there in the first place? The critical apparatus of the
Biblia Hebraica Stuttgartensia suggests the former. They argue that,
since each of these districts ends with the same Hebrew word, וחצריהן,
'and their villages', that a scribe copying the end of v. 59 skipped down
to the end of v. 59a, thereby omitting this district in the Masoretic Text
through a process of homoioteleuton. Here is an example where,
despite the predilection of the UBS committee for the Masoretic Text,
there is agreement that the Septuagint preserves an older reading.[6]

3. *Dead Sea Scrolls.* Another group of early texts that need to be considered in any translation are the Dead Sea Scroll biblical texts. Fragments of the book of Joshua are preserved. The most controversial is
4QJoshua[a]. Ulrich published the fragments, noting that they contain the
following verses and additional non-biblical text (= X) in this order:
8.34-35; X; 5.2-7; 6.5-10; 7.12-17; 8.3-14, (18?); 10.2-5, 8-11.[7] Josh.
8.34-35 describes the building of the altar on Mt Ebal. It is out of its
Masoretic sequence in the Qumran text. It occurs immediately after the
crossing of the Jordan River. In the Septuagint at 8.30-35, the text is
also at a different place from the Masoretic Text. However, there it has
moved only one verse and now follows 9.1, a text similar to 5.1. These
differences of position have led Rofé to find here the presence of several different recensions by different editors.[8] Auld argues that this

6.   See D. Barthélemy, *Critique textuelle de l'Ancient Testament: Tome 1,
Josué, Juges, Ruth, Samuel, Rois, Chroniques, Esdras, Néhémìe, Esthèr* (OBO,
50.1; Fribourg, Switzerland: Éditions Universitaires; Göttingen: Vandenhoeck &
Ruprecht, 1982), p. 44.
7.   E. Ulrich, '4QJoshua and Joshua's First Altar in the Promised Land', in G.J.
Brooke and F. García Martínez (eds.), *New Qumran Texts and Studies: Proceed-
ings of the First Meeting of the International Organization for Qumran Studies,
Paris 1992* (Studies in Texts from the Desert of Judea, 15; Leiden: E.J. Brill, 1994),
pp. 89-104.
8.   A. Rofé, 'The Editing of the Book of Joshua in the Light of 4QJosh[a]', in

demonstrates that 8.30-35 is a late text inserted by different editors into different places in an otherwise fixed text.[9] Where should the translator include this text? Following the principles of the UBS Hebrew Bible committee, it belongs at the place where the text received by the community of faith placed it, at 8.30-35. This probably remains the preferred location in the textual tradition of the book of Joshua. The fragmentary nature of the Qumran text, and the presence of the X material that follows, raise questions about the nature of the Qumran document. Perhaps this is an example of a midrashic style of text, a 'parabiblical' text, containing a collection of various biblical quotations along with additional notes and explanations?

4. *Intertextual Translation.* The choice of a text to translate can also raise intertextual questions. For example, consider the name of the perpetrator of the theft of items committed to the ban at Jericho.[10] In Joshua 7 his name is Achan, עכן. The same figure is described in 1 Chron. 2.7 and there he is given the name, Achar, עכר. In the Septuagint his name in both Joshua and 1 Chronicles is Achar. How should the translator render this name? It is a question of spelling rather than interpretation of the name. Nevertheless, it is a translation issue. The simple answer is to follow the spelling in the Masoretic Text and this is what most translations do. However, could the Masoretic Text have transmitted a spelling error in Joshua 7? After all, the Hebrew nun and resh can interchange in other names, the most famous example being Nebuchadnezzar who is also spelled Nebuchadrezzar. In this case, however, the name Achan is probably correct. Achan is supported by three reasons. First, 'Achan' probably does occur as a personal name in a text of the West Semitic world, specifically from Alalakh.[11] However, there is no attestation of a Hebrew root for עכן in Classical Hebrew. Secondly, Achar does not occur as a personal name but the root, עכר, 'disaster', is well-known in Hebrew. It occurs in 1 Chron. 2.7 where the

Brooke and García Martínez (eds.), *New Qumran Texts and Studies*, pp. 73-80.

9. A. Graeme Auld, 'Reading Joshua after Kings', in J. Davies, G. Harvey and W.G.E. Watson (eds.), *Words Remembered, Texts Renewed: Essays in Honour of John F.A. Sawyer* (JSOTSup, 195; Sheffield: JSOT Press, 1995), pp. 167-81.

10. For the following, see R.S. Hess, 'Achan and Achor: Names and Wordplay in Joshua 7', *HAR* 14 (1994), pp. 89-98.

11. Spelled as *a-ka-an*. For questions about the initial 'ayin in the Hebrew name and for the specific location of this name, see Hess, 'Achan and Achor: Names and Wordplay in Joshua 7', p. 91.

name Achar is given a pun, for it is said, 'Achar brought disaster' upon Israel, עכר עוכר. This is the same root that occurs in the name of the place of Achan's execution and burial, the Valley of Achor. Thus the name, Achar, is best understood as a nickname of an original Achan, used to describe the fate of the name bearer. Thirdly, the name, Achan, also occurs in the Syriac Peshitta. Thus, Achan remains the best way in which to render the text.

It may be concluded that the translator of the Old Testament must make choices about which text to use in translation. This occurs on the level of the canonical text of the Old Testament, where the translator must decide whether to translate the Old Testament as reflected in the Hebrew canon or in the Greek canon. It is found on the level of an individual book of the Old Testament, as to whether the translator will translate the Septuagint or the Masoretic Text. The choice must be made wherever significant variants occur within a text, especially where scribal errors are identified. Will the translator translate the error, select a version or manuscript that has a 'better' reading, or choose to emend the text? An additional aspect of this question arises when the text to be translated is cited or referred to elsewhere in the Old Testament, as in the case of Achan in Joshua and 1 Chronicles. What weight does the additional citation have on the Joshua text? Some of these decisions are already made in the case of most translators. They are committed to a particular version and sometimes to a particular text from that version. Whatever the case, a decision must be made before translation can proceed. Indeed, it is necessary even for this essay. For purposes of the discussion here, it is assumed that the Masoretic Text will form the basis of the translation issues that arise in the following sections.

b. *The Translation of the Text*
A second aspect of translation that focuses upon the original text asks questions about the translational approach to be used. The student of Classical Hebrew will find that much of the Hebrew Bible conforms to expected lexical, grammatical and syntactical forms and patterns that may be obtained from study of the standard grammars and lexicons. However, this is by no means true of all of the language. It is the unusual forms that occupy the translator at this stage. At the lexical level, these are those words that occur only once (*hapax legomena*) or twice. At the grammatical and syntactical level, they are forms that also occur only once or infrequently. In the past, they were too easily

considered errors. However, they may represent distinctive dialects or idiomatic expressions unique to a group or social context. These forms lie outside the accepted parameters of the language. At a broader level there are questions of stylistic features that can convey important features and nuances intended by the text. This issues are all the more significant when dealing with a text in a dead language, one that no longer has living speakers. Although modern Israeli Hebrew possesses many similarities to Classical Hebrew, it is of little help at several points where the issue of translation becomes most difficult. There are examples of these types of questions in the book of Joshua.

1. *Hapax Legomena*. Although the exact number depends on how they are counted, there are many *hapax legomena* in the Hebrew Bible. Part of the reason for this is that the Hebrew Bible forms the largest corpus of literature that constitutes Classical Hebrew. Outside of the Hebrew Bible there are relatively few inscriptions that can be added to the corpus. The other significant collection of Classical Hebrew is the Hebrew Dead Sea Scrolls and fragments. However, many of these are themselves biblical texts or use biblical language. Even when all these additional texts are considered, the Hebrew Bible remains the largest collection of Classical Hebrew. Therefore, a *hapax legomenon* in the Bible is likely also one in Classical Hebrew.

The presuppositions behind the translator's interpretation of a given passage can often determine the way in which a word is translated. For example, the word translated 'secretly' (חרש) in Josh. 2.1 appears to be part of the description of how Joshua sent out the spies. This word does not appear elsewhere in biblical Hebrew. Hebrew lexicons list either three or four roots spelled the same way.[12] They place the Josh. 2.1 reference with the root meaning, 'to be silent, dumb, deaf'. However, a homonym of this root can mean, 'to cut, engrave'. Other similarly spelled nouns can mean 'magic, magician'. Thus in Isa. 3.3, a word spelled in exactly the same way in the Masoretic Text appears as a noun, translated as 'craftsman' in the New International Version and New Jewish Publication Society Version and as 'magician' in the

---

12. F. Brown, S.R. Driver and C.A. Briggs, *A Hebrew and English Lexicon of the Old Testament* (Oxford: Clarendon Press, 1907; corrected, 1953), pp. 360-61; L. Koehler, W. Baumgartner, J.J. Stamm *et al.*, *The Hebrew and Aramaic Lexicon of the Old Testament*. I. א–ח (trans. M.E.J. Richardson *et al.*; Leiden: E.J. Brill, 3rd edn, 1994), pp. 357-58.

Revised Standard Version, depending on which of several homonymic roots is preferred. While 'secretly' is used in occurrences of this root in later Hebrew, it is not clear that this is the best translation here. There are several reasons for this. First, as noted, other homonymic roots carry different meanings. Some of these include similar vocalizations of a noun form. Could this word refer to the spies as 'skilled' in their task? The context would allow for it. A second reason to question this translation assumes that one does follow Brown, Driver and Briggs and assign the form in Josh. 2.1 to the root meaning 'to be silent, dumb, deaf'. None of the usages of this root require a meaning such as 'secretly'. Why not simply translate the word, 'quietly', a word less charged with underlying motives than 'secretly'? A third reason that this word might allow another translation has to do with the absence of a translation for it in the Septuagint and the Peshitta. This suggests that the original meaning of the occurrence in Josh. 2.1 was unknown in the Hellenistic period.

Why then do all the translations render the word in Josh. 2.1 as 'secretly'? Probably because it is assumed that the spies undertook a secret mission. This may be, but that does not necessarily mean that the word should be translated this way. Bolstering an assumption by an otherwise unjustifiable translation of a *hapax legomenon* is not necessarily the translator's task. It is true that the translator must make a decision. It seems that three possibilities exist: (1) leave the translation as 'secretly' and insert a footnote that admits ignorance or at least allows for other possibilities; (2) choose a translation closer to the root upon which 'secretly' is based, such as 'quietly'; or (3) choose to translate from one of the other homonymic roots that does attest nominal forms, such as 'skilful' or 'trained in their task'. The second or third option seems preferable as they allow for a rendering of the form based on actual attested usages of roots elsewhere. Whatever choice is made, the uncertain nature of the translation should be noted. This becomes important when it is argued that the sending of the spies was contrary to God's will.[13] Therefore, the argument goes, Joshua did it secretly to avoid the objections of pious Israelites or even of God. Whether the sending of the spies was according to God's will, a *hapax legomenon* should not be called into service in order to support it.

13. R. Polzin, *Moses and the Deuteronomist: A Literary Study of the Deuteronomistic History. Part One. Deuteronomy, Joshua, Judges* (New York: Seabury Press, 1980), pp. 86-87.

2. *Syntax.* A distinctive element of syntax that sometimes troubles readers of the text is also found prominently in Joshua 2. This is an aspect of narrative style that repeats many of the salient features of the text. On some occasions, there is no apparent problem. For example, the mission of the spies is described twice, in v. 1 where Joshua charges them and again in v. 2 where the mission is reported to the leader of Jericho. More problematic are the double accounts of the spies' act of lying down in vv. 1 and 8 and Rahab's act of hiding them in vv. 4 and 6. Some commentators regard these as unnecessary repetitions and additions.[14] Others identify here a feature of Hebrew style in which an initial summary statement of the action is followed by a detailed discussion of both the dialogue and the activity that led to that point in the action. Thus the statement that the spies lay down in v. 2 anticipates the whole process of their being hidden and then being led to the roof that is detailed in vv. 3-8. The point that Rahab hid the spies in v. 4 prepares for her discussion with the royal messengers of vv. 4-6, which culminates in a return to the observation that she had hidden the spies.[15]

This stylistic feature of Hebrew is not marked in any observable manner by the morphology of the verb, or by the word order, or by particles.[16] Nevertheless, it functions in these texts and should be reflected in any translation. For example, the New American Bible renders the actions of Rahab in hiding the spies in the form of pluperfects in vv. 4 and 6. Although the morphology of these verbs is that of the standard narrative form of waw consecutive plus prefix conjugation, the rendering of the English pluperfect, that is, 'she had...hidden them', is required by the structure of the Hebrew text at these points. The means of rendering how the men lie down twice in vv. 1 and 8 must be different, however. Since v. 1 anticipates an action that only begins to occur in v. 8, it cannot be rendered by a pluperfect. Indeed, v. 8 suggests that the spies never did 'lie down' because Rahab moved them

14. V. Fritz, *Das Buch Josua* (HAT, 1.7; Tübingen: J.C.B. Mohr, 1994), pp. 33-41.

15. W. Moran, 'The Repose of Rahab's Israelite Guests', in *Studi sull'Oriente e la Bibbia: Offerti al p. Giovanni Rinaldi nel 60j compleanno da allievi, colleghi, amici* (Genova: Studio e vita, 1967), pp. 273-84 (275).

16. B.K. Waltke and M. O'Connor, *An Introduction to Biblical Hebrew Syntax* (Winona Lake, IN: Eisenbrauns, 1990), pp. 552-53 para. 33.2.3, argue that Hebrew narrative can accept the pluperfect tense in the middle of a narrative section as well as at the beginning. The waw + prefix conjugation is the customary verbal form used.

out of her house before they had the opportunity. Therefore, many translations render the same verb, 'to lie down' (root שׁכב), in two different ways in these two verses. In v. 1 it is rendered by the more general, 'they lodged there'. In v. 8 it is usually translated, 'before they lay down' or 'before they went to sleep'. This translation accurately reflects the intent of the narrative even if it does not render literally the same Hebrew word by the same English equivalent.

A similar issue pertains to vv. 15 to 24 of Joshua 2. After Rahab's confession and the spies' promise of her salvation, v. 15 begins a new narrative sequence with the waw consecutive plus prefix conjugation: ותורדם 'she let them down'. This describes how Rahab aids the spies in their escape, by providing a way through her window on the town wall. What follows, however, is puzzling. Verses 16-21 relate a final conversation between Rahab and the spies in which she details the method by which they can escape the notice of Jericho's agents, and the spies set conditions for the rescue of Rahab and her family. Since the speaking is introduced by the normal narrative forms of waw consecutive plus prefix conjugation, the impression the reader has is that this conversation takes place after the spies have passed out of Rahab's window. The spies either dangle on a rope outside the window or shout their secret message to Rahab from the ground beneath her. Is this an instance of ironic humour in which the spies reveal one more example of their incompetence when it comes to their task of spying?[17] Again, it appears best to understand v. 15 as a proleptic summary of the action that is recounted in detail in vv. 16-21.[18] This time, however, there is an additional problem. It is found in v. 18, where the spies relate what Rahab must do to save her family. Using a suffix conjugation form of the same

17. T.C. Butler, *Joshua* (WBC, 7; Waco, TX: Word Books, 1983), p. 31; Y. Zakovitch, 'Humor and Theology or the Successful Failure of Israelite Intelligence: A Literary-Folkloric Approach to Joshua 2', in S. Niditch (ed.), *Text and Tradition: The Hebrew Bible and Folklore* (SBL Semeia Studies; Atlanta: Scholars Press, 1990), pp. 92-93. Zakovitch recounts Josephus and Rabbinic commentators who also observed this difficulty. He notes that Abarbanel used a legal argument to resolve it, that the spies would not have been bound by their oath while they were within Rahab's house since an oath taken under coercion is not valid. Josephus, on the other hand, resolves the issue by placing the events of vv. 16-20 before the spies' departure. Compare the solution proposed here.

18. Moran, 'The Repose of Rahab's Israelite Guests'; W.J. Marti, '"Dischronologized" Narrative in the Old Testament', in *Congress Volume: Rome 1968* (VTSup, 17; Leiden: E.J. Brill, 1969), pp. 179-86.

Hiphil verb as in v. 15 they relate what appears to be an action that has already taken place: הורדתנו '[this cord with which] you have let us down'. If this action has already occurred, then clearly the spies must be outside the window when they are speaking. Although some commentators posit an interpolation from v. 20 and an early scribal error,[19] for translators this option does not commend itself. A sampling of recent translations shows that some choose not to address the issue and render the verb in v. 17 almost as though it has no tense. So the New International Version, the New Jewish Publication Society and the New Revised Standard Version translate, 'through which you let us down'. This allows the reader to understand that the spies had already been let down through the window but it also allows for a translation that it is happening at the time that the spies are speaking. The New American Bible takes a more committed stance and translates the second of these two options, 'through which you are letting us down'. However, if the narrative structure of the text that pertained in the first half of ch. 2 also occurs in vv. 15-21, then one would expect an English future perfect translation of this suffix form, 'through which you will have let us down'. Waltke and O'Connor refer to this as an accidental perfect, related to the better-known prophetic perfect.[20] This is the best translation, fitting both the overall structure of the narrative as already observed and allowing for a logical understanding of the events and dialogue of vv. 15-21.

3. *Style.* Do larger issues of the style of the original text have a place in translation? The answer is yes, although it is often difficult to reflect style in the target language. Thus Nida and Taber comment:

> Though style is secondary to content, it is nevertheless important. One should not translate poetry as though it were prose, nor expository material as though it were straight narrative. For example, the fast-moving

---

19. J.A. Soggin, *Joshua* (OTL; Philadelphia: Westminster Press, 1972), p. 42.

20. Waltke and O'Connor, *An Introduction to Biblical Hebrew Syntax*, p. 490, para. 30.5.1. 'Accidental perfect' is an odd term. It is not clear from their brief description what is 'accidental' about the form. The 'perfect' refers, of course, to the Hebrew suffixed verbal form, not to the English perfect tense. Waltke and O'Connor do not cite Josh. 2.17. For this translation, see D.J. McCarthy, 'The Theology of Leadership in Joshua 1–9', *Bib* 52 (1971), pp. 165-75 (171); N. Winther-Nielsen, *A Functional Discourse Grammar of Joshua: A Computer-Assisted Rhetorical Structure Analysis* (ConBOT, 40; Lund: Almqvist & Wiksell, 1995), pp. 140-41.

brisk style of Mark is quite different from the much more polished and structured style of Luke. Similarly, the First Epistle of Peter has some of the most elaborately organized sentence structure of the New Testament, while the Second Epistle of Peter is almost the exact opposite.

It is usually quite impossible to represent some of the stylistic subtleties of the original, e.g., plays on words (such as the meanings of certain Old Testament names: Isaac, Abraham, Sarah, Cain, and Abel), acrostic poems…, rhythmic units (e.g., phrases and lines of poetry). In many instances, one can indicate something about these stylistic peculiarities of the original by means of marginal notes, which will assist the reader to understand why the text reads as it does. This is particularly essential in the case of plays on words, where the meaning of a passage so often depends upon knowing the double meaning or the allusion.[21]

One of the interesting features of Hebrew narrative style is its use of certain key words that recur in a variety of contexts throughout the narrative. This phenomenon has long been noticed. Martin Buber referred to a *leitwort*, the 'leading word' that was used to unify a narrative and to guide the reader to recognize the major theme of the author.[22] More recently, H.J. Koorevaar has divided the entire book of Joshua into four sections, each of which is dominated by a key word: עבר 'cross' in 1.1–5.12; לקח 'take' in 5.13–12.24; חלק 'divide, apportion' in chs. 13–21; and עבד 'serve' in chs. 22–24.[23] The first of these, עבר 'cross', fits well as an example of a *leitwort*. It occurs some thirty-one times in the first section of Joshua. However, it also appears another forty-nine times in the remaining parts of the book.

עבר 'cross' is a root whose verbal formations can occur in a variety of contexts. In the first five chapters of Joshua, it frequently refers to a physical movement from one place to another. This can include passing through the camp of the Israelites (1.11; 3.2) and across the Jordan River (1.2; 2.23; 3.1, 4, 11, 14, 16, 17; 4.1, 3, 5, 7, 8, 10, 11, 12, 13, 22, 23 twice; 5.1). The verb can be used to describe the passing before

---

21. E.A. Nida and C.R. Taber, *The Theory and Practice of Translation* (Helps for Translators, 8; Leiden: E.J. Brill, 1969), pp. 13-14.

22. Y. Amit, 'The Multi-Purpose "Leading Word" and the Problems of Its Usage', *Prooftexts: A Journal of Jewish History* 9 (1989), pp. 99-114. On Buber's method, see M. Buber, *II. Schriften zur Bibel* (Munich: Kösel; Heidelberg: Lambert Schneider, 1964); *idem, Pointing the Way* (trans. M. Friedman; New York: Harper, 1963).

23. H.J. Koorevaar, *De Opbouw van het Boek Jozua* (Heverlee: Centrum voor Bijbelse Vorming België, 1990), p. 294.

others in a military review (1.14; 4.12) or in bearing the ark before the people (3.6) or in passing before Yahweh (4.13). It can function as a preposition in 'across the Jordan River' (1.14, 15; 2.10). The crossing can be done by Israel (1.2; 3.1, 4, 14, 16, 17; 4.1, 10, 11, 22, 23 twice; 5.1), the officers of Israel (1.11; 3.2), the Transjordanian tribes (1.14, 15), the spies (2.23), priests (3.6; 4.11), the ark (3.11; 4.7, 11), and the twelve representatives who carry the memorial stones (4.3, 5, 8).

Once across the Jordan, the verb describes how Israel passes around Jericho (6.7, 8) and moves from one town to another in the southern campaign (10.29, 31, 34). Thus the same movement that brought Israel across the Jordan continues in the occupation of the Promised Land. In the tribal allotments the root occurs frequently as both a verb (15.3, 4, 6, 7, 10, 11; 16.2, 6; 18.9, 13, 18, 19; 19.13) and a preposition (13.8, 27, 32; 14.3; 17.5; 18.5, 7; 20.8) to indicate boundaries. The preposition 'across' is always used in relation to the Jordan River, as it is in the dispute about the Transjordanian altar in Joshua 22 (vv. 4, 7 and 11). The verb is used theologically in the sense of 'transgress' in 7.11 and 15, where it describes how Achan sinned against the covenant by taking what was devoted to God alone. At the end of the book, it has theological significance in three occurrences. In 22.19 Phinehas and the ten tribal representatives from west of the Jordan River exhort the Israelites who live east of the Jordan to consider leaving their unclean land and to 'cross over' west of the Jordan to the land that Yahweh possesses and where his dwelling stands. In 23.16 Joshua warns the people not to worship other gods and thereby 'transgress' their covenant with Yahweh. In the final chapter Joshua uses עבר in v. 17 to describe Yahweh's preservation of Israel among all the peoples through whom they 'passed'.

What does this have to do with translation? It demonstrates the difficulty with which the translator is faced when attempting to capture this theologically and thematically significant word. There is no English equivalent that would allow the same translation of this root every time it occurs. The translations render the verb alone by a variety of English equivalents: cross, pass, break, transgress. Yet this root is so important because it ties together the book and demonstrates connections essential to understanding the argument and message of the text. If there is no English translational equivalent, perhaps the best alternative would be to insert a brief footnote at 3.1 and 7.11 (and 24.17?) that explains the significance of this *leitwort*.

2. *The New Translation*

a. *The Audience*

If the original text provides the focus for the task of the translator, it must also compete with the translated text. This is a new text, created by the translator. Every translation is an interpretation and there can be no exception with the Bible. This is all the more true when the original text is from a culture that has no living informants and that is removed in time and geography from the translator and the translated text. This latter text will reflect a variety of concerns. Foremost is the community who will read the new text. Translators who translate texts for themselves can translate with much greater freedom and experimentation. This sometimes can be seen in translations that appear in commentaries where the commentator is given freedom to write the translation judged to be the best. These translations are often much more idiosyncratic than those that appear in Bibles. This is not only because the latter tend to be products of committees. Often that fact itself is the result of a concern to reflect the interests of the community for whom the translation is prepared. The goal is to translate in a manner that is acceptable to as wide a group from that community as possible. For Old Testament translations of Joshua, the community is usually one that has a faith commitment, whether Jewish or Christian, whether conservative or liberal, whether reflecting one or another theological concern and priority.

Another important consideration is the use that will be made of the translation by the community. Some translations are intended for liturgical reading in a formal worship setting while others have as their purpose personal or classroom reading and study. Some are intended for beginners, others for those who are doctrinally literate. Some seek to address the needs of a specific age group, while others are directed at those who speak a particular dialect or variant of the target language.

b. *Gender-Inclusive Language*

At present, many English translations are in the process of updating and revising their translations. In part, this is a reflection of the speed with which language has changed in this generation. It is also a reflection of new emphases and concerns in the prevailing values of the society. Most important among these has been the question of gender and the use of masculine pronouns to represent both genders in the translations. Older translations used the same pronouns for both masculine and common genders, and a different set of pronouns for the feminine. It is irrelevant that this corresponds to the use of pronouns in Classical Hebrew. The goal of the translator is to accurately communicate the text in the target language, not to reflect particular forms or idioms of Hebrew in a manner that is not the convention of the culture and time of the readership for whom the translation is created. For this reason many of the present Bible translation projects are concerned with removing perceived examples of sexist language from existing translations. This has already taken place with the appearance of the Revised English Bible (for the New English Bible), the new edition of the New International Version, the New Revised Standard Version, and the planned new edition of the New American Bible.[24]

1. *Pronouns.* The question of gender in the book of Joshua includes several areas. There are examples where שׁ×ישׁ is a pronoun, 'each', instead of 'man'. Thus Josh. 24.28 has been changed from the Revised Standard Version to the New Revised Standard Version:[25]

Revised Standard Version	*New Revised Standard Version*
So Joshua sent the people away, **every man to his** inheritance.	So Joshua sent the people away **to their** inheritances.

The problem occurs in performative language such as may be found in the oath of the spies in Joshua 2 and the exception clause of v. 19:

Revised Standard Version	*New Revised Standard Version*
If any one goes out of the doors of your house into the street, **his blood shall be upon his head,** and we shall be guiltless; but if a hand is laid upon any one who is with you in the house, **his blood shall be on our head**.	If any of you go out of the doors of your house into the street, **they shall be responsible for their own death,** and we shall be innocent; but if a hand is laid upon any who are with you in the house, **we shall bear the responsibility for their death**.

Examples occur in other performative statements such as Joshua's curse about whoever rebuilds Jericho (6.26):

24. See D. Coggan, 'Preface to the Revised English Bible', in *The Revised English Bible* (Oxford: Oxford University Press; Cambridge: Cambridge University Press, 1989), p. ix; B.M. Metzger, 'Preface', in *The Holy Bible: New Revised Standard Version* (Grand Rapids: Zondervan, 1995), pp. viii-ix; and The Committee on Bible Translation, 'Preface', in *The Holy Bible: New International Version. Inclusive Language Edition. The New Testament, Psalms and Proverbs* (London: Hodder & Stoughton, 1995), pp. ix-x. The last one provides the most complete explanation of its translation process.

25. Josh. 22.14 also uses this particle, but the Revised Standard Version uses inclusive gender language.

Revised Standard Version
Joshua laid an oath upon them at that time, saying, 'Cursed before the LORD be **the man that rises up and rebuilds this city, Jericho.** At the cost of his first-born shall he lay its foundation, and at the cost of his youngest son shall he set up its gates'.

New Revised Standard Version
Joshua then pronounced this oath, saying, 'Cursed before the LORD be **anyone who tries to build this city—this Jericho**! At the cost of his first-born shall he lay its foundation, and at the cost of his youngest son shall he set up its gates.'

It is not clear why the translators do not carry through the revision to the second half of the verse.

Formulae in legal texts have also been the subject of gender-free translations. This includes: God's judgment against the one(s) who violated the ban of Jericho (7.15) and the judgment for the unintentional killer who comes to a town of asylum (20.4-6):

Revised Standard Version
Josh. 7.15 And he who is taken with the devoted things shall be burned with fire, **he and all that he has, because he has** transgressed the covenant of the LORD, and **because he has done a shameful** thing in Israel.
Josh. 20.4 **He** shall flee to one of these cities and shall stand at the entrance of the gate of the city, and explain **his** case to the elders of that city; then **they shall take him into the city, and give him** a place, and he shall remain with them.
Josh. 20.5 And if the avenger of blood **pursues him**, they shall not give up the slayer **into his hand; because he killed his neighbor unwittingly, having had no enmity against him in times past.**
Josh. 20.6 **And he** shall remain in that city until **he has stood** before the congregation **for judgment**, until the death of him who is high priest at the time: then the slayer may **go again to his own town and his own** home, to the town **from which he fled.**

New Revised Standard Version
Josh. 7.15 And **the one** who is taken as having the devoted things shall be burned with fire, **together with all that he has, for having** transgressed the covenant of the LORD, and **for having done an outrageous** thing in Israel.
Josh. 20.4 **The slayer** shall flee to one of these cities and shall stand at the entrance of the gate of the city, and explain **the** case to the elders of that city; then **the fugitive shall be taken into the city, and given** a place, and shall remain with them.
Josh. 20.5 And if the avenger of blood **is in pursuit**, they shall not give up the slayer, **because the neighbour was killed by mistake, there having been no enmity between them before.**
Josh. 20.6 **The slayer** shall remain in that city until **there is a trial** before the congregation, until the death of **the one** who is high priest at the time: then the slayer may **return** home, to the town **in which the deed was done.**

Like 6.26, 7.15 is not thoroughly consistent in revising to a common gender translation. On the other hand, 20.4-6 is an example of the way in which the whole text has been rendered throughout in a common gender.

2. *Citizens, Armies and Professions.* A second area for the change to gender-inclusive language is found in the narratives where the army or citizens in general are referred to as 'men', whether from Israel (8.12, 19; 9.6-7; 10.24), Jericho (24.11), Ai (8.16-17, 20-22, 24), Gibeon (10.2, 6) or warriors in general (10.21). There are also representatives who are commissioned to gather stones (3.12; 4.2, 4) or guard them (10.18), or sent as scouts (2.4, 14, 17; 6.22; 7.2) or as mapmakers (18.4) who are referred to as men. The nature of their function suggests an alternative translation.

3. *Allies.* Finally, there is the example, especially in Josh. 22.3-4 and 7-8, of references to 'brothers' or 'kinsmen'. This chapter describes a crisis that could have led to civil war. In the delicate negotiations the close relationship of the two sides required emphasis. This could be translated by using an expression such as 'companions' or 'allies' which captures the point of the relationship. It is not that the two sides were literally brothers. The concern of the text is to emphasize their covenant commitment to one another in fighting together and, at that point in time, living together. The same is true of the usage of this expression in 1.14-15. However, its occurrence in 17.4 is a different matter. There the daughters of Zelophehad are given an inheritance along with their 'kinsmen'. Since the point of this passage is to emphasize the unusual nature of Israelite inheritance arrangements, in which females as well as males can inherit, it is important to see that the daughters inherit along with other 'men' of their clan.

These texts provide examples of an attempt to revise an existing translation in order to update it for the cultural expectations of late twentieth-century English readers.

3. Conclusion

This essay has attempted to present examples of the various aspects of work involved in the translation of Old Testament texts. By focusing on the text of the book of Joshua, it was possible to consider specific examples of choosing a text for translation, of translating on lexical, syntactical and stylistic levels, and of an instance of rendering the biblical text into a translation that reflects contemporary concerns of the readership.

JUDGES 1–5 AND ITS TRANSLATION

Richard S. Hess

The first five chapters of the book of Judges provide the translator with a variety of problems that can be described in terms of the genres of the material found therein. To the reader of Joshua, the first chapter of Judges is a pastiche of notes that repeat or change and summarize items found in the previous book. The second chapter forms a Deuteronomistic introduction with the language customary to that (or those) author(s)/editor(s). The third chapter is a good example of a narrative set within a specific historic context, and challenging the reader to recreate the scene using special vocabulary. The fourth and fifth chapters provide an example of two narratives purporting to describe the same event, the first in terms of prose and the second in terms of poetry. How are the differences and similarities between these two accounts to be dealt with in translation? The Song of Deborah in the fifth chapter is also notorious for containing many rare words and expressions that are not easily translated.

For the purposes of this study the Masoretic Text as preserved in the *Biblia Hebraica Stuttgartensia* will form the primary original text. This is Codex Leningrad, dating from the beginning of the eleventh century and providing one of the best witnesses to the Masoretic tradition. As in *BHS*, the versions may be noted when the Masoretic Text itself is not decipherable and there is need of another source to provide interpretation.

The New International Version is a recent English translation. It claims to be the best-selling of all Bible translations and will be used here as an example of a translation. The NIV version of the verse will be cited and comment will follow. Footnotes to the translation are incorporated into the cited translation. In the discussion, consideration will be made of recent discoveries and analyses that affect the translation of the biblical text.

1. *Translation Problems in Judges 1–5*

a. *Judges 1.1–2.5*

1. *Judges 1.2.* 'The LORD answered, "Judah is to go; I have given the land into their hands".' Judges 1.2 is similar to the second part of 20.18 ('They said, "Who of us shall go first to fight against the Benjamites?" The LORD replied, "Judah shall go first".'). Should the two statements of God be translated in the same way? In fact, the Hebrew of what the Lord says is different. In 20.18, 'Judah' is followed by the adverbial 'first' (בתחלה) while in 1.2 it is followed by the verb, 'will ascend' (יעלה). Therefore, it is best to translate these two phrases differently, though the similar form might prefer the wording 'Judah shall go' in 1.2. Note that the existing translation, 'Judah is to go', does reflect a possible volitional sense to the verb (יעלה). While this is possible, this is not the main emphasis of the two words of the Lord's response. If it were, one might expect the jussive form, יעל. The placement of 'Judah' at the beginning of the Hebrew response suggests that the emphasis in the text is on the choice of Judah, not on a command to ascend and fight. Therefore, I would not worry about a translation like, 'is to go', but allow for a style that is less of a command and more of a declaration. 'Judah shall go up' provides a happy compromise that allows the emphasis to remain on Judah and permits a sufficient agreement with the similar phrase in 20.18.

2. *Judges 1.3.* 'Then the men of Judah said to the Simeonites their brothers, "Come up with us into the territory allotted to us, to fight against the Canaanites. We in turn will go with you into yours." So the Simeonites went with them.'

In light of literary analysis of this first chapter (see Younger 1994, along with other literary studies cited in the article), the actions of 1.3 are not to be understood as an obedient response to God's charge in 1.2 or even as a logical consequence, but as the first example in the book of disobedience. Judah alone was commanded to go up first. Instead of straightforward obedience, Judah seeks additional human assistance from Simeon. Therefore, I would translate the first word, 'Then', as 'But'. This represents an adversative use of the waw consecutive and is reasonable in this context. It stresses the disobedience of Israel from the very beginning of the narrative, a theme that will build throughout the book. At the same time, it eliminates too great an emphasis on the privileged place given to Judah and its presentation as an ideal tribe in this book (contra Brettler 1990). Judah was not without fault.

3. *Judges 1.4.* 'When Judah attacked, the LORD gave the Canaanites and Perizzites into their hands and they struck down ten thousand men at Bezek.'

Has the time come to accept the views of a variety of scholars that Hebrew, like Akkadian, Ugaritic, and Canaanite (Rainey 1996: I, 190), uses 'thousand' to refer to 'clan' in domestic and social contexts and to 'company' in military ones? (See Mendenhall 1958; Wenham 1981: 62-64; Hess 1996: 146.) Boling (1975) translates 'contingents'. Lindars (1995: 17-18) retains the numbers in thousands but argues that they are 'obviously exaggerated'. It is better to understand the specifics of the text as an authentic attempt at the recreation of an incident, historical or otherwise. See also Judg. 3.29; 4.6, 14.

4. *Judges 1.14.* 'One day when she came to Othniel, she urged him[1] to ask her father for a field. When she got off her donkey, Caleb asked her, "What can I do for you?" '

I would retain the Masoretic Text with Achsah requesting Othniel to make the request for the land and then making the request herself for the water supplies. The versions represent secondary attempts to resolve the apparent contradiction of one person being encouraged to ask for something and someone else doing the asking. For recent discussion and literature that defends this 'ambiguity' in the light of Hebrew legal and social practice, see Westbrook 1991: 152-53. Westbrook argues that while the wife retains some control over her dowry it also becomes part of the husband's property. This ambiguity is found in the text. Achsah persuaded her husband, Othniel, to request the dowry from her father. However, she then requested the water rights from her father. Both exercised some authority over this dowry of the land.

5. *Judges 1.19.* 'The LORD was with the men of Judah. They took possession of the hill country, but they were unable to drive the people from the plains, because they had iron chariots.'

Do 'iron chariots' (רכב ברזל; also Judg. 4.3, 13, and Josh. 17.16) describe chariots made of iron? This is most unlikely due to the rarity

---

1. NIV {footnote: Hebrew; Septuagint and Vulgate <Othniel, he urged her>}.

of iron and especially the weight of the resultant vehicle. Horses would not be able to pull them easily. (See Millard 1995: 194-95 with references to earlier literature.) Nor is it necessary to assume a construct chain, *rekeb barzel,* or, even if there is one, to translate it as, 'chariots of iron', 'iron chariots'. It is better to see here 'chariots with iron' or something similar that emphasizes the presence of iron without necessarily insisting that iron was the primary element of manufacture for the chariot itself. In this regard there is an interesting text from fifteenth-century Alalakh which includes among a list of items, 1 *narkabtu* (ᴳᴵˢGIGIR) *iḫ-zu*, which may be translated, 'one chariot with mountings' (AT 177 line 31). These mountings may have been ornamental or they may have served some practical purpose. Whatever the case, they demonstrate the sequence of the word 'chariot' followed by a word describing something attached to the chariot. This is the same sequence in the Masoretic Text: *rekeb barzel* 'chariot(s) with iron'.

6. *Judges 1.21.* 'The Benjamites, however, failed to dislodge the Jebusites, who were living in Jerusalem; to this day the Jebusites live there with the Benjamites.'

The translation, 'failed to dislodge' (הורישו לא), is anomalous, as the same phrase occurs in vv. 19, 27, 29, 30, 31, and 33 where it is consistently translated 'did not drive out'. This is a key phrase in the chapter (Younger 1994: 219) and its repetition should be translated consistently. The same is true for v. 32.

7. *Judges 1.23.* 'When they sent men to spy out Bethel (formerly called Luz) ...'

In the light of the change to inclusive language and the concern for accuracy in translation it is surprising to find the expression, 'they sent men to', in this verse. This expression nowhere appears in the Masoretic Text. Instead, I would translate: 'the House of Joseph spied out' (בית־יוסף ויתירו). Compare the corresponding account of the investigation of Ai in Josh. 1.2: So the men went up and spied out Ai. There a different verb (רגל in piel) is used; however, the parallel is similar: before attack there is reconaissance.

8. *Judges 1.35.* 'And the Amorites were determined also to hold out in Mount Heres, Aijalon and Shaalbim, but when the power of the house of Joseph increased, they too were pressed into forced labor.'

Stylistically, 'to hold on to' may be better than 'to hold out in' for
לשבת.

9. *Judges 2.3*. 'Now therefore I tell you that I will not drive them out
before you; they will be [thorns] in your sides and their gods will be a
snare to you.'

Van der Kooij (1995) translates, 'I also said', rather than 'Now therefore I tell you', for וגם אמרתי. He argues that this is not an announce-
ment of judgment but a reminder of the dangers in covenants with other
nations. However, this is not likely because this proposal would result
in the continuation of a sequence begun with the waw consecutive,
ואמר 'I said', in v. 1. In other words, one expects a waw consecutive for
the proposal. The formation that exists, a particle introducing a perfect
form, suggests a change of aspect, here from what was recounted to
what now will be the situation.

b. *Judges 2.6–3.6*
Judges 2.12 'They forsook the LORD, the God of their fathers, who
had brought them out of Egypt. They followed and worshiped various
gods of the peoples around them. They provoked the LORD to anger.'

Is 'forsook' a good modern translation for the עזב root? Would not
'abandoned' or 'deserted' communicate better?

c. *Judges 3.7-31*
1. *Judges 3.15*. 'Again the Israelites cried out to the LORD, and he
gave them a deliverer—Ehud, a left-handed man, the son of Gera the
Benjamite. The Israelites sent him with tribute to Eglon king of Moab.'

Halpern (1988: 39-75) notes that, as with its use in Ps. 69.15 [16], the
verb in the phrase translated 'left-handed' (אטר יד ימינו) should be rendered as 'close [to his side]' or 'bound' with respect to the right hand.
Koehler and Baumgartner's lexicon translates, 'impeded on the right
side'. Perhaps a rendering such as 'left handed' with a note, 'literally,
"bound or prevented from using his right hand"'. The implication is
that this is not a phenomenon with which Ehud was born but one that
involved training him to use his left hand rather than his right for
fighting.

2. *Judges 3.18*. 'After Ehud had presented the tribute, he sent on their
way the men who had carried it.'

The expression, 'dismissed', might better convey the piel of שׁלח than 'sent on their way'. Again, 'tribute bearers' might more easily be read than 'the men who had carried it'. Both phrases in the NIV are unnecessarily periphrastic and vaguer than need be.

3. *Judges 3.19.* 'At the idols[2] near Gilgal he himself turned back and said, "I have a secret message for you, O king". The king said, "Quiet!" And all his attendants left him.'

The term, הפסילים 'idols', is translated by Koehler and Baumgartner as 'Gottesbild'. The term is always used elsewhere in the Bible for divine images. The suggestion of 'boundary markers', while preserving the essential feature of marking the boundary of Eglon's territory, does not do justice to the general usage of the expresssion. Boundary markers have their own terminology (e.g. Deut. 27.17 גבול). The same is true for quarries (Josh. 9.5 השברים). Perhaps 'stone images' comes closer to the mark as a representation of Eglon's hegemony. Clearly, the word translated as 'quiet' (הס) carries here the sense that the room must be cleared so that a secret message can be conveyed. 'Leave me in peace' might convey this sense, although it is too periphrastic.

4. *Judges 3.20.* 'Ehud then approached him while he was sitting alone in the upper room of his summer palace[3] and said, "I have a message from God for you". As the king rose from his seat …'

For 'the upper room of his summer palace' (עלית המקרה), Halpern (1988) examines a common offical structure of the second and first millennia, the bit hilani. This structure included an outer porch which surrounded and led into a rectangular room to which was joined (at one end) a raised room with a clerestory allowing light into it. This is the 'upper room'. It is the throne room. Halpern compares the second word with Ps. 104.3 where it refers to 'beams' or 'boards' as part of a structure built over waters. Here Halpern believes that they are placed over the private latrine of the king. The phrase can be translated, 'the raised throne room above the latrine area'. The interpretation of the first word is plausible. The second word is possible but the evidence is circumstantial and depends upon other allusions in the story which Halpern develops. The translation, 'the raised throne room over the beams', might be possible.

2. NIV {[19] Or <the stone quarries>; also in verse 26}.
3. NIV {footnote The meaning of the Hebrew for this phrase is uncertain.}

5. *Judges 3.22*. 'Even the handle sank in after the blade, which came
out his back. Ehud did not pull the sword out, and the fat closed in over
it.'

The expression, 'which came out', is not adequate for the last phrase
in the verse (ויצא הפרשדנה). The second word is a *hapax legomenon*,
but that does not exclude a translation that agrees wth the traditional
rendering of this expression as 'the bowels discharged', an expression
for a statement whose 'earthiness' was perhaps intended to shock the
listener. It certainly fits the context.

6. *Judges 3.23*. 'Then Ehud went out to the porch;[4] he shut the doors of
the upper room behind him and locked them.'

For 'the porch' (המסדרונה) I follow Halpern (1988) here and see
Eglon's palace as composed of three parts, the porch, the audience hall,
and the raised throne room. The servants, who were in the audience
hall, waited outside on the porch at Eglon's command. Ehud crossed
from the audience hall to the high throne room, ostensibly to tell Eglon
a secret, when in fact he killed him. He then locked the doors between
the high throne room and the audience hall from inside the throne
room. He escaped from the throne room into the audience hall via a
janitor's door beneath the boards of the throne room, an area that may
have functioned as a royal latrine. This led him to the audience hall and
he departed from there in full view of the guards whom he passed as he
exited through the porch. Translate the verse, 'When Ehud departed
through the cleaner's side door, he closed the doors of the raised throne
room behind him and locked them'.

7. *Judges 3.31*. 'After Ehud came Shamgar son of Anath, who struck
down six hundred Philistines with an oxgoad. He too saved Israel.'

For 'Shamgar son of Anath' (שמגר בן־ענת) it is better to render this
whole sequence in transliteration, Shamgar Ben-Anath, in which Ben-
Anath is another name for Shamgar. This would mean, 'son of Anath',
in the sense of a disciple of the goddess. Although not appropriate for a
Yahwist worshipper, it could have been given to him by heterodox par-
ents and Shamgar then added his own name, preserving Ben-Anath as a
name by which he was already known. More likely, as the name Shamgar itself is not Semitic and may originate to the north of Palestine in

---

4.   NIV {footnote: The meaning of the Hebrew for this word is uncertain.}

Anatolia or elsewhere, Shamgar himself comes from a heterodox background. There are many examples of 'son of X' names throughout the history of ancient Israel, especially attested in inscriptions outside the Bible.

d. *Judges 4*

1. Judges 4.2. 'So the LORD sold them into the hands of Jabin, a king of Canaan, who reigned in Hazor. The commander of his army was Sisera, who lived in Harosheth Haggoyim.'

I would suggest dropping the 'a' here as it is not necessarily correct, that is, Jabin seems to have been king over all of northern Canaan rather than just one among several Canaanite kings in the area. Thus Hazor was the capital of his kingdom and Harosheth Haggoyim was Sisera's military base (cf. Josh. 11.10). So the latter part of this verse should be translated 'Jabin, king of Canaan, who reigned in Hazor. Sisera, the commander of his army, was based in Harosheth Haggoyim'.

2. Judges 4.4. 'Deborah, a prophetess, the wife of Lappidoth, was leading Israel at that time.'

I agree with Stek (1986: 56) that this section begins just like the one at the start of v. 11. Both should be translated, 'Now Deborah' and 'Now Heber'.

3. Judges 4.6-7. 'She sent for Barak son of Abinoam from Kedesh in Naphtali and said to him, "The LORD, the God of Israel, commands you: 'Go, take with you ten thousand men of Naphtali and Zebulun and lead the way to Mount Tabor. I will lure Sisera, the commander of Jabin's army, with his chariots and his troops to the Kishon River and give him into your hands.'"'

I agree with Stek (1986: 63) that the use of מָשַׁךְ in both verses is an intentional wordplay. To make this explicit in the translation, I would change 'lead the way' into 'direct them'. Then 'I will lure Sisera' becomes 'I will direct Sisera'.

4. Judges 4.9. ' "Very well", Deborah said, "I will go with you. But because of the way you are going about this,[5] the honor will not be

---

5. NIV {footnote Or <But on the expedition you are undertaking>}.

yours, for the LORD will hand Sisera over to a woman. So Deborah
went with Barak to Kedesh ...'

With Stek (1986: 65), ימכר ביד 'hand over', should be rendered as
'sell in the hands of' according to the same expression in v. 2.

5. *Judges 4.10.* '...where he summoned Zebulun and Naphtali. Ten
thousand men followed him, and Deborah also went with him.'

With Stek (1986: 56), the last phrase of v. 9 should be distinguished
from v. 10: 'Deborah went with Barak to Qedesh'. Verse 10 should
begin, 'There Barak summoned Zebulun and Naphtali'. Then 'Ten
companies of foot soldiers went up, and Deborah went with them'. It
may seem that the Hebrew, 'to go up' (עלה), does not require only this
one translation. Frequently, this verb occurs in the movement of someone or a group of people from one place to another. It seems that here
the meaning is that Deborah and the army assembled with Barak at the
same place. However, this must be balanced by the repeated use of
'descend' (ירד) that occurs throughout this chapter. The 'going up'
describes the preparations for war[6] while the 'descending' describes the
engagement in battle and the aftermath. Therefore, it is important to
include this in the translation. See also v. 12.

6. *Judges 4.13.* 'Sisera gathered together his nine hundred iron chariots
and all the men with him, from Harosheth Haggoyim to the Kishon
River.'

Translate 'summoned' in place of 'gathered' in agreement with the
same verb in v. 10, which compares and contrasts the two armies and
their commanders.

7. *Judges 4.15.* 'At Barak's advance, the LORD routed Sisera and all
his chariots and army by the sword, and Sisera abandoned his chariot
and fled on foot.'

The word play of 'descend' (וירד) in vv. 14 and 15 is not significant
enough to warrant the same translation in both cases. The NIV's translation is good as it stands since the descent from Tabor had a different
purpose (attack) than the descent from the chariot (flight). The parallel
use of this verb in vv. 15 and 16 is much more important.

---

6.   Parallel forms occur in the Amarna texts, e.g., forms of *elû* 'to go up', with
the meaning 'to attack' when used with certain prepositions. See Rainey 1996: III,
60.

8. *Judges 4.16.* 'But Barak pursued the chariots and army as far as Harosheth Haggoyim. All the troops of Sisera fell by the sword; not a man was left.'

With Stek (1986) the adversative 'But' at the beginning of v. 16 is not the best choice. It seems to want to contrast Sisera's flight of v. 15 with Barak's success. However, this may not be the main focus of the waw + noun that begins v. 16. Rather, I would suggest 'Meanwhile', which provides both a hint of contrast and also affirms that vv. 15 and 16 were simultaneous.

9. *Judges 4.17.* 'Sisera, however, fled on foot to the tent of Jael, the wife of Heber the Kenite, because there were friendly relations between Jabin king of Hazor and the clan of Heber the Kenite.'

With Lindars (1995: 197) something stronger than 'friendly relations' between Jabin and Heber is required for שלום בין...ובין. Either 'there was an alliance between' or perhaps smoother in style 'X and Y were allies'. Here בית חבר is an extended family over which Heber exercises control (on this social structure see Stager 1985: 17-22) so John's Stek's 'Heber the Kenite's household' is to be preferred.

10. *Judges 4.18-19.* 'Jael went out to meet Sisera and said to him, "Come, my lord, come right in. Don't be afraid." So he entered her tent, and she put a covering over him. "I'm thirsty", he said. "Please give me some water." She opened a skin of milk, gave him a drink, and covered him up.'

There is an emphasis on the covering of Sisera which is repeated using the same verb. Thus, I would translate the end of v. 18, 'she covered him with a blanket' (ותכסהו בשמיכה), and the end of v. 19, 'and covered him' (ותכסהו).

e. *Judges 5*

1. *Judges 5.2.* ' "When the princes in Israel take the lead, when the people willingly offer themselves—praise the LORD!" '

Surely ברכו יהוה is 'Bless the LORD' not 'Praise the LORD'? The two concepts may be related but they should be distinguished for accuracy of translation. See also v. 9.

2. *Judges 5.3.* ' "Hear this, you kings! Listen, you rulers! I will sing to[7] the LORD I will sing; I will make music to[8] the Lord, the God of Israel." '

The middle phrase, אנכי ליהוה אנכי אשירה, is not 'I will sing to the LORD, I will sing' (much less is there evidence for 'of'). It could be translated, 'As for me, to the LORD I will sing'. The option 'with song I will praise' is not in the Hebrew or the versions.

3. *Judges 5.4.* ' "O LORD, when you went out from Seir, when you marched from the land of Edom, the earth shook, the heavens poured, the clouds poured down water." '

נטפו with the subject of the heavens and the clouds may mean to 'quake, shake'. Coogan (1978: 146) refers to Albright (1936) and to Boling (1975) as incorporating this meaning. Thus 'the heavens shook, and the clouds shook water'. Although the root נטף can mean 'drip', I am unaware of the usage, 'pour'.

4. *Judges 5.6-7.* ' "In the days of Shamgar son of Anath, in the days of Jael, the roads were abandoned; travelers took to winding paths. Village life[9] in Israel ceased, ceased until I[10] Deborah, arose, arose a mother in Israel." '

Schloen (1993) rejects Chaney's (1976) *ḥdl* II 'to grow plump' in v. 7 in favour of T.J. Lewis's (1985) *ḥdl* I 'to cease' here 'to restrain' (also Craigie). There is no need to posit a second homonymous root with the meaning, 'to grow plump'. The first root is sufficient. It carries the idea, 'to cease', more specifically, 'to restrain'. So vv. 6-7:

> Caravans and travelers held back,
> They went on winding tracks,
> Villagers in Israel held back,
> They held back,
> until I arose, Deborah,
> until I arose, a mother in Israel.

Note that פְּרָזוֹן 'villagers' seems increasingly to be the agreed upon translation of this word. (See Stager 1988: 224-25; 1989: 54.) Although 'Perizzite' originally referred to a group of Hurrian-related people from

---

7.   NIV {footnote: Or <of>}.
8.   NIV {footnote: Or <with song I will praise>}.
9.   NIV {footnote: Or <Warriors>}.
10. NIV {footnote: Or <you>}.

the north (Hess 1996: 27), its common noun (used here) is best understood as people living in unwalled villages around the countryside, that
is, exactly the archaeological picture of the first settlement areas of the
Israelites. See also v. 11.

5. *Judges 5.8.* ' "When they chose new gods, war came to the city gates,
and not a shield or spear was seen among forty thousand in Israel." '

I would follow P.C. Craigie, who has done many studies on this text
(Craigie 1968; 1969; 1972a; 1972b; 1977a; 1977b; 1978)[11] and
translate the first part of this verse, 'God chose new ones'. The first half
of the line follows the Masoretic Text with the understanding that, as
elsewhere in this ancient poem, the initial Hebrew 'imperfect' (יבחר) is
actually a preterite form not unlike the yiqtal preterite of the sort found
in the Canaanite Amarna texts of the fourteenth century BCE (see
Rainey 1996: II, for a complete discusssion). Lindars (1995: 240-41)
agrees with the first phrase, noting that it follows logically from the
preceding verse by describing the preparations for war once Deborah
arose. This is more likely than the introduction of a description of
apostasy (they chose new gods) in a victory poem that nowhere else
mentions it. The second half of the phrase, 'then there were five cities'
(אז לחם שערים), preserves the consonants and their sequence in the
Masoretic Text but divides them differently and revocalizes the middle
word (לחמש). The present NIV 'war came to the city gates' reads a word
for 'war' (לחם) that is a *hapax legomenon*. Nevertheless, it is better
than the introduction of a new concept, 'five cities', that occurs
nowhere else in the poem. The words, 'then' and 'gates', appear
together again three verses later. Therefore, the NIV here is a preferable,
if not certain, proposal and I would translate the whole verse:

> God chose new ones,
> then war came to the city gates,
> but not a shield or spear was seen
> among forty companies in Israel.

6. *Judges 5.10.* ' "You who ride on white donkeys, sitting on your
saddle blankets, and you who walk along the road, consider" '

---

11. The whole question of the place of Anat in Judges and comparisons with
Jael, Shamgar ben-Anath, and the battle of chs. 4–5 must be re-evaluated in the
light of the discovery that the name of the goddess does not exist in one of the
crucial texts used to establish her character as warlike. See Lewis 1996.

צחרות is 'tawny, red-gray' not 'white'. See Koehler and Baumgartner's lexicon and the bibliographical discussion there.

'You who sit enthroned over Midian' instead of 'sitting on your saddle blankets' has been proposed for יֹשְׁבֵי עַל־מִדִּין. This is because it allows יֹשְׁבֵי to carry the nuance of rulership for the local kings of Canaan and surrounding regions (see Gottwald 1979; Boling 1975: 110; and Coogan 1978: 148). Nevertheless, it remains best to translate this in line with the preceding and following phrases as one of several references to modes of transport. In conjunction with vv. 6-7 it describes the trade economy that was so important to the Jezreel Valley and concerning which the battle may have been fought (see Stager 1988).

7. *Judges 5.11.* ' "The voice of the singers[12] at the watering places. They recite the righteous acts of the LORD, the righteous acts of his warriors[13] in Israel.

' "Then the people of the LORD went down to the city gates." '

The translation is 'At the watering places' but בֵּין is 'between the watering places'. As in vv. 6-7, I would translate 'villagers', not 'warriors'.

8. *Judges 5.13.* 'Then the men who were left came down to the nobles; the people of the LORD came to me with the mighty.'

The alternative possibility of reading the two occurrences of יֵרַד in this verse according to the Masoretic Text's pointing should be noted, that is, from רדה 'to rule'. So: 'Then survivors ruled the nobles; the people of the LORD ruled the warriors for me'. This makes good sense within the context as it describes Israel's victory over the enemy.

9. *Judges 5.14.* ' "Some came from Ephraim, whose roots were in Amalek; Benjamin was with the people who followed you. From Makir captains came down, from Zebulun those who bear a commander's staff." '

The last word, סֹפֵר, is difficult in this context. It normally means scribe. *BHS* suggests repointing as סֵפֶר, 'book' or the Akkadian word for 'bronze', *siparru.* Albright (1936) is followed by Coogan (1978) in

12. NIV {footnote: Or <archers>; the meaning of the Hebrew for this word is uncertain.}

13. NIV {footnote: Or <villagers>}.

rendering it as 'marshal' which is probably the basis for the NIV's 'commander'. This agrees with Tsevat's (1952–53) proposal to read here 'ruler' following the Akkadian *šapāru*. In this military context the reference to a 'marshal' or 'commander' would be best. Lindars (1995: 255) follows Gray (1986) in arguing that this is the officer in charge of enlistment, the ספר as in 2 Kgs 25.19. However, there the ספר is one of a group of officers whereas in Judges 5 the figure emerges prominently. This is better understood as a leader, a position which Lindars never actually refutes.

10. *Judges 5.15.* ' "The princes of Issachar were with Deborah; yes, Issachar was with Barak, rushing after him into the valley. In the districts of Reuben there was much searching of heart." '

The phrase that describes Issachar as 'rushing after him into the valley' in the NIV significantly alters the Masoretic Text (בעמק שלח ברגליו). First, the verb is a pual and therefore passive, that is, 'sent forth', here 'spread out'. Secondly, the Hebrew expression, ברגליו, literally, 'at his feet', never carries the meaning, 'after him'. Other suggestions include 'instantly' (Gerleman) or 'with his footsoldiers' (Ehrlich and Weiser). Issachar was a client of Naphtali (Lindars 1995: 257-58) or, more likely in view of biblical (Judg. 10.1; 1 Chron. 7.1-2) and settlement survey evidence, in the central hill country of Manasseh (Stager 1988; 1989: 63; Gal 1992: 91). Not able to obtain its own allotment in the Jezreel Valley, this tribal group was sent out first under the command of Barak. Thus the translation:

> The princes of Issachar were with Deborah,
> so Issachar was with Barak,
> sent out under his command into the valley.

11. *Judges 5.16.* ' "Why did you stay among the campfires[14] to hear the whistling for the flocks? In the districts of Reuben there was much searching of heart." '

The NIV renders המשפתים as 'campfires' with a note, 'Or saddlebags'. The one other occurrence of this word, applied to Issachar in Gen. 49.14, translates 'saddlebags' with a note, 'Or campfires'. As Lindars (1995: 260-61) reviews the evidence he notes that a similar noun, השפתים, occurs in Ps. 68.14 and Ezek. 40.43. In all cases, except

---

14. NIV {footnote: Or <saddlebags>}.

the Ezekiel passage which seems to describe an object fastened to a table, the two options could be used as could a third, 'folds, sheepfolds'. The dual ending implies that 'campfires' is least likely while either two saddle bags on either side of a donkey or two walls erected to create a pen or fold seem preferable. The second half of the phrase, which describes flocks (עדרים), weights the argument here in favour of 'folds'. Although Gen. 49.14 uses the word in the context of a donkey, there the five Hebrew words, including 'donkey' (חמר) and משפתים, are a small context to establish the meaning of this word. Indeed, in Gen. 49.14 the meaning of the word describing the donkey (גרם) is uncertain. The remaining three words in the Genesis text, רבץ בין המשפתים, can be translated 'crouching between/within the folds'.

12. *Judges 5.18*. ' "The people of Zebulun risked their very lives; so did Naphtali on the heights of the field." '

Concerning 'the heights of the field', מרומי שדה, it is better here (and in 2 Sam. 1.21) to follow Stager (1985: 6; 1989: 55) and to translate as 'the terraces' (or 'the terraces of the field'). The region, including Mt Tabor, has many terraces dating before Israel's settlement. It would describe likely battlegrounds on the sides of the mountains and hills.

13. *Judges 5.19*. ' "Kings came, they fought; the kings of Canaan fought at Taanach by the waters of Megiddo, but they carried off no silver, no plunder." '

This suggests that the battleground was at Taanach whereas ch. 4 implies a place near Mt Tabor. In fact, this verse is two separate sections: the first describes the battle, while the second part describes the period after the battle. Taanach was a place where the victorious Egyptian army would hold its prize giving and booty division. That practice is reflected here. Taanach was not the site of the battle but of the booty distribution after the battle; a distribution that did not take place because of the Canaanite defeat. See Rainey (1981), and Younger (1991: 133-34). I would translate something like Rainey:

> Kings came, they fought,
> > then the kings of Canaan fought.
> At Taanach, by the waters of Megiddo,
> > they took no plunder of silver.

14. *Judges 5.22*. ' "Then thundered the horses' hoofs—galloping, galloping go his mighty steeds." '

NIV's 'galloping, galloping go his mighty steeds' omits both the min-preposition and the construct relationship of אביריו דהרות מדהרות. Better is 'from the galloping, galloping of his mighty steeds'. (See Coogan 1978; Lindars 1995 *et al.*).

15. *Judges 5.27.* ' "At her feet he sank, he fell; there he lay. At her feet he sank, he fell; where he sank, there he fell—dead." '

For כרע, 'he sank', surely the dramatic effect would be heightened and there would be no violation of the verb if it were translated (with commentators) as 'he collapsed'. Also I would translate 'between her feet' in accordance with the preposition, בין.

2. *Summary*

This survey of translation problems in the first five chapters of Judges has demonstrated the variety of problems that can be encountered in texts that possess a great variety of difficulties in translation. Reviewing the issues encountered, the following results may be noted:

1. The smallest number of problems was found in the text most identified as a composition of the Deuteronomist, Judg. 2.6–3.6. This text yielded only one problem. The largest number of problems was found in the one poetic text, Judges 5. Not only is poetry difficult to translate but this is a notoriously difficult text with many features of archaic forms that are not familiar to the reader of Classical Hebrew. Judges 5 contained fifteen problems. The narrative stories of the Judges in the prose of chs. 1, 3 and 4 yielded nine, seven and ten problems respectively.

2. If it is possible to divide the problems into issues of vocabulary, syntax, and style, vocabulary had seventeen problems, larger than syntax (nine) or style (fourteen). The largest groups of vocabulary issues were found in chs. 3 and 5. The latter is no surprise with nine problems. The five in ch. 3 certainly reflect the essay of Halpern and the incorporation of its insights into this survey. Stylistically, the largest group of problems, six of them, was found in ch. 4. This may reflect the study of Stek which was largely concerned with literary structure and problems of translation reflecting that structure.

3. The nine most significant exegetical issues that were addressed by the discussion above were found in Judg. 1.3, 14; 3.20, 23; 4.17; 5.6-7, 8, 15, and 19. The last one, in 5.19, is the only one to deal with an apparent contradiction in the text (here between the narratives of chs. 4

and 5). The remainder were mostly concerned with vocabulary and how recent insights and discoveries have changed the translation of texts in the NIV.

In conclusion, it seems reasonable to say that the NIV provides a good translation for Judges 1–5, but it is one that could be improved upon in many ways. Particular attention to recent studies relating to some of the obscure vocabulary items would yield a more reliable rendering of some of the more difficult passages. Examples of this include Halpern's analysis of the bit hilani ('throne room') and its application to the Ehud narrative of ch. 3, and Judg. 1.19 where the suggestion of a new interpretation of 'iron chariots' may move the reader away from untenable assumptions about mobile warfare and provide a reading within the contemporary context of the biblical world.[15]

BIBLIOGRAPHY

Albright, W.F.
1936   'The Song of Deborah in the Light of Archaeology', *BASOR* 62: 26-31.
Boling, R.G.
1975   *Judges* (AB, 6A; Garden City, NY: Doubleday).
Brettler, M.
1990   'The Book of Judges', *JBL* 108: 395-418.
1991   'Never the Twain Shall Meet? The Ehud Story as History and Literature',
            HUCA 62: 285-304.
Chaney, M.L.
1976   'ḤDL-II and the "Song of Deborah": Textual, Philological, and Sociolog-
            ical Studies in Judges 5, with Special Reference to the Verbal Occur-
            rences of ḤDL in Biblical Hebrew' (PhD dissertation, Harvard
            University).
Coogan, M.D.
1978   'A Structural and Literary Analysis of the Song of Deborah', *CBQ* 40:
            143-66.
Craigie, P.C.
1968   'A Note on Judges V 2', *VT* 18: 397-99.
1969   'The Song of Deborah and the Epic of Tukulti-Ninurti', *JBL* 88: 253-65.
1972a   'A Reconsideration of Shamgar Ben Anath (Judg 3.31 and 5.6)', *JBL* 91:
            239-40.
1972b   'Some Further Notes on the Song of Deborah', *VT* 22: 349-53.
1977a   'Parallel Word Pairs in the Song of Deborah', *JETS* 20: 15-22.

15. Thanks to the Biblical Studies Research Cluster of Roehampton Institute London's Theology and Religious Studies Department for reading and making helpful comments on this essay; especially S.E. Porter and J. Jarick.

| 1977b | 'Three Ugaritic Notes on the Song of Deborah', *JSOT* 2: 33-49. |

1978   'Deborah and Anat: A Study of Poetic Imagery (Judges 5)', *ZAW* 90: 374-81.

Gal, Z.

1992   *Lower Galilee during the Iron Age* (American Schools of Oriental Research Dissertation Series, 8; Winona Lake, IN: Eisenbrauns).

Gottwald, N.K.

1979   *The Tribes of Yahweh: A Sociology of the Religion of Liberated Israel 1250–1050 BCE* (Mary Knoll, NY: Orbis Books).

Gray, J.

1986   *Joshua, Judges and Ruth* (NCB; London: Routledge, 2nd edn).

Halpern, B.

1988   *The First Historians: The Hebrew Bible and History* (San Francisco: Harper & Row).

Hess, R.S.

1996   *Joshua* (TOTC; Leicester: IVP).

Koehler, L., and W. Baumgartner

1967–90   *Hebräisches und Aramäisches Lexikon zum Alten Testament* (4 vols.; Leiden: E.J. Brill; English translation of volume one, by M.E.J. Richardson, Leiden: E.J. Brill, 1994).

Kooj, A. van der

1995   ' "And I also said": A New Interpretation of Judges ii 3', *VT* 45: 294-306.

Lewis, T.J.

1985   'The Songs of Hannah and Deborah: *ḥdl*-II ("growing plump")', *JBL* 104: 107.

1996   'The Disappearance of the Goddess Anat: The 1995 West Semitic Research Project on Ugaritic Epigraphy', *BA* 59.2: 115-21.

Lindars, B.

1995   *Judges 1–5: A New Translation and Commentary* (ed. A.D.H. Mayes; Edinburgh: T. & T. Clark).

Mendenhall, G.

1958   'The Census of Numbers 1 and 26', *JBL* 77: 52-66.

Millard, A.R.

1995   'Back to the Iron Bed: Og's or Procrustes' ', in J.A. Emerton (ed.), *Congress Volume Paris 1992* (VTSup, 61; Leiden: E.J. Brill, 1995): 193-201.

Rainey, A.F.

1981   'The Military Campground at Taanach by the Waters of Megiddo', *Eretz-Israel* 15: 61-66.

1996   *Canaanite in the Amarna Tablets: A Linguistic Analysis of the Mixed Dialect Used by the Scribes from Canaan* (4 vols.; Handbuch der Orientalistik, 1.25; Leiden: E.J. Brill).

Schloen, D.

1993   'Caravans, Kenites, and *Casus Belli:* Enmity and Alliance in the Song of Deborah', *CBQ* 55: 18-38.

Stager, L.E.

1985   'The Archaeology of the Family in Ancient Israel', *BASOR* 260: 1-35.

| 1988 | 'Archaeology, Ecology and Social History: Background Themes to the Song of Deborah', in J.A. Emerton (ed.), *Congress Volume Jerusalem 1986* (VTSup, 40; Leiden: E.J. Brill): 221-34. |

1989   'The Song of Deborah: Why Some Tribes Answered the Call and Others Did Not', *BARev* 15.1: 50-64.

Stek, J.
1986   'The Bee and the Mountain Goat: A Literary Reading of Judges 4', in W.C. Kaiser, Jr and R. Youngblood (eds.), *A Tribute to Gleason Archer* (Chicago: Moody): 53-86.

Tsevat, M.
1952-53   'Some Biblical Notes', *HUCA* 24: 107-14.

Wenham, G.
1981   *Numbers* (TOTC; Leicester: IVP).

Westbrook, R.
1991   *Property and the Family in Biblical Law* (JSOTSup, 113; Sheffield: Sheffield Academic Press).

Younger, K.L., Jr
1991   'Heads! Tails! Or the Whole Coin?! Contextual Method & Intertextual Analysis: Judges 4 and 5', in K.L. Younger, Jr, W.W. Hallo and B.F. Batto (eds.), *The Biblical Canon in Comparative Perspective: Scripture in Context IV* (Ancient Near Eastern Texts and Studies, 11; Lewiston, NY: Edwin Mellen Press): 109-46.

1994   'Judges 1 in Its Near Eastern Literary Context', in A.R. Millard, J.K. Hoffmeier and D.W. Baker (eds.), *Faith, Tradition, and History: Old Testament Historiography in Its Near Eastern Context* (Winona Lake, IN: Eisenbrauns): 207-27.

Part III

NEW TESTAMENT

TRANSLATION AND THE EXEGETICAL PROCESS, USING MARK 5.1-10, 'THE BINDING OF THE STRONGMAN', AS A TEST CASE

Matthew Brook O'Donnell

1. *Introduction*

A provisional translation of the Greek text often serves as one of the first stages in the exegetical process, as suggested by a number of the standard New Testament exegetical manuals.[1] By working through the text and providing a translation, the interpreter is confronted with the text-critical, grammatical, contextual, historical and other interpretative issues raised by the text under consideration. Through the process of translation, the exegete begins to understand the text, with understanding the text being one of the goals of exegesis. Yet, at the beginning of the exegetical process, the interpreter is unable to answer many of the questions raised by this initial translation. Lührmann suggests that, 'translation comes at the beginning of understanding the text, and at the same time reflects newly-gained understanding'.[2] There is a cyclic process at work: translation raises exegetical questions, and answering

---

1. In outlining an exegetical method for interpreting the New Testament, Conzelmann and Lindemann suggest that, 'It is best to begin with a provisional translation'. See H. Conzelmann and A. Lindemann, *Interpreting the New Testament: An Introduction to the Principles and Methods of N.T. Exegesis* (trans. S.S. Schatzmann; Peabody, MA: Hendrickson, 1988), p. 36. Kaiser lists translation as one of the preparatory tasks to carrying out exegesis; see W.C. Kaiser, *Toward an Exegetical Theology: Biblical Exegesis for Preaching and Teaching* (Grand Rapids: Baker Book House, 1981), p. 51. See also B. Chilton, *Beginning New Testament Study* (Grand Rapids: Eerdmans, 1987), pp. 95-119; G.D. Fee, *New Testament Exegesis: A Handbook for Students and Pastors* (Louisville, KY: Westminster/John Knox, rev. edn, 1993), pp. 36-37.

2. D. Lührmann, *An Itinerary for New Testament Study* (trans. J. Bowden; London: SCM Press, 1989), p. 17.

those questions informs translation. However, an interpretative translation is rarely presented as the *result* of the exegetical process.[3] A number of commentary series have elected to include a new translation of each pericope as part of their format; examples of such series are the Anchor Bible commentaries and the Word Biblical Commentary series. These translations often reflect interpretative decisions made in the verse by verse comments, though they are placed *before* the comments section.

The purpose of this study is to explore the role of the translation as the final or result stage in the exegetical process. A passage from Mark 5 has been selected as a test case. The article begins with an initial translation of the passage that represents a relatively literal rendering of the text. Brief comments are made at this point concerning the problems encountered and exegetical issues raised during this initial translation process. The next sections present a detailed exegesis of the passage, paying particular attention to its literary context, that is, its role within the Gospel author's theological narrative. It is argued that Mark[4] wishes to portray the ministry of Jesus as a battle between the kingdom of Satan and the kingdom of God, and this understanding shapes the interpretation and final translation of 5.1-10. Specific attention is also given to the tense-forms utilized by the author in the light of recent work on verbal aspect in the New Testament.[5] A combination of these two elements provides a different understanding of Mk 5.8 than argued for by the majority of commentators. The final section of the paper presents an interpretative translation of Mk 5.1-10 that aims to reflect the points brought out in the preceding exegesis.

2. Initial Translation of Mark 5.1-10

1 And they came to the other side of the sea to the region of the Gerasenes. **2** And after he had come out of the boat, immediately met

---

3.   Note that Fee does suggest the preparation of a 'finished translation' at the end of the exegetical process (Fee, *New Testament Exegesis*, p. 58). However, he labels this stage as 'optional'.

4.   For the purpose of this paper, the author of Mark shall be referred to as 'Mark' and 'he'; however, this is merely for convenience. A discussion of the authorship of the second Gospel is beyond the scope of this study.

5.   Here I adopt the systemic understanding of the Greek tense-forms developed in S.E. Porter, *Verbal Aspect in the Greek of the New Testament, with Reference to Tense and Mood* (New York: Peter Lang, 1989).

him out of the tombs a man with an unclean spirit, **3** who was having his home in the tombs, and no longer was anyone able to bind him with a chain. **4** Because often he had been bound with shackles and chains and the handcuffs had been broken and feet chains had been shattered, and no one was strong enough to bind him. **5** And constantly night and day in the tombs and in the graves he was crying out and cutting himself with stones. **6** And after seeing Jesus from far away he ran and worshipped him. **7** And crying out in a loud voice he says, 'What to you and to me, Jesus Son of the Most High God? I beg you, do not torment me!' **8** Because he was saying to him, 'Unclean spirit come out of the man'. **9** And he was asking him, 'What is your name?' And he says to him, 'Legion is my name, because we are many'. **10** And he was begging him many times that he might not send them out the area.

a. *Notes on the Initial Translation*

I have used the standard English renderings for translating Greek verb forms, that is, simple-past for the aorist indicative (e.g. ἦλθον in v. 1, rendered 'they came') and the progressive past for the imperfect indicative (e.g. ἐπηρώτα in v. 9, 'he was asking'). The perfect passive infinitives in v. 4 have been rendered with the past perfect (e.g. αὐτὸν...δεδέσθαι 'he had been bound'). Already it is clear that translation cannot take place without adopting a particular view of the Greek tense-forms, whether that be a traditional time-based, *Aktionsart* or aspect-oriented understanding. The genitive absolute (ἐξελθόντος αὐτοῦ ἐκ τοῦ πλοίου) in v. 2 has been rendered with a past perfect plus a temporal adverb, 'after he had come out of the boat'. Traditional elementary grammars suggest that, when translating a participle, the student should add '-ing' to the lexical stem and then use 'while' for a present participle and 'after' for an aorist. In the case of a genitive absolute construction, such as we find in Mk 5.2, the participle is rendered with a finite English clause, following a time-based understanding.

The Greek word order has been retained for the second half of v. 2, 'met him out of the tombs a man with an unclean spirit'. Though this appears awkward, it allows the following three verses (vv. 3-5), which add to the description of the man, to continue directly on from his introduction into the narrative. There are also a number of textual variants that are significant for the exegesis of this passage, particularly the number of the verb ἔρχομαι in v. 1, ἦλθον 'they came' or ἦλθεν 'he came'. Another significant variant is the person and number of αὐτός in v. 10, 'that he might not send them (αὐτά) / him (αὐτόν) out the area'.

For the initial translation I have followed the main text in the Nestle–Aland[27]. However, it may be necessary to adjust the translation on the basis of text-critical decisions made during the exegetical process.

b. *Some Problems of Translating Hellenistic Greek*

In making the translation above, I have attempted to provide a relatively literal rendering of the Greek. However, the concept of a *literal* translation is not without problems. Every translation is an interpretation, and, therefore, even when making a quick, initial translation the exegete is forced to make interpretative decisions. One of the main difficulties facing the exegete wishing to produce a translation at the beginning of their work is the linguistic and temporal gap between Hellenistic Greek and the receptor language, which for the purposes of this paper is English. There are, unfortunately, no living speakers of Hellenistic Greek, so it is not possible to find bilingual individuals and ask them to translate, as it would be in the case of translating from, say, French to English. Our knowledge of Hellenistic Greek is restricted to the corpora of texts transmitted from the ancient world. Considering the linguistic system of each language, one notices many differences. Greek is a highly inflected language, while English forms do not exhibit regular or consistent inflection patterns. This has implications for word order in each language. It is a common misconception that word order in Greek is almost completely free, while word order in English is almost completely fixed. However, it is better to view word order variation among languages on a continuum, one end of the scale representing languages with relatively fixed ordering and the other representing those with free, or grammatically unrestricted, ordering.[6] Even in English, the position of a word can indicate more than simply its grammatical category.[7] Equally, there are certain restrictions and patterns of word order in Greek, which render overly simplistic the common assertion that elements occurring at the start of a clause are being emphasized by the author.[8]

---

6. See J. Lyons, *Language and Linguistics: An Introduction* (Cambridge: Cambridge University Press, 1981), pp. 104-109.

7. See M.A.K. Halliday, *Functional Grammar* (London: Edward Arnold, 2nd edn, 1994). Halliday discusses thematization at the clause level, and asserts that the first element of a clause makes up the Theme and the remainder the Rheme.

8. See S.E. Porter, 'Word Order and Clause Structure in New Testament Greek: An Unexplored Area of Greek Linguistics Using Philippians as a Test

Particular problems are caused for translators by the Greek verbal system. Greek verbs carry considerable semantic information just within the individual verb form. Aspect, voice, mood, person and number are all communicated by a single form. That is, these semantic categories are form-based or synthetic.[9] When using a verb, the user of the language must select values for each of these five categories.[10] In contrast, many of these categories in English are not form based, that is, they are analytic semantic categories. For example, it is necessary to add an explicit subject to the verb form in order to indicate person and number. Much recent study of the Greek of the New Testament has focused on the semantic category of verbal aspect.[11] Porter asserts that the tense-forms in Hellenistic Greek do not grammaticalize temporality but aspect, that is, the 'author's reasoned subjective choice of conception of a process'.[12] This provides a significant challenge in the translation of Greek tense-forms. A Greek verb form cannot be directly mapped onto an English equivalent. λαλεῖ cannot automatically be rendered 's/he says' and ἐλάλησεν 's/he said'. There is not a one-to-one relationship between a Greek verb form and an English verb group. Neither is there a clear one-to-many relationship as has been assumed by many Greek grammars. That is, an aorist can be either inceptive, gnomic, or temporal and so on, whereas a present can be durative, iterative, historic, or narrative and so on. Porter draws a helpful distinction between the semantics of the tense-forms, operating at the level of code, and the virtually unlimited pragmatic uses of the tense-forms at the level of text.[13] Traditionally, when faced with a verb form,

---

Case', *FN* 6 (1993), pp. 177-206; also *idem, Idioms of the Greek New Testament* (BLG, 2; Sheffield: Sheffield Academic Press, 2nd edn, 1994), pp. 286-97.

9.   See Porter, *Verbal Aspect*, p. 88; *idem, Idioms of the Greek New Testament*, pp. 21, 52, 62.

10.   See Porter, *Verbal Aspect*, p. 86.

11.   See, particularly, Porter, *Verbal Aspect*; B.M. Fanning, *Verbal Aspect in New Testament Greek* (Oxford: Clarendon Press, 1990). For a summary of Porter and Fanning's views, and a response from a number of scholars, see S.E. Porter and D.A. Carson (eds.), *Biblical Greek Language and Linguistics: Open Questions in Current Research* (JSNTSup, 80; Sheffield: JSOT Press, 1993), pp. 7-81. For an attempt to apply aspectual theory to an intermediate level grammar, see K.L. McKay, *A New Syntax of the Verb in New Testament Greek: An Aspectual Approach* (SBG, 5; New York: Peter Lang, 1994).

12.   Porter, *Verbal Aspect*, p. 88.

13.   Porter, *Verbal Aspect*, p. 82.

for example ἔλεγεν in Mk 5.8, the exegete might turn to one of the grammars and ask the question, 'What kind of imperfect is this?' The options might include: Progressive Imperfect, Customary Imperfect, Iterative Imperfect, Tendential Imperfect, Voluntative Imperfect or Inceptive Imperfect.[14] These possibilities provide limits to how the verb could be operating in the passage under consideration. Having discovered their options, the interpreter is then free to select the one that best fits their understanding of the passage.

There are a number of problems with this traditional approach to translating and interpreting the tense-forms. One problem is that it tends to view the verb form in a clause, and specifically the tense-form in which it occurs, as communicating all the temporal and procedural (*Aktionsart*) information for the clause. So we find categories like the Historic Present, because it is assumed that, although the present tense-form usually communicates present time and continuing action, its presence in a narrative section requires special explanation. Or in a situation where the context indicates that the process described by the verb is beginning, and the verb is in the aorist tense-form, it must be explained as an Inceptive Aorist, because the verb is responsible for all procedural information of this nature. This overloading of the tense-forms should fall under the same criticisms given to the word-concept or word-theology understanding of lexical semantics by Barr, among others.[15]

Another problem with the traditional understanding of the tense-forms is that the semantics of each tense-form are not described in relationship to the other tense-forms. The strength of Porter's treatment is that he analyses the Greek tense-forms as a system, utilizing systemic linguistics.[16] From this perspective it is not possible to talk about the semantics of the aorist tense-form without discussing its semantic relationship to the present and perfect tense-forms as well. For example, when translating ἔλεγεν in Mk 5.8 it is important to study the pattern

14. These are taken from H.E. Dana and J.R. Mantey, *A Manual Grammar of the Greek of the New Testament* (New York: Macmillan, 1927), pp. 186-91. Similar categories are found in most of the standard grammars of the Greek of the New Testament.

15. See J. Barr, *The Semantics of Biblical Language* (Oxford: Oxford University Press, 1961); cf. A. Gibson, *Biblical Semantic Logic: A Preliminary Analysis* (Oxford: Basil Blackwell, 1981).

16. See Porter, *Verbal Aspect*, pp. 7-16.

of tense-forms in the preceding and proceeding context. Does it come after a string of aorist verbs? If so, it may be functioning to bring the process of speaking into the foreground of the discourse.[17] Unfortunately, the majority of commentaries adopt a verse by verse methodology, which makes decisions on the way in which a tense-form is being used simply on the basis of the verse in which it occurs. Thus, discourse considerations are rarely brought out in either the comments or the translations they present.

Similarly the voice system of Hellenistic Greek provides significant challenges for the translator. The English language has active and passive voices, but not a middle voice. It is not possible to see the English active and passive as direct or literal renderings of a Greek active or passive form. In the same way as with the tense-forms, it is necessary to view the voices in Greek in a systemic manner, and to define them in relationship to each other.[18] There are particular problems in translating the middle and passive voice forms. For example, the verb ἐγείρω ('rise up') is translated inconsistently by many standard English Bible translations. For example, in Matthew's account of the raising of the synagogue leader's daughter, it states, 'Going in he took hold of her hand, καὶ ἠγέρθη τὸ κοράσιον' (Mt. 9.25). The NRSV has 'and the girl got up' for καὶ ἠγέρθη τὸ κοράσιον. The passive form is translated with an active sense. Likewise, throughout the Gospel the adverbial aorist participle ἐγερθείς is translated with an active sense, 'after getting up' (Mt. 1.24; 9.7-8). However, in the three passion predictions (Mt. 16.21; 17.22-23; 20.17-19) passive forms of ἐγείρω are rendered with passive constructions. For example, Mt. 20.19 has καὶ τῇ τρίτῃ ἡμέρᾳ ἐγερθήσεται, which is translated by the NRSV as, 'and on the third he will be raised'. The same verb in the same voice form within the same New Testament book is translated in two different ways. There may well be sound contextual reasons for sometimes rendering a passive verb with an active sense, but one suspects that it is more likely that theological concerns are at work here in the case of ἐγείρω.[19]

17. For a discussion of foregrounding and its realization in the New Testament through the verb tense-forms, see Porter, *Verbal Aspect*, pp. 89-93; cf. also his discussion of planes of discourse in *Idioms of the Greek New Testament*, pp. 23-25.

18. See Porter, *Idioms of the Greek New Testament*, pp. 64-73.

19. For a more detailed discussion of the New Testament occurrences of ἐγείρω and some suggestions for the reassessment of the Greek voice system, see M.B. O'Donnell, 'Some New Testament Words for Resurrection and the Company They

The previous discussion illustrates the need for at least two considerations in carrying out a translation of a New Testament text: (1) a systemic approach to the language, and particularly the verbal system, and (2) a discourse approach that takes into consideration the surrounding textual context (that is, the co-text). These two considerations will help to prevent an atomistic, word-by-word treatment and translation of the passage. In the following section, I present an exegesis of Mk 5.1-10 that attempts to apply these principles, paying particular attention to the way in which the exegetical decisions made can be brought out in the final translation.

3. *Exegesis of Mark 5.1-10*

a. *Introduction*

In his Gospel, Mark is not unconcerned with the teachings of Jesus, but there is a definite focus upon his actions. Jesus begins his ministry by claiming 'the kingdom of God has come' (1.15). On what basis can this claim be sustained? From Mark's perspective it is the actions of Jesus. Particularly prominent in Mark are the exorcisms that Jesus performs. Mark portrays the ministry of Jesus as a battle between two kingdoms: the reign of evil and the reign of God. The Pharisees fail to understand this when they accuse Jesus of using the power of Satan to drive out demons (3.22). Jesus answers the accusation with a parable (3.27): Satan is the Strong Man; his house is this world which he rules in this age; the coming of the kingdom of God involves Jesus binding Satan and plundering his belongings (sinful humanity). Luke includes some additional words of Jesus: 'If by the finger of God I am driving out demons then the kingdom of God has come upon you' (Lk. 11.20).

The story of the Gerasene demoniac recorded in Mk 5.1-20 is the longest exorcism account in the Synoptic Gospels and, given the central place of the spiritual battle between Jesus and Satan in Mark, it is key to understanding the ministry of Jesus. Graham Twelfree summarizes it well:

> For Jesus his ministry of exorcism was not preparatory to the kingdom, nor a sign of the kingdom nor an indication that the kingdom had arrived, nor even an illustration of the kingdom, but actually the kingdom of God itself in operation.[20]

Keep', in S.E. Porter, M. Hayes and D. Tombs (eds.), *Resurrection* (RILP; JSNTSup; Sheffield: Sheffield Academic Press, forthcoming).

20. G.H. Twelftree, 'Demon, Devil, Satan', in J.B. Green, S. McKnight and

In the exegesis of this passage, I attempt to demonstrate that Mark's record of the Gerasene exorcism communicates his theological understanding of the ministry of Jesus as a confrontation between Jesus and Satan. The story, while recording a particular event, is symbolic of this broader reality. The focus of this study is upon vv. 1-10, which records the 'battle' between Jesus and the demoniac. The remainder of the passage (vv. 11-20), which will not be treated here, describes the punishment of the demons (vv. 11-13) and the response of the local people to the exorcism (vv. 14-20). Jesus allowed the demons to enter the pigs and continue their destructive existence because it was not yet time for their final judgment and destruction. The exorcism caused the people to fear Jesus and they urged him to leave (vv. 14-17). This ended his direct ministry in that area; yet through the ministry of the healed demoniac the word of God spread throughout the region (vv. 18-20).

b. *The Scene Set (vv. 1-2)*

Mark 5 begins with the fulfilment of Jesus' request 'Let us go to the other side' (4.35). Between 4.35 and 5.1 is a story that demonstrates Jesus' sovereignty over nature, particularly the sea, which is often associated with the activity of Satan.[21] This event left the disciples confused and fearful. Their question regarding the identity of Jesus is left unanswered (4.41). The exact location where the following story takes place is uncertain, except to say that it is on the coast of the east side of the sea of Galilee.[22] Mark sets the scene for the battle about to take place. As soon as the boat reaches the other side and Jesus sets foot on

I.H. Marshall (eds.), *Dictionary of Jesus and the Gospels* (Downers Grove, IL: InterVarsity Press, 1992), p. 168.

21. See Pss. 74.13-15; 89.8-10; Isa. 27.1; 51.9 (God delivered the Israelites from the power of Egypt by dividing the sea). The beasts in Daniel (Dan. 7.1-8, esp. vv. 2-3) and in Revelation 13 come up out of the sea. See also W. Lane, *The Gospel of Mark* (Grand Rapids: Eerdmans, 1974), pp. 173-76. He says 'The sea is understood as a manifestation of the realm of death, with overtones of the demonic in its behavior' (p. 173). Kee, discussing Mk 4.35-41, says 'The central core of the pericope presents Jesus as speaking the word of command by which the evil πνεῦμα is overcome', in H.C. Kee, 'The Terminology of Mark's Exorcism Stories', *NTS* 14 (1968), p. 244.

22. Mark says 'In the region of the Gerasenes'. The parallel passage in Matthew has 'Gaderenes' linking it to Gadera, a city of the Decapolis 5 miles SE of the sea of Galilee. Whatever the exact location, the story is set among the predominantly Gentile Decapolis.

dry land, he is confronted by a demon-possessed man.[23] 'Immediately (εὐθύς) a man with an unclean spirit came to oppose him (ὑπαντάω)' (5.2). The word ὑπαντάω does not always refer to meeting someone with hostile intent;[24] however, it can be used in the context of a battle, where two sides meet each other on the battle field.[25] Considering both the content of this story and Mark's broader concern to communicate the coming of the kingdom as a battle between the powers of Satan and the power of God, a translation something like 'he came out to confront him' communicates this sense. The man has 'an unclean spirit' (πνεύματι ἀκαθάρτῳ),[26] and he comes out from the tombs (ἐκ τῶν μνημείων). In the mountains which surround the sea of Galilee are numerous caves which served as tombs and often provided homes for the poor and other social outcasts. The mention of the tombs also strengthens the notion of ceremonial uncleanness suggested by ἀκάθαρτος. In the first two verses, Mark has set the scene for the

23. The genitive absolute ἐξελθόντος αὐτοῦ though aorist need not signify antecedent action. The verb only occurs five times in the New Testament as a present participle (52 aorist). Mt. 9.32 is the only genitive absolute in the present (NRSV 'After they went out...'). See Porter, *Verbal Aspect*, p. 370, for the view that tense-forms in genitive absolutes communicate verbal aspect and not time relative to the main verb of a clause. The point here is the immediacy of the action of the demoniac, which is communicated better by a translation, 'While Jesus was coming out of the boat'.

24. For example, Jesus' meeting of the disciples after the resurrection (Mt. 28.9). John uses the word with this non-threatening sense (Jn 4.51; 11.20; 11.30; 12.18). However, the emphasis always seems to be on the initiative of the subject going out to meet someone.

25. In Lk. 14.31, for example, where a king going out (ὑπαντάω) to meet another king should consider the size of his army in comparison to his opponent's. BAGD cites Josephus, *War* 1.177; *Ant.* 7.128, as examples of this use. Louw and Nida include the secondary use of the word in domain 55 Military Activities; see J.P. Louw and E.A. Nida, *Greek–English Lexicon of the New Testament Based on Semantic Domains* (2 vols.; New York: United Bible Societies, 1988), I, p. 549. See also Acts 16.16-17, where the slave girl with a spirit of divination (πνεῦμα πύθωνα) meets Paul as he is going to pray and then follows him and cries out revealing his identity.

26. Mk 1.23; 1.26; 1.27; 3.11; 3.30; 5.2; 5.8; 5.13; 6.7; 7.25; 9.25; It is used only once by Matthew, and not in two of the parallels, Mt. 8.28 (δύο δαιμονιζόμενοι) and Lk. 8.27 (ἀνήρ τις ἔχων δαιμόνια). Matthew's mention of two demoniacs is striking but will not be discussed here. The phrase 'unclean spirit' is Mark's main description of 'demons' (9.17, 25—he uses 'deaf and dumb spirit' to describe physical symptoms).

conflict which will follow: Jesus is confronted by the powers of Satan (and death), represented by the tomb-dwelling demoniac.[27]

c. *The Enemy Described (vv. 3-5)*

In the next three verses, Mark leaves the primary story line to provide further information about the demoniac. He carefully constructs a vivid description of the grip of the demon(s), and thus for Mark, Satan, upon the man.[28] Setting the scene in vv. 1-2, Mark has used three aorist tense-forms (the perfective aspect is suited to setting the background).[29] Now he switches to the imperfective aspect (εἶχεν) and repeats the reference to the tombs. Not only did the man come out of the tombs, 'he lives among them'. The vividness and emphatic nature of these verses has led many to suggest that Mark's source was an eye-witness account, perhaps from inhabitants of the town from which the demoniac came.[30]

The first part of Mark's description describes the past attempts (presumably by the local people) to restrain the demoniac (vv. 3-4). The series of three negatives brought to the front of the clause emphasizes the history of failure in dealing with the demoniac.[31] The words, 'No-one was able to bind (δέω) him', are clearly linked with Jesus' parable

27. Gundry comments on v. 2, 'According to word order, some emphasis falls on the demoniac's dwelling in the tombs and thus makes the ensuing contest one of Jesus versus the power of death', in R. Gundry, *Mark: A Commentary on His Apology for the Cross* (Grand Rapids: Eerdmans, 1993), p. 248.

28. Mark devotes far more space to this description than either Matthew or Luke. Mt. 8.28 describes the demoniacs as 'exceedingly violent', so much so that 'no one was able to pass through that way'. Assuming Markan priority, Luke has condensed Mk 5.3-5 into one verse and placed it after Jesus' command 'to come out' (Lk. 8.29).

29. See Porter, *Idioms of the Greek New Testament*, p. 23, for a discussion of planes of discourse: 'The aorist is the background tense, which forms the basis for the discourse; the present is the foreground tense, which introduces significant characters or makes appropriate climactic references to concrete situations; and the perfect is the frontground tense, which introduces elements in an even more discrete, defined, contoured and complex way.'

30. See, for example, Lane, *Gospel of Mark*, p. 180.

31. Porter offers a literal rendering: 'no, no one no longer was able to bind him with a chain'. See his section on multiple negatives in *Idioms of the Greek New Testament*, pp. 283-84. Gundry (*Mark*, p. 249) suggests 'not even with a chain' for οὐδὲ ἁλύσει (cf. KJV, NASB, NRSV). In my translation I have tried to bring out the emphatic nature without adding the further phrase 'not even'.

of the plundering of the 'strong man' (3.27). There 'no-one is able' (οὐ δύναται οὐδείς) to enter into the strong man's house unless they bind him (δέω). Here, Mark states that 'no-one is able' to bind the man (5.3) and 'no-one is strong enough to tame him' (5.4). Verse 3b could be rendered something like: 'there was no one any longer who was at all able to bind him with a chain'. The adverb οὐκέτι may imply that at one time people had been able to bind him, or that they had just given up trying; whatever the case, it is clear that they no longer made these attempts.[32]

Mark continues his vivid description. He provides more historical information to explain why the man could not be restrained. He moves from the imperfective to the stative aspect, utilizing three perfect infinitives[33] in a row governed by διὰ τό ('because').[34] The traditional understanding of the perfect tense ('past action with continuing effects') does not adequately explain the use of these three verb-forms.[35] The view that the perfect grammaticalizes the stative aspect is more satisfactory.[36] The adverb πολλάκις ('many times') explains the

---

32. Gundry thinks that the adverb signifies the demon(s) exercising increasing power over the man: 'The second of the negatives implies increasing strength on the part of the demoniac: not even the short-lived successes of past efforts to chain him are possible any more' (*Mark*, p. 249).

33. The perfect infinitive is rare in the New Testament (49x, approximately 2% of the infinitives). It occurs only here in Mark, not at all in Matthew. Luke (in the Gospel and Acts) uses it 16x, John 3x, Paul 19x, and Hebrews 6x.

34. Burton suggests that though the usual use of διὰ τό + infinitive is to show cause, in Mk 5.4 it 'expresses the evidence rather than the cause strictly so called'; E.D.W. Burton, *Syntax of the Moods and Tenses in New Testament Greek* (Chicago: University of Chicago Press, 1900), p. 161. Robertson questions why it cannot signify both 'cause' and 'evidence' here; see A.T. Robertson, *A Grammar of the Greek New Testament in the Light of Historical Research* (Nashville: Broadman, 1934), p. 966; though he agrees with Burton later in his discussion, p. 1069.

35. Even if they are translated by English pluperfects, 'Many times he had been bound but the chains had been torn apart...', it seems forced.

36. See Porter, *Verbal Aspect*, chap. 5 for discussion of the perfect tense. Also pp. 392-94 for his discussion of the perfect infinitive. He cites Mk 5.4 as an example of a verse which cannot be explained by 'a traditional time-based understanding of the Greek Perfect' and suggests that verbal aspect (specifically the stative aspect) provides a more satisfactory explanation. Commenting on the verse, he writes, 'The author stresses the state of violence in which the demoniac lived, using the Perfect as the narrative label as well as the supporting description'.

presence of οὐκέτι in the previous verse.[37] Satan's power over the man
was so extreme that they had to bind both hands and feet. ἅλυσις can
simply refer to 'chains' (as in v. 3) or, when paired with πέδη ('foot
shackles'), it can be rendered 'handcuffs'.[38] However, he could not be
kept in this state.[39] Just as Samson, bound (δέω Judg. 15.7, 11 LXX)
with cords and bowstrings, was able to break (διασπάω) his bonds
without effort, the demoniac was able to leave the 'cuffs torn apart'
(διεσπάσθαι) and the 'shackles smashed apart' (συντετρῖφθαι). The
use of the perfect infinitives draws a contrast between the attempt to
place the demoniac in a state of boundness and the state in which he
leaves his bonds. In the light of Mark's broader portrayal of the conflict
between two kingdoms, the stative aspect signifies that, despite
attempts to 'bind the strong man', Satan's kingdom prevails; the strong
man has remained in a state of unboundness. Mark concludes the history of failure with a similar construction to that in v. 3b.[40]

The second part of Mark's historical description focuses on the
'unbound' existence of the demoniac before his encounter with Jesus.
Emphatically, he places adverbs and locatives in a series at the beginning of the sentence. He mentions the tombs for a third time and introduces the fact that the demoniac spent time roaming through the
mountains, which were considered dangerous places (cf. the Good
Samaritan in Luke 10), and often associated with demonic activity.
Mark uses the imperfective aspect to bring the reader inside the action:
'Constantly[41] he was crying out and cutting himself with stones'. The

---

37. There does not seem to be a link between the use of the adverb πολλάκις
and the tense of the verb(s) it modifies. This is the only time it is found with a perfect verb. See Mk 9.22 with an aorist but the parallel with present (Mt. 17.15). The
'repeated-action' sense communicated by the adverb should not be imposed onto
the tense form as has often been done; e.g. by calling the aorist in 9.22 a constative
aorist.

38. See Acts 12.7, καὶ ἐξέπεσαν αὐτοῦ αἱ ἁλύσεις ἐκ τῶν χειρῶν ('The cuffs
fell off his wrists').

39. Luke says that he was 'bound in handcuffs and shackles while being
guarded (φυλασσόμενος)' (8.29), suggesting that he was placed under guard in his
state of boundness.

40. Negative + Imperfect Indicative + Aorist Complementary Infinitive - καὶ
οὐδεὶς ἴσχυεν αὐτὸν δαμάσαι. The two constructions form a sort of inclusio.
' "No one was strong enough to tame him" wraps up the emphasis on failure'
(Gundry, *Mark*, p. 249).

41. διὰ παντός ('always') is made more explicit with the phrase 'night and

periphrastic construction is most likely more emphatic than the simple imperfect indicative forms would be.[42] Porter offers the gloss 'He was in progress crying and cutting himself with stones'.[43] The reference to self-mutilation may strengthen the description of demonic activity; demon worshippers often cut themselves in their frenzied rituals (cf. Baal worshippers in 1 Kgs 18.28). According to Jewish tradition, the behaviour of this man matched that of a mad person.[44]

Within the larger theological context, Mark uses this detailed and vivid description of the power of the demon over the man as an illustration of the power of Satan (the 'Strong Man') over 'this age'. Jesus' confrontation with the demoniac represents the broader conflict between Jesus and Satan, signifying that 'the kingdom has come near' (1.15).

d. *The Demon's Attack (vv. 6-7)*
Mark returns to the narrative, which he left in v. 2, having provided a vivid description of the enemy.[45] This return is indicated by a switch back to verb forms in the perfective aspect, as in vv. 1-2.[46] The power

day', similar to the repetition of negatives in v. 3, perhaps indicating the eyewitness nature of Mark's sources.

42. κράζω is used by Mark 3 times (3.11; 10.48; 11.9) and it is interesting that direct speech follows each one. Perhaps the periphrastic construction in 5.5 focuses more on the process of 'crying out' than on the context (a more detailed study would need to be carried out to confirm this). For a discussion of periphrastic constructions and their possible emphatic nature, see Porter, *Idioms of the Greek New Testament*, p. 46; also *idem*, *Verbal Aspect*, pp. 452-78.

43. Porter, *Verbal Aspect*, p. 480. He states that, 'Though preceded by a series of temporal and locative phrases, this combination of the narrative auxiliary and Present Participle emphasizes the histrionics in which the demoniac was involved'. He argues that εἰμί is 'aspectually vague' and, in these constructions, aspect is communicated by the participle. There is a functional difference between a present and imperfect auxiliary in that the imperfect is more suited to narrative contexts.

44. 'Our Rabbis taught: "Who is considered to be an imbecile? He who goes out alone at night, and he who spends the night on a cemetery, and he that tears his garments".' See *t. Ter.* 1.3; *y. Ter.* 1.1. (40b) and *Giṭ* 7.1 (48c). Note, also, Luke's mention that, 'He was not clothed in a garment' (Lk. 8.27).

45. Hooker describes vv. 3-5 as 'somewhat intrusive' and suggests that the passage as a whole has 'an embarrassing amount of detail'. See M.D. Hooker, *The Gospel According to Saint Mark* (Peabody: Hendrickson, 1991), p. 141.

46. In vv. 3-5, he has used only two aorists, both complementary infinitives with imperfect auxiliaries.

of the demon is demonstrated by its instant recognition of the presence of Jesus 'from afar'. At first glance, it seems that in the presence of Jesus demons can do nothing but run towards him and submit to him. However, neither Mark's narrative construction, nor his language, portrays the demon as surrendering automatically. As noted in v. 2, ὑπαντάω is used in military contexts and this gives the neutral 'run' (τρέχω) of v. 6 a more confrontational sense.[47] Upon reaching Jesus, the demoniac knelt before him. The word προσκυνέω is often translated as 'worship' but in this context the focus of the word is simply on the physical action of bending or kneeling down.[48] Mark only uses προσκυνέω twice: here in 5.6 and in 15.19, where the soldiers mocking Jesus 'knelt down in homage to him' (NRSV). Everything up until this point has depicted the demoniac mounting an attack upon Jesus, so it is unlikely that he is either submitting to Jesus or begging for mercy at this point.[49]

The next verse confirms this suggestion. The attack posed by the demoniac consists of three elements. First, he addresses Jesus with a phrase commonly used in battle situations: literally 'What to me and to you?' (τί ἐμοὶ καὶ σοί;). From a study of the biblical use of this phrase,[50] I suggest that the demoniac interprets Jesus' arrival in the area

47. Gundry suggests that the demon is running towards Jesus, 'to get rid of him' (*Mark*, p. 249).

48. There are other words which are more suited to communicating reverent or devotional worship than προσκυνέω, for example σέβομαι or λατρεύω. For a helpful consideration of the different words used for worship in the New Testament, see the article by K.H. Jobes in M. Silva, *Biblical Words and Their Meaning* (Grand Rapids: Zondervan, 2nd edn, 1994), pp. 201-11. She identifies three senses in the New Testament: (1) Worship of deity, (2) Paying political homage, and (3) Entreaty, often accompanied by kneeling or prostration. She adds 'For this reason, προσκυνέω should not be translated "worship" in every instance' (p. 205). However, she does not address the use of the word in Mk 5.6. I suspect she would place it in the third category. It is interesting that in the parallel passage Luke uses the word προπίπτω ('fall before' Lk. 8.28). Perhaps Luke wanted to avoid the impression that the demon was fully submissive to Jesus at this point.

49. Contra Gundry who suggests that 'The doing of obeisance shows recognition of Jesus' divine majesty' (*Mark*, p. 250). He points to Jas 2.19 where the demons are said to shudder in recognition of the existence of God.

50. Examples of extra-biblical use of the phrase are Josephus, *Ant.* 7.625 and Epictetus, *Discourses* 2.19.1. In the LXX see particularly Judg. 11.12 and 2 Chron. 35.20; also 2 Sam. 16.5-15; 19.18-23; 1 Kgs 17.18; 2 Kgs 3.13; 1 Esd. 1.24. In the New Testament the phrase occurs in: Mt. 8.29; Mk 1.24; 5.7; Lk. 4.34; 8.28; Jn 2.4.

as an act of war. By using this phrase, he is inquiring why Jesus has come and makes it clear that he is ready for battle.

Secondly, the demon invokes the name of Jesus: 'What to me and to *you Jesus Son of the God Most High*'. There was a common belief, especially associated with magic, that knowledge of a person's name gave power over that person.[51] By revealing the true identity of Jesus, the demon is trying to gain the upper hand over him. From a literary standpoint, Mark uses this declaration in two ways: (1) in the immediate context it answers the question of the disciples in 4.41 and (2) it serves as a reminder of who Jesus really is.[52] The phrase 'Most High God' (τοῦ θεοῦ τοῦ ὑψίστου) is found in the Old Testament (cf. Dan. 4.34) and is usually used by non-Israelites in reference to Yahweh.

Finally, the demon attempts to cast a spell upon Jesus. The word ὁρκίζω occurs only twice in the New Testament (Mk 5.7 and Acts 19.13). In the LXX it (and its compound forms) is used to translate שבע ('to swear an oath'),[53] which does not seem to be the way Mark uses it

A close examination of these passages reveals the following points: (1) The person who uses the phrase does so in response to some action or suggestion on the part of another which affects them. (2) There is often a sense that the person who uses the phrase is in a more powerful position than the person to whom it is addressed. (3) There is a definite hostile flavour to the phrase in almost all the occurrences. (4) In the LXX the phrase is a direct translation from the Hebrew, though this does not explain its use by Epictetus.

51. See entry on 'Demons' by P.L. Hammer in G.A. Buttrick (ed.), *The Interpreter's Dictionary of the Bible* (Nashville: Abingdon Press, 1962), p. 824. See also Hooker, *Gospel According to Saint Mark*, p. 143; Lane says 'The full address is not a confession of Jesus' dignity but a desperate attempt to gain control over him or to render him harmless' (*Gospel of Mark*, p. 183).

52. 'Through the cries of the demons, Mark is able to remind his readers who Jesus is' (Twelftree, 'Demon, Devil, Satan', p. 169). See Mk 1.24-25, 34; 3.11-12; 5.7. Unlike the other Gospel authors, Mark does not provide any editorial clues as to who Jesus is. He introduces Jesus by simply saying, 'Jesus came from Nazareth' (1.9). Throughout the first half of the Gospel, people are constantly asking, 'Who is this person?', climaxing with Jesus' question in 8.27 ('Who do you say that I am?') and Peter's confession.

53. It occurs 31 times: 24 aorist, 4 present and 3 future. ὁρκίζω occurs in the active voice 30 times and often translates a Hiphil form, which has a causative sense: 'to cause someone to take an oath'. Particularly interesting are the occurrences in the present tense in 1 Kgs 22.16 = 2 Chron. 18.15. The king of Israel hates Micaiah, the prophet of the Lord (2 Chron. 18.7); but Jehosephat urges him to inquire from Micaiah about success in battle. When Micaiah at first gives the same answer as the false prophets, the king says 'How many times must I adjure you

here. The other New Testament reference is instructive because it records that 'certain Jewish exorcists (ἐξορκιστῶν)' were travelling around attempting to use the name of Jesus over those who were possessed (Acts 19.13). They were using the following formula: ὀρκίζω ὑμᾶς τὸν Ἰησοῦν ὃν Παῦλος κηρύσσει 'I adjure you by Jesus whom Paul is preaching'. They assumed that they could insert the name of Jesus into a standard exorcism spell. The common use of ὀρκίζω in such spells is demonstrated by its frequent occurrence in the Greek Magical Papyri. Of most interest for the present study is the 'Charm of Pibechis for those possessed by daimons (πρὸς δαιμονιαζομένους)' (*PGM* 4.3007-86).[54] The text contains repeated occurrences of ὀρκίζω σε (3019, 3029, 3037, 3045) followed by a description of God. The demoniac's use of this spell formula represents the demon's attempt to, as Gundry says, 'exorcise Jesus out of exorcising [it]'.[55] The content of the spell is the desperate attempt by the demon(s) to avoid, at least for Mark and perhaps his readers, the inevitable: 'You will not torment me!'[56]

e. *Jesus' Response (vv. 8-9)*

Mark has structured the narrative up to this point to demonstrate the vicious battle taking place between Jesus and the demons (representative of the larger battle between Satan and Jesus). Far from falling before Jesus whimpering, the powerful demoniac (vv. 3-5) has mounted a formidable, though futile, attack.

(ὀρκίζω σε) to speak to me nothing but the truth in the name of the LORD?' (35.15). The king's dislike for Micaiah and his frustration with him seem to bring a sense of 'curse' to or 'cast a spell' on the word. It is as if he is saying, 'How many times must I cast a spell on you to get you to tell the truth?'

54. See H.D. Betz (ed.), *The Magical Papyri in Translation: Including the Demotic Spells* (vol. 1; Chicago: University of Chicago Press, 1986), pp. 96-97 for translation. The spell to exorcise a demon begins: ὀρκίζω σε κατὰ τοῦ θεοῦ τῶν ἑβραίων Ἰησοῦ 'I adjure you by the God of the Hebrews, Jesus' and continues with the description of the demon's expulsion. The use of the substantival participle of δαιμονιάζω here matches that of Mk 5.15-16.

55. Gundry, *Mark*, p. 250.

56. Matthew's record of the incident has the demons saying 'Have you come here before the allotted time (πρὸ καιροῦ) to torment us?' (Mt. 8.29). The demons understand that Jesus will bring final judgment upon them yet they are surprised by his coming now. Note use of βασανίζω in Rev. 20.10, 'The devil and the one leading them astray...will be tormented (βασανισθήσονται) day and night for ever and ever'.

I depart from the majority of commentators in my understanding of the chronology of v. 8. Many interpret ἔλεγεν γὰρ αὐτῷ as indicating a previous action of Jesus before the demon spoke (v. 7). They suggest an English pluperfect sense for the ἔλεγεν: 'Because he had been saying...'[57] There are three implications of understanding v. 8 in this manner:

(1) Mark's presentation of the event is out of chronological order and he has inserted v. 8 as an explanation for v. 7.
(2) The action of the demoniac in v. 7 is not one of attack as I have argued above, but it is in fact a self-defensive manoeuvre in response to the command of Jesus in v. 8.
(3) Jesus' first attempt to perform an exorcism was a failure because the demon resists in v. 7.

There is no reason why Mark should not break the chronology in his presentation. Perhaps he was carried along with the eye-witness account he used as his source and suddenly realized that v. 7 required some explanation. He recognized that those reading the account may not understand what was happening and decided to insert an explanatory note (as in 6.52).[58] However, it has been argued that vv. 6-7 record

---

57. Gundry, for example, says, 'γάρ "for", implies that Jesus' command to come out preceded the demoniac's self-defensive question and adjuration (contrast 1.23-25) and therefore that ἔλεγεν means "he had been saying" ' (Gundry, *Mark*, p. 251). See also V. Taylor, *The Gospel According to St Mark* (London: Macmillan, 2nd edn, 1966), p. 281; C.E.B. Cranfield, *The Gospel According to Saint Mark* (Cambridge: Cambridge University Press, 1963), pp. 177-78; H.B. Swete, *The Gospel According to St Mark* (London: Macmillan, 1909), p. 95. While a minority view the imperfect as communicating repeated action, warranting a translation: 'Because he was repeatedly/continually saying...', for example, C.S. Mann, *Mark* (AB, 27; New York: Doubleday, 1986). He suggests Jesus is repeating the injunction: 'a simple command was insufficient, given the gravity of the case' (p. 279). Gundry also mentions J.A. Klesit 'who translates ἔλεγεν "he was about to say" ', indicating an inceptive nuance.

58. See Lane, *Gospel of Mark*, pp. 183-84 and n. 16; also Cranfield, *The Gospel According to Saint Mark*, p. 178. Schweizer suggests that 'Vs. 8...is a clumsy insertion, in the course of transmission, by some narrator who did not understand that demons experience agony by merely being in the presence of Jesus (as in 1:24) and not only at the command to come out', in E. Schweizer, *The Good News According to Mark* (Richmond: John Knox Press, 1970), p. 112. Gundry comments, 'that Mark advances the demoniac's question and adjuration out of chronological order (if we take ἔλεγεν in v. 8 as having the force of a pluperfect) puts great weight on the strength of the demonical self-defense' (*Mark*, p. 251).

the 'first-strike' attack of the demoniac against Jesus, and I think this is supported by the language of both v. 7 and the whole narrative.[59]

More problematic is the suggestion that Jesus' initial attempt to exorcise the demoniac (v. 8) had failed (indicated by the demoniac's response in v. 7). Gundry suggests that Jesus' 'failure was due to his commanding a single unclean spirit to come out when in fact the victim needed to be dispossessed of a large number of unclean spirits'.[60] Hence his question in v. 9. It is true that Mark records another incident where Jesus does not instantly work a miracle but does so in stages—that of the blind man in 8.22-26. However, it does not seem to be due to a failure of Jesus' knowledge.[61] It is possible that γάρ has a consecutive sense 'then' or 'so then'.[62] Verse 8 would then signify Jesus' response to the demoniac's attack. There is also a textual variant in ℵ, with καί in place of γάρ, which indicates that a certain scribe thought a consecutive connection between vv. 7 and 8 more appropriate than the causal or support sense usually associated with γάρ.[63] On the other

---

59. See Lane, *Gospel of Mark*, p. 182 n. 10, who notes Eitrem's objection to the chronology as presented by Mark because 'it is inconceivable that the man would have addressed himself to Jesus at once with an adjuration so strong'. Eitrem reconstructs the dialogue so that it would read: vv. 7b, 8b, 9, 8a, 7c, 10. See S. Eitrem, *Some Notes on Demonology in the New Testament* (Oslo, 1950), p. 55. Accepting this reconstruction would place Jesus' question, 'What is your name?', before his command to come out of the man.

60. Gundry, *Mark*, p. 251.

61. It is not necessarily Jesus' lack of knowledge of the blind man's condition that led to the initial partial healing, since Mark uses this story in a symbolic way to illustrate the confusion of the disciples as to the mission of Jesus (cf. 8.21). The account forms an *inclusio* with the account of Blind Bartimaeus in 10.46-52. Between these two accounts is the series of three predictions by Jesus concerning his suffering. It is conceivable that Mark is using the narrative in 5.1-10 for a theological purpose in a similar way.

62. Bauer suggests that γάρ can express 'continuation or connection' as his fourth possible meaning; see BAGD, pp. 151-52. Louw and Nida include γάρ in domain 91A Markers of Transition; see Louw and Nida, *A Greek–English Lexicon of the New Testament*, I, pp. 811-12.

63. Though one must then explain why the majority of texts have γάρ and not καί. Note that this variant is not shown in Nestle-Aland[27] but can be found in Aland's Synopsis. I am not trying to argue that this is the original reading, simply that it indicates that others have seen problems with the usual understanding of γάρ (indicating a causal or supporting clause). The parallel in Lk. 8.29 has γάρ and no noted variant.

hand, perhaps there is not a strict order implied. In this 'battle' between the demon and Jesus we need not assume there was a civil exchange of words. Mark indicates the great noise (v. 6), perhaps they were shouting at each other. A string of imperfective verb forms (λέγει... ὀρκίζω...ἔλεγεν...ἐπηρώτα...λέγει...παρεκάλει) is used by Mark to bring the listener/reader into the midst of the action.[64] It is a fiery confrontation, a showdown between the two figures representing the kingdom of darkness and the kingdom of God. Gundry may be correct to speak about Jesus' 'failure' to drive out the demon; however, an uncertain understanding of the significance of the imperfect tense-form, and an assumption that γάρ always constitutes a causal clause, are weak evidence for such a position. Perhaps Mark does not think that Jesus needed to call for silence from the demon because he was in a private setting.[65]

Many commentators have seen v. 8 as an afterthought by Mark to explain the absence of an explicit command for the demon to come out, or as the work of a later redactor who was confused by the ordering of the account. Guelich acknowledges the suggestion by a number of commentators that v. 8 comes from the hand of a later redactor, admitting that:

> Without doubt, the comment stands in awkward tension with what has gone before by implying a previous ineffectual command for the unclean spirit to come out of the man.[66]

However, he does not see this option as fitting 'the story's repeated emphasis on the servile position of the unclean spirit towards Jesus'.[67] Thus he suggests that it serves as an explanatory comment for the demon's adjuration in the previous verse. I have argued in the preceding discussion that the demon is in fact adopting anything but a 'servile position' towards Jesus. With this understanding it is difficult to see how Jesus' command in v. 8 could serve as an explanation for the

---

64. Translating into English continuous presents brings out this sense.

65. Only the disciples are present (or so Mark has told us at this point; though others are nearby, e.g. pig herders). Later on (v. 20) it appears that, on this side of the sea of Galilee (in mainly Gentile territory), Jesus is less concerned to keep his identity hidden than elsewhere in the Gospel.

66. R.A. Guelich, *Mark 1–8:26* (WBC, 34A; Dallas: Word Books, 1989), p. 280.

67. Guelich, *Mark*, p. 280.

demon's vicious attack, in attempting to cast a spell upon him. Interestingly, Guelich also suggests that the γάρ in v. 8 was added in a redactional stage that brought together the story of the drowning of the pigs in the sea and the exorcism account. He comments that:

> 5.8 without the explanatory conjunction 'for' (γάρ) and with a different tense of λέγειν may well have expressed the original exorcism order per se by having Jesus, who disregards the adjuration of 5.7b (similarly in 1.25), simply order the unclean spirit out.[68]

Adopting the aspectual understanding of the Greek tense-forms used in this study takes away the necessity that λέγω be placed in a different tense-form, and allowing for a simple continuative sense for γάρ removes the need to posit various stages of redaction.

Ultimately the question of how v. 8 should be chronologically related to v. 7 does not alter the overall effect of Jesus' command. He does not ask for the name of the demon in order to use it in a spell. None of the exorcism accounts in the Synoptic Gospels shows Jesus using contemporary exorcism spells. He does not use the ὀρκίζω formula, invoke a name or use mechanical objects to aid in the exorcism.[69] What is striking about the exorcisms performed by Jesus is the power of his spoken word. He simply commands the demon to leave its victim.[70] It is unclear in Mark's account exactly why Jesus asks for the demon's name. However, Mark uses the response to emphasize again the power of the demon ('we are many'; cf. vv. 3-5).[71]

---

68. Guelich, *Mark*, p. 280.

69. See Tob. 8.1-3 for a description of an exorcism in which the demon is driven away by the odour of burning fish liver. Cf. Josephus's record of an exorcism performed by Solomon in which a ring was used to draw the demon out of the nostrils of a demoniac (*Ant.* 7.46-47).

70. See Kee, 'Terminology', pp. 232-46, for a discussion of the unique use of ἐπιτιμάω by Jesus. He states, 'Where texts have been preserved which tell how one should control demons ἐπιτιμάω does not appear' (p. 241).

71. Contra Gundry, *Mark*, p. 251: 'The something that is needed beyond the usual command to shut up is the knowledge of the unclean spirit's name, which will expose Jesus' mistake in addressing one unclean spirit when he issued the command to come out, whereupon the spirits seized a temporary advantage through using their accurate knowledge of Jesus' name and title...the failure was due to his commanding a single unclean spirit to come out when in fact the victim needed to be dispossessed of a large number of unclean spirits'.

f. *Demon's Surrender (v. 10)*

Another difficulty with Gundry's view that Jesus makes two attempts at the exorcism, is the absence of a further command by Jesus after v. 9. The demon is utterly defeated, in spite of its tremendous power. It is reduced to repeatedly begging Jesus for mercy.[72] If Gundry's assertion of initial failure were plausible would one not expect to see Jesus repeat the command to come out, but this time using τὰ πνεύματα τὰ ἀκάθαρτα ('unclean spirits') instead of τὸ πνεῦμα τὸ ἀκάθαρτον ('unclean spirit') as in v. 8?[73] Notice the use of verbal aspect from v. 6 to v. 10. The demoniac sees (perfective) Jesus and runs towards him (perfective) and crouches before him (perfective) and cries out (perfective), saying (imperfective) 'What to you...' Jesus speaks to him (imperfective)... asking him (imperfective). Then the demoniac pleads with Jesus (imperfective). The shift from perfective to imperfective fits the development of the confrontation, reaching a climax in the defeat of the demon. The following verses (vv. 11-13) describe the punishment of the demon(s), and with a switch back to the perfective aspect (παρεκά-λεσαν in v. 11).

g. *Summary of Exegesis of Mark 5.1-10*

Mark uses the exorcism of the Gerasene demoniac to illustrate the larger battle between the kingdom of Satan and the kingdom of God. In the first half of his Gospel Mark presents the actions of Jesus as proof of the claim of Jesus in 1.15 that 'the kingdom of God has come near'; particularly prominent are the exorcisms of Jesus.[74] The 'strong man' (Satan) has carried out a destructive reign over humanity and no one

---

72. The adverbial πολλά ('frequently') modifying παρακαλέω in v. 10 is in stark contrast to the adverb πολλάκις ('frequently') in v. 4 (see above). The constant failure of the attempts to bind the demoniac is contrasted with the power of Jesus to defeat the demon (thereby 'binding the strong man').

73. It would be unwise to make too much of the singular noun (πνεῦμα) in v. 8. It does not necessarily signify that Jesus perceived only one demon at this point. Even after the 'revelation' of the numerous demons (v. 9) the passage shows a switch between the singular and plural: v. 10—καὶ παρακαλεῖ (singular) αὐτὸν πολλὰ ἵνα μὴ αὐτὰ (plural) ἀποστείλῃ...(N.B. variant for αὐτά)... v. 12—παρε-κάλεσαν (plural) αὐτόν...

74. Kee asserts that, 'There can be no mistaking Mark's intention: it is in the exorcisms that the authority of Jesus is supremely manifest, and it is through the exorcisms that the kingdom can be seen as having drawn near (1.15)' ('Terminology', p. 242).

has been able to bind him. Jesus' ministry is a vicious conflict between himself and Satan, symbolized in the violent conflict between Jesus and the demoniac (5.1-13). Far from collapsing in defeat before Jesus, the demons possessing the man make a veritable first-strike. Yet, the power of Jesus is such that he succeeds in doing what no one else was able to do. Contrary to many commentators, this study has argued that the command of Jesus in v. 8 follows the first-strike attack of the demoniac in v. 7. If this position is accepted, it is not necessary to posit initial failure by Jesus due to his lack of knowledge concerning the number of demons possessing the man.

4. *Interpretative Translation of Mark 5.1-10*

1 And they arrived at the other side of the sea in the region of the Gerasenes. **2** Straightaway, as Jesus was getting off the boat, a man possessed by an unclean spirit came out of the tombs to attack him. **3** Now this man lived among the tombs, and there was no-one any longer who was at all able to bind him with a chain. **4** The reason for this is that many times he had been put in cuffs and chains in a bound state but the cuffs had been left torn apart by him and the chains were left shattered. So there was no-one strong enough to contain him. **5** As a result of this night and day he was always among the tombs and in the mountains wailing and cutting himself with stones. **6** This man saw Jesus from a distance and rushed to confront him and he crouched before him. **7** He cries out in a loud voice shouting, 'What business do you have here with me, O Jesus Son of God the Most High! I cast a spell on you in the name of God, "You will not torment me!"' **8** Then Jesus says, 'Unclean spirit, come out of the man!', **9** asking, 'What is your name?' He says, 'My name is "Legion", because we are many'. **10** Many times the demon was pleading with Jesus that he might not send them out of the region.

Having carried out a detailed exegesis of the passage, it is now possible to offer an interpretative translation that attempts to illustrate the exegetical decisions that have been made. To achieve this goal it may at places be necessary to provide English words or phrases that cannot be directly drawn from the Greek. That is to say, taken atomistically a particular Greek verb form or noun group would not easily be rendered by the interpretative equivalent that arises out of the contextual and co-textual features discovered in the exegetical process. For instance, the verb προσκυνέω is commonly seen to carry the sense of 'worship' or 'give reverence', and where bodily posture is in mind, it is a bending down in reverence to another. However, in section 3 I suggested that, in the context of the demoniac's dramatic attack upon Jesus, it is unlikely that he is falling down before Jesus to worship him. It is therefore more likely that the physical sense of προσκυνέω is prominent in this verse, and not in the sense of 'falling down to worship' or 'in surrender'. For this reason I have chosen to render προσεκύνησεν αὐτῷ with 'he crouched before him', in an attempt to communicate the full-frontal attack the demoniac is mounting upon Jesus. Some might object that this represents an unacceptable stretching of the possible senses of προσκυνέω, by pointing out that the word is often used in contexts of worship of Jesus, or at least where subjects of some authority are showing deference to him.[75] Mark's only other use of the word is in ch. 15: 'And they began saluting him, "Hail, King of the Jews!" They struck him with a reed, spat upon him, and knelt down in homage to him (τιθέντες τὰ γόνατα προσεκύνουν αὐτῷ)' (Mk 15.18-19 NRSV), which might suggest a similar nuance in 5.6, that the demon is actually mocking Jesus. However, given the collocation of προσκυνέω with τρέχω ('to run/rush'),[76] and the surrounding context, including the use of ὑπαντάω in v. 2 and the extended description of the power of the demoniac (vv. 3-5), I would still wish to argue for a more combative, physical sense for προσκυνέω.

Making translational decisions on the basis of contextual and exegetical/interpretative decisions raises a number of interesting issues for both translational and lexicographical theory. For instance, do words have basic meanings, that is, core semantic values that are found in all contextual uses of the word? In the case of προσκυνέω the basic meaning might involve the act of deference or worship, whether motivated by genuine devotion or by mockery. A more basic problem concerns how exactly these basic meanings might be discovered. Many of these

75. Nützel concludes that: 'The use of προσκυνέω in the NT is based on that of the OT, with a stronger concentration of the meaning in the direction of worship. What is new in the NT is that now the exalted Christ emerges next to God as the one worshipped' (J.M. Nützel, 'προσκυνέω', in H. Balz and G. Schneider [eds.], *Exegetical Dictionary of the New Testament* [vol. 3; Grand Rapids: Eerdmans, 1993], p. 175). Addressing the use of προσκυνέω in Mk 5.6, he suggests that the word there communicates 'the demonic gesture of submission' (Nützel, 'προσκυνέω', p. 174).

76. Louw and Nida suggest that the use of τρέχω places 'emphasis upon relative speed in contrast with walking' (Louw and Nida, *Greek–English Lexicon of the New Testament*, I, p. 209).

questions are beyond the scope of this study.[77] However, there are shortcomings both in the traditional lexicons, such as Bauer, which fail to see the relationships between words in the language system, and in a linguistically informed approach utilizing semantic field theory, such as that taken by Louw and Nida, which relies more heavily on sense relations instead of noting collocational patterns within texts.[78]

The significance of the preceding discussion for the use of an interpretative translation as the result of the exegetical process, is that it may not be possible for a reader to look at the final translation and at the original text and to understand how the translation was arrived at, without reference to the exegetical discussion. This may make some interpreters uncomfortable, feeling that the underlying original has been misrepresented or made to say something it could not possibly do if one was observing the standard 'rules' of grammar and the glosses found in the lexicon. In a response to an article by J.D. Kingsbury concerning the figure of Jesus in the Gospel of Matthew,[79] David Hill criticizes Kingsbury for suggesting that in Matthew the phrase ὁ υἱὸς τοῦ ἀνθρώπου ('The Son of Man') should be translated as 'this man'.[80] He argues that:

> The translational equivalent which, according to Kingsbury, best conveys the consistent meaning the 'Son of man' bears in Matthew, namely 'this man' or 'this human being', is simply not an available option. The Greek ὁ υἱὸς τοῦ ἀνθρώπου might, under strain, permit the definite rendering, '*the* man', but it will not permit 'this man', for which there is perfectly acceptable Greek, οὗτος ὁ ἄνθρωπος.[81]

Though he offers an alternative Greek phrase that would more literally capture Kingsbury's translation 'this man', Hill does not provide any indication whether Matthew uses this construction, or whether it is used

77. For a concise summary of Greek lexicography and seminal suggestions for future work in this area, see S.E. Porter, 'Linguistic Issues in New Testament Lexicography', in S.E. Porter, *Studies in the Greek New Testament* (SBG, 6; New York: Peter Lang, 1996), pp. 49-74.

78. For a more detailed discussion of the merits and shortcomings of both traditional and modern approaches to New Testament lexicography, see Porter, 'Linguistic Issues', *passim*; also Silva, *Biblical Words and Their Meanings*.

79. J.D. Kingsbury, 'The Figure of Jesus in Matthew's Story: A Literary-Critical Probe', *JSNT* 21 (1984), pp. 3-36.

80. D. Hill, 'The Figure of Jesus in Matthew's Story: A Response to Professor Kingsbury's Literary Critical Probe', *JSNT* 21 (1984), pp. 37-52.

81. Hill, 'The Figure of Jesus in Matthew's Story', p. 94.

in the New Testament at all. His assertion that this translation is 'not an available option' and his certainty that Greek will and will not *permit* certain options is a little perplexing. He seems to have missed the point that Kingsbury was not arguing that a first-pass translation would render ὁ υἱὸς τοῦ ἀνθρώπου with 'this man', or even that the phrase should be translated in this way in Mark's Gospel, or anywhere else in the New Testament. Kingsbury makes the suggestion on the basis of a detailed literary analysis of the Gospel of Matthew, focusing particularly on the figure of Jesus. This wider framework and investigation, rightly or wrongly, has led him to believe that 'the Son of man' is used by Jesus in Matthew not as 'a confessional title to set forth the identity of Jesus, but as a "public title"'.[82] From this understanding of the function of the phrase within Matthew's narrative, he suggests that the interpretative translation 'this man' best captures that understanding. He is not claiming that, in whatever sense one uses the term 'meaning', ὁ υἱὸς τοῦ ἀνθρώπου means 'this man', simply that its function within Matthew is best conveyed with 'this man'. In his response to Hill he states:

> On the question of the meaning of 'the Son of man', my position, which Hill misrepresents, is that the proper translation of the Greek that underlies 'the Son of man' is 'the man', or 'the human being'. But technically accurate as this translation is, one encounters a problem if one attempts simply to substitute, in each Son-of-man passage in Matthew, the expression 'the man' for 'the Son of man'.[83]

I have included a discussion of Kingsbury's articles on the figure of Jesus in Matthew, and Hill's response, not because I necessarily agree with Kingsbury's assertions about ὁ υἱὸς τοῦ ἀνθρώπου, but because his articles demonstrate the approach to translation presented in this paper. There are those, similar to Hill, who will not accept my overarching interpretation of the significance of Jesus' encounter with the demoniac within the Gospel of Mark, and so object to many of the translations I have suggested shaped by this understanding. However, the interpretative and subjective nature of any translation makes this virtually unavoidable, especially if one ventures to use exegetical, literary and discourse information in undertaking the translation process.

82. Kingsbury, 'The Figure of Jesus in Matthew's Story: A Literary-Critical Probe', pp. 75-76.

83. J.D. Kingsbury, 'The Figure of Jesus in Matthew's Story: A Rejoinder to David Hill', *JSNT* 25 (1985), p. 109.

5. *Conclusion*

Translation of the Greek text is an important, even essential, part of the exegetical process. It most often takes place in the early stages of this process, and serves to raise the key issues and central problems found in the text. In this article, I have suggested that translation should also be seen as one way of communicating the results of exegetical study. Through the use of interpretative translation it is possible to summarize the conclusions and interpretative decisions that have been made, and to communicate the overall understanding of the passage under consideration, in a way that is not possible through the use of verse-by-verse comments. The treatment of Mk 5.1-10 presented here has sought to demonstrate the use of interpretative translation in this way, by presenting translations of the passage at both the beginning and end of an exegetical study that, taking a systematic approach to the language of the New Testament, sees discourse considerations as essential to the process of exegesis and interpretative translation.

FOREGROUNDING AND ITS RELEVANCE FOR INTERPRETATION AND TRANSLATION, WITH ACTS 27 AS A CASE STUDY

Gustavo Martín-Asensio

Since its origin in the context of Russian formalism, the concept of linguistic foregrounding has motivated a large volume of work from a variety of angles. As has already been pointed out,[1] the differing theoretical frameworks that have thus far been brought to the discussion, together with the lack of agreement as to a basic definition, have greatly limited the fruitfulness of this notion. It is not surprising, then, that New Testament Greek scholarship has only recently begun its own reticent forays into this exciting new area of linguistic research, and this on a fairly limited scale.[2] The basic structure of this article is as follows. First, I shall attempt to summarize and assess various recent theories of linguistic foregrounding within the framework of functional grammar. Secondly, I shall refer to the notion of functional equivalence in the translation of foregrounding as discussed in the work of V. Procházka and E. Nida. Lastly, I shall turn my attention to the self-contained story of Paul's shipwreck in Acts 27, exploring the significance of foregrounded elements therein, and offering some suggestions for their

---

1. See H.A. Dry, 'Foregrounding: An Assessment', in S.J.J. Hwang and W.R. Merrifield (eds.), *Language in Context: Essays for Robert E. Longacre* (Dallas: Summer Institute of Linguistics, 1992), pp. 435-50.
2. See J.E. Grimes, 'Signals of Discourse Structure in Koine', in *Society of Biblical Literature 1975 Seminar Papers* (ed. G. MacRae; Missoula, MT: Scholars Press, 1975), pp. 151-64; R.D. Bergen, 'Text as a Guide to Authorial Intention: An Introduction to Discourse Criticism', *JETS* 30 (1987), pp. 327-36; S.E. Porter, *Verbal Aspect in the Greek of the New Testament, with Reference to Tense and Mood* (New York: Peter Lang, 1993), pp. 92-93; B.M. Fanning, *Verbal Aspect in New Testament Greek* (Oxford: Clarendon Press, 1990), pp. 72-77; J.T. Reed, 'Identifying Theme in the New Testament: Insights from Discourse Analysis', in S. Porter and D. Carson (eds.), *Discourse Analysis and Other Topics in Biblical Greek* (JSNTSup, 113; Sheffield: Sheffield Academic Press, 1995), pp. 75-101.

translation into the receptor language of Spanish, with reference to the Reina-Valera translation. I will attempt to demonstrate that research into foregrounding in New Testament Greek, a largely neglected area of study, has significant potential for both New Testament interpretation and translation, and requires much further study, along the lines here proposed.

1. *Linguistic Foregrounding in Recent Discussion: 1917–1990*

The phenomenon of foregrounding[3] has been a focus of study in over forty years of literary criticism and discourse analysis in a wide variety of genres and languages. In producing a text, a writer encounters several constraints. There is limited space and time for its composition; it is necessary to abide—if communication is to take place with the readers—by the lexico-grammatical conventions of the receptor speech community; lastly, a particular perspective must be imposed on the text, a 'patterning of patterns' that unifies the composition, investing it with at least a minimal amount of structure and direction.[4] Through

---

3.   The key works on the subject of foregrounding are: J. Mukarovsky, 'Standard Language and Poetic Language', in P.R. Garvin (ed.), *A Prague School Reader on Esthetic, Literary Structure and Style* (Washington, DC: Georgetown University Press, 1964), pp. 17-30; R. Jakobson, 'Linguistics and Poetics', in T.A. Sebeok (ed.), *Style in Language* (Cambridge, MA: MIT Press, 1960), pp. 350-68; G.N. Leech, 'Linguistics and the Figures of Rhetoric', in R. Fowler (ed.), *Essays on Style and Language* (London: Routledge and Kegan Paul, 1970), pp. 135-56; M. Halliday, 'Linguistic Function and Literary Style', in his *Explorations in the Functions of Language* (London: Edward Arnold, 1976), pp. 103-38. See also G. Leech 'Foregrounding and Interpretation', in his *A Linguistic Guide to English Poetry* (London: Longman, 1969), pp. 56-72; S. Wallace 'Figure and Ground: The Interrelationships of Linguistic Categories', in P.J. Hopper (ed.), *Tense–Aspect: Between Semantics and Pragmatics* (Amsterdam: John Benjamins, 1982), pp. 201-23; S. Fleischmann, 'Discourse Functions of Tense-Aspect Oppositions in Narrative: Toward a Theory of Grounding', *Linguistics* 23.6 (1985), pp. 851-82; Fleischmann, *Tense and Narrativity* (Austin: University of Texas Press, 1990); Fleischmann and L. Waugh (eds.), *Discourse Pragmatics and the Verb* (London: Routledge, 1991); (the last four works focus on tense-aspect); W. van Peer, *Stylistics and Psychology, Investigations of Foregrounding* (Croom Helm Linguistics Series; London: Croom Helm, 1986), esp. chap. 1; R. Hasan, *Linguistics, Language and Verbal Art* (Oxford: Oxford University Press, 1989), esp. pp. 29-106; H. Dry, 'Foregrounding' For a complete bibliography, see van Peer, *Stylistics*.

4.   In the words of Grimes, this can no more be avoided than a photographer

linguistic means such as lexico-grammatical structures or tense-aspect morphology, the writer attempts to guide the readers through the text, highlighting various levels of meaning or drawing attention to the episodes or themes that matter most in the light of the overall rhetorical[5] strategy employed.

An adequate understanding of the theory of foregrounding requires at least a basic acquaintance with a small number of works that have dealt with it from the 1920s to the present. The discussion that follows will concentrate on seminal essays by Mukarovsky, Jakobson, Leech, and Halliday (see n. 3), all of whom have left their imprint upon the notion in somewhat predictable ways.

The notion of linguistic foregrounding can be traced to insights developed within Russian formalism in the second decade of our century. Formalism's concern for differentiating between non-poetic and poetic works led Viktor Slovskij and others to the conclusion that the distinguishing mark of the latter is their potential for defamiliarization (Russian *ostranenie*), for causing readers and hearers to perceive elements of the poem with heightened awareness. Consequently, much of the energy of the formalists was dedicated to the investigation of the linguistic devices that activate such defamiliarization. Thus began the tendency to see foreground fundamentally as the departure from an established norm, a figure against a ground, to use the terms of subsequent psychological investigation.

The discussion reached a point of significant development in the early sixties, primarily at the hands of two Prague structuralists, Jan Mukarovsky and Roman Jakobson. Their two highly influential essays[6] mentioned above have much in common, as well as significant differences at various points. Both scholars saw the primary aim of their respective papers as the definition of the *'differentia specifica'* of poetic language vis-à-vis ordinary, standard language.[7] Both emphasize that

can choose to 'take his picture from nowhere or from everywhere'. Grimes, 'Signals', p. 153.

5. The term 'rhetorical' is used here in its widest sense of *ars bene dicendi*, the art of addressing a situation effectively by means of speech. See N.E. Enkvist, 'Text and Discourse Linguistics, Rhetoric, and Stylistics', in T.A. Van Dijk (ed.), *Discourse and Literature* (Amsterdam: John Benjamins, 1985), p. 11.

6. This is particularly true of Mukarovsky's 'Standard Language', as translated and edited by Garvin in 1960. To Garvin we owe the English word 'foregrounding', his rendering of Mukarovsky's Czech term *aktualisace*.

7. Jakobson, 'Linguistics', p. 350; Mukarovsky 'Standard Language', p. 17.

the poetic function is a concentration on the message 'for its own sake', while ordinary language points rather to the referent or the subject matter. Further, Jakobson and Mukarovsky seem to share a determination to distinguish between the purely aesthetic in poetic language, and the pragmatic focus of non-poetic language. Lastly and most importantly, both Jakobson and Mukarovsky see some form of foregrounding as the essence of poetic language.[8] Their differences are no less considerable. While Mukarovsky insists on a strong dichotomy between poetic and standard language, arguing that the former cannot be considered a brand of the latter, Jakobson would tone down the differences by affirming that poetics is an integral part of linguistics, and that every speech event, poetic or not, fulfills not one but several functions. For Mukarovsky, the essence of the poetic function is foregrounding, understood as the opposite of 'automatization', that is, the departure from a norm.[9] Jakobson, however, sees parallelism as the fundamental element of poetic language, that is, repetition of the same elements where a departure would have been expected.[10] Parallelism, argues

8.   Though Jakobson does not use the term foregrounding nor its Czech equivalent, he does rely on one of the common metaphors for the notion such as 'palpability'. Jakobson, 'Linguistics', p. 356.

9.   Thus, for example, in his short introductory story to his trilogy *U.S.A.*, John Dos Passos seeks to underline that it is its peculiar language that is the essence of America. This effect is achieved syntactically by a departure from an established pattern at two points. One example will suffice. The author embarks upon an extended list of negative statements: 'It was not in the long walks through jostling crowds at night that he was less alone, or in the training camp at Allentown, or in the day at the docks at Seattle...[this continues for 12 lines]...but in his mother's words...it was the speech that clung to the ears, the link that tingled in the blood, U.S.A'. In this short story, this device can be shown to be motivated and consistent in its two instances. John Dos Passos, *The Big Money* (New York: Signet, 1979), p. xix.

10.   In the anonymous fifteenth-century Spanish poem 'Romance del Rey Moro que perdió Alhama', the author presents a poetic justification of the Moorish loss of Granada ('Bien se te emplea, buen rey' etc.). Throughout these 56 lines, the narrator depicts the last moments of Moorish occupation of southern Spain from his Christian perspective. However, his repetition of the Moorish king's lament '¡Ay de mi Alhama!' (11X) gives the whole poem the feel of a dirge, and its effect is that of evoking sympathy for the defeated. The device of foregrounding serves here to undermine what would otherwise be clearly seen as the theme of this poem. *Las Mil Mejores Poesias de la Lengua Castellana* (ed. J. Bergua; Madrid: Ediciones Ibéricas, 30th edn, 1991), p. 108.

Jakobson, is the primary means of promoting the 'palpability of signs' in a text.

Though the contribution made by these two essays to the theory of foregrounding makes them veritable landmarks in the history of the discussion, at least two serious objections must be raised against their commonly held views. The difference between a focus on the message 'for its own sake' (the poetic function) and a focus on the referent or subject matter (non-poetic, referential function) seems very difficult to demonstrate, as van Peer has noted.[11] Does the aesthetic nature of poetic language necessarily make it non-pragmatic? Does poetic language not communicate in the manner that 'ordinary' language communicates? Hasan has argued convincingly for the pragmatic import of verbal art.[12] Secondly, both scholars fail to provide adequate criteria for determining what is *significant* parallelism (Jakobson) or departure from a norm (Mukarovsky). Mukarovsky is aware of the need to develop such criteria, affirming that foregrounding is not a capricious, random, breaking of norm(s), but must be systematic and consistent. However, he seems unclear as to whether the norms are set up locally by the text or poem in question, or whether they are derived from the standard language.[13]

The publication of Geoffrey Leech's essay 'Linguistics and the Figures of Rhetoric' (see n. 3) represents the first of several key contributions to foregrounding theory by scholars of University College, London.[14] The main thrust of Leech's paper is his proposal for an integration of the two types of foregrounding discussed above, namely, by parallelism (Jakobson) and by deviation from norm(s) (Mukarovsky). This integration is achieved by means of applying Saussure's dichotomy of the paradigmatic and syntagmatic axes: while paradigmatic foregrounding would involve the selection of an item not permitted or expected at a particular point, syntagmatic foregrounding is the repeated selection of an item where a single selection is expected. The unifying element is that of selection along the two axes.

Michael Halliday's essay entitled 'Linguistic Function and Literary Style'[15] represents the foremost contribution of the London School of

11. van Peer, *Stylistics*, p. 9.
12. R. Hasan, *Linguistics, Language and Verbal Art*, p. 99.
13. See especially Mukarovsky, 'Standard Language', p. 21.
14. With Halliday and Hasan, see below.
15. In Halliday, *Explorations in the Functions of Language*, pp. 103-38. See

Linguistics[16] to the discussion of foregrounding. In what could be Halliday's most persuasive presentation of his functional grammar,[17] the author provides a thorough account and interpretation of foregrounded transitivity patterns in William Golding's novel *The Inheritors*. Following Leech, Halliday affirms that foregrounding need not be understood exclusively in terms of deviation, and that whether it is seen as the transgression or the establishment of a norm is only a matter of point of view. Two points make Halliday's contribution to the discussion particularly significant. The author sets out to discover not only foregrounded patterns of language in a specific text such as Golding's, but, more importantly, criteria for relevant prominence that may be applied across the board. In fundamental agreement with Mukarovsky, Halliday seeks to distinguish between mere linguistic prominence, and that prominence which can be shown to be motivated or relevant in light of the overall theme or purpose of the text. The author affirms that the terms 'foreground' and 'foregrounding' can only be properly predicated of the latter. In addition, Halliday establishes his criteria within the framework of 'a functional theory of language' capable of relating every item of lexico-grammar in a text to the specific functions it has in the language system.[18]

The Inheritors is a story of the contrasting worldviews and lifestyles of two tribes of primitive men, of their encounter and conflict, and of the eventual survival of the more advanced group. In his analysis of the text, Halliday shows that the differing perspectives on reality of both tribes are skillfully conveyed by means of choices in the transitivity network at the rank of clause. Stemming from the ideational 'macro-function' of language, transitivity choices have to do with the representation of experience, and are realized by the functional elements of

also Ruqaiya Hasan's analyses of a poem and a story in Hasan, *Linguistics, Language and Verbal Art*, esp. pp. 29-106.

16. For a critical introduction to the London School, see T. Langendoen, *The London School of Linguistics: A Study of the Linguistic Theories of B. Malinowski and J.R. Firth* (Research Monograph, 46; Cambridge, MA: MIT Press, 1968).

17. See C. Butler, *Systemic Linguistics: Theory and Applications* (London: Batsford, 1985), p. 198.

18. The importance of relating individual elements of style to a 'higher level functional framework' has been acknowledged by linguists outside the London School. See P.J. Hopper and S.A. Thompson, 'Transitivity in Grammar and Discourse', *Language* 56.2 (1980), p. 280.

'process', 'participants', and 'circumstances'.[19] These elements together define the typical clause used by Golding to characterize the first tribe (clause type 'A'): only one participant, action in simple past tense, almost complete absence of complements, overabundance of adjuncts. This clause type becomes the norm for the bulk of the narrative and has the effect of conveying the limited understanding and ability, indeed, the frustrated existence of the Neanderthal tribe. In stark contrast, the last sixteen pages of the novel depict the superiority of the Homo Sapiens group by means of a vastly different clause type: human subjects predominate in transitive clauses of action, encoding a far more complex perception of reality. Halliday concludes that the unexpected frequency of clause type 'A' throughout the work is related to an interpretation of the text's overall theme and subject matter, and can therefore be considered relevant, motivated prominence. That the foregrounded structures are choices arising from the transitivity network is not surprising to Halliday, who affirms that 'transitivity is really the cornerstone of the semantic organization of experience'.[20]

In her evaluative assessment of the state of the art in foregrounding research as of 1992, Helen Dry notes the difficulties presented by the seemingly incompatible assumptions brought into the discussion by the disciplines of psychology, literary criticism and discourse analysis. It is my contention that Halliday's functional grammar is capable of integrating insights from these three approaches into one coherent theory of foregrounding which is widely applicable. Halliday's analysis of *The Inheritors* bears this point out. First, functional grammar enables us to recognize and study foregrounding in all kinds of texts, the only necessary condition for its identification being its demonstrable motivation and consistency, in light of an interpretation of the theme or purpose of the text in question. According to Halliday's theory, the three 'macrofunctions' known by him as ideational, interpersonal, and textual are a universal of language.[21] The qualities that make a text what it is, for

---

19. See M.A.K. Halliday, *An Introduction to Functional Grammar* (London: Edward Arnold, 1990), pp. 101-44.

20. Halliday, *Explorations in the Functions of Language*, p. 134.

21. Halliday, *Functional Grammar*, p. xxxiv. Cf. Jakobson, 'Linguistics and Poetics', p. 353, and J. De Waard and E.A. Nida, *From one Language to Another* (Nashville: Thomas Nelson, 1986), pp. 26, 43, 119. But Halliday adds that the particular realizations of these macrofunctions are language relative: 'while all languages are assumed to have a "textual" component, whereby discourse achieves a texture that relates it to its environment, it is not assumed that in any given

example, include cohesiveness and coherence, and these, whether exhibited by a poem or a newspaper article, are the product of the *textual* macrofunction. Likewise, consistent, motivated prominence of the sort discernible in Golding's novel or Dos Passos's story (n. 9 above) is fundamentally contributive to the *texture* of those works, that is, it plays an essential role in their semantic organization. Functional grammar shows us, therefore, that the famous distinction between 'standard' and 'poetic' language is in fact much more tenuous than has been traditionally believed.[22] Secondly, Halliday's framework demonstrates that insights from discourse analysis and psychology need not be incompatible. Since the seminal ethnolinguistic work of Bronislaw Malinowski, functional grammarians[23] have been profoundly aware of the fact that the meaning of every utterance is inseparably tied to its function in a specific context of situation. In the light of this, Halliday's model aims to relate linguistic patterns of texts (the domain of discourse analysis) to the effects they have in their readers (the province of psycholinguistics).[24] 'Meaning, therefore, is function in context', not primarily the function of the individual elements of a text, but that of their strategically structured sum total. The implications of this insight for translation will be dealt with in the next section.

2. *Foregrounding: 'A Hard Nut for the Translator'*[25]

In his stimulating and ground-breaking 1942 essay on the translation of foregrounding, Vladimir Procházka suggests three essential qualifi-

language one of the ways of achieving texture will be by means of a thematic system...' (*Functional Grammar*, p. xxxiv).

22. 'The search for the language of literature is misguided; we should look instead at language in literature'. Hasan, *Linguistics, Language, and Verbal Art*, p. 94. See also pp. 92-100. Though Hasan maintains a distinction between non-poetic and poetic language, this is strictly on the basis of the motivated nature of foregrounding in the latter. Furthermore, she calls for the 'demystification' of linguistic analysis of literature (p. 92), and affirms the potential for the widest use of foregrounding: 'once a novel patterning of patterns is introduced, it can become a currency...something that is available to the community for use in other textual environments' (p. 100).

23. Though the term is Halliday's, it is equally applicable to his teacher and predecessor at University College, John Rupert Firth, who first defined meaning as 'function in context'.

24. Halliday, 'Linguistic Function', p. 112.

25. This is Vladimir Procházka's translation of the Czech title of R. Wellek's

cations of a 'good translator': (1) 'Understand the original work thematically and stylistically'; (2) 'Overcome by his own means of expression the differences between the two linguistic structures', and (3) 'Reconstruct the stylistic structure of the original work in translation'. The last qualification is considered by the writer 'the center of gravity of the translator's work'.[26] Consequently, argues Procházka, it is unhelpful to define translations in terms such as 'free', 'literal', or 'halting', for these designations fail to address the fundamental problem, namely, whether or not words, clauses and larger units in the source text are translated adequately in the light of the total stylistic structure of the work. The final aim of a translation, continues the author, is not the literal rendering of words, clauses and sentences (that is, the formal elements of language) from source into receptor language, but rather, the search for linguistic elements in the receptor that are *functionally analogous* to those of the source.[27] This principle is illustrated by means of the example of Procházka's translation of a German novel into Czech:

> First of all, I had to face the basic problem: whether, and to what extent, it is necessary to preserve Scholz's complicated compound sentences and in general the baroque qualities of his style. After long reflection, I came to the conclusion that this complexity, baroqueness, almost lack of clarity, belongs to the basic structure and therefore must be preserved. It could, of course, not be done mechanically; Scholz's sentences and entire passages had to be, as it were, melted down in my mind, and then recreated in Czech...I... have the impression that my reconstruction has been relatively successful, and that *the Czech reader gathers a similar impression from the translation to that of the German reader from the original* (emphasis mine).[28]

Procházka's notion of functional analogy makes his essay a significant precursor of the work of Eugene Nida, the dean of modern Bible translators. Though Nida recently confessed to this writer that he was not aware of Procházka's essay, he openly admitted his indebtedness to Prague functionalism as a whole.[29] Nida's approach to translation may

article 'Prekladatelsky Orisek', published in 1935; cited in Procházka, 'Notes on Translating Technique', in Garvin (ed.), *Prague School Reader*, pp. 93-112.

26. Procházka, 'Notes', p. 97.

27. Procházka, 'Notes', pp. 97, 99, 104.

28. Procházka, 'Notes', p. 104.

29. Telephone conversation held on 17 April 1996. I wish to express my thanks to Dr Nida for his phone call, fax, and letter shortly thereafter in response to my

be summarized by reference to three fundamental points made in his recent work, *From One Language to Another*. First, Nida's is a socio-semiotic approach. In essence, this means that linguistic signs such as verb forms or relative clauses are understood within a larger framework of signs: linguistic (e.g. other verb forms and clauses), para-linguistic (e.g. punctuation), and extra-linguistic (e.g. the symbolic meaning of eating a meal in the ancient Mediterranean world).[30] Secondly, his is a functional approach. Nida posits eight distinct universal functions in language: expressive, cognitive, interpersonal, informative, imperative, performative, emotive and aesthetic, arguing that their universality across languages is what makes the translator's task possible.[31] Lastly, the work of translation involves for Nida not primarily a transfer of forms from one language to another, but rather a process of searching for functional equivalents between languages at the lexical, grammatical, and rhetorical levels.[32]

Though De Waard and Nida make only a brief specific reference to foregrounding in their book,[33] the authors pay due attention to what they call 'rhetorical functions', that is, the varying degrees of selection and arrangement in a text together with the effects that these have upon the reader. The writers affirm that the rhetorical level is 'more inclusive' than the syntactical level, and that the meaning of rhetorical patterns cannot be fully appreciated without reference to the total context. Foregrounding is, therefore, subsumed by the authors within the rhetorical level of linguistic structure.[34]

questions to him. That two linguists with similar interests arrive at strikingly similar notions independently of each other is not as surprising as some may think. A classic example of this is the nearly simultaneous and wholly independent founding of semiotics by Charles S. Peirce (who used the term 'semeiotics') and Ferdinand de Saussure (who coined the term *sémiologie*).

30. De Waard and Nida, *From One Language to Another*, pp. 73-77. Cf. M.A.K. Halliday, *Language as Social Semiotic* (London: Edward Arnold, 1978).

31. De Waard and Nida, *From One Language to Another*, pp. 26, 43, 119; E.A. Nida, J.P. Louw, A.H. Snyman and J.W.V. Cronje, *Style and Discourse* (Cape Town: Bible Society, 1983), p. 168. Though Nida is generally very appreciative of Halliday's work, he adamantly rejects the latter's reduction of functional components to three. Telephone conversation, see n. 29.

32. De Waard and Nida, *From One Language to Another*, p. 68.

33. De Waard and Nida, *From One Language to Another*, p. 84.

34. De Waard and Nida, *From One Language to Another*, pp. 78-85. The specific rhetorical functions discussed by the authors are 'wholeness', 'aesthetic appeal', 'impact', 'appropriateness', 'coherence', 'cohesion', 'focus' and 'emphasis'.

I wish to argue that the theory of functional equivalence as presented by Nida represents a strong confirmation of the seminal insights of Vladimir Procházka referred to above, and provides translators with an ideally suited conceptual framework for the translation of foregrounding schemes in texts such as the Acts of the Apostles. Following my analysis of the shipwreck narrative, I shall offer some suggestions for the translation of foregrounding into the receptor language of Spanish.

3. *Modern Luke–Acts Study: From Source to Literary Criticism*

Of the immense amount of scholarly work dedicated to the study of Luke–Acts[35] over the last 200 years, the question of purpose may well be the most important to have been asked.[36] As Gasque has pointed out, though the conclusions of the Tübingen school have long been rejected in and outside Germany, it must be recognized that it was Ferdinand Christian Baur who first pointed to the significance of the 'why question' in the study of Luke–Acts. Since Baur first presented his theory of the Paulinist–Jewish feud as the fundamental polemic behind the composition of Acts, the question of purpose has been pursued primarily along the lines of source criticism and *tendenz*-criticism.[37]

With the establishment of form and redaction criticism as widely accepted methods in the second half of this century, greater attention began to be paid to the text of Luke–Acts as a two-volumed literary unit, and to its final form as composed by the author with specific aim(s) in mind. Though this development often came at an unacceptable price,[38] the shift in focus from speculation about sources[39] to the

35. Since H.J. Cadbury coined this designation and argued convincingly for it, the unity of the two volumes has not been seriously challenged. See R. Maddox, *The Purpose of Luke–Acts* (Studies in the New Testament and its World; Edinburgh: T. & T. Clark, 2nd edn, 1985), pp. 3-6.

36. Thus W.W. Gasque, *A History of the Criticism of the Acts of the Apostles* (Beitrage Zur Geschichte der Biblischen Exegese, 17; Tübingen: J.C.B. Mohr, 1975), p. 50.

37. Haenchen provided a memorable summary of this development, paraphrasing Schwanbeck: '...either the author of Acts was *unwilling*, or he was *unable*, to say more. The latter possibility led to source criticism, the former...to so-called "tendency-criticism"'. E. Haenchen, *The Acts of the Apostles* (trans. B. Noble and G. Shinn; Oxford: Basil Blackwell, 1971), p. 15.

38. Martin Dibelius was very much a pioneer of this new thrust in Luke–Acts scholarship, primarily through his essays 'Style Criticism of the Book of Acts' (1923) and 'The Acts of the Apostles in the Setting of Early Christian Literature'

text of Luke–Acts as a literary unit is a welcome and healthy turn of events in the investigation of the purpose of this work. Few scholars have done more to bring this shift about than Henry Joel Cadbury. In his celebrated monograph, *The Making of Luke–Acts*, Cadbury distances his new approach from that of previous scholars, whose

> ...ultimate interest is not the author and his times, but the subject matter of his history. His own interests are considered merely as they colour or adulterate his story. He is someone to be allowed for, eliminated and discounted, not someone to be studied and appreciated for his own sake. His literary methods are examined in order that we may discover the earlier sources behind them, or the facts and personalities behind the sources.[40]

In the early 1970s literary critics, primarily American, began arguing that redaction criticism had not gone far enough in its appreciation of the compositional artistry of the New Testament writings.[41] Though

(1926). Dibelius's focus on Acts as a literary work was primarily due to his belief that: (1) the author lacked any significant source materials, and (2) the early Christians expected an immediate eschaton and were therefore uninterested in recording history. Consequently, Dibelius believed that '...we cannot, in the first place, consider this work from the aspect of "Formgeschichte" but only from that of its style'. M. Dibelius, 'Style Criticism', in *Studies in the Acts of the Apostles* (trans. M. Ling; London: SCM Press, 1956), p. 4. Following Dibelius, Haenchen has embraced a strong dichotomy between that which is historical and that which is literary. See Haenchen, *Acts*, pp. 41, 44. Disputing Haenchen's belief in the absence of traditions behind Acts, Max Wilcox points out that all we are entitled to say is that if these existed, 'they are no longer extant as separate entities'. M. Wilcox, 'A Foreword to the Study of the Speeches in Acts', *Studies in Judaism in Late Antiquity*, 12.1 (1975), p. 210. On the issue of the false dichotomy of history and literature, see also Gasque, *History*, p. 266; C.J. Hemer, *The Book of Acts in the Setting of Hellenistic History* (Tübingen: J.C.B. Mohr, 1989), pp. 34-35.

39. See Dibelius, 'Style Criticism', p. 1.

40. H.J. Cadbury, *The Making of Luke–Acts* (London: SPCK, 3rd edn, 1968), p. 7. Cadbury has rightly been called the 'patron of the literary approach to Luke'. R.I. Pervo, 'On Perilous Things: A Response to Beverly Gaventa', in M. Parsons and J. Tyson, *Cadbury, Knox and Talbert: American Contributions to the Study of Acts* (SBL Centennial Publications; Atlanta: Scholars Press, 1992), p. 39. Pervo adds that Cadbury was a 'forerunner of redaction criticism', and one who 'prepared the ground for its natural heir: literary criticism' (p. 41).

41. See C.H. Talbert, *Literary Patterns, Theological Themes, and the Genre of Luke–Acts* (SBLMS, 20; Missoula, MT: Scholars Press, 1974), p. 5; W.A. Beardslee, *Literary Criticism of the New Testament* (Philadelphia: Fortress Press, 1970); F.S. Spencer, 'Acts and Modern Literary Approaches', in B. Winter and A. Clarke

several scholars within this new stream have dealt with various aspects of the language of Luke–Acts,[42] none have, to my knowledge, pursued consistently a study of its composition from a modern linguistics perspective. It remains to be seen, therefore, whether linguistic analysis has any contribution to make to the study of Luke–Acts as literature, and to the investigation of its purpose in particular. It is hoped that the following exploration of foregrounding in Acts 27 will confirm that the answer is affirmative on both counts.

4. Foregrounded Syntax in Acts 27: Its Nature and Implications for Interpretation and Translation

The account of Paul's shipwreck off the coast of Malta has rightly been described as being 'among the most literary sections of Acts'.[43] A self-contained narrative, it commences with the decision to set sail (27.1), and ends with the colophon-like statement: καὶ οὕτως ἐγένετο πάντας διασωθῆναι ἐπὶ τὴν γῆν (27.44). A first reading of this story may yield

(eds.), *The Book of Acts in its Ancient Literary Setting* (The Book of Acts in its First Century Setting, 1; Grand Rapids: Eerdmans; Carlisle: Paternoster Press, 1994), pp. 385-86. Other works that have approached Luke–Acts from a literary standpoint are P. Schubert, 'The Final Cycle of Speeches in the Book of Acts', *JBL* 87 (1968), pp. 1-16; J. Kilgallen, 'Acts: Literary and Theological Turning Points', *Bulletin de Théologie Biblique* 7 (1977), pp. 177-80; R.C. Tannehill, *The Narrative Unity of Luke–Acts: A Literary Interpretation* (2 vols.; Minneapolis: Fortress Press, 1990); Maddox, *The Purpose of Luke–Acts*; P.E. Satterthwaite, 'Acts Against the Background of Classical Rhetoric', in Winter and Clarke (eds.), *The Book of Acts in Its Ancient Literary Setting*, pp. 337-79; S.M. Sheeley, *Narrative Asides in Luke–Acts* (JSNTSup, 72; Sheffield: Sheffield Academic Press, 1992); see also the essays in the section entitled 'Issues of Literary Criticism' in B. Witherington (ed.), *History, Literature and Society in the Book of Acts* (Cambridge: Cambridge University Press, 1996), pp. 283-362.

42. P. Schubert, 'The Place of the Areopagus Speech in the Composition of Acts', in J.C. Rylaarsdam (ed.), *Transitions in Biblical Scholarship* (Essays in Divinity, 6; Chicago: University of Chicago Press, 1968), pp. 235-61; J. Kilgallen, *The Stephen Speech, a Literary and Redactional Study of Acts 7:2-53* (AnBib, 67; Rome: Biblical Institute Press, 1976); E. Richard, *Acts 6:1–8:4, The Author's Method of Composition* (SBLDS, 41; Missoula, MT: Scholars Press, 1978); C.M. Tuckett (ed.), *Luke's Literary Achievement* (JSNTSup, 116; Sheffield: Sheffield Academic Press, 1995).

43. Dibelius, 'The Acts', p. 205; See also his 'Style Criticism', p. 7, though see my caveat in note 27; Haenchen, *Acts*, p. 710, though I disagree that 'it is precisely the Pauline speeches...which give this section its literary character'.

the following further observations: the 'we' subject[44] continues from previous material, beginning at verse one and being discontinued after v. 37, where the referent is the totality of the crew and passengers; there are four brief speeches attributed to Paul, of which the second is by far the longest; Paul's speeches appear in the 'I style';[45] the writer has been particularly detailed in his description of both nautical equipment and its (ineffective) use to overcome the elements; besides 'we' and Paul, other subjects in the narrative are Julius the centurion, the soldiers and the sailors. These preliminary observations suggest several possible themes for this narrative: the survival of the crew and passengers through Paul's (or Julius's) intervention; the perils of first-century navigation during the winter months; the condition of prisoners in Roman custody, etc. Unless, however, these intuitions can be grounded in more precise linguistic data, we are bound to be influenced primarily by historical or theological preconceptions of what the author 'could' or 'could not' be saying. This was the bane of much of German Luke–Acts scholarship in the nineteenth century.[46]

The analysis that follows is a search for motivated prominence in this narrative, that is, an investigation of the author's foregrounding strategy and of how it has shaped the raw elements of lexico-grammar at his disposal into what Hasan has termed 'a second order semiosis',[47] a 'larger' meaning that transcends that of the individual elements. Following the pioneering works of Porter and Fanning in the discourse-pragmatic use of verbal aspect in the New Testament,[48] I shall first turn

44. For a recent discussion of the 'we' sections, see S.E. Porter, 'Excursus: The "We" Passages', in C. Gempf and D.W.J. Gill (eds.), *The Book of Acts in its Graeco-Roman Setting* (The Book of Acts in its First Century Setting, 2; Grand Rapids: Eerdmans; Carlisle: Paternoster Press, 1993), pp. 545-74. See also A.J. Mattill, Jr, 'The Value of Acts as a Source for the Study of Paul', in C.H. Talbert (ed.), *Perspectives on Luke-Acts* (Danville, VA: Association of Baptist Professors of Religion, 1978), pp. 76-98, who shows how one's evaluation of Acts as a source for the study of Paul is directly related to one's assessment of the 'we' sections; V.K. Robbins, 'By Land and by Sea: The We-Passages and Ancient Sea-Voyages', in Talbert (ed.), *Perspectives*, pp. 215-42.

45. On the 'I style', see Schubert, 'The Final Cycle', p. 4. Schubert's conclusion is that the 'I style' is characteristic of his 'cycle III' of speeches in Acts 22.1–28.22, and that this is motivated by the judicial nature of the situation.

46. See Gasque, *History*, p. 106.

47. Hasan, *Linguistics*, p. 98.

48. Porter, *Verbal Aspect in the Greek Language and Verbal Art*, pp. 92-93; Fanning, *Verbal Aspect in New Testament Greek*, pp. 72-77.

to the use of the present and aorist tense forms in this passage. Secondly, and using Porter's method for clause structure analysis,[49] I shall investigate the possible use of contrasting clause types as a means of grounding in Acts 27. Last of all, I shall turn to the author's use of transitivity patterns and provide an interpretation of my findings.

a. *The Discourse Use of the Aorist and Present Tense Forms in Acts 27*
The use of tense-aspect morphology to mark grounding has been a subject of recent study in a variety of languages and genres.[50] Fleischmann, for example, has noted that the ways that verbal forms perform when used in language is by no means exhausted by their 'basic grammatical functions', and suggests that discourse-pragmatic considerations are essential for an adequate understanding of tense forms.[51] Stanley Porter's and Buist Fanning's volumes on verbal aspect in the Greek of the New Testament both include a brief discussion of the discourse function(s) of aspect, based largely on Stephen Wallace's 1982 essay 'Figure and Ground' (see my n. 3).[52] It seems appropriate, then, to

49. S.E. Porter, 'Word Order and Clause Structure in New Testament Greek', *FN* 6 (1993), pp. 177-206. In this essay, Porter follows, in large measure, the work of Margaret Berry, *Introduction to Systemic Linguistics*. I. *Systems and Structures* (London: Batsford, 1977), esp. pp. 62-90.

50. See for example the study of the *pretérito imperfecto de subjuntivo* in journalistic Spanish by P. Lunn and T. Cravens, 'A Contextual Reconsideration of the Spanish -ra "Indicative"', in Fleischmann and Waugh (eds.), *Discourse Pragmatics*, pp. 147-78; G. Centineo, 'Tense Switching in Italian: The Alteration between *Passato Prossimo* and *Passato Remoto* in Oral Narratives', in Fleischmann and Waugh (eds.), *Discourse Pragmatics*, pp. 55-85; R.E. Longacre, *The Grammar of Discourse* (New York: Plennum, 1983), p. 27, for a discussion of the use of Hebrew tenses in the Genesis flood narrative.

51. Fleischmann and Waugh, 'Introduction', in Fleischmann and Waugh (eds.), *Discourse Pragmatics*, p. 2.

52. It must be said that Fanning's wholesale adoption of Wallace's scheme is ill-informed given that Fanning's subject is New Testament Greek. Wallace's argument is that '...part of the meaning of the perfective aspect, at least in narration, is to specify major, sequential, foregrounded events, while part of the meaning of the contrasting non-perfective aspects, particularly an imperfective, is to give supportive, background information' (Wallace, 'Figure and Ground', in Hopper [ed.], *Tense–Aspect*, p. 209). Wallace is here making a metalinguistic claim, preceded by examples from Latin, Greek and Zapotec. In his defense of this scheme's validity for the Greek of the New Testament, Fannning offers examples that are unconvincing. Mark 5.1-20 is, among other passages, offered as evidence that the aorist narrates 'main' or 'foreground' events, while the imperfect or present is used to

begin my search for relevant prominence in Acts 27 with a look at what has been designated 'the core of aspect',[53] the aorist–present opposition.

record subsidiary or 'background' ones. But in the Mark passage we could also argue that the aorist is used to set the scene for the two dialogues between the demonized man and Jesus (5.7-10, 18-19) in both of which the present and imperfects dominate. Another climactic point in this passage is 5.15, again built upon the present tense: καὶ ἔρχονται πρὸς τὸν Ἰησοῦν, καὶ θεωροῦσιν τὸν δαιμονιζόμενον καθήμενον ἱματισμένον καὶ σωφρονοῦντα, τὸν ἐσχηκότα τὸν λεγιῶνα, καὶ ἐφοβήθησαν. These events can hardly be said to be 'subsidiary'. Fanning, *Verbal Aspect*, p. 191. In contrast to Fanning, Porter argues that in New Testament Greek, it is the aorist (perfective aspect) that is the 'background tense', Porter, *Verbal Aspect*, p. 92; *idem, Idioms of the Greek New Testament* (Sheffield: Sheffield Academic Press, 1992), p. 23. Among the examples offered by Porter in support of his view is Acts 16.1-5. Porter writes that in this passage, 'aorist tense-forms are used for the narrative events, present tense-forms are used for selected or highlighted events, and the perfect tense-form is reserved for selective mention of a few significant items...' (*Idioms*, p. 23). Even if we accept Porter's interpretation of vv. 1-7, consistency becomes very near impossible in the following verses. In the brief account of Paul's vision of the 'man of Macedonia', Porter's hypothesis would require us to understand 'they tried to go [πορευθῆναι] into Bythinia (6.7) and, immediately following, 'but the Spirit of Jesus did not allow [εἴασεν] them' as a 'narrative event'; further, 'a certain Macedonian man was standing [ἑστὼς]' would be understood as 'significant', and, immediately following, 'and urging [παρακαλῶν] him and saying [λέγων]', as 'selected or highlighted' (16.9); lastly, the words of the Macedonian 'come to Macedonia and help [βοήθησον] us!' (16.9b) would be merely a 'narrative event'. A further difficulty with the application of Porter's theory to Acts 27 lies in the use of the imperfect tense forms in this story, a use indistinguishable from that of the aorist forms. Haenchen called upon A. Debrunner to solve this problem, but the latter was unable to do so. See E. Haenchen '"We" in Acts and the Itinerary', *Journal for Theology and the Church* 1 (1965), p. 93. Porter's and Fanning's treatments of the discourse use of aspect in the Greek of the New Testament are generally helpful and draw attention to a function of verb forms that is consistent in many languages (see above). However, the lack of *text-specific criteria* in both presentations appears to be a serious flaw and seems to question the validity of their proposals. On what basis can we argue (besides the presence of a present or imperfect verb form!) that a clause is foregrounded or 'highlighted'? If we wish to argue that this is an intentional literary strategy by the author, how does this alleged choice(s) relate to his overall theme or aim? How does one instance of foregrounded morphology or syntax cohere with others throughout the text? Without at least a serious attempt at answering these questions, arguing for various degrees of grounding based on contrasting tense-aspects leads inevitably to a distressing circularity.

53. D. Schmidt, 'Verbal Aspect in Greek: Two Approaches', in Porter and

As is the case in the New Testament as a whole, aorist forms predominate over present forms in the shipwreck narrative (88 to 60, or 59.4 per cent to 40.5 per cent of present tense forms). This distribution, however, is reversed in the speeches attributed to Paul, where present tense forms predominate by a 69 per cent to a 31 per cent margin. Before suggesting a possible interpretation of this variation in terms of foregrounding, it is important to note the likely possibility that present tense forms naturally predominate in direct speech. If this possibility is confirmed as a result of studying the rest of the speeches in Acts, the mentioned variation in distribution will require no further explanation.[54] As for the use of the aorist and present tense forms elsewhere in the narrative, it seems clear that the lines between those that are 'narrative events', 'highlighted' and 'significant' (if, indeed, such lines exist) cannot be drawn on the basis of these tense forms alone.[55]

b. *Clause Structure in Acts 27*
As has been noted by Robert Longacre among others, contrasting clause structures are frequently used to mark grounding in a variety of languages.[56] Nevertheless, and in spite of the insights yielded by recent research into foregrounding as discussed above, the studies of clause structure from this angle have been relatively few. Among the possible reasons for this, I venture to suggest, is the strong interest in 'language universals' that Joseph Greenberg's work has created among linguistic

---

Carson (eds.), *Biblical Greek Language and Linguistics* (Sheffield: JSOT Press 1993), p. 72.

54. Thus, Halliday writes: 'prominence...is not significant if the linguistically unpredicted configuration is predictable on other grounds' ('Linguistic Function and Literary Style', p. 118).

55. A few examples are sufficient to bear this out. In vv. 15-16 there are five aorist forms (bold) and three present forms (underlined): **συναρπασθέντος** δὲ τοῦ πλοίου καὶ μὴ <u>δυναμένου</u> <u>ἀντοφθαλμεῖν</u> τῷ ἀνέμῳ **ἐπιδόντες** ἐφερόμεθα. νησίον δέ τι **ὑποδραμόντες** <u>καλούμενον</u> Καῦδα **ἰσχύσαμεν** μόλις περικρατεῖς **γενέσθαι** τῆς σκάφης. My question is, simply, on what basis (apart from the tense-forms themselves) can we argue that 'being seized' is a narrative event, while 'not being able to face the wind' is highlighted? or that 'we were hardly able to control the dinghy' is a narrative event, but '[the ship] was not able to face the wind' is highlighted?; see also, e.g., v. 35.

56. Longacre, *Grammar*, p. 17, who cites examples in Anglo-Saxon, Biblical Hebrew and Trique; Hopper and Thompson, 'Transitivity in Grammar', pp. 280-86.

researches since 1963.[57] To the degree that one focuses on hypo-
thesizing linguistic 'laws' of universal application across languages,
careful attention to linguistic usage in individual texts must recede to
the background. In the light of this—I would argue—unfortunate
development in recent linguistic thought, students of New Testament
Greek have grounds for a measured optimism. Stanley Porter's essay
'Word Order and Clause Structure in New Testament Greek' (see n. 49
above)[58] must be considered a success on at least two counts. First, it
has achieved its stated purpose, namely, to 'clear the ground' for
further specialized projects on the subject. Secondly, it has made a
significant contribution to the ongoing debunking of Greenberg's
'universals'.[59]

Three of Porter's conclusions seem particularly insightful. First,
given the fact that Greek need not grammaticalize all of the clause

57. J.H. Greenberg, 'Some Universals of Grammar with Particular Reference to
the Order of Meaningful Elements', in Greenberg (ed.), *Universals of Language*,
(Cambridge: MIT Press, 2nd edn, 1963), pp. 73-113. Greenberg's 45 universals
were based on samples of thirty languages with which the author had 'some previous acquaintance or for which a reasonably adequate grammar was available to
[him]' (p. 59).

58. See also M.E. Davison, 'New Testament Greek Word Order', *Literary and
Linguistic Computing* 4.1 (1989), esp. pp. 24ff; I. Larsen, 'Word Order and Relative Prominence in New Testament Greek', *Notes on Translation* 5.1 (1991),
pp. 29-34. Davison's essay is of very limited usefulness, due to the very limited
data incorporated into his study. Davison includes only main clauses with an indicative verb which have an explicit subject other than a pronoun. In the two pages
that Larsen dedicates to clause structure, the writer limits himself to rather generic
comments on the findings of other scholars.

59. See, e.g., Porter's n. 22 in regard to universals 18 and 19. Greenberg
affirmed that, given the six possible permutations of clause order, the three which
never occur or at least are extremely rare are VOS, OVS, and OSV. Further,
Greenberg's universal #1 asserted that 'in declarative sentences with nominal subject and object, the dominant order is almost always one in which the subject precedes the object' (Greenberg, 'Universals', p. 61). This has been refuted with
convincing evidence from several languages. See A. Romero-Figueroa, 'OSV as
the Basic Word Order in Warao', *Linguistics* 23 (1985), pp. 105-21; D.C. Derbyshire and G.K. Pullum, 'Object Initial Languages', *International Journal of American Linguistics* 47.3 (1981), pp. 192-214. Both these essays explicitly address and
refute Greenberg in regard to his first 'universal', Derbyshire and Pullum arguing
that the geographical spread of SVO order is due first and foremost to the colonial
expansion of speakers of European languages, rather than to the alleged 'natural-
ness' of such an order (p. 193).

constituents (including subject, object and verb), the structure of the Greek clause must be formulated on the basis of the elements that are explicit in each instance.[60] This fundamental fact has been largely ignored, with predictable results, in many of the older Greek grammars. Secondly, the predicate is the fundamental or basic element of the Greek clause.[61] Thirdly, Porter notes that, in Philippians, the subject is the most significant element that can be introduced in order to mark or highlight a clause.[62]

My study of clause structure in Acts 27 strongly confirms the first and second points above. In the shipwreck narrative the predicate element (i.e. a verb form) is the only clause constituent that is present in every instance, in both independent and dependent clauses. When the object constituent is grammaticalized, it follows the predicate in a majority of instances.[63] My findings in regard to the subject constituent, however, are at variance with the (mostly) Philippians data as presented in Porter's essay. This confirms Porter's expressed suspicion,[64] and is likely a result of the characteristic idiosyncrasies of the narrative genre. Among these idiosyncrasies is the high priority given to the distinction

60. Porter, 'Word Order', pp. 187, 190.
61. Porter, 'Word Order', p. 192. However, Porter's data may need to be revised. On page 193, for example, speaking of participial clauses with a predicate structure, he cites Phil. 3:4, **καίπερ ἐγὼ ἔχων πεποίθησιν καὶ ἐν σαρκί. εἴ τις δοκεῖ ἄλλος πεποιθέναι ἐν σαρκί, ἐγὼ μᾶλλον**, which is actually a subject-predicate-object structure. See Porter's footnote 65, p. 193.
62. Porter, 'Word Order', pp. 200-201.
63. Independent clauses: P-C [19x] as in 27:10, θεωρῶ ὅτι μετὰ ὕβρεως καὶ πολλῆς ζημίας…; C-P [5x, though 39b is a split construction] as in 27.18b, τῇ ἑξῆς ἐκβολὴν ἐποιοῦντο; Dependent clauses: (1) Infinitival: P-C [6x] as in 27.21, κερδῆσαί τε τὴν ὕβριν ταύτην καὶ τὴν ζημίαν; C-P [3x] as in 27.3 ἐπιμελείας τυχεῖν; (2) Participial: P-C [20x] as in 27.17 χαλάσαντες τὸ σκεῦος; C-P [8x] as in 27.33, τεσσαρεσκαιδεκάτην σήμερον ἡμέραν προσδοκῶντες; (3) Other (dependent clauses with finite verbs) P-C [1x], 27:25 λελάληταί μοι; C-P [2x] as in 27.42 ἵνα τοὺς δεσμώτας ἀποκτείνωσιν.
64. Porter, 'Word Order', p. 203. Unfortunately, Porter's essay gives no exact figures in regard to the subject constituent in his text, and states only that 'the subject constituent is apparently not used in the majority of clauses' (p. 194). If one is to argue that 'the subject is the most important element that an author can introduce to mark a given structure' (p. 200), a more precise summary of the data is required. Longacre also points to the likely possibility that word order and clause structure differ from genre to genre within a language (*Grammar*, pp. 1, 17). See also Nida, Louw, Snyman and Cronje (eds.), *Style and Discourse*, p. 137.

of participants, a factor that acquires particular relevance in Acts 27, as I will show below.

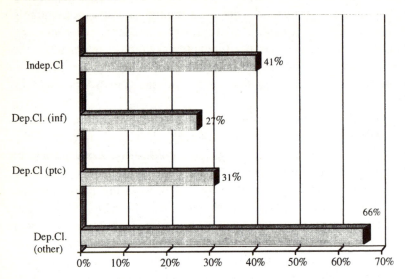

Figure 1. Distribution of grammaticalized subjects
within various clause types in Acts 27

Besides the greater number of grammaticalized subjects in the ship-wreck narrative, my findings for Acts 27 differ from Porter's Philippi-ans data in other related respects. When the subject is explicit in Philippians, Porter notes that the strong tendency is for it to be placed first in the cause,[65] and that its placement in second or third place (after predicate and/or object) seems to indicate a proportionate decrease in emphasis.[66] In the shipwreck story, however, explicit subjects at initial and non-initial positions are nearly equal in number, in both dependent and independent clauses.[67] If these findings are shown to be consistent throughout Luke–Acts and other narrative texts, Greenberg's universal #1 would be brought further into question (see note 50).

65. Porter, 'Word Order', p. 188.
66. Porter, 'Word Order', p. 201.
67. Placement of explicit subjects within the clause in Acts 27:

	Subject Initial	Non-Subj. Initial
Indep. Clauses	13	12
Dep. Clauses (inf)	3	3
Dep. Clauses (ptc.)	10	10
Dep. Clauses (other)	6	2

In summary, both the number of explicit subjects and their even placement in initial and non-initial positions within the clause make any interpretation of their possible 'highlighting' role difficult to prove in the shipwreck narrative.[68] Though Porter's essay has done much to encourage and lay the foundation for further research into clause structure in the Greek of the New Testament, a word of criticism seems in order. As is the case with Mukarovsky's essay discussed above, the reader of Porter's article is left wondering whether the norms from which (for instance) an explicit subject is a departure are set up locally by the writers of individual texts or, rather, extend to the language as a whole. In section III.2, for example, Porter comments on the use of the clause initial explicit subject to mark a new subject in Philippians 2, or a 'heightened' statement by Paul in 3.13. Yet, the overall aim that is apparently being pursued by Porter is to discover 'marked' structures in the language of the New Testament as a whole.[69] It seems to me that the fundamental problem at this point is one of vague usage of a difficult term. The word 'marked' is being used by Porter as synonymous with highlighted, emphasized and other related terms, all akin to 'foregrounded'. But to make such 'markedness'[70] claims for the

68. See also Levinsohn's findings in regard to 'emphatic' fronted subjects in Acts, cited in Reed 'Identifying Theme', p. 76.

69. See Porter, 'Word Order', pp. 190, 203.

70. Markedness theory was pioneered by N. Trubetzkoy and R. Jakobson in the 1920's. The central notion behind this method of phonological and grammatical analysis is based on the observation that phonemes, cases, or verbal aspects have what are known as distinctive features (in the case of phonemes) or conceptual features (in the case of cases or verbal aspects, for example), which define their minimal semantic content. This semantic content is gleaned from all the uses of the item in question, which is then said to be 'marked' or 'unmarked' in relation to the particular feature that defines it. See R. Jakobson, 'Zur Struktur des russischen Verbums', 'Shifters, Verbal Categories and the Russian Verb', in Roman Jakobson, *Roman Jakobson: Selected Writings,* II (The Hague: Mouton, 1971), pp. 3-16, 130-47; E. Battistella, *Markedness: The Evaluative Superstructure of Language* (Albany: The State University of New York, 1990), p. 33; E. Andrews, *Markedness Theory: The Union of Asymmetry and Semiosis in Language* (Durham: Duke University Press, 1990), p. 137. A significant departure from previous work in markedness theory was brought about by Greenberg and Comrie, who defined 'marked' not in terms of a feature, but on the basis of such 'criteria' or 'characteristics' (Greenberg uses these words interchangeably) as being less frequent, or having greater morphological bulk. J.H. Greenberg, *Language Universals* (The Hague: Mouton, 1966), esp. pp. 26ff; B. Comrie, *Aspect* (Cambridge: Cambridge Univer-

language of the New Testament as a whole seems at best extremely
difficult to prove. Further, if an exegete wishes to argue that a particular
linguistic item (e.g. an explicit, fronted subject) is being used in
Philippians to highlight a key protagonist, such an argument must be
supported by a discussion of the author's 'highlighting strategy' elsewhere *in that text,* and of how that strategy relates to his aim(s) in
writing. This is, as I pointed out above, Halliday's central thesis in his
analysis of Golding's *The Inheritors.*

c. *Foregrounded Transitivity Patterns in the Shipwreck Narrative*
Hopper and Thompson's essay 'Transitivity in Grammar and Discourse' did much to highlight the crucial role that transitivity systems
play in many of the world's languages. Working with a revised version
of the classic notion of transitivity in western linguistics, the authors
present a scale of transitivity features such as 'participants', 'volition-
ality', and 'agency', as a means of gauging clauses in terms of their
high or low transitivity. Secondly, Hopper and Thompson argue convincingly that it is at the discourse, rather than at the sentence or clause
level, where the main function of transitivity is found. Their data point
to high transitivity clauses being used consistently to foreground material in texts, while low transitivity clauses carry out the backgrounding
function.[71]

As I mentioned above, the notion of transitivity also plays a central
role in Michael Halliday's functional grammar. For Halliday, however,
the term has two distinct interpretations. According to the first and
more generic interpretation, the system of transitivity includes the various types of processes that exist in a language, together with the structures that realize these processes. A process consists of three basic
elements: the process itself, participants and circumstances. The second
and narrower interpretation of transitivity is roughly equivalent to the
classic notion as presented by Hopper and Thompson, though in Halliday's scheme it is limited to his 'material processes'.[72] In this process

sity Press, 1976), pp. 111-22. Porter follows the latter model of markedness theory.
    71. Hopper and Thompson, 'Transitivity in Grammar', p. 284.
    72. Halliday, *Functional Grammar*, pp. 101-105. Halliday affirms that the tra-
ditional understanding of transitivity is an accurate interpretation, so long as it is
understood (1) that the concept applies to clauses rather than to individual verb
forms, and (2) that it is only applicable to certain clauses, namely, material process
clauses.

type, the elements of actor (subject) and process (predicate) are obligatory, and that of goal (object) is optional. When the element of goal is present (i.e. A is doing something to G) the transitive interpretation applies.

Of particular relevance for my present purpose, however, is Halliday's notion of *ergativity*, a somewhat more abstract explanation of the transitive/intransitive concept. In both the classic notion of transitivity and Halliday's 'narrow' definition of it, the question being asked of a clause is 'does the process in question extend beyond the actor to a goal?' Here the variable is *extension*. In Halliday's ergativity model, however, the question being asked is 'is the process in question being brought about from within or from outside?' The variable in this case is *causation*. In the ergative analysis, the nucleus of the clause is made up of process and medium, as in

Ergative Interpretation	**Transitive Interpretation**
τὸ πλοῖον ἀνήχθη	τὸ πλοῖον ἀνήχθη
The ship (medium) sailed (process)	The ship (actor) sailed (process)

where the medium is the key element, the entity through the medium of which the process occurs. In addition to the medium, there may be another participant functioning as a cause external to the medium, which Halliday calls the agent, as in

Ergative Interpretation	**Transitive Interpretation**
ἀνήχθημεν τὸ πλοῖον	ἀνήχθημεν τὸ πλοῖον
we (agent) sailed (process) the ship (medium)	we (actor) sailed (process) the ship (goal)

The process may, then, be represented either as self-engendering, in which case there is no external agent (non-ergative clause) or as brought about from the outside, in which case the presence of an agent is obligatory. It is important to note that, in reality, there may well have been an external agent in such processes as *the plant withered* (e.g. the sun's rays), or *the window broke* (e.g. a football); nevertheless, non-ergative clauses represent these processes as self-engendered, or, more accurately, make no reference to causation.[73] With this framework in place, we now return to the shipwreck narrative.

---

73. In Jakobsonian markedness theory, we would say that non-ergative clauses are unmarked as to the feature [causation], or [Ø Causation], while ergative clauses are marked as to the same feature, or [+ Causation].

In the analysis of narrative, the number, means of introduction and roles assigned to participants acquire an importance unparalleled in the study of other genres. In Acts 27, human participants may be divided into two groups: (1) primary: the 'we' participant and Paul; and (2) secondary: Julius, and the soldiers and ship's crew, often referred to simply by means of third-person plural verb suffixes.

One of the most striking features of this story is the peculiar use made of the 'we' participant. Beginning at the start of the narrative, it appears regularly through to 27: 8, reappearing at vv. 15 to 29, and surfacing one last time at v. 37. Its referent in the beginning clauses could be the captive group of Paul's companions (esp. vv. 2 and 6). However, from v. 7 on, 'we' is clearly inclusive of the totality of the ship's passengers and crew, for it is the whole ship which 'the wind does not allow to move forward' (v. 7), 'pass[es] Crete with difficulty' (v. 8), '[is] being carried along' (v. 15), '[is] violently storm-tossed' (v. 18), etc. A close reading of all the 'we' clauses reveals that the fundamental feature they have in common is not primarily their referent,[74] but rather, the sense of powerlessness created by their non-ergative structures. That is, the processes depicted in these clauses are represented without reference to an external agent, and therefore the 'we' participant is consistently perceived as a passive medium, who is literally carried along by the course of events, rather than affecting them in any way. The cumulative effect of these clauses is accurately summarized by 27.15b: ἐπιδόντες ἐφερόμεθα, 'having given way, we were being carried'.[75]

---

74. Haenchen expressed uncertainty as to the referent of 'we': 'is it Paul's group or all the passengers?' ('"We" in Acts', p. 93.)

75. This cumulative effect is best appreciated as a result of a continuous reading of these clauses: Ὡς δὲ ἐκρίθη τοῦ ἀποπλεῖν ἡμᾶς (27.1)...ἀνήχθημεν (2)...κατήχθημεν (3)...ἀναχθέντες ὑπεπλεύσαμεν τὴν Κύπρον (4)...διαπλεύσαντες κατήλθομεν εἰς Μύρα (5)...βραδυπλοοῦντες καὶ μόλις γενόμενοι κατὰ τὴν Κνίδον... ὑπεπλεύσαμεν τὴν Κρήτην (7)...μόλις τε παραλεγόμενοι αὐτὴν ἤλθομεν εἰς τόπον τινὰ (8)...ἐπιδόντες ἐφερόμεθα. (15)...νησίον δέ τι ὑποδραμόντες... ἰσχύσαμεν μόλις περικρατεῖς γενέσθαι τῆς σκάφης (16)...σφοδρῶ` δὲ χειμαζομένων ἡμῶν (18)...τοῦ σῴζεσθαι ἡμᾶς (20)...διαφερομένων ἡμῶν... (27)...φοβούμενοί τε μή που κατὰ τραχεῖς τόπους ἐκπέσωμεν (29)...ἤμεθα δὲ αἱ πᾶσαι ψυχαὶ (37): 'When it was decided that we set sail...we sailed...we sailed down to...we sailed under the shelter of Cyprus...having sailed through (Cilicia and Pamphilia) we came to Myra...navigating slowly and passing with difficulty in front of Knidos...we sailed under the shelter of Crete...passing by it with difficulty,

In stark contrast, soldiers and crew (often simply 'they') appear from beginning to end involved in unflagging and assiduous activity, beginning immediately after Paul advises them not to sail from 'Beautiful Havens' (27.10). Paul's warning notwithstanding, 'the majority' made the decision to set sail from there (v. 12), and appear from that point on enmeshed in a struggle that spirals downward from sailing in rough weather (vv. 13-17), to seeking to save the ship at the expense of the ship's gear (v. 18), to attempting to escape (v. 30), to seeking to save the ship at the expense of the grain cargo (v. 38), to finally trying to run the ship aground onto a beach (v. 39). It is interesting to note, first, that the actions of 'they' are the result of their 'supposing to have achieved *their* purpose' (v. 13); secondly, that although the vast majority of these clauses are ergative, with 'they' playing the role of a highly dynamic agent, all their actions lead eventually to failure.[76] Verses 15b and 17, for example, contain respectively a clause typical of each participant: ἐπιδόντες...(v. 15b) predicated of 'we', and χαλάσαντες τὸ σκεῦος...

we came to a certain place...having given way, we were being carried...running under the shelter of a certain island...we were hardly able to exercise control... being violently storm-tossed...[all hope was abandoned] that we be saved...being carried through...fearing lest we may run aground in a rocky coast...we were in all [276] souls'. It is important to note that the consistent non-ergativity of the 'we' clauses is not due to the prisoner status of their referent. I have already shown that the referent of 'we' in the story is for the most part the totality of the ship's passengers and crew (as in v. 37); secondly, v. 16 has 'we' being 'unable to maintain control of the dinghy', an unnecessary statement, if prisoners on a ship were always inactive; thirdly, note the variant reading for v. 19, which has the 'we' participant doing the jettisoning. In connection with this textual variant, William Ramsay pointed out that such an action by prisoners on a ship was by no means unthinkable. W. Ramsay, *Saint Paul the Traveller and the Roman Citizen* (London: Hodder & Stoughton, 1896), p. 332; see also B. Rapske, 'Acts, Travel and Shipwreck', in Gempf and Gill (eds.), *The Book of Acts in its Graeco-Roman Setting*, pp. 32-33.
76. ἄραντες ἆσσον (27.13)...ἦν ἄραντες βοηθείαις ἐχρῶντο ὑποζωννύντες τὸ πλοῖον...χαλάσαντες τὸ σκεῦος (17)...τῇ ἑξῆς ἐκβολὴν ἐποιοῦντο(18)... αὐτό-χειρες τὴν σκευὴν τοῦ πλοίου ἔρριψαν (19)...βολίσαντες (2x, 28)...ἐκ πρύμνης ῥίψαντες ἀγκύρας τέσσαρας (29)...χαλασάντων τὴν σκάφην (30)...ἀπέκοψαν οἱ στρατιῶται τὰ σχοινία τῆς σκάφης καὶ εἴασαν αὐτὴν ἐκπεσεῖν (32)...καὶ αὐτοὶ προσελάβοντο τροφῆς (36)...ἐκούφιζον τὸ πλοῖον ἐκβαλλόμενοι τὸν σῖτον εἰς τὴν θάλασσαν. (38)...καὶ τὰς ἀγκύρα᾿ περιελόντες εἴων εἰς τὴν θάλασσαν, ἅμα ἀνέντες τὰς ζευκτηρίας τῶν πηδαλίων, καὶ ἐπάραντες τὸν ἀρτέμωνα τῇ πνεούσῃ κατεῖχον εἰς τὸν αἰγιαλόν. (40)...ἐπέκειλαν τὴν ναῦν (41).

(v. 17b) with 'they' as agent. Yet, the same is concluded about each: we/they *were being carried.* The role of Julius in the shipwreck narrative is a somewhat ambiguous one. From the outset, he is inclined to act kindly toward Paul, allowing him the privilege of obtaining assistance from friends while at Sidon (27.3). At a crucial juncture, however, Julius is swayed by the resoluteness of the ship's captain and navigator to set sail, ignoring Paul's warning about the approaching winter season (v. 11). From that point on the focus of the story is placed squarely on the ship's crew, and Julius does not appear again until the end, when he prevents the killing of the prisoners, and commands all who are able to swim to safety (vv. 43-44). Though the nine clauses in which Julius appears as participant are largely ergative in their structures,[77] the 'affectedness' of the mediums is rather low in most instances.[78]

Before addressing the nature and significance of Paul's role in the story, reference must be made to a set of participants that is notable in terms of the amount of space they occupy in the narrative. I am referring to the 24 inanimate participants that range from the ship and the port of Beautiful Havens, to various natural elements such as the wind (3 times) and the waves.[79] Except for one (μὴ προσεῶντος ἡμᾶς τοῦ

77. φιλανθρώπως τε ὁ Ἰούλιος τῷ Παύλῳ χρησάμενος (27.3a); ἐπέτρεψεν πρὸς τοὺς φίλους πορευθέντι ἐπιμελείας τυχεῖν (27.3b); κἀκεῖ εὑρὼν ὁ ἑκατοντάρχης πλοῖον Ἀλεξανδρῖνον (6a); ἐνεβίβασεν ἡμᾶς εἰς αὐτό (6b); ὁ δὲ ἑκατοντάρχης τῷ κυβερνήτῃ καὶ τῷ ναυκλήρῳ μᾶλλον ἐπείθετο (11); ὁ δὲ ἑκατοντάρχης βουλόμενος διασῶσαι τὸν Παῦλον (43a); ἐκώλυσεν αὐτοὺς τοῦ βουλήματος (43b); ἐκέλευσέν τε τοὺς δυναμένους κολυμβᾶν...(43c); καὶ τοὺς λοιποὺς οὓς μὲν ἐπὶ σανίσιν οὓς δὲ ἐπί τινων τῶν ἀπὸ τοῦ πλοίου (44)

78. This is one of Hopper and Thompson's parameters that is applicable to Halliday's model. Thus, the affectedness of Paul in v. 27b above ([Julius] allowed [him] to obtain help) is much lower than the affectedness of the 'we' participant in v. 6b ([Julius] placed us on board). It seems clear to me that other parameters suggested in Hopper and Thompson's essay (e.g. kinesis) may be used with profit to refine Halliday's ergative/non-ergative distinction. A comparison of the ergativity of the clauses in the previous paragraph ('they' clauses) with that of the clauses in which Julius participates points to the need for such a refinement. See also Hasan, *Linguistics, Language, and Verbal Art*, pp. 45-46; Halliday, 'Linguistic Funtion', pp. 127-28, where Halliday discusses a notion akin to affectedness.

79. πλοίῳ (27.2); τοὺς ἀνέμους (4); πλοῖον (6); τοῦ ἀνέμου (7); Ἱκανοῦ δὲ χρόνου (9); τοῦ πλοὸς (9); τὴν νηστείαν (9); τὸν πλοῦν (10); τοῦ λιμένος (12); νότου (13); ἄνεμος τυφωνικὸς (14); τοῦ πλοίου (15); μήτε δὲ ἡλίου μήτε ἄστρων (20); χειμῶνός τε οὐκ ὀλίγου (20); ἐλπὶς πᾶσα (20); Πολλῆς τε ἀσιτίας (21);

ἀνέμου, v. 7), all these clauses are clearly non-ergative and encode for the most part processes of being. Lastly, the role of Paul must be considered. Though from ch. 13 onwards Paul is clearly *the* protagonist of Acts, his role clearly reaches its climactic point in the final section of the book (Acts 21–28), where his arrest and imprisonment are related in detail. In what amounts to nearly one fourth of Acts (23.5%),[80] the writer recounts Paul's seizure and appearance before a Roman tribune and the Jewish council (21.22–23.11), his escape from a Jewish conspiracy to kill him (23.12-35), the trial before Felix (24.1-26), his appearance before Festus and appeal to Caesar (25.1-12), and his defense before Herod Agrippa (25.13–26.32). The shipwreck story represents the last great episode before Paul's arrival in Rome, where he will appear before the emperor and fulfill Jesus' last commission to him: ὁ κύριος εἶπεν, Θάρσει, ὡς γὰρ διεμαρτύρω τὰ περὶ ἐμοῦ εἰς Ἰερουσαλὴμ οὕτω σε **δεῖ καὶ εἰς Ῥώμην μαρτυρῆσαι** (23.11).

Paul's participation in the shipwreck narrative is essentially limited to four separate addresses, all of which convey direction to the ship's crew and passengers for the safe completion of the journey.[81] The nature and significance of Paul's role, however, becomes clear when we look at the clauses wherein he himself is a participant, that is, a subject in the traditional sense, or an agent or medium in Halliday's ergative/non-ergative model. In these 12 clauses Paul's activity centers on communicating to the ship's crew the necessary conditions for a safe journey, and encouraging all aboard the ship with the thought of God's protection.[82] Of particular significance is Paul's second and longest address in vv. 21-26, which comes immediately after 'all hope of salvation was abandoned':

ἀποβολὴ γὰρ ψυχῆς (22); τεσσαρεσκαιδεκάτη νὺξ (27); ἡμέρα (33); ἡμέρα (39); ἡ μὲν πρῷρα (41); ἡ δὲ πρύμνα (41); βουλὴ (42).

80. Maddox, *The Purpose of Luke–Acts*, p. 66. Maddox notes that the section dedicated to 'Paul the prisoner' is slightly longer than that dedicated to 'Paul the missionary'.

81. 27.10, 21-26, 31, 33-34.

82. παρήνει ὁ Παῦλος λέγων αὐτοῖς (27.9b-10a); θεωρῶ ὅτι μετὰ ὕβρεως καὶ πολλῆς ζημίας...(10); σταθεὶς ὁ Παῦλος ἐν μέσῳ αὐτῶν εἶπεν (21); παραινῶ ὑμᾶς εὐθυμεῖν (22); πιστεύω γὰρ τῷ θεῷ (25); εἶπεν ὁ Παῦλος τῷ ἑκατοντάρχῃ (31); παρεκάλει ὁ Παῦλος ἅπαντας (33); παρακαλῶ ὑμᾶς μεταλαβεῖν τροφῆς (34); εἴπας δὲ ταῦτα (35a); καὶ λαβὼν ἄρτον (35b); εὐχαρίστησεν τῷ θεῷ (35c); κλάσας ἤρξατο ἐσθίειν (35d).

Men! in order to have avoided the present damage and loss it would have been necessary to listen to me and not have sailed from Crete. Now I urge you to take courage, for there shall be no loss of life, though the ship itself will be lost. For this night appeared to me an angel of the God to whom I belong and whom I worship, who said to me: 'Do not be afraid Paul! It is necessary that you appear before Caesar, and God has graciously given you all those who sail with you'. Therefore, cheer up men! for I believe God, and that it shall be just as He said to me. It is necessary that we run aground on some island.

Three points made in this speech are essential for an adequate understanding of the shipwreck story. First, the angelic oracle affirms that 'it is necessary' for Paul to stand before Caesar (cf. Acts 23.11), one of three instances of the impersonal verb δεῖν in these five verses alone. The fondness of the author of Luke–Acts for this verb has been a subject of specialized study in recent years, and has often been explained in light of what appears to be one of his favorite themes in the work, namely, the unstoppable unfolding of God's sovereign plan.[83] Secondly, because of Paul's presence on the vessel, the lives of all his fellow travelers will be spared. Lastly, Paul's response to the oracle is simply to believe God, and to encourage all to do likewise.

In the light of the above, it seems fair to say that the literary function of Paul's role in the shipwreck narrative is not that of an agent in the ergativity sense of the word (his only action in Acts 27 is that of breaking bread!),[84] but rather, that of an interpreter, a Hermes-like figure (cf. Acts 14.12) who understands (θεωρῶ, v. 10) and elucidates events from a divine perspective. In the light of God's plan as revealed in vv. 21-26, certain things are 'necessary', and the only proper human response is to believe and await their unfolding. Human attempts to resist God's plan are, therefore, irrevocably bound to fail.

---

83. Luke–Acts has 65.5% of the instances of δεῖν in the New Testament. On the theme of 'necessity' in Luke–Acts, John Squires writes, 'Inherent in the life and passion of Jesus and in the missionary deeds of the apostles, there is a necessity which had been foreordained by Jesus. Juxtaposed along this theme of necessity is the role of human agents in carrying out the plan of God; some may oppose this plan, but those who are obedient to the will of God play key roles in God's plan'. J.T. Squires, *The Plan of God in Luke–Acts* (SNTSMS, 76; Cambridge: Cambridge University Press, 1993), p. 3; see also pp. 4-6; Cadbury, *Making*, p. 303; Haenchen, *Acts*, p. 159 n. 8; C.H. Cosgrove 'The divine ΔΕΙ in Luke-Acts', *NovT* 26 (1984), pp. 168-90.

84. But see his more active role after landing in Malta.

It is my contention that this theme is embodied in the author's fore-grounding scheme in the shipwreck narrative. In their seminal essay referred to above, Hopper and Thompson note that narrative story lines are usually carried by people who intentionally initiate events.[85] In Halliday's terms, it is agents who are represented as bringing about events in ergative clauses, while their absence in non-ergative clauses leaves the question of causation unanswered. In the shipwreck story, against the background of the non-agentive participants ('we', Paul, and the 23 inanimate participants), the author foregrounds the highly dynamic 'they' agent who appears to be actively involved in the shaping of events. The resolve of the ship's crew and captain to sail is strong enough to sway Julius, who from that point until the end of the narrative fades into the background. As the story progresses, however, the utter futility of the sailors' efforts is revealed, as the ship begins to drift, helplessly carried by wind and waves. The conclusion of the narrative sees the safe rescue of all the ship's passengers and crew at the expense of the ship and its cargo, in strict fulfillment of the divine message conveyed to Paul. Thus the writer utilizes the syntax of Greek to work out the theme of the supremacy of divine will and necessity as revealed in vv. 21-25.

At the outset of the present section, I expressed confidence that modern linguistic analysis would be shown to be a valuable tool in both the study of Acts as literature, and the investigation of its purpose in particular. Although the shipwreck narrative is, admittedly, a very small fragment of the vast work that is Luke–Acts, I believe it is large and stylistically varied enough to serve as an adequate indicator of the validity of these claims. In regard to the first issue, I hope to have shown that a solid understanding of modern linguistics is essential for the full appreciation *and* appraisal of a literary work. Without grounding our claims regarding such issues as the 'theme' of Luke–Acts on a careful study of the language system and the author's choices in that system, one scholar's guess may be as good as that of the next.[86] Concerning my second claim, the linguistic analysis of foregrounding is not likely to add new theories to the long and prolific discussion of the purpose of Acts. Its value resides, rather, in its role as a relatively objective test of the plausibility of such theories. If we accept that the meaning of

85. Hopper and Thompson, 'Transitivity', p. 286.

86. See on this R. Hasan 'Linguistics and the Study of Literary Texts', *Etudes de Linguistique Appliquée* 5 (1967), p. 107.

such clauses as δόξαντες τῆς προθέσεως κεκρατηκέναι (27.13), or διαφερομένων ἡμῶν ἐν τῷ Ἀδρίᾳ (27.27), is determined by their function in the larger context of Acts 27, and that the story as a whole has been shaped artfully and intentionally by the writer to produce a specific effect in his readers, then any theory of the purpose of this work must be tied, in one way or another, to a type of linguistic analysis similar to the one I have proposed in the present paper. Thus, if my conclusions in regard to foregrounding in the shipwreck narrative are accepted and are found confirmed in the rest of Acts, Squires' proposal in regard to the purpose of Luke–Acts[87] would find fresh support from a new angle, while Haenchen's would certainly become more difficult to accept.[88]

5. *Some Suggestions for the Translation of Foregrounding: From Hellenistic Greek to Modern Castillian Spanish*

In a very recent study of transitivity in Spanish, José Mᵃ García-Miguel offers the following trenchant criticism of Hopper and Thompson's essay discussed above:

> It must be recognized that transitivity cannot be determined by means of a mere counting of properties on a scale (whichever scale that may be), that the various parameters each have different 'weight', *and that that relative 'weight' may vary from one language to another* (emphasis mine).[89]

Of the three objections to Hopper and Thompson's thesis raised by García-Miguel, the last two seem particularly well grounded. Although many of their insights are extremely valuable, the reader of Hopper and Thompson's essay is certainly left with the impression that all that is involved in gauging the transitivity of a clause is counting the number

---

87. Namely, the edification of Christian believers through an exposition of God's providence in the face of human opposition. Squires, *Plan*, pp. 191-92.

88. Haenchen's proposal was essentially a rehashing of the 'apology before the Roman powers' thesis. Haenchen, *Acts*, pp. 90-110.

89. ['Habra que admitir que la transitividad no puede determinarse mediante un simple recuento de rasgos en una serie (sea cual sea ésta), que los diferentes parámetros tienen distinto "peso", y que este "peso" relativo puede variar de una lengua a otra.'] J.Mᵃ García-Miguel, *Transitividad y Complementación Preposicional en Español* (Verba, 40; Santiago: Universidade de Santiago de Compostela, 1995), p. 57.

of 'parameters' present in it, without discriminating, for example, between 'kinesis' and 'punctuality'. García-Miguel does well, therefore, to point us to the unequal 'weight' that the various properties carry within a language, as well as to the fact that the relative value of individual parameters varies from one language to another. This last point must be extended to foregrounding as a whole, whether it be realized by transitivity patterns as is the case in the shipwreck narrative, or contrasting tense–aspect morphology. Having studied the nature and function of foregrounded structures in the Greek of Acts, the translator must turn his attention to the receptor language system, and determine which linguistic structures therein (if any) are functionally analogous to those in the original. Thus Nida says,

> In view of the fact that we cannot match rhetorical forms, it is essential that careful consideration be given to the equivalent rhetorical functions, for these functions can in large measure be matched if one bears in mind carefully the respective degree of impact and appeal in the source and receptor texts. The question is basically 'what is the function of the rhetorical feature or features?' ... Though the features may not be universal, the functions are, for all languages have devices for such functions as emphasis, marking similarities and contrasts, foregrounding and backgrounding... [90]

Though the 'universality' of foregrounding has not yet been demonstrated, its presence in Spanish texts of various genres has been the subject of several recent studies. The focus of the translator's work may, therefore, narrow down to the particular elements within the Spanish language system that may best 'promote the palpability' of the foregrounding scheme in our text. As I mentioned in the previous section, the core of foregrounding in Acts 27 is the contrast between the ergativity of the 'they' clauses and the comparatively passive role of the rest of the participants in the story. With the Reina-Valera[91] translation as a reference point, I shall now highlight several features of both Spanish and Greek that may be profitably exploited in our translation task.

(1) As is the case in Greek, Spanish verb forms are, for the most part, person and number specific. Consequently, the subject constituent is normally absent from the clause, and appears grammaticalized as an

---

90. Nida *et al.*, *Style and Discourse*, p. 168.

91. *Sagrada Biblia* (trans. Reina-Valera; Buenos Aires: Sociedades Bíblicas Unidas, 1960).

explicit subject only when its presence is felt to be required, for example, for the introduction of a new participant. A degree of ambiguity is introduced in both languages when non-finite verbs such as participles are used. Such forms as χειμαζομένων and (Reina-Valera's rendering) *siendo combatidos* (27.18), for example, are number, but not person, specific. In vv. 18 and 27, however, the author of Acts wishes to distinguish the 'we' and 'they' participants which appear in the same clauses, and does so by means of an explicit first-person plural subject. The Reina-Valera translators have missed this entirely, and by their choice of the ambiguous participial forms *siendo combatidos* (18) and *siendo llevados* (27) without explicit subjects, the 'they' participant is in effect made the subject of the entire clause in each instance:

Reina-Valera	***UBS GNT⁴* 3rd Edition**
27.18. Pero siendo combatidos por una furiosa tempestad, al siguiente dia empezaron a alijar. [But being besieged by a mighty storm, the following day they began to make a jettisoning.]	σφοδρῶς δὲ χειμαζομένων ἡμῶν τῇ ἑξῆς ἐκβολὴν ἐποιοῦντο,
27.27. Venida la decimocuarta noche, y siendo llevados a través del mar Adriático, a la medianoche los marineros sospecharon que estaban cerca de tierra. [After the fourteenth night came, being carried through the Adriatic sea, at midnight the sailors suspected they were near land.]	Ὡς δὲ τεσσαρεσκαιδεκάτη νὺξ ἐγένετο διαφερομένων ἡμῶν ἐν τῷ Ἀδρίᾳ, κατὰ μέσον τῆς νυκτὸς ὑπενόουν οἱ ναῦται προσάγειν τινὰ αὐτοῖς χώραν.

Participant distinction in the Greek text is further obscured by Reina-Valera at v. 29, where the aorist subjunctive form ἐκπέσωμεν is translated by means of the Spanish infinitive *dar en escollos,* with the same result as above. Lastly, Reina-Valera has made a very poor textual choice at v. 19, and introduces a first-person plural subject where the best available witnesses have none.[92] The end result of these poor choices by Reina-Valera is the partial defusing of the foregrounding scheme employed by the author in the source language.

(2) The wide semantic range of the Greek conjunctions δέ and καί may be exploited with a view to highlighting the contrast between the ergative and non-ergative clauses in the story. Here too the work of the Reina-Valera translators stands in need of improvement. The over-

92. On this issue see my n. 74.

abundance of the *y* conjunction in the Spanish text creates at best a highly unnatural style and tends to obscure the logical and temporal relations in the story. In light of the strong contrast between the 'they' agent and the rest of the participants in our narrative, the translator would be well advised to reserve the rather colorless *y* conjunction for the backgrounded 'we' participant as much as possible, while using disjunctive conjunctions or temporal adverbs to highlight the role of 'they' at key points. Verse 13 is a case in point:

> **Y** (Gk. δέ) soplando una brisa del sur, pareciendoles que ya tenían lo que deseaban, levaron anclas e iban costeando Creta. [And, a south wind blowing, supposing they had what they wanted, they raised the anchors and were sailing along Crete.]

Having also begun vv. 12, 15, 16 and 17 with *y*, the translators are failing to mark an important transition in the story, and have created a highly artificial Spanish. Instead, I suggest the following: 'Entonces,[93] soplando una brisa del sur, y cuando ellos suponían que habían logrado su propósito, levaron anclas e iban costeando Creta' [then, a soft wind blowing, when they thought they had achieved their purpose, they raised the anchors and were sailing along Crete].

(3) Once the translator has decided that transitivity is an issue of particular significance in the shipwreck narrative, the transitivity system in the receptor language must be carefully considered. The recent work of García-Miguel proves invaluable at this point. He notes, for example, that processes that include two participants may be realized in Spanish by any of the following clause structures: SUBJ.-PRED.-DIRECT OBJECT (María compró lotería), SUBJ.-PRED.-INDIRECT OBJECT (el premio le tocó a María) and SUBJ.-PRED.-PREPOSITIONAL CLAUSE (María disfrutó del premio).[94] García-Miguel notes, furthermore, that although these three clause types may all be considered 'transitive' insofar as each makes reference to two participants, the first (that is, SUBJ.-PRED.-D.O.) is by far the most frequent in Spanish. On the basis of his data,[95] the writer argues that the two less frequent

---

93. The adverb *entonces* (then) seems amply justified here in light of both the contrastive role of δέ and the likely adverbial function of the genitive absolute. See also Reina-Valera at v. 42, where δέ is also translated by *entonces*.

94. García-Miguel, *Transitividad*, p. 10.

95. Data taken from 'Archivo de Textos Hispanicos de la Universidad de Santiago' (ARTHUS): narrative: 37%; Essay 18%; Plays/Theater 15%; oral speech 19%; newspapers 11%.

constructions often present 'a certain kind of semantic "deviation" with respect to the transitivity prototype'.[96] García-Miguel then proposes a transitivity continuum for Spanish in which the three clause types mentioned are given values ranging from high to low transitivity, with the SUBJ.-PRED.-PREP.C. standing in a middle position. On the basis of the data presented in this important essay, the translator must carefully consider the choices that the Spanish transitivity system offers when translating a clause such as βοηθείαις ἐχρῶντο ὑποζωννύντες τὸ πλοῖον (27.17), together with the various semantic nuances attached to each choice. In translating the clause just cited, Reina-Valera has chosen a PRED.-PREPOSITIONAL CLAUSE rather than a PRED.-DIRECT OBJECT structure, where either option was equally valid, though, according to García-Miguel, not equal in its transitivity.[97] Such choices must be justified in the light of the use made of transitivity patterns in the source text, and, insofar as this is possible, the relative degree or transitivity discernible in various clauses within the source text must be preserved in the translation.

During the telephone conversation referred to above, Eugene Nida mentioned to me that although the translation of foregrounding is an issue of 'extreme importance', modern translations generally ignore it because they are too strongly tied to previous versions of the biblical text to make stylistic innovations of this nature. Nida's assessment holds true for the Reina-Valera translation. I hope that analyses of the biblical text such as the one carried out in this paper will encourage new translation projects that aim to be lexically, grammatically, as well as stylistically, faithful renderings of the source text.

6. *Conclusion*

I began this essay with a reference to Helen Dry's recent evaluation of the state of the art in foregrounding theory as of 1992. Though a helpful summary in more than one way, Dry's article tended to emphasize

96. García-Miguel, *Transitividad*, p. 96.

97. Thus Reina-Valera, 'usaron de refuerzos para ceñir la nave', instead of 'usaron refuerzos'. García-Miguel has this to say in regard to the semantic value of the Subj-Pred-D.O. structure: 'la relación entre el verbo y la frase nominal que le sirve de argumento deja de der directa para ser mediatizada por la preposicion. La consecuencia en el plano de contenido es que las denotaciones de verbo y complemento se presentan como relativamente mas independientes, obedeciendo a un principio de iconicidad en la sintaxis' (p. 97).

some of the perceived problems in this complex and multi-faceted area of linguistic research. The author's conclusion, not surprisingly, was an attempt at a minimal definition of foregrounding that would be flexible and generic enough to encompass insights from the various disciplines that have contributed to its study:

> In the absence of an agreed upon definition of the central concept, we may identify as foreground whatever textual feature strikes us as prominent.[98]

I hope that my paper has shown the inadequacy of such a definition. Beginning with a rather complete discussion of the multi-faceted theoretical background of foregrounding, I have argued that Michael Halliday's Functional Grammar is a method capable of integrating the most fruitful insights from literary criticism, psycholinguistics and discourse analysis into one coherent theory of foregrounding, as presented in Halliday's analysis of *The Inheritors*. My study of the shipwreck narrative was intended as a demonstration of Halliday's central claim, namely, that foregrounding is linguistic prominence that can be shown to be consistent and motivated in the light of the overall theme(s) of the work in question. Lastly, my concluding sections was aimed at showing that, insofar as foregrounding is part and parcel of the meaning of a text, translators cannot escape its careful consideration without a loss to the receptor language readers.

98. Dry, 'Foregrounding', p. 447.

THE PERFECT TENSE-FORM IN COLOSSIANS: VERBAL ASPECT, TEMPORALITY AND THE CHALLENGE OF TRANSLATION

Thomas R. Hatina

The perfect tense-form, like other verbal forms in the Greek of the New Testament, has recently undergone fresh analysis. Though most contemporary grammarians view verbal tense-forms aspectually, the issue of temporality is far from resolved. Some like S.E. Porter deny that temporality should be seen as a semantic feature, while others like B.M. Fanning still wish to retain a time element. If we are to move forward beyond the initial theoretical stage of the discussion toward a resolution, application of the theories must ensue. This means that verbal tense-forms need to be analyzed within the confines of a given work; that is, the contextual strictures should be pushed beyond adjacent sentences to the entirety of a given literary work. This approach will allow for an informed evaluation of the language user's choice of verbal tense-forms. In this study I examine the function of every perfect tense-form in Colossians in the light of recent research. I argue that the perfect tense-form in this epistle does not inherently convey temporality. Instead, the temporal element is governed by external factors, known as deictic indicators—such as temporal adverbs, references to person, place and time, and discourse features. Depending on the context, the perfect can refer to the past, the present, and even to the future. In fact, it rarely refers to both the past and the present (i.e. a past action with continuing result), contrary to what most grammarians maintain. Many translators have unfortunately operated from the premise that temporality is a semantic feature of tense-forms and consequently limited the importance of deictic indicators. Translators and commentators alike have also largely ignored the potential for temporal tensions when this premise is adopted. The study begins with a brief history of the perfect tense-form and concludes with some reflections on the temporal function of the perfect with reference to exegesis and translation.

1. *A Brief History of the Perfect Tense-Form: From Temporality to Aspect and Back*

Since the nineteenth century the perfect tense-form in the Greek of the New Testament has been understood in three ways, each on the basis of a different grammatical model. The first model was temporally based and described all verbal tense-forms as merely tenses which function to describe a given time referent of an action, in much the same way as English verbs function. The perfect tense-form was described as expressing a past action which has come to completion in the present. The result of the action was often regarded as having enduring significance.[1] Given the compatibility between the function of the English verb and that of the Greek verb, translation posed little problem. The innovative work of G. Curtius, however, caused many grammarians to abandon the time-based model.[2] In its place a new model, which eventually came to be known as the *Aktionsart* model, was proposed. Within this construct the verb was viewed as primarily expressing not 'time of action' but 'kind of action'. While a temporal feature still remained active within the new perspective, it took a subordinate position.[3] In the *Aktionsart* model the action of the verb reflects or corresponds to reality. The perfect tense-form was commonly described as expressing a completed action, incorporating both the punctiliar function of the aorist and the durative function of the present, though the emphasis was allowed some flexibility.[4] Today the vast majority of New Testament exegetes still rely on the *Aktionsart* model. And the

---

1. E.g. G.B. Winer, *A Treatise on the Grammar of New Testament Greek, Regarded as a Sure Basis for New Testament Exegesis* (trans. W.F. Moulton; Edinburgh: T. & T. Clark, 3rd edn, 1882), pp. 331, 338.

2. G. Curtius, *The Greek Verb: Its Structure and Development* (trans. A.S. Wilkins and E.B. England; London: John Murray, 1880).

3. J.H. Moulton, *A Grammar of New Testament Greek*. I. *Prolegomena* (Edinburgh: T. & T. Clark, 3rd edn, 1908), p. 140; A.T. Robertson, *A Grammar of the Greek New Testament in the Light of Historical Research* (Nashville: Broadman Press, 1934), pp. 823-24; H.E. Dana and J.R. Mantey, *A Manual Grammar of the Greek New Testament* (New York: Macmillan, 1957), p. 178; C.F.D. Moule, *An Idiom Book of New Testament Greek* (Cambridge: Cambridge University Press, 2nd edn, 1959), pp. 13-14; F. Blass, A. Debrunner and R.W. Funk, *A Greek Grammar of the New Testament and Other Early Christian Literature* (Chicago: University of Chicago Press, 10th edn, 1961), §342.

4. E.g. Robertson, *A Grammar of the Greek New Testament*, p. 893.

grammars which have advocated this model still remain as key reference works for students and teachers. It goes without saying that translating Greek verbs into English verbs from this perspective proves to be a challenging endeavour. In practical terms, however, the English translations of the New Testament completed within the framework of this second stage of grammatical models (e.g. NASB, NIV) did not exhibit many differences from translations completed within the framework of the first stage (e.g. ASV, KJV).

The third model is based on verbal aspect. Its impetus largely lies in the work of J. Holt which drew attention to the differences between verbal forms and their functions.[5] Holt's structural linguistic approach began to be adopted by grammarians of New Testament Greek some three decades later, most notably J. Mateos and K.L. McKay.[6] More recently two full length monographs on verbal aspect in New Testament Greek have appeared on the scene almost simultaneously.[7] The works by Porter and Fanning not only have contributed significantly to the advancement of this third grammatical model, but have also caused a degree of discussion due to their respective independent approaches.[8] While both agree that verbal aspect is concerned with the language user's viewpoint of how an action is represented by the verbal tense-

---

5.   J. Holt, *Etudes d'aspect* (Acta Jutlandica Aarskrift for Aarhus Universitet, 15.2; Copenhagen: Universitetsførlaget i Aarhus, 1943). Prior to Holt, verbal aspect theory was commonly applied to Slavonic languages.

6.   J. Mateos, *El aspecto verbal en el nuevo testamento* (Madrid: Ediciones Cristiandad, 1977); K.L. McKay, *Greek Grammar for Students: A Concise Grammar of Classical Attic with Special Reference to Aspect in the Verb* (Canberra: Australian National University, 1974); *idem*, 'Syntax in Exegesis', *TynBul* 23 (1972), pp. 39-57; *idem*, 'On the Perfect and Other Aspects in the Greek Non-Literary Papyri', *Bulletin of the Institute of Classical Studies* 27 (1980), pp. 23-49; *idem*, 'The Use of the Ancient Greek Perfect down to the End of the Second Century AD', *Bulletin of the Institute of Classical Studies* 12 (1965), pp. 1-21; *idem*, 'On the Perfect and Other Aspects in New Testament Greek', *NovT* 23 (1981), pp. 289-329; *idem*, 'Time and Aspect in New Testament Greek', *NovT* 34 (1992), pp. 209-28.

7.   S.E. Porter, *Verbal Aspect in the Greek of the New Testament, with Reference to Tense and Mood* (SBG, 1; New York: Peter Lang, 1989); B.M. Fanning, *Verbal Aspect in New Testament Greek* (OTM; Oxford: Clarendon Press, 1990).

8.   See, for example, the essays in S.E. Porter and D.A. Carson (eds.), *Biblical Greek Language and Linguistics: Open Questions in Current Research* (JSNTSup, 80; Sheffield: JSOT Press, 1993); McKay, 'Time and Aspect in New Testament Greek', pp. 209-28; *idem*, *A New Syntax of the Verb in New Testament Greek* (SBG, 5; New York: Peter Lang, 1994), pp. 35-38.

form, as opposed to *Aktionsart* which equates the verbal form with reality, they disagree about the meaning which is conveyed by verbal tense-forms.

Porter argues that verbal tense-forms in every mood only grammaticalize aspect and not temporal or *Aktionsart* features.[9] The most radical part of his approach is the denial that verbal tense-forms inherently convey temporality regardless of contextual features. Porter argues that temporality is conveyed only by deictic indicators.[10] The perfect tense-form, including participles functioning verbally, is described by Porter as that form which the language user uses to express a given state of affairs (i.e. stative aspect). Even if translation into English cannot fully convey this overriding semantic component, Porter urges that this notion must be retained.[11] Porter also views the perfect in terms of planes of discourse.[12] The perfect is described as the frontground plane which is used in a discourse to introduce the most discrete, defined and contoured elements, as opposed to the background plane of the aorist which forms the basis of a discourse and the foreground plane of the present which introduces semi-significant characters and situations or noteworthy descriptions.[13] In other words, the perfect, since it points to details and particularities, may serve as an emphatic marker so as to highlight a given action or state of affairs.

By contrast, Fanning argues that the meaning of a verbal tense-form is determined by a variety of interacting features which are part of the

9. Porter, *Verbal Aspect*, pp. 75-97.

10. Porter, *Verbal Aspect*, pp. 98-102.

11. Porter, *Verbal Aspect*, pp. 251-59. J.P. Louw's ('Die Semantiese Waarde van die Perfektum in Hellenistiese Grieks', *Acta Classica* 10 [1967] 27) definition of 'stative' is noteworthy: 'By *stative* I mean that *not the events but the whole affair is established as completed*' (translation of the Afrikaans is taken from Porter, *Verbal Aspect*, p. 258 n. 9).

12. Porter (*Verbal Aspect*, pp. 245-51) distinguishes four ways in which markedness can occur: (1) distributional markedness shows the relative infrequency of the tense-form; (2) material markedness lends attention to the perfect's morphological bulk; (3) implicational markedness points to the morphological regularity in comparison to the aorist and present forms; and (4) semantic markedness takes into account the consistent function, described as 'resultative state' which subsumes either or both the aorist and the present. In general, more heavily marked structures appear less frequently, are less prone to change in form and structure, and indicate greater semantic significance.

13. Porter, *Verbal Aspect*, p. 92; *idem*, *Idioms of the Greek New Testament* (BLG, 2; Sheffield: JSOT Press, 1992), p. 23.

verbal form such as lexical meaning carried by the verb, singular versus plural references, contextual elements, discourse structuring (e.g. articles, personal pronoun references and mood), and time values in the indicative form. At the same time Fanning curiously maintains a theoretical distinction between aspect and *Aktionsart*.[14] For Fanning the meaning of the perfect tense-form incorporates the combination of three elements: 'there is an *Aktionsart*-feature of *stative* situation, an internal tense-feature of *anteriority*, and an aspect-feature of summary viewpoint concerning an occurrence. Put together, these result in a sense usually described as denoting "a condition resulting from an anterior occurrence"'.[15] Fanning adds that in the indicative forms the result of the anterior occurrence should be understood as the expression of present-time or the time of speaking. Concerning the perfect participle, Fanning claims that it 'preserves the basic sense of the other perfect forms in denoting a state or condition resulting from an anterior occurrence...it often emphasizes the resulting state and only implies the anterior occurrence'.[16] The most noteworthy remark that Fanning makes regarding the meaning of the perfect is with regard to its inherent temporal quality. He writes:

> One element of meaning in the perfect which is clear from a study of usage is the dual 'time'-reference inherent in virtually all its occurrences. The forms, with few exceptions, juxtapose two related situations: an occurrence and a consequence of that occurrence.[17]

When the definitions of the perfect tense-form by Fanning and Porter are compared, it is the issue of inherent temporality which clearly separates them.[18]

---

14. Fanning, *Verbal Aspect*, pp. 126-96.
15. Fanning, *Verbal Aspect*, pp. 290-91.
16. Fanning, *Verbal Aspect*, p. 416.
17. Fanning, *Verbal Aspect*, p. 112.
18. Some mention should also be made of McKay's (*A New Syntax*, pp. 31, 49) approach. He understands the perfect tense-form, with respect to aspect, as expressing 'the state or condition of the subject of the verb, as a result of an action (logically a prior action), but most often with comparatively little reference to the action itself'. As far as the temporal feature is concerned, McKay simply states that the perfect is 'mostly found in present-time contexts and those without specific time reference'. McKay's description does not rest on linguistic foundations, but simply on usage, which results in a plethora of various examples, but no unifying semantic or linguistic structure whereby some unifying understanding can be reached.

2. *The Perfect Tense-Form in Colossians*

The following analysis of the perfect tense-form in Colossians concentrates on the temporal features of the verbal form. Does the perfect in and of itself express temporality as Fanning claims it does? Or are all temporal references solely determined by deictic indicators as Porter advocates? Porter's description of the perfect is preferable because it allows tense-forms to function in a larger spectrum of contexts. In other words, Porter's theory can accommodate more data than competing theories. As I pointed out in an earlier study on the perfect tense-form in Galatians, Porter's approach virtually eliminates the temporal tensions which are associated with the use of two or more verbal forms that share a common reference.[19] In other words, if temporality is not a semantic feature, difficulties do not arise when the same event is expressed in different verbal forms. The opposite is the case when time is a semantic feature of verbal forms. In the following analysis I also interact with Porter's view of the perfect as the frontground plane, though this is of secondary importance and only receives passing comments.

Since the function of tense-forms should be analyzed within their literary contexts—in this case the context of the epistle as a whole—I have divided the analysis according to a recognized structure.[20] Though the demarcations among the sections presented here are slightly fluid and not universally accepted, they nevertheless provide a working structure within which grammatical investigation can take place. Most scholars agree that Colossians exhibits a unified structure with regard to both content and form, regardless of the demarcations they propose.[21]

a. *Colossians 1.1-14: Greeting, Thanksgiving and Intercession*
As is the case with many other epistles in the New Testament, Paul begins with a greeting (1.1-2) coupled with a thanksgiving for the spiritual state of the community (1.3-8).[22] This is followed by a section

---

19. T.R. Hatina, 'The Perfect Tense-Form in Recent Debate: Galatians as a Case Study', *FN* 8 (1995), p. 7.

20. The structure followed is taken from M. Barth and H. Blanke, *Colossians* (trans. A.B. Beck; AB, 34B; New York: Doubleday, 1994), p. 42.

21. E.g. E. Lohse, *Colossians and Philemon* (trans. W.R. Poehlmann and R.J. Karris; Hermeneia; Philadelphia: Fortress Press, 1971), p. 90.

22. I refer to Paul as the author for the sake of convenience.

which recalls the intercessory prayer of the author who seeks the continued progress in the Colossians' knowledge of God's will and conduct of life. It is difficult to determine whether this section ends at v. 14 or v. 11.

Although there are no perfect tense-forms in this section, there is an aorist form which functions and is often translated as a perfect (if we assume Fanning's definition). I bring attention to the function of this aorist for the purpose of demonstrating that the assignment of temporal values to verbal forms creates the potential for numerous inconsistencies in the author's choice of forms.

In v. 6 Paul uses the aorist ἐπέγνωτε in the phrase ἀφ᾽ ἧς ἡμέρας ἠκούσατε καὶ ἐπέγνωτε τὴν χάριν τοῦ θεοῦ ἐν ἀληθείᾳ ('from the day you heard it and came to know the grace of God in truth'). In this case the perfect could have also been used if, as Fanning claims, it contains a temporal feature since the knowledge gained in the past continues in its effects. The implication of ἐπέγνωτε is not a developed knowledge, but an active conscious recognition.[23] The ongoing occurrence of the knowledge of God's will is clearly expressed in v. 3 where the author uses the present tense-forms to express his thanksgiving for the Colossians' spiritual state. Further, in v. 4 we are reminded of the present form of ἔχετε which expresses the ongoing love which the Colossians have toward the saints. Both the author's thanksgiving and the community's love for the saints should be seen as the result of the knowledge which the Colossians acquired in the past as expressed by the deictic indicator ἀφ᾽ ἧς ἡμέρας. One would assume that if the perfect contains a time element, it would have been the most appropriate choice in this situation.

A number of commentators suggest that ἐπέγνωτε is an inceptive aorist which should be translated as an English perfect.[24] E.D.W. Burton makes a distinction between a 'true' perfect and an inceptive aorist by claiming that the former affirms the present state of the action and implies the past, while the latter affirms the 'becoming' of the action and leaves the present action to be suggested.[25] This distinction,

23. T.K. Abbott, *A Critical and Exegetical Commentary on the Epistles to the Ephesians and to the Colossians* (ICC; Edinburgh: T. & T. Clark, 1897), p. 199.

24. E.g. P.T. O'Brien, *Colossians, Philemon* (WBC, 44; Waco, TX: Word Books, 1982), p. 13.

25. E.D.W. Burton, *Syntax of the Moods and Tenses in New Testament Greek* (Chicago: University of Chicago Press, 1900), p. 29.

however, needs to be validated. On what basis can we say that the language user wanted to leave the present action to be suggested or implied? In this context the current, ongoing knowledge of God's will among the Colossians is clearly in effect. It is not merely implicit. This use of the aorist provides an excellent example of how verbal forms can undergo a variety of exceptions if temporality is a semantic feature. All in all, if temporality is a semantic feature, one wonders why the language user would not have opted for the perfect in this case.

b. *Colossians 1.15–2.3: Praise for Reconciliation Through the Blood of Christ*

This section begins with a hymn about the primacy of Christ and his reconciliatory work (1.15–20). The hymn is followed by an application of the reconciliation to the Colossian community (1.21-23) and then by an extended proclamation by Paul about his commissioning and sufferings for the purpose of the advancement of the gospel (1.24–2.5). This section may conclude with either 2.3 or 2.5; it is difficult to be certain. If v. 4 is seen as the beginning of the warnings against false teachers, then the section concludes with v. 3. But if the warning against false teachers is connected with the preceding verses, then this section probably concludes with v. 5. Nevertheless, this section contains seven perfect tense-forms, the highest concentration of any section.

The first perfect to appear in the epistle is the passive form of κτίζω ('create') in the phrase τὰ πάντα δι' αὐτοῦ καὶ εἰς αὐτὸν ἔκτισται ('all things were created through him and in him') in 1.16. Fanning cites this text as an example of a 'perfect with accomplishments', meaning that the result of the verbal action is here clearer than the activity of the action.[26] He also claims that the perfect in this case describes a 'present condition or state of affairs produced by the action of the verb'.[27] While I am in agreement with Fanning that the perfect expresses a state of affairs, I am skeptical about the notion of accomplishment or result, or any implications of temporality inherent in the verbal form itself.

The use of the aorist passive form of κτίζω at the beginning of v. 16 in the phrase ὅτι ἐν αὐτῷ ἐκτίσθη τὰ πάντα ἐν τοῖς οὐρανοῖς καὶ ἐπὶ τῆς γῆς ('For in him all things were created in the heavens and on earth') raises questions about the choice of verbal forms by Paul. Why did he choose two different verbal forms of the same verb to express

---

26. Fanning, *Verbal Aspect*, pp. 153-54.
27. Fanning, *Verbal Aspect*, pp. 293-94.

the same creative work of God? N. Turner has tried to answer this question by suggesting that the concept of πρωτότοκος ('first born') introduced in v. 15 'necessarily involves two other conceptions, viz. (1) a past act which is punctiliar (grammatically) because one aspect of creation is past for ever, and (2) a second action which is not merely punctiliar but also perfective'.[28] But to suggest that the aorist was chosen to convey a completed past action, whereas the perfect was chosen to show the ongoing result of that action is not convincing. Why would Paul describe the creative action of God as concluded or complete at the beginning of the verse and as ongoing at the end of the verse? There is nothing in the context to warrant Turner's explanation. Certainly if Paul understood the perfect as being semantically temporal, why did he not choose the perfect for both uses of κτίζω? According to this scheme the perfect would have incorporated the features of the aorist. I think a better explanation is to suggest that the perfect was chosen by Paul as an emphatic device, or for the purpose of expressing a front-ground plane whereby the act of God's creativity is given prominence in the hymn. If this is the case, then the perfect functions as a peak in the discourse.[29] As far as temporality is concerned, both forms can be translated into English as past tenses, but this is solely based on the context.

In the next verse (1.17) Paul uses the perfect συνέστηκεν in the phrase καὶ αὐτός ἐστιν πρὸ πάντων καὶ τὰ πάντα ἐν αὐτῷ συνέστη-κεν ('and he is before all things and in him all things exist [or hold together]'). If temporality is a semantic feature of verbal forms, it is perplexing why Paul chose a perfect to express the existence of all things in Christ. Are we to understand that συνέστηκεν indicates a past action with ongoing results? Or does the perfect in this case simply indicate a continuous sustaining activity?[30] If it is the latter, would not a present tense-form have been more appropriate, especially since the preceding phrase αὐτός ἐστιν πρὸ πάντων uses a present? The choice of the perfect was probably motivated by the use of the same tense-form in the previous verse where Paul emphasizes the divine creation and its relationship to Christ. Since a corresponding concept is expressed here, both perfects can be viewed as operating in tandem to

---

28. N. Turner, *Grammatical Insights into the New Testament* (Edinburgh: T. & T. Clark, 1965), p. 125. See also Barth and Blanke, *Colossians*, p. 199.

29. See Porter, *Idioms of the Greek New Testament*, pp. 23, 302.

30. As suggested in O'Brien, *Colossians*, p. 47.

express the frontground of the hymn. But unlike in 1.16 where creation is perceived as a past event, the perfect in 1.17 is best translated into English as a present, given the focus on the existence or cohesion of creation.

The perfect is used again in 1.21 in the phrase καὶ ὑμᾶς ποτε ὄντας ἀπηλλοτριωμένος ('and you who were once alienated'). Grammarians and commentators have tried to explain the use of this perfect by suggesting that the periphrastic construction (ὄντας + ἀπηλλοτριωμένος) expresses more forcibly the persistence of an existing state. Thus the perfect is regarded as expressing the past state or condition of the Colossians' alienation from God.[31] Grammarians must admit that ἀπηλλοτριωμένος does not fit into the standard functional definition of the perfect. It cannot imply an ongoing temporal reference or a result from a past action. The deictic indicator ποτέ places the action clearly in the past, probably in reference to the time when the Colossians had no part in the inheritance of the 'holy ones in light' (1.12). This is further underscored in the next verse, where Paul uses the deictic indicator νυνί to explain that the alienation is no longer effective since Christ has 'now' reconciled the Colossians through his death provided they persevere in the faith. But if the result of the Colossians' alienation has been negated by the deictic indicator, why did not Paul use an aorist or an imperfect form of ἀπαλλοτριόω?[32] In fact, if temporality is inherent in verbal forms, as Fanning claims, it would have been ideal for Paul to substitute the aorist ἀποκατήλλαξεν in 1.22 for a perfect since reconciliation is clearly portrayed as an ongoing phenomenon, continuing in its results. The result of the action (i.e. ἀποκατήλλαξεν) is expressed not only by means of νυνί, but also by the ethical conditional statement immediately following in 1.23. The choice of the perfect in 1.21 (and the aorist in v. 22) must have been made for reasons other than temporality.[33] I would even venture to say that, in this context, the perfect

31. E.g. Blass, Debrunner and Funk, *Greek Grammar*, §352; Burton, *Syntax of the Moods and Tenses*, §155; O'Brien, *Colossians*, p. 66.

32. This is exactly what we find in Col. 3.7 where both an aorist (περιεπατήσατε) and an imperfect (ἐζῆτε) are used to likewise describe the Colossians' misguided condition prior to their restoration through Christ. The Colossians' conduct in 3.7 clearly points to the past through the use of ποτε coupled with the contrasting use of νυνὶ δέ in 3.8.

33. On the use of the aorist form of καταλλάσσω, see S.E. Porter, *Καταλλάσσω in Ancient Greek Literature, with Reference to the Pauline Writings* (Estudios de Filología Neotestamentaria, 5; Cordoba: Ediciones el Almendro, 1995), p. 178.

in 1.21 express a state of affairs in the same manner that the aorist does in the next verse. The choice of the perfect may have been made for the purpose of emphasizing the Colossians' state of alienation prior to Christ's reconciliation. The pre-Christian state serves as a peak in the discourse for Paul. It may be that he wants the Colossians to take special notice of their condition before they entered into obedience to Christ as a kind of warning, which would fit quite well with the ethical conditional statement in v. 23.

In 1.23 Paul uses the perfect passive participle τεθεμελιωμένοι in the conditional statement εἴ γε ἐπιμένετε τῇ πίστει τεθεμελιωμένοι ('provided that you remain in the faith, firmly grounded'). Once again it is difficult to see how the perfect participle expresses a result from an anterior occurrence. At least two deictic indicators in the immediate context restrict the action to the present and possibly the future. First, in the previous verse Paul uses νυνί to draw attention to the Colossians' new condition in Christ. In the past they were alienated from God, but *now* they are reconciled. Given the conditional nature of v. 23, it is clearly connected to v. 22. Secondly, the combination of εἴ γε + ἐπιμένετε in v. 23 further underscores a present-time reference. The conditional statement implies an ongoing and even a future reference. The Colossians are now reconciled (or are in a state of reconciliation) provided that they remain firmly grounded. If an implication regarding a past occurrence is indicated by the perfect, as Fanning claims, how would it be expressed in translation? One would have to translate the flow of thought something like this: 'And you who were once alienated..., he has now reconciled...provided that you remain in the faith, having been and continuing to be firmly grounded...' But this suggestion simply creates unnecessary tension in temporality. The temporal contrast which Paul creates by means of deictic indicators is the Colossians' alienation in the past and their reconciliation in the present. Verse 23 clearly fits with a reconciliation in present time. It is likely that Paul chose the perfect form of θεμελιόω to draw out the importance of the conditional statement.

In 1.26 Paul uses the perfect passive participle ἀποκεκρυμμένον ('hidden') to describe the mystery which was hidden from past generations. He writes, τὸ μυστήριον τὸ ἀποκεκρυμμένον ἀπὸ τῶν αἰώνων καὶ ἀπὸ τῶν γενεῶν—νῦν δὲ ἐφανερώθη τοῖς ἁγίοις αὐτοῦ ('the mystery which was hidden from the ages and from the generations, but now it has been revealed to his holy ones'). In this context the perfect refers only to past time and cannot indicate an ongoing result.[34] The use of νῦν δέ immediately following ἀποκεκρυμμένον creates a contrast between the past hidden mystery and the present manifestation of it. The perfect here expresses a state of affairs in the past. But could not the same concept have been expressed by means of the aorist or the imperfect? Certainly, as far as temporality is concerned, there would have been no problem, but this is obviously not the governing factor for Paul's choice of verbal forms.

Unlike the previous uses of the perfect, the choice here is probably not motivated by a need for emphasis. Within the discourse, emphasis appears to be placed on the current manifestation of the mystery to God's holy ones in 1.26b. The discourse which follows focuses on the present expression of the revealed mystery and not on its past concealment. Without straying too far from the issue of temporality, it is interesting to note that in the closest parallels Paul likewise uses the perfect to describe the concealment of the mystery to past generations (Rom. 16.25-26; 1 Cor. 2.7; Eph. 3.9).[35] It may be that Paul chose the perfect to express the long duration of the concealment. But if this is the reason, why did he use the aorist in 3.7 to describe the pre-Christian conduct of the Colossians?[36] Is the duration of immorality in 3.7 to be understood as shorter than the duration of the concealed mystery in 1.26 simply on the basis of the tense forms? This seems highly unlikely since both notions are two sides of the same coin. It may be, as Fanning claims, that in some cases verbal forms may be dependent on lexical meanings carried by verbs. Certain subjects, like mystery, which are virtually always found in connection with revelation, may for some reason require a perfect form.[37]

In 2.1 Paul uses two perfect tense-forms, εἰδέναι and ἑόρακαν, when he writes θέλω γὰρ ὑμᾶς εἰδέναι ἡλίκον ἀγῶνα ἔχω ὑπὲρ ὑμῶν καὶ τῶν ἐν Λαοδικείᾳ καὶ ὅσοι οὐχ ἑόρακαν τὸ πρόσωπόν μου ἐν

---

34. Fanning (*Verbal Aspect*, p. 116) claims that the perfect in Col. 1.26 still maintains its dual sense of 'occurrence with consequence'.

35. Unlike 1 Cor. 2.7, Eph. 3.9 and Col. 1.26 where the perfect form of ἀποκρύπτω is used, Rom. 16.25 has the perfect form of σιγάω.

36. Col. 3.7 reads, ἐν οἷς καὶ ὑμεῖς περιεπατήσατε ποτε ὅτε ἐζῆτε ἐν τούτοις ('in which you also once walked when you lived in these').

37. On 'mystery' and its connection with terms denoting revelation, see J.B. Lightfoot, *Saint Paul's Epistles to the Colossians and to Philemon* (London: Macmillan, 1879), p. 168.

σαρκί ('for I want you to know how great a struggle I have for you and for those in Laodicea and all who have not seen my face in the flesh'). The first is an anarthrous infinitive form of οἶδα ('to know'), a verb which has been the focus of much discussion in lexical semantics. Although it has traditionally been considered as one of the oldest perfect forms in Hellenistic Greek, the verb has raised questions regarding its aspectual characterization. Some argue that οἶδα is aspectually vague since it does not seem to be found in more than one verbal form. Others suggest that οἶδα should be regarded as a present form since it often appears to be translated into the English present and often lacks reference to a past event with present results.[38] The latter suggestion, however, has serious implications in light of the variety of temporal functions of the perfect which have been observed thus far in Colossians. Fanning admits that οἶδα—since it only appears to preserve a present state without any reference to a past occurrence—is one of those lexical items which does not coincide with his description of the perfect.[39] But οἶδα need not be viewed as an exception. One can simply avoid any reference to temporality as a semantic feature altogether and echo McKay in suggesting that οἶδα is a perfect tense-form expressing a state of knowledge.[40] In this light Col 2.1 expresses Paul's desire for the Colossians to know—that is, to be in a state of knowing—that he is struggling for them and all those who have not personally seen him.

The second perfect, ἑόρακαν (from ὁράω; 'see'), is used in reference to all those who have not personally met Paul, including the Colossians, the Laodiceans and other Christians in the Lycus valley. In this context the perfect is used primarily to refer to the past since Paul is in prison during the time of writing (4.10, 18), and is not in a position to see any of these groups. Although the past is in view, it does not nullify a result or continuation of the past action. Since Paul is in prison, it is obvious that those who have not seen him in the past continue in not seeing him in the present. For those who advocate dual temporality as a semantic feature of the perfect, this text can undoubtedly serve as a key example. But was the perfect chosen because it inherently expresses an anterior occurrence with a resulting condition? Is this the reason why

---

38. See the summary of viewpoints in Porter, *Verbal Aspect*, p. 283.

39. Fanning, *Verbal Aspect*, p. 112 n. 74.

40. McKay, 'On the Perfect and Other Aspects in New Testament Greek', pp. 302-303.

Paul did not opt for the aorist εἶδον?[41] The aorist was an option despite its absence in Colossians. If Paul had used the aorist, one would still assume that the audience continue in not seeing him personally. Although the immediate context of ἑόρακαν allows for both anteriority and result, it does not determine that dual temporality is a semantic feature—especially since this is not a common context in which the perfect is found. It does, however, establish that dual temporality is a pragmatic feature of the perfect. When a stative aspect is the only semantic feature ascribed to the perfect, one can account for temporal flexibility on pragmatic grounds and thus eliminate a number of so-called exceptions. In translation the stative aspect can be lost. The translation which best captures both the stative aspect and the temporal function of ἑόρακαν is the NEB: 'all who never set eyes on me'. The inclusion of 'never' coupled with the slight temporal ambiguity allows for a fair degree of temporal breadth.

c. *Colossians 2.6–3.4: The Superiority of Life in Christ Over and Against Man-made Religions*
In this section Paul contrasts the life in Christ with the life based on human teaching. Since God has raised Christ from the dead and exalted him over all earthly rulers, Paul urges his fellow followers of Christ to shun pagan rituals, legalism and mysticism. The recipients of the epistle are exhorted with a warning to abandon the physical and mental participation in competing religions. They are reminded that they have died to this way of life and been raised to a higher order, a life in obedience to Christ. In this section Paul chooses to use a total of five perfects. Four of them are used to describe the significance of the Colossians' life in Christ.

The first perfect in this section is the passive participle ἐρριζωμένοι in 2.7. It appears as the first of four plural masculine nominative participles which describe the Colossians' grounding and conduct in Christ whom they received some time back. Following the admonition to proper discipleship in v. 6, v. 7 reads: ἐρριζωμένοι καὶ ἐποικοδομούμενοι ἐν αὐτῷ καὶ βεβαιούμενοι τῇ πίστει καθὼς ἐδιδάχθητε, περισσεύοντες ἐν εὐχαριστίᾳ ('being rooted and built up in him and established in the faith just as you were taught, abounding in thanksgiving').

41. The aorist form εἶδον does not appear in Colossians.

The perfect ἐρριζωμένοι refers temporally to the present, and not to an anterior action with present results as suggested, for example, by M.J. Harris.[42] Nor does it simply refer to an antecedent condition of the imperative περιπατεῖτε in v. 6 as Abbott maintains. Abbott causes an unnecessary temporal disjunction between ἐρριζωμένοι, which is regarded as a past event, and the other participles, which supposedly convey a continual and advancing development.[43] The present temporal function of all four participles has already been determined in v. 6 where Paul uses the combination of ὡς οὖν with an imperative. Paul exhorts the Colossians to now walk in Christ on the basis of their past acceptance of Christ. The exhortation to walk in Christ in the next verse is qualified by the four participles in much the same fashion as is observed in Col. 1.10-12. It is also possible that the four participles are themselves functioning as commands, which likewise supports a present time reference (e.g. NEB, JB).

If Fanning's definition of the perfect is ascribed to ἐρριζωμένοι, theological disjunctions begin to emerge between this participle and the subsequent participles. In other words, if temporality is inherently present in verbal forms, is Paul suggesting that in the past the Colossians were 'rooted' (ἐρριζωμένοι) in Christ, given the perfect form, but they were not 'built up in him' (ἐποικοδομούμενοι), 'established in the faith' (βεβαιούμενοι), or 'abounding in thanksgiving' (περισσεύοντες), given the present forms? Is the notion of being 'rooted' somehow disjointed from the qualities which the other participles convey? If this is so, how does the concept of being 'rooted' differ from that of being 'established'? As is quickly observed, a host of questions like these begin to surface—all of which are needless if temporality is restricted to contextual factors and not to verbal forms.

Although ἐρριζωμένοι is syntactically and temporally linked with the subsequent participles, it must at the same time remain unique given its differing verbal form. Despite the difficulty in expressing the notion in translation, the perfect tense-form depicts a state of affairs.

---

42. M.J. Harris, *Colossian and Philemon* (Exegetical Guide to the New Testament; Grand Rapids: Eerdmans, 1991), p. 90.

43. Abbott, *Epistles to the Ephesians and to the Colossians*, p. 244. The NASB translation seems to imply anteriority when it adds the deictic indicator 'and now' immediately following the perfect. The translation reads: 'having been firmly rooted *and now* being built up in Him and established in your faith, just as you were instructed...'

The Colossians are commanded to walk in Christ by remaining firmly rooted in him; that is, by being in a state of 'rootedness'. The perfect conveys emphasis by projecting more detail and information than the subsequent present participles. The perfect participle probably functions as the head term in a series of participles.

The next perfect form is πεπληρωμένοι in 2.10 where Paul encourages the Colossians that their fullness of life is found in Christ. He writes: ἐστὲ ἐν αὐτῷ πεπληρωμένοι, ὅς ἐστιν ἡ κεφαλὴ πάσης ἀρχῆς καὶ ἐξουσίας ('you are complete in him, who is the head over every rule and authority'). Though it is possible to regard the first clause as having two predicates (i.e. 'you are in him, being [or having been made] complete'), the periphrastic construction is preferable. When the question of temporal reference is raised, scholars differ, despite their common definition of the perfect. For example, in O'Brien's translation ('and you have been filled in him') the emphasis appears to be placed on the past action.[44] Harris, on the other hand, translates the clause as 'you have your completeness in him', which emphasizes the present time of action or the present state.[45] Despite the differing temporal emphases, neither scholar would abrogate the lesser temporal element. Both still retain the notion of anteriority and continuing result in their understanding of the perfect.

Anteriority, or a past temporal reference, is irrelevant in this case. The clause should be translated as 'you are complete in him' or 'you are fulfilled in him'. The fulfillment or completion need not be regarded as the result of a past action of filling or completing. The Colossians are described as being in a state of completeness. If temporality is ascribed as a semantic feature to tense-forms, a certain degree of tension arises in the immediate context between the perfect πεπληρωμένοι in v. 10 and the present κατοικεῖ in v. 9. One would have to posit that the fullness of deity dwells in Christ in the present, whereas the fullness that the Colossians have in Christ is experienced in both the past and the present. The question which immediately arises is: how could the Colossians be fulfilled in Christ in the past when the fullness of deity dwells in Christ only in the present? Granted, this may seem to be an awkward question, but its point is to draw attention to the temporal disjunction when verbal forms are semantically defined as containing time references. A better solution is to allow the context to set the temporal

---

44. O'Brien, *Colossians*, pp. 102, 113.
45. Harris, *Colossians and Philemon*, p. 112.

parameters. The perfect was chosen by Paul not only to draw attention
to the religious state or condition of the Colossians, but also to make it
a point of emphasis. The Colossians' state of fullness is of primary
importance to him, more than the warning in v. 8 or the indwelling of
deity in Christ in v. 9.

The third perfect form in this section appears in 2.14 where Paul
writes, ἐξαλείψας τὸ καθ' ἡμῶν χειρόγραφον τοῖς δόγμασιν ὃ ἦν
ὑπεναντίον ἡμῖν, καὶ αὐτὸ ἦρκεν ἐκ τοῦ μέσου προσηλώσας αὐτοῦ
τῷ σταυρῷ ('having canceled against us the bond with its decrees
which was opposed to us, he has also taken it away from our midst by
nailing it to the cross'). Paul chooses ἦρκεν, the perfect form of αἴρω,
to metaphorically describe the removal of the Colossians' past debt,
namely the accusation of sin leveled against them by God. Although
the pragmatic use of the perfect points to a past action, many scholars
strive to maintain the conventional view of the perfect. For example,
Harris claims that the perfect 'points to present freedom from indebtedness after the complete abrogation of the bond'.[46] Both his translation
and paraphrase, however, simply stress the past action of the bond's
removal. Respectively, they read: 'he has set it aside by nailing it to the
cross' and 'in fact he has removed it altogether from sight by nailing it
to the cross'.[47] Though O'Brien likewise translates ἦρκεν as a reference to a past action, he claims that the shift from the aorist
(ἐξαλείψας) to the perfect 'points to the permanence of the removal'.[48]

The difficulty with these explanations is that they create unnecessary
temporal tensions between parallel concepts. If we grant that the perfect
form of αἴρω refers to a past removal of the bond as well as to its continuing or permanent removal, does this at the same time imply that the
aorist ἐξαλείψας only refers to the past cancellation of the bond and
not to its continuation? In other words, does the aorist form of
ἐξαλείφω exclude the results of the bond's cancellation in the present?
Is O'Brien, in his distinction between the aorist and the perfect,
suggesting that Paul specifically chose the aorist ἐξαλείψας to avoid or
negate the notion of the permanence of the 'cancellation'? One can
extend the comparison among tense-forms to the adjacent verses. In
2.13 Paul begins the flow of thought by metaphorically contrasting the

---

46. Harris, *Colossians and Philemon*, p. 109. See also Abbott, *Epistles to the
Ephesians and to the Colossians*, p. 256.

47. Harris, *Colossians and Philemon*, pp. 112-13.

48. O'Brien, *Colossians*, p. 126.

Colossians' pre-conversation, when they were 'dead in transgressions', with the new life they have in Christ. In the process, Paul uses two aorist forms, συνεζωοποίησεν ('he made alive') and χαρισάμενος ('forgiven'), to describe God's past action of grace toward the Colossians. Did Paul choose these two aorist forms to indicate that the Colossians' new life in Christ and forgiveness of sins, though performed by God in the past, have no continuing results? No, Paul's choice of verbal forms was governed by other matters. On a temporal level, the perfect ἦρκεν is indistinguishable from the list of actions which God has performed in the past. But on the level of priorities, Paul opted for ἦρκεν instead of the aorist ἦρε to draw attention to the particularity of this divine action.[49]

The fourth perfect form in this section of the epistle is ἑόρακεν, found in 2.18 where Paul writes: μηδεὶς ὑμᾶς καταβραβευέτω θέλων ἐν ταπεινοφροσύνῃ καὶ θρησκείᾳ τῶν ἀγγέλων, ἃ ἑόρακεν ἐμβατεύων, εἰκῇ φυσιούμενος ὑπὸ τοῦ νοὸς τῆς σαρκὸς αὐτοῦ ('let no one disqualify you by insisting on humility and the worship of angels, taking his stand on that which he saw, being inflated without reason by his fleshly mind'). Though this is a difficult verse to translate and allows for several possibilities, the point of Paul's admonition is clear. He warns the Colossians not to allow anyone who indulges in cultic worship, no matter what their experiences might be, to rob them of the benefits they have in Christ. For these kinds of visionary experiences merely lead to conceit.

The difficulty of trying to assess the temporal reference of this perfect tense-form is compounded by the ambiguity of the meaning of the participle ἐμβατεύων. Harris lists three possibilities: (1) 'taking his stand on [that which he saw]', (2) 'going into detail about [that which he saw]', and (3) 'entering into [that which he saw]'. In all three cases, the relative clause serves as the object of ἐμβατεύων.[50] O'Brien, taking his lead from the third option, views the participle circumstantially: 'delighting in humility and the angelic worship [of God], which he has seen upon entering'.[51] With regard to temporality, however, the function of ἑόρακεν remains equally ambiguous. If the participle is to be

---

49. The perfect form of αἴρω only appears twice in the New Testament, here as a finite verb and in Jn 20.1 as a participle. By contrast the aorist form occurs about 67 times. Thus Paul's choice appears to be quite deliberate.

50. Harris, *Colossians and Philemon*, pp. 120-21.

51. O'Brien, *Colossians*, p. 135.

taken as circumstantial, then Paul may be referring either to a past visionary incident which is experienced when the cultic participant undergoes initiation, or to an ongoing cultic experience whenever the participant enters a religious sanctuary. As a result, one can translate the clause as 'which he saw when entering' or 'which he sees when entering'. There is nothing in the context to suggest that either is preferred. If we view the relative clause as the object of the participle, both temporal references are also possible, but a past action is probably preferred, especially for options (1) and (2). In these two options the action of seeing forms the basis of either the stand which the cultic participant is taking, or the detail into which he is going. Nevertheless, much uncertainty remains. Paul could have chosen the present or the aorist, but he opted for the perfect to lay stress on the visionary experience. The sole perfect tense-form in this context is contrasted with numerous present tense-forms.

The final perfect form to appear in this section is κέκρυπται in 3.3 where Paul encourages the Colossians of their security in Christ: ἀπεθάνετε γάρ, καὶ ἡ ζωὴ ὑμῶν κέκρυπται σὺν τῷ Χριστῷ ἐν τῷ θεῷ ('for you died, and your life is hidden with Christ in God'). In this context the perfect expresses a present state of affairs. The notion of the Colossians' new life being hidden with Christ follows not only the exhortations by Paul in 3.1-2 to live and think according to the new life they now have, but also the reminder in v. 3 that they have died in the past to the elementary principles of the world (cf. 2.20-23). The entire discussion focuses on the Colossians' new and present status as converts to Christ. One feature of the present status is that the Colossians' life is now concealed with Christ for a time until Christ is revealed (3.4). It is surprising that even the NASB—which presupposes that verbal forms have an inherent temporal reference and thus often equates the Greek perfect with the English perfect—translates κέκρυπται as 'is hidden' instead of 'has been hidden'. For the same reason, it is equally surprising to read Harris's translation: 'For you died, and so your life is now hidden with Christ in God'.[52] The addition of 'now' certainly excludes the notion of anteriority. It instead draws attention to the contrast between the Colossians' death and their new life in Christ.

If we apply Fanning's definition of the perfect, then κέκρυπται refers to both the past and continuous concealment of the Colossians' life with Christ. J.D.G. Dunn comes close to this understanding when

---

52. Harris, *Colossians and Philemon*, p. 141.

he writes, 'The perfect tense as usual indicates a continuing state which is the result of a past action'.[53] One can only speculate that the past action refers to the initial point of concealment when the Colossians died to their former life. And since Christ has not yet been revealed, their life with Christ continues to be hidden. Although this understanding of κέκρυπται is pragmatically possible in the context, it raises serious temporal tensions if the perfect is thus described semantically. One example is the tension between the aorist συνηγέρθητε in 3.1 and the perfect κέκρυπται.[54] If temporality is a semantic feature, it implies that the raising of the Colossians with Christ does not have any continuing results attached to it, despite the subsequent (or resulting) exhortations by Paul in the immediate context. Theologically, we are faced with trying to reconcile, on the one hand, the continuous results of concealment with Christ, and, on the other, the anteriority of being raised with Christ. Surely, Paul does not imply that the Colossians do not remain raised in the present?[55]

Why did Paul choose the perfect instead of the present? One of the reasons is that he wanted to express the state or condition of the Colossians' hidden life with Christ. He also wanted to draw attention to this particular feature of their condition. The Colossians were probably growing skeptical or even bored of their new life with Christ since it was not accompanied by visions or other physical manifestations which the competing religions in Colossae offered.

d. *Colossians 3.5–4.6: A Call for True Worship*
This section largely consists of the characteristics of the Colossians' new life in Christ. Paul instructs the converts to abandon the immoral and unjust practices in which they engaged when they lived according to their so-called earthly passions. Since they are now in Christ, resurrected with him to a new life and renewed to a true knowledge of God, they are to live accordingly. The admonitions go well beyond ethical strictures; they extend to the attitude and imply an expected change in

---

53. J.D.G. Dunn, *The Epistles to the Colossians and to Philemon* (NIGTC; Grand Rapids: Eerdmans; Carlisle: Paternoster Press, 1996), pp. 202, 207.

54. Some have suggested the rising here refers to the past event of baptism. See, for example, Lightfoot, *Saint Paul's Epistles to the Colossians*, p. 208.

55. Once again the NASB strays from its premise by translating the aorist συνηγέρθητε as 'you have been raised' instead of 'you were raised'. The former implies an ongoing quality.

the Colossians' worldview. Paul expects his converts to live a life of thanksgiving, prayer and love for one another. Paul uses six perfect tense-forms in this section. Since I have discussed the temporal function of οἶδα above, I will omit comments on εἰδότες in 3.24 and 4.1, and εἰδέναι in 4.6. It suffices to note that all three refer to the present.

The first perfect in this section is ἠγαπημένοι in 3.12 where Paul commands the Colossians to ἐνδύσασθε οὖν ὡς ἐκλεκτοὶ τοῦ θεοῦ, ἅγιοι καὶ ἠγαπημένοι, σπλάγχνα οἰκτιρμοῦ, χρηστότητα, ταπεινοφροσύνην, πραΰτητα, μακροθυμίαν ('therefore, as God's elect, who are holy and loved by him, put on heartfelt compassion, kindness, humility, gentleness, patience'). This translation (as opposed to the NASB, NEB and NRSV) reflects the verbal qualities of the perfect passive participle and, as Harris notes, distinguishes it from ἀγαπητοὶ θεοῦ (e.g. Rom. 1.7).[56] Aside from highlighting the verbal features of ἠγαπημένοι, commentators generally ignore the potential significance of the participle. Since the adjective ἀγαπητός is used more often by Paul than the participle, the question of its import should be raised.[57]

So, why did Paul choose the participle and not the adjective? It may well be that Paul wanted to include the idea of action and thus draw attention to God's love for the Colossians. The emphasis of ἠγαπημένοι stands out when it is compared to the neighbouring descriptions of the Colossians, ἐκλεκτοί and ἅγιοι. Though all three concepts are similar, for they point to the Colossians' new status, the participle stands out linguistically on the basis of its morphological bulk and its aspectual quality. In other words, unlike the other substantives, the participle contains more information. On the basis of the immediate context, it is fitting for Paul to emphasize God's love for the Colossians, instead of their sainthood or their election. It is God's love which becomes the foundation not only for all the subsequent character traits and social duties demanded by Paul (3.12-4.6), but for the overarching characteristic of their new life, namely love (3.14). It is also noteworthy to point out that ἠγαπημένοι is the most isolated perfect tense-form in the epistle. It is the only perfect to appear between 3.4 and 4.2. Consequently, the emphasis is further confirmed since it lies in opposition to the largest number of other tense-forms.

In this context the perfect refers temporally to present time, and not to an anterior action with continuing results. Fanning also admits that

56. Harris, *Colossians and Philemon*, p. 161.
57. In Colossians the adjective outnumbers the participle 4 to 1.

the present condition is at the forefront, though he still wants to retain a prior action of God's love as a basis for present time.[58] The perfect participle, however, appears in the midst of a series of imperatives which point to an immediate temporal situation. In other words, the imperatives demand an immediate response. Paul exhorts (commands?) the Colossians to adopt the characteristics of their calling right away in the present. There is no implication of delay in the context. Paul uses the perfect form, instead of the present, to depict the action as a state of affairs. Thus he views the Colossians in a state of being loved by God.

The next perfect tense-form in this section is δέδεμαι in 4.3 where Paul recounts that the reason for his imprisonment was his preaching about the mystery of Christ—that is, the salvation of the Gentiles (cf. 1.26-27). The final clause of 4.3 reads: δι ' ὃ καὶ δέδεμαι ('for which also I am imprisoned'). It is difficult to determine the exact temporal function of δέδεμαι since the context can adequately support either a past reference with a continuing effect (i.e. that Paul was imprisoned and continues to be imprisoned) or a present reference. It is noteworthy, however, that most commentators support a present temporal reference. For example, Harris, who views the perfect in much the same way as does Fanning, omits any reference to the past in his translation and simply views the action as taking place in the present. His translation and paraphrase respectively read: 'because of which I am in chains' and 'It is, in fact, because of this open secret that I am now a prisoner in chains'.[59] Although Harris claims that the perfect tense-form emphasizes a present consequence of a past act of binding, he is not willing to adopt the NASB's translation which reflects the conventional (dual temporal) definition of the perfect: 'for which I have also been imprisoned'.[60]

But since the immediate context is not helpful in determining the temporal function of δέδεμαι, why do so many commentators and translators opt for a present reference? While the majority are correct in their assessment of δέδεμαι, one is hard pressed to read a supporting

58. Fanning, *Verbal Aspect*, p. 148.

59. Harris, *Colossians and Philemon*, p. 198. See also Barth and Blanke, *Colossians*, p. 451; Lohse, *Colossians and Philemon*, p. 165; F.F. Bruce, *The Epistles to the Colossians, to Philemon, and to the Ephesians* (NICNT; Grand Rapids: Eerdmans, 1984), pp. 172, 174 n. 15; O'Brien, *Colossians*, p. 239; Dunn, *The Epistles to the Colossians and to Philemon*, p. 261.

60. Harris, *Colossians and Philemon*, pp. 194-95.

argument for this translation. It is possible, however, to argue for a present reference on the basis of other texts in Colossians where Paul speaks of his imprisonment. Specifically, in 1.24 he speaks of the joy he now has in his sufferings for the Colossians' sake. In 2.1, which is discussed above, Paul again refers to his present struggle. And in 4.18 Paul, in his own hand, asks the Colossians to remember his imprisonment—an obvious reference to his current state. Since Paul refers to his imprisonment in these texts as a current hardship, one can assume the same temporal reference in 4.3.

Paul chose the perfect instead of the present to depict the state of affairs in which he found himself. Had he decided on the present tense-form, he would have viewed his imprisonment as being in progress. This aspectual distinction, however, between the perfect and the present, remains vague since it is unclear how being in the 'state' of imprisonment differs from being in the 'progress' of imprisonment. Did Paul choose the perfect because he saw an eventual end to his imprisonment? Or did he simply choose the perfect form of δέω because this was the standard passive form used with this verb? There do not appear to be any present passive forms of δέω in Hellenistic literature or non-literary papyri.[61] It is also likely that the perfect form may be a point of emphasis in the immediate context. It may have been chosen (instead of the aorist, for example) to highlight the extent to which Paul has gone in informing the Gentiles of their inclusion in the body of Christ. In essence, the Colossians are reminded that Paul has risked being imprisoned for the sake of the Gentiles. As a result, they should view their new life with seriousness and thanksgiving.

The last perfect tense-form in this section appears in 4.6 where Paul writes: ὁ λόγος ὑμῶν πάντοτε ἐν χάριτι, ἅλατι ἠρτυμένος, εἰδέναι πῶς δεῖ ὑμᾶς ἑνὶ ἑκάστῳ ἀποκρίνεσθαι ('let your speech always be with grace, seasoned with salt, so that you may know how to answer each person'). The perfect participle ἠρτυμένος refers pragmatically to present time given the preceding exhortation and the adverb πάντοτε. I suppose one could also argue that the perfect tense-forms refer to the future if the exhortation is viewed as a pre-condition of the action. Nevertheless, what is important is that no major translation or commentary translates ἅλατι ἠρτυμένος as 'having been seasoned with salt' so as to express both anteriority and continuing result. In fact, the major

61. The present passive of δέω was probably avoided since it would have been indistinguishable from the present forms of the verb δέομαι ('to beseech').

commentaries are silent on the temporal significance of ἠρτυμένος. Both dative phrases—ἐν χάριτι and ἅλατι ἠρτυμένος—can be viewed as complementing the predicate (i.e. the verb, which is supplied here, and the modifier). It is also possible that ἅλατι ἠρτυμένος is epexegetic of ἐν χάριτι. If this is the case one could translate the opening clause as 'let your speech always be seasoned with the salt of grace'. In any event, the temporal function of the participle is not affected.

It is obvious in this context that Paul's choice of the perfect was not governed by some inherent temporal quality. If temporality was an issue, he would have been better off with the present tense-form. Paul's choice was instead governed by aspectual factors. He expected the Colossians' speech to be in a state of being 'seasoned with salt'. Paul viewed this feature of their speech as an essential characteristic. The perfect also highlights 'speech seasoned with salt' as a vital characteristic of the Colossians' new life. It is a characteristic which is, in Paul's view, vital for his audience's interaction with 'outsiders' (cf. 4.5).

e. Colossians 4.7-18: Final Greetings

Much of this concluding section of the epistle consists of personal remarks about Paul's assistants who have been a constant source of encouragement to him. The list of names is followed by greetings and instructions about the circulation of the letter. The final verse is somewhat detached since it serves as a greeting and signature in Paul's own hand, written below the dictated letter. In this section, Paul uses only one perfect tense-form.

In 4.12 Paul uses the perfect πεπληροφορημένοι to describe the content of Epaphras's prayers for the Colossians. Paul writes: ἀσπάζεται ὑμᾶς Ἐπαφρᾶς ὁ ἐξ ὑμῶν, δοῦλος Χριστοῦ [Ἰησοῦ], πάντοτε ἀγωνιζόμενος ὑπὲρ ὑμῶν ἐν ταῖς προσευχαῖς, ἵνα σταθῆτε τέτειοι καὶ πεπληροφορημένοι ἐν παντὶ θελήματα τοῦ θεοῦ ('Epaphras, who is from among you, a slave of Christ [Jesus], greets you. He always labours for your sake in prayers so that you may stand perfect and be fully assured in every desire of God').[62] Since the perfect participle πεπληροφορημένοι agrees with the subjunctive σταθῆτε, it cannot express anteriority or a continuing result. Rather, it functions temporally as a hypothetical reference and thus depicts future time. Although

---

62. For survey of possible translations, see Harris, *Colossians and Philemon*, p. 210; Lightfoot, *Saint Paul's Epistles to the Colossians*, p. 240.

O'Brien translates πεπληροφορημένοι as 'be filled' instead of 'be fully assured', he likewise views the participle as depicting a future time.[63] O'Brien suggests that since the Colossians have already been filled in Christ, Epaphras now prays that they may attain eschatological perfection and fullness on the last day.[64] While O'Brien is correct that the Colossians have already been filled with Christ, there is no need to view Epaphras's prayer as eschatological. Even if one translates πεπληροφορημένοι as 'be filled', Epaphras may simply be praying that the Colossians attain God's will more fully in the immediate future. Since I translate πεπληροφορημένοι as 'be fully assured', I view Epaphras's prayer as a request that the Colossians may attain fuller assurance or conviction of God's will in their new life. A plea for assurance in the immediate future appears to be more consistent with the list of exhortations Paul has conveyed throughout the epistle.

Once again, commentators are silent on the temporal function of the perfect. While no one appears to translate πεπληροφορημένοι in a way that expresses both anteriority and continuing result, there are no explanations offered to support this shift from the conventional meaning of the perfect. If we utilize Fanning's understanding of the perfect participle and apply temporality as an inherent feature of the tense-form, we are faced with a syntactical difficulty given the preceding construction of ἵνα + subjunctive. But if we separate the semantic features of the perfect (that is, its aspectual significance) from its pragmatic features (namely, temporal function), we can allow for a variety of temporal uses, including, as in this case, a reference to future time.

Why did Paul opt for the perfect form instead of the present? Most likely, Paul perceived the 'full assurance' for which Epaphras prayed as a state of affairs or a frame of mind, and not as a progressive action. Alongside all the other greetings and descriptions of Paul's assistants, Epaphras's prayer for 'full assurance' on behalf of the Colossians stands out as a point of emphasis. In light of the whole epistle, which aims at encouraging the Colossians to live according to their new life in Christ, this emphasis is not surprising.

---

63. Although πεπληροφορημένοι is the preferred reading, most cursives, 𝔓[46], and D[1] read πεπληρωμένοι.

64. O'Brien, *Colossians*, p. 254.

3. *Assessment*

According to this survey, the majority of perfect tense-forms do not conform pragmatically to Fanning's definition. Of the nineteen perfect tense-forms, six refer to the past (cf. 1.16, 21, 26; 2.1, 14, 18). Two of these (cf. 2.1, 18), however, are tenuous and could very well refer either to the present or to both the past and the present. The largest number of perfect tense-forms—twelve in total—refer to the present (cf. 1.17, 23; 2.1, 7, 10; 3.3, 12, 24; 4.1, 3, 6 [x2]). Two of these, however, are less than certain. One may incorporate the past (cf. 4.3) and the other may refer to the future (cf. 1.23). There is even one perfect tense-form which refers to the future (cf. 4.12). In other words, only three out of nineteen perfects possibly exhibit both anteriority and continuous result (ἑόρακαν in 2.1; ἑόρακεν in 2.18; and δέδεμαι in 4.3), and these are by no means firm. In this regard Porter's model is more suitable than Fanning's (or than the conventional definition) since it allows for the temporal flexibility of tense-forms at the pragmatic level. Incorporating temporality as a semantic feature unfortunately results in (1) the need to allow for exceptions, such as οἶδα, and (2) the inevitability of temporal tensions among tense-forms—an issue rarely discussed by commentators.

The implications resulting from this kind of study are potentially far reaching. If we move beyond the temporal flexibility of the perfect to its function in relation to other tense-forms at the level of discourse, we can examine its relative position of importance from the perspective of the author. As I briefly mentioned above, Porter has introduced into the field of New Testament Greek grammar the notion of planes of discourse. Taking his lead from structural linguistics he argues that since the perfect/pluperfect is the most heavily marked tense-form, it implies more semantic weight than the other tense-forms. The perfect is regarded as the frontground tense which introduces elements in the most 'discrete, defined, contoured and complex way'.[65] In short, the perfect points to those features in the discourse which are very significant. While this contention needs to be tested in a thorough examination of the relationship of tense-forms in the New Testament (and all Hellenistic literature for that matter), I have observed that in Colossians

---

65. Porter, *Idioms of the Greek New Testament*, pp. 22-23; *idem*, *Verbal Aspect*, ch. 2.

at least, the hypothesis is plausible in some cases at this preliminary stage (e.g. ἀπηλλοτριωμένος in 1.21; κέκρυπται in 3.3; ἠγαπημένοι in 3.12; πεπληροφορημένοι in 4.12). What is more, the evidence based on contextual and discourse features certainly does not discredit the hypothesis. It is generally not the case that the perfect is found in a comparatively insignificant position. The verb/participle which Paul chooses to take on the form of the perfect usually plays an important role in the immediate discourse, and sometimes in the broader discourse of the epistle as a whole. But obviously more work is required if the hypothesis is to be thoroughly tested.

If the perfect expresses emphasis, then interpretation is necessarily affected. This may appear obvious, but in an age when Greek grammar is often overshadowed by current literary or social-scientific approaches in New Testament interpretation, it needs to be stressed. While current approaches have their place in clearing new ground for understanding not only the text, but also ourselves as readers, the language of the New Testament must be the starting point for the exegete. Without it, the exegete is dependent on translations which he or she cannot properly evaluate. Moreover, the exegete finds him- or herself in a situation where identifying tense-forms, moods, cases, and a host of other essential features is next to impossible. Consequently, fresh insights, and even creativity, are significantly limited.

If Paul chose the perfect as a mark of importance, it allows us to gain a clearer understanding of his own thought. It is somewhat analogous to reading a document which contains select words that are highlighted or underlined for the purpose of emphasis. An investigation into this kind of interplay between tense-forms can potentially shed more light on Paul's more opaque arguments. When we examine the displacement of perfects in Colossians, we notice that the highest concentration occurs in the second section of the epistle where Paul discusses the supremacy of Christ and the reconciliation of the Colossians through Jesus' sacrifice. Given this high concentration of perfects, Paul probably viewed this section as the most important. On a broader scale this kind of investigation might also help us to resolve the illusive quest for the centre of Paul's theology.

Another important implication arising from this study has to do with translation. At least three challenges are posed. First, temporality must be decided on the basis of context, however broad or narrow this may prove to be. As I have emphasized throughout this study, the perfect tense-form functions in a variety of ways—it refers to the past, present and future. And, on occasion, it may express dual temporality. Although context has long been recognized as an indicator of temporality, it has not served as the rule. Consider, for example, the NASB which presupposes temporality as a semantic feature of Greek verbs. The default translation of the perfect, so to speak, expresses both anteriority and continuous result by means of the English construction 'has/ have been...' Only when faced with no other alternatives does the NASB opt for another English equivalent, such as a simple past or the present (e.g. κέκρυπται in Col. 3.3).

Secondly, we are faced with the challenge of expressing the perfect's stative aspect into English, a language whose verbal system is time based. With some terms the challenge can be met. Take, for example, γέγραπται which occurs in numerous quotation formulas in the New Testament. Instead of agonizing over the most appropriate temporal reference—'was written', 'has been written' or 'is written'—the term can simply be translated as 'stands written'. This alternative best brings out the stative aspect. It is noteworthy how often the inclusion of the verb 'to stand' expresses the stative aspect in English in a variety of situations. In Colossians, expressing a state of affairs in translation is sometimes fairly straightforward. For example, the phrase καὶ τὰ πάντα ἐν αὐτῷ συνέστηκεν in 1.17 can simply be translated as 'and in him all things exist'. The state of existence is expressed without the need of saying 'and in him all things are in a state of existence'. In other cases, however, the challenge seems insurmountable. How are we, for example, to express a state of affairs when translating ἔκτισται in 1.16 while at the same time remaining fairly literal? The phrase in which it appears is best translated as 'all things were created through him and in him' and does not easily lend itself to a stative aspect in English translation if a past temporal reference is used. A state of affairs can be expressed into English more easily if the English present tense is used in translation (i.e. 'all things are created through him and in him'), but if the context favours a past reference, the tension between aspect (Greek) and time (English) becomes apparent. Instead of searching for a solution, it is best to allow for this kind of tension. In principle, every feature of the Greek verb does not need to be expressed in translation. To do so would inevitably distort one of the two poles in the tension. The exegete, however, who ideally works in conjunction with current translations, should be aware of those features of the

Greek language which cannot be expressed into English.

The third challenge which the perfect tense-form poses for translators has to do with its emphatic character. If the perfect marks a high degree of significance in comparison to other tense-forms neighbouring it, how is this to be expressed into English? Since English verbs are not marked to the same degree as Greek verbs, this appears to be an impossible challenge—short of underlining every perfect in the translation. Once again, the reality is that translations can only take us so far. Translations must be accompanied by teachers who are competent in Greek. For this purpose commentators—who are consulted most often by the laity—must be aware of current insights into the Greek of the New Testament.

ASSUMPTIONS IN THE CRITICISM
AND TRANSLATION OF PHILEMON

Brook W.R. Pearson

1. *Introduction*

The letter to Philemon is amongst the shortest in the New Testament, and, of all the Pauline letters, most like the thousands of papyrus personal letters from Egypt. Nevertheless, it has still managed to elicit its fair share of critical concern. For the most part, this concern has revolved not so much around authorship and theology[1] (as it has for other Pauline and 'deutero-Pauline' letters), but, more fundamentally, around the *Sitz im Leben* of the letter—the actual situation which called forth this tiny scrap of communication from the Apostle to the Gentiles. In some ways, it is an anomaly within the Pauline corpus—unlike other Pauline epistles, the simple fact of its inclusion in the New Testament argues convincingly for its authenticity. Its contents are not, on the surface, theologically significant, although they may be some of the most significant when it comes to the discussion of the social reality of the Pauline churches.[2] However, it is this latter significance which, in the

1. E.g. the recent J.M. Bassler (ed.), *Pauline Theology. I. Thessalonians, Philippians, Galatians, Philemon* (Philadelphia: Fortress Press, 1991) virtually ignores the theology of Philemon. Each of the other texts is given an entire section of the book, as well as dedicated bibliographies, whereas Philemon seems to be treated only by N.T. Wright in his essay, 'Putting Paul together Again: Toward a Synthesis of Pauline Theology (1 and 2 Thessalonians, Philippians, and Philemon)' (pp. 183-211). Philemon figures only in the title of two other essays in the volume (R.B. Hays, 'Crucified with Christ: A Synthesis of the Theology of 1 and 2 Thessalonians, Philemon, Philippians, and Galatians', pp. 227-46; and D.J. Lull, 'Salvation History: Theology in 1 Thessalonians, Philemon, Philippians, and Galatians: A Response to N.T. Wright, R.B. Hays, and R. Scroggs', pp. 247-66).
2. A fact noticed by, for instance, N.R. Petersen, *Rediscovering Paul: Philemon and the Sociology of Paul's Narrative Thought World* (Philadelphia: Fortress Press, 1985).

light of current research and debate, becomes very difficult to quantify. Much of the discussion surrounding the significance of Philemon has typically revolved around the question of the ethics of slavery, and of Paul's position thereon. This is perhaps because the situation behind the letter has, since patristic times, been understood thus: Onesimus, a slave of the church leader Philemon in Colossae, absconded with valuables belonging to his master, and fled. For some reason, he decided that the safest place to flee would be to wherever the apostle Paul, his master's spiritual father and friend, was in prison. Another way of formulating this part of the story is that, somehow, with Paul in prison and Onesimus 'on the lamb', they somehow met and were able to have enough discourse for Paul to convert Onesimus, and for Onesimus to then become a useful co-worker in the spread of the gospel—as Lightfoot put it, the apostle 'spread his net' for the runaway slave.[3]

What is the most interesting aspect of this reconstructed story is that, for the largest part, it does not derive *directly* from the text of Philemon itself. This narrative derives from inferences drawn from certain of its elements, which are then read back into the text of Philemon itself, and used as an assumptive foundation for both translation and interpretation. This, like many historical 're-constructions', has led readers of the letter to think that more is known about the situation behind it than is actually the case. My primary purpose is thus to examine the positions on either side of the debate surrounding the background of Philemon. On the one side are those who support the traditional story concerning the flight of Onesimus, and, on the other, those who would posit that the situation behind Philemon has nothing to do with a *runaway* slave, and everything to do with the complex relationship between an imprisoned apostle and his free, wealthy, 'partner', Philemon.[4] It is my position that complete certainty can not be achieved

---

3.   J.B. Lightfoot, *Saint Paul's Epistles to the Colossians and to Philemon* (London: Macmillan, rev. edn, 1879), p. 312. However, original modern scholarship (rather than simple commentary) has turned somewhat away from this paradigm. See J.A. Harrill, *The Manumission of Slaves in Early Christianity* (HUT, 32: Tübingen: J.C.B. Mohr [Paul Siebeck], 1995), who purposely leaves discussion of Philemon out of his investigation, as the evidence surrounding the issue of manumission (and, by extension, the whole background story which would go along with this issue) 'proves too slim to support a positive conclusion' (p. 3).

4.   The reader will note that elements of this alternative view, which was first voiced by J. Knox (in *Philemon among the Letters of Paul* [London: Collins, 1960]), are not discussed, such as his theory that Archippus was the actual recipient

concerning this issue—the exact situation addressed in the letter is simply too obfuscated to posit a definite solution. However, because of this obfuscation, it is important that the question of the situation remain open, both at a scholarly level and at the level of translations made by and for experts and non-experts alike. Thus, the second part of the article will consist of an examination of some significant factors which surround the translation of Philemon, in an attempt to see where translators' and editors' judgments in their translation and presentation of Philemon have been clouded by dependence upon the traditional historical reconstruction.

2. *Textual and Grammatical Issues Relating to the Situation which Elicited the Letter to Philemon*

Those who would posit that a particular background of Philemon should be seen as the proper reading must take stock of several elements in the text of the letter. The first nine verses of this twenty-five verse letter do not typically figure in the tendentious aspects of the discussion, usually being brought in to bolster a case built on the entreaty, beginning in v. 10. This entreaty, or at least the part seemingly concerned with Onesimus in some direct way, extends for ten verses, to v. 19. The most significant issues with regard to these verses are: (a) the sense of the verb παρακαλῶ in v. 10 with the preposition περί with a genitive object—τοῦ ἐμοῦ τέκνου, (b) the sense of ὃν ἀνέπεμψά σοι in v. 12, (c) the sense of τάχα γὰρ διὰ τοῦτο ἐχωρίσθη πρὸς ὥραν in v. 15, (d) what Paul means by οὐκέτι ὡς δοῦλον ἀλλ᾽ ὑπὲρ δοῦλον, ἀδελφὸν ἀγαπητόν in v. 16, (e) the nature and sense of the conditionals εἰ οὖν με ἔχεις κοινωνόν, προσλαβοῦ αὐτὸν ὡς ἐμέ in v. 17 and εἰ δέ τι ἠδίκησέν σε ἢ ὀφείλει, τοῦτο ἐμοὶ ἐλλόγα in v. 18, (f) the reason why Paul should entreat Philemon to προσλαβοῦ αὐτὸν [Onesimus] ὡς himself in v. 17, and finally, (g) for what exactly Paul expects to possibly be held bond in v. 19. Some have, of course, brought up different

of the letter, and that the letter to Philemon is actually the missing letter to the Laodiceans, mentioned in Colossians. These are passed by simply because they have (1) received virtually no support, and (2) because they rest on a historical reconstruction even more tenuous than the traditional view. Much gratitude is due to Knox, however, for illuminating several difficulties with the traditional view of Philemon's situation that have spurred later studies, even if this later discussion is more of a by-product of his study than the original goal.

aspects of the letter as significant (some of which will be discussed in the course of this article), but it seems that these seven issues are the basis of all other inquiry, and the starting point for any interpretation of the situation underlying the letter. All other outside information brought to bear on the issue of background must first establish a base among these verses and their problematic nature, before sallying forth into various cognate writings and historical reconstructions. Translation, too, is unable to be completed without some sort of decision regarding the nature of these verses and their background—even such an ideal translation that would keep the question completely open must make a decision *not* to read one or the other suggested backgrounds into the text and its translation.

In discussing the relative merits of the two major options for the understanding of the background of Philemon, it seems prudent to determine how they establish at least provisional answers to these seven issues.

a. παρακαλῶ σε περὶ τοῦ ἐμοῦ τέκνου

There are two specific issues to take into account concerning the meaning of this clause: the meaning of παρακαλῶ, and the sense of the preposition περί with the genitive. Basic English glosses for the verb παρακαλῶ are 'entreat, beseech, ask', although the sense of 'exhort, urge' is also attested.[5] In Paul's usage, Phlm. 10 is the only occurrence of this verb with an object preceded by the preposition περί. The verb, however, occurs twice in Philemon, the first time in v. 9: διὰ τὴν ἀγάπην μᾶλλον παρακαλῶ, τοιοῦτος ὢν ὡς Παῦλος πρεσβύτης νυνὶ δὲ καὶ δέσμιος Χριστοῦ Ἰησοῦ. Because of the proximity of these two usages of the verb in Philemon, and because of the lack of Pauline cognates to the usage with περί, it is probably best to begin with trying to understand παρκαλῶ in its immediate context in Philemon.[6]

---

5. See Moulton–Milligan (M–M) *s.v.* παρακαλέω, as well as Liddell–Scott–Jones (LSJ) *s.v.* παρακαλέω. See also Louw–Nida (domain) 33.168, 310, 315 'communication', and 25.150 'attitudes, emotions'.

6. This is not the opinion of J.G. Nordling, whose essay, 'Onesimus Fugitivus: A Defense of the Runaway Slave Hypothesis in Philemon', *JSNT* 41 (1991), pp. 97-119, is the most cogent defense of the traditional view concerning the background of Philemon in recent scholarship. He suggests that we should carefully consider 'the 52 occurrences [this figure, from Moulton–Geden, seems inaccurate, as, using the full Pauline corpus, including the "deutero-Pauline" material, the count is 54, or, only using the *Hauptbriefe*, it is 40] of this verb in Paul will reveal

In v. 9, Paul's entreaty is rather confusing, since he seems not to specify the object of the request. Unlike any other usage in the Pauline corpus, this usage of παρακαλέω seems to have no object. παρακαλέω, used in the first person (singular or plural) and active voice, is generally found in one of two constructions. The first construction is with an accusative object (most common in Paul and the rest of the New Testament is ὑμᾶς, usually translated something like, 'I/we entreat/exhort/ encourage you'; Rom. 12.1; 15.30; 16.17; 1 Cor. 1.10; 4.16; 16.15; 2 Cor. 2.8; 6.1; 10.1; etc.)—often as part of a catenative construction (e.g. 2 Cor. 2.8 διὸ παρακαλῶ ὑμᾶς κυρῶσαι εἰς αὐτὸν ἀγάπην). The second is with an object in either the accusative or dative cases, accompanied by a ἵνα clause (e.g. 2 Cor. 12.8 ὑπὲρ τούτου τρὶς τὸν κύριον παρεκάλεσα ἵνα ἀποστῇ ἀπ᾽ ἐμοῦ with the accusative; or 2 Thess. 3.12 τοῖς δὲ τοιούτοις παραγγέλλομεν καὶ παρακαλοῦμεν ἐν κυρίῳ Ἰησοῦ Χριστῷ, ἵνα μετὰ ἡσυχίας ἐργαζόμενοι τὸν ἑαυτῶν ἄρτον ἐσθίωσιν, with the dative). There are two places in Pauline usage where the first-person active is used without being complemented in the above manners: one is possibly Phlm. 9, under consideration here, and the other is 1 Cor. 4.13: δυσφημούμενοι παρακαλοῦμεν· ὡς περικαθάρματα τοῦ κόσμου ἐγενήθημεν, πάντων περίψημα ἕως ἄρτι ('being slandered, we apologize…'). In 1 Cor. 4.13, the exact sense of the verb is difficult to ascertain, but, if translated as I have done, there are parallels in the New Testament (Acts 16.39 καὶ ἐλθόντες παρεκάλεσαν αὐτοὺς καὶ ἐξαγαγόντες ἠρώτων ἀπελθεῖν ἀπὸ τῆς πόλεως), the *Letter of Aristeas* (§229 παρακαλέσας δὲ καὶ τοῦτον

that the apostle used the word in two ways: (1) "to exhort/beseech"…; and (2) "to comfort/encourage" ' (p. 112). Nordling then apparently reads these two related meanings back into Philemon, and comes up with the translation, 'I encourage you …' (extrapolated from p. 112, as he never actually states how he thinks this clause should be translated, but the material he does submit leads one to imagine that this is the translation/sense he wishes παρακαλέω to carry). Unfortunately, Nordling ignores both the initial occurrence of παρακαλέω in Philemon as well as the typical meaning of περί with the genitive. Although he discusses the importance of the context of the two preceding verses in the paragraph following his discussion of v. 10, he does not mention the occurrence of παρακαλέω in this discussion. He suggests that περί is a 'semantically uncertain preposition', and thinks that it 'is difficult to avoid the suspicion that the whole argument [that περί with the genitive should be taken in its typical Hellenistic sense of content] has been ingeniously invented to suit an alien interpretation of the text' (p. 112). See discusson of this issue below.

ἐπυνθάνετο καὶ τοῦ μετέπειτα τί καλλονῆς ἄξιόν ἐστιν; 'and encouraging that one, he inquired of the following one, "What is like beauty?"'; also in §§235, 238 and 264), as well as in Menander (*Fragment*, p. 241: οὐχὶ παρακληθέντας ὑμᾶς δεῖ γὰρ ἡμῖν εὐνοεῖν, ἀλλ' ὑπάρχειν τοῦτο) (see M–M *s.v.* παρακαλέω, for references in the papyri). There are, however, two further examples to note: the lack of an object in Heb. 13.19, περισσοτέρως δὲ παρακαλῶ τοῦτο ποιῆσαι, ἵνα τάχιον ἀποκατασταθῶ ὑμῖν, and in 1 Pet. 2.11 ἀγαπητοί, παρακαλῶ ὡς παροίκους καὶ παρεπιδήμους ἀπέχεσθαι τῶν σαρκικῶν ἐπιθυμιῶν αἵτινες στρατεύονται κατὰ τῆς ψυχῆς. Although without an explicit object, in both of these instances παρακαλέω still functions as a part of a catenative construction. That it does not do so in Phlm. 9 seems to suggest that they may not provide legitimate parallels to explain its use in this verse.

So, while we have some near parallels to Phlm. 9, we do not have exactly the same syntax in either Paul or wider New Testament usage. If we look more carefully at the text of Philemon, however, we might think that vv. 9 and 10 are more intricately linked than is usually thought. Verses 9 and 10 read: διὰ τὴν ἀγάπην μᾶλλον παρακαλῶ, τοιοῦτος ὢν ὡς Παῦλος πρεσβύτης νυνὶ δὲ καὶ δέσμιος Χριστοῦ Ἰησοῦ· παρακαλῶ σε περὶ τοῦ ἐμοῦ τέκνου, ὃν ἐγέννησα ἐν τοῖς δεσμοῖς, Ὀνήσιμον κ.τ.λ. The typical reading of v. 9 supplies the pronoun 'you' (or, with the preposition, 'to you') after παρακαλῶ (NKJV, NEB, JB/NJB, CEV, NASB, NIV, Lattimore, RSV/NRSV etc.).[7] However, if we remove this translational emendation, we are left with something which (given the usual pattern of παρακαλέω being found with some kind of object and/or role to play within a catenative construction and/or following a ἵνα clause) should probably be associated with the subsequent usage of παρακαλέω in v. 10. The intervening material would then be seen as parenthetical, with the repetition of the verb in v. 10 signalling the resumption of the request, this time with an object, as expected. Translated, this reads, 'on account of love, rather, I ask—being as [I am] Paul, old now, and even in chains for Christ Jesus—I ask you…' The sense of this request, having something to do with Onesimus is, of course, also a matter of some dispute, revolving mostly around the sense of περί. It is to this which we will now turn.

---

7.   This is also the case for Heb. 13.19 and 1 Pet. 2.11, which is, perhaps, more defensible than in Phlm. 9, as they are both parts of catenative constructions.

John Nordling's article, mentioned above, displays the continued uncritical usage of the traditional background story of Philemon to interpret the letter.[8] As a result, he characterizes attempts to understand

8. As Nordling puts it, 'I would like to defend the hypothesis that Onesimus was a runaway slave. Not only does that hypothesis suit the evangelical character of Philemon, but there is important extra-biblical evidence which ought to be considered before an informed decision can be reached about Onesimus...' ('Onesimus Fugitivus', p. 99). He then goes on to lay out the plan for his paper: '1. extra-biblical texts that mention runaway slaves; 2. passages in Philemon that support the runaway slave hypothesis; 3. the runaway slave problem in light of Roman law; 4. conclusion' (p. 99). However, there was no need to place section four of this paper at the end, as his conclusions are assumed right from the beginning. Rather than attempt to establish the basis from which a 'runaway slave hypothesis' could be formed on the basis of the text of Philemon itself (as is the approach advocated in the present article), he begins by discussing texts which may or may not have anything to do with the text of Philemon—if Onesimus was *not* a runaway, then those texts have *no* relevance to the discussion of the background of the letter. Although the sympathies in my article most definitely lie with some form of the alternative hypothesis—that Onesimus had been *sent* by Philemon to help Paul in some capacity during his imprisonment—it is also my concern to show how unacknowledged and invalid assumption can cloud scholarship. The simple substitution of one slanted translation and presentation (through translation, sub-titling, commentary, etc.) of an epistle for another will do nothing but perpetuate a climate where questions are closed before they are even asked. This is Sara Winter's approach. Besides the fact that her Greek grammar is based on an *Aktionsart* (and even time-based!) approach to the Greek verb outdated now for several years, her argumentation suffers from the same wish to combat one set of presuppositions by substituting her own. She fallaciously appeals to Hans-Georg Gadamer's *Truth and Method* (trans. J.C. Weinsheimer and D.G. Marshall; London: Sheed and Ward, 2nd rev. edn, 1989) to undergird this aspect of her programme (S.W. Winter, 'Methodological Observations on a New Interpretation of Paul's Letter to Philemon', *USQR* 39 [1984], p. 211 n. 19).
Another good example of this process in the interpretation of Philemon, enshrined at the level of method, is in Petersen's study, *Rediscovering Paul*, in the chapter entitled 'From Letter to Story—and Back: Toward a Narratology and Sociology of Letters', pp. 43-88. His process is such that, assuming he knows the background story concerning Onesimus and Philemon's relationship, he sets out to 'discover' this in the text of Philemon, and, unsurprisingly, does indeed find it there. Although the book was published in 1985, we can assume that, given publication queues and such, he will have had no access to Winter's first article on the subject ('Methodological Observations'), but aspects of the alternative hypothesis were put forward as early as 1935 with the first publication of Knox's *Philemon among the Letters of Paul*, and later, after the second edition of Knox's book in

the function of περί in v. 10 as the result of 'alien interpretation[s]'.[9] He may indeed be correct in asserting that the Knox/Winter hypothesis[10] brings alien elements into the interpretation of the text, but no more so than the traditional hypothesis. What is important in the understanding of περί with a genitive object, however, has little to do with historical reconstructions, and more to do with grammar and syntax. It is the sense of this construction that may help us discern the sense of the preceding verb(s) παρακαλῶ, and may give us the best window on the nature of the request being made by Paul—is this a request being made *on behalf of* Onesimus, for whatever reason, or is it *for* Onesimus, that is, with Onesimus himself as the *content* of the request? As Nordling's argument is the most recent, and as it handily surveys the previous attempts at solving this issue,[11] it will form the basis of my analysis.

Nordling responds to the suggestion on Knox's part (followed by Winter and, for different reasons, F.F. Bruce[12]) that the phrase παρακαλῶ σε περὶ τοῦ ἐμοῦ τέκνου should be translated 'I ask you for my child',[13] by discussing the semantic overlap of περί with ὑπέρ:

1959/60, in J.L. Houlden's *Paul's Letters from Prison* (Baltimore: Penguin, 1970), which is less ambitious than Knox's hypothesis and more measured than Winter's: 'That he was a runaway slave and that this is why Paul is so delicate and charming in this letter aimed at assuaging his master's wrath is a legend without foundation. We just do not know how he came to be with Paul...probably he had been lent Paul to be of service to him over a difficult period. And the reason for Paul's delicacy is simply that he wishes to retain his services longer...' (p. 226).

9.   Nordling, 'Onesimus Fugitivus', p. 112.

10.   So designated because Winter's hypothesis, while rejecting Knox's idea that Philemon was the letter to the Laodiceans, is essentially built upon his work.

11.   Cited without analysis in J.D.G. Dunn, *The Epistles to the Colossians and to Philemon* (NIGTC; Grand Rapids: Eerdmans; Carlisle: Paternoster, 1996), p. 328 n. 20.

12.   F.F. Bruce, *The Epistles to the Colossians, to Philemon, and to the Ephesians* (NICNT; Grand Rapids: Eerdmans, 1984), pp. 212-13. Nordling does not acknowledge Bruce.

13.   Knox, *Philemon*, p. 20. On the same page he explains, 'Moule [*Colossians and Philemon* (CGTC; Cambridge: Cambridge University Press, 1957)] writes that I take "the παρακαλῶ σε περὶ...of v. 10 to mean 'I request you for...'", as though Paul were not making a request *concerning* Onesimus but rather *for the gift of him*". Professor Moule neither accepts nor rejects this proposal, but his sentence does not seem to me to state the relationship between the two possibilities quite correctly. One does not need to decide that Paul is not making a request *concerning*

The more traditional translation cannot stand, claims Winter, because there is a substantial difference in the NT between the παρακαλῶ…περὶ construction (which she contends occurs only at Phlm 10) and παρακαλῶ…ὑπέρ. Winter also claims that the παρακαλῶ […] ὑπέρ construction occurs three times (2 Cor. 12.8; 5.20; 1 Thess. 3.2) and that these passages demonstrate the differing sense 'request *on behalf of*'.

It is necessary to point out, however, that in the third passage that Winter uses to support her position, περὶ (*not* ὑπέρ!) occurs: παρακαλέσαι ὑμᾶς περὶ [*sic*—see discussion below] τῆς πίστεως ὑμῶν… (1 Thess. 3.2). This fact alone severely damages Winter's argument that there *must* be a difference in meaning between the παρακαλῶ […] περὶ and παρακαλῶ […] ὑπέρ constructions. To be sure, NT grammarians do make a slight distinction between περί and ὑπέρ with the genitive case.[14] Yet it is widely acknowledged that the two prepositions overlap semantically, at least in epistolary and *Koine* Greek.[15]

There are several difficulties with this response on the part of Nordling. The first is his citation of 1 Thess. 3.2 with περί on the basis of a very weak variant reading, of which he has no discussion. The textual apparatus of the Nestle–Aland[27] edition records that the reading περί does indeed exist, but supported only in the Majority text and the hand of the second corrector of Codex Bezae. The reading ὑπέρ is, however, found in Sinaiticus, Alexandrinus, Vaticanus and the original hand of Bezae, as well as many other later codices and minuscules. So, while there may be grounds for discussion of this as a textual variant, it in no way deserves to simply replace ὑπέρ in the text without mention—the *UBSGNT*[4] committee did not even deem it necessary to include περί as

Onesimus in order to recognise that he is asking *for* him. It may be argued, and agreed, that περί with the genitive always means "about", or "with reference to"; what I am saying is that after παρακαλῶ the "about" can often be sharpened. A request *for* Onesimus would certainly also be a request *concerning* him' (p. 20 n. 8). It is very possible that Nordling never saw this note, as he seems to have been using the original, 1935, edition of the book (see his p. 98 n. 1), which could not have included this comment upon Moule's 1957 commentary. (Somewhat strangely, given that her work seems to have been part of a dissertation largely based on Knox's earlier investigations, it appears that Winter is also unaware of this later edition of Knox's work.)

14. He cites S.G. Green, *Handbook to the Grammar of the Greek New Testament* (New York: F.H. Revell, 1904), pp. 250-52, and E. Van Ness Goetchius, *The Language of the New Testament* (New York: Charles Scribner's Sons, 1965), pp. 155-56.

15. Nordling, 'Onesimus Fugitivus', p. 111.

a discussed variant. It is difficult to discern exactly how it was that Nordling arrived at this reading, unless he relied upon a printed text of the Greek New Testament based on the Majority text. The semantic overlap upon which Nordling would like to build his case for ὑπέρ and περί being very similar with this verb is unsupported in Paul, and indeed, in the entire New Testament.

A second problem with Nordling's argumentation here is that, in the sources he cites for the 'semantic overlap' of these two prepositions, he is very selective. There is indeed good evidence that, at times, ὑπέρ and περί are used in very similar circumstances, and it has even been suggested by Moule that they may be 'synonymous'.[16] However, it is important that the partial 'synonymy' of these two terms is not confused with complete synonymy—it is better to think of them as semantically overlapping. In fact, the semantic overlap goes in both directions—it is not only the case that περί appears in the same contexts in which we might expect to find ὑπέρ, but also that ὑπέρ appears in contexts in which we might expect to find περί. Louw–Nida (90.24) lists several examples of this reverse linking, including Jn 1.30 οὗτός ἐστιν ὑπὲρ οὗ ἐγὼ εἶπον, and 2 Cor. 7.4 πολλή μοι καύχησις ὑπὲρ ὑμῶν. Their note to this section is helpful: 'The general equivalence of meaning of περί and ὑπέρ in contexts introducing content can be readily seen from the tendency of scribes to interchange these terms in manuscripts. However, there may be certain subtle distinctions in

---

16. C.F.D. Moule, *An Idiom Book of New Testament Greek* (Cambridge: Cambridge University Press, 2nd edn, 1959), p. 63, on the basis of Eph. 6.18, 19 δεήσει περὶ πάντων τῶν ἁγίων καὶ ὑπὲρ ἐμοῦ, ἵνα μοι δοθῇ λόγος ἐν ἀνοίξει τοῦ στόματός μου, ἐν παρρησίᾳ γνωρίσαι τὸ μυστήριον τοῦ εὐαγγελίου, and Heb. 5.1-3 πᾶς γὰρ ἀρχιερεὺς ἐξ ἀνθρώπων λαμβανόμενος ὑπὲρ ἀνθρώπων καθίσταται τὰ πρὸς τὸν θεόν, ἵνα προσφέρῃ δῶρά τε καὶ θυσίας ὑπὲρ ἁμαρτιῶν, μετριοπαθεῖν δυνάμενος τοῖς ἀγνοοῦσιν καὶ πλανωμένοις, ἐπεὶ καὶ αὐτὸς περίκειται ἀσθένειαν καὶ δι' αὐτὴν ὀφείλει, καθὼς περὶ τοῦ λαοῦ, οὕτως καὶ περὶ αὐτοῦ προσφέρειν περὶ ἁμαρτιῶν. There is no question that these two prepositions are semantically related; however, in differing circumstances, this semantic relation may or may not translate into semantic *overlap*—the very fact that the writers of these two passages have used *two* semantically related prepositions, rather than simply one of them, may argue for a lack of complete synonymy (if such can exist). Nuances in word variation are, of course, difficult to discern when there are no native language users to interrrogate, but, by the same token, it is important that we do not simply conflate similar terms, and so lose any chance at determining the nuances that may exist.

meaning, but these cannot be determined from existing contexts.' It seems, then, that we are no further ahead in the determination of the sense of Paul's request of Philemon by recourse to the preposition. However, if we read 'on behalf of...', we are doing so in a context where there is no syntactical reason why we must do so, and are in fact doing exactly that of which Nordling accuses Knox and Winter, namely importing a reading which, although possible, is by no means the best option.

Given that the grammar here has not moved us one way or the other on the issue, it would be worthwhile at this juncture to examine the evidence adduced by Winter to support her argument that the language here in Philemon reflects that of summons formulae in extra-biblical Greek. She adduces four examples (following Knox's lead),[17] to which, despite the potential damage to his own argument, Nordling offers three more.[18] These clearly show a pattern, in Greek of the Hellenistic period, of a formula using παρακαλῶ and περί that is very similar to Paul's usage here in Philemon. Although this formula is used only once in Paul and the New Testament, it seems to have been quite clearly established elsewhere, at least enough to militate against the construction in Phlm. 10 necessarily being understood in the sense of 'on behalf of', which translation seems to be necessary to establish the sense of the request required for the traditional hypothesis. Of course, given the semantic overlap mentioned above, it remains a possibility.

b. ὃν ἀνέπεμψά σοι
The sense of ὃν ἀνέπεμψά σοι in v. 12 is also important in the discussion of the sense of Paul's request. This is one of the phrases which Knox and Winter have tried to understand on the basis of both New Testament and extra-biblical legal settings. In fact, when used in the

17. S.C. Winter, 'Paul's Letter to Philemon', *NTS* 33 (1987), pp 1-15, here p. 14 n. 45: *P. Oxy.* 1070.7-10 μεῖζον [ν]ῦν ἐν τῷ μεγάλω Σαραπείῳ | προσκυνεῖ, τὸν μέγαν θεὸν Σαρᾶπιν πα|ρακαλῶ περί τε τῆς ζωῆς ὑμῶν καὶ τῶν | ἡμῶν πάν[τ]ων καὶ τῶν χρηστῶν...; *P. Tebt.* 1.58.52-55 (a letter from a tax-farmer) πάλιν προσεντέλλο|μαί σοι προσεδρεῦσα | καὶ προσπαρακλέσαι Νίκωνα | περὶ τῆς λογ[ί]ας; Aur. Sakaon 37.15-17 (although this uses ὑπέρ); and Appian, *Punic Wars* 136.
18. Nordling, 'Onesimus Fugitivus', p. 111 n. 4, printed on p. 112: *P. Sarap.* 92 παρακαλῶ σε γράψαι μοι περὶ τῆς ὑγιείας σου; *P. Sarap.* 95 παρακαλῶ οὖν σε...γράφε περὶ τῆς σωτηρίας; *SB* 10.102 παρακαλῶ οὖν ἀντιγράψαι μοι περὶ τῆς σωτηρίας σου.

New Testament, not considering Phlm. 12, this phrase seems to be used by Luke exclusively in legal contexts, namely, the referring of either Jesus' (Lk. 23.7, 11,[19] 15) or Paul's (Acts 25.21) cases to a different or more suitable authority. In extra-biblical Greek, the word is indeed used in the sense argued for by Knox and Winter (although neither of them cites any examples, this work being done, again, by Nordling[20]), as 'send up/refer [to a higher/more suitable authority]', but there is also a frequently used sense of 'send back'.[21] Just because the word has a clear legal sense (amongst others), it is not, as Knox would suggest, clear that we should read this sense into the text of Philemon, which, after all, is *not* a clear legal setting![22] In fact, even in the Lukan data brought to bear by Knox and Winter, there is some equivocation. Although Knox would suggest that 'in the New Testament period it was commonly employed to indicate the reference of a case from a lower to a higher court',[23] the Lukan 'legal' examples are not examples of references of Jesus' case from a *lower* to a *higher* court, but simply the reference of Jesus' case *back* to the court from which it was previously referred. Arguably, Lk. 23.7 is an instance where the word is used in the sense for which Knox and Winter argue.[24] However, if one

19. ἀνέπεμψεν is the form chosen by Nestle–Aland[27] for the text, though they list ἔπεμψεν as a *v.l.* supported by 𝔓[75], ℵ*, L, and two minuscules. Winter ('Paul's Letter', p. 7) lists Lk. 23.22 as an example of ἀναπέμπω, which must be a misreading for 23.11, although it is difficult to determine exactly how her numbers tally, as she mentions a *v.l.* at Acts 27.1 which Nestle–Aland[27] have not included in their list of variants. In addition to this, it must be noted that Acts 25.21 also has a *v.l.* of πέμψω, supported by H, L, P, among other sources.

20. Nordling, 'Onesimus Fugitivus', p. 108 n. 1. Winter does cite BAGD, but does not list any of the examples they have adduced.

21. See M–M *s.v.* ἀναπέμπω, and the texts listed there, as well as Plutarch, *Sol.* 4.6, listed in BAGD, and Pindar, *I.* 7 (6).10, listed in LSJ.

22. Knox, *Philemon*, p. 21: 'That the term has the same legal connotation in the Philemon passage there is not the slightest reason to doubt'. To pre-determine that Philemon is a legal text is, however, to again assume unproven conclusions.

23. Knox, *Philemon*, p. 21.

24. However, it is somewhat questionable as to whether or not Herod's court was really a *higher* court, or simply the court with initial jurisdiction, through which Jesus' case, to abide by legal precedent (as well as political expediency), should first go. The mention in Lk. 23.12 of Pilate and Herod's previous enmity and subsequent friendship as a result of Jesus' case being first referred to Herod's court (as Herod had legal jurisdiction over Jesus), and then, prudently, sent back to

argues for the sense of *lower* to *higher* in the use of the word in 23.7, by definition, one cannot argue for the same sense in 23.11, as Jesus is sent from Herod's court (ostensibly the *higher* court, or at least the court with jurisdiction) *back* to Pilate. Is Pilate's court magically transformed through some legal chicanery into a higher court while Jesus is being interrogated by Herod? By no means. In fact, what one is forced to do, on either one or both of these occasions, is translate the word either simply 'refer', 'send', or, in the second instance (as well as in 23.15), 'send *back*'. The reference in Acts 25.21 is, perhaps, the clearest example of the sense for which Knox and Winter argue, but this may simply be because, unlike the Luke references, Caesar is clearly a higher authority than Festus. This fact may not, in truth, be anything more than coincidence, however, and the verb there may simply mean 'refer' or 'send'. Of course, it cannot mean 'send *back*', as Paul has not yet been to Rome, let alone to Caesar's court.

At the end of this discussion, one is left with the clear impression that the Knox/Winter hypothesis, where based on the particular meaning for which they argue for this verb, loses support. Of course, the traditional hypothesis gains nothing by this investigation, as we are left with a verb which can only be surely translated as 'send' or 'send *back*'. Since we know that Onesimus did indeed come from Philemon at one point, the latter translation seems perfectly acceptable, and this fact also seems to provide the best explanation for Paul's use of the prefixed form of this verb, rather than the simple πέμπω. The lack of legal context and the lack of any clear reason *why* Onesimus left in the first place mean that this cannot, as Nordling puts it, 'provide solid support for the runaway slave hypothesis in Philemon',[25] nor, as Winter puts it, 'support the argument that ἀναπέμπω is being used in the legal sense in Phlm. 12'.[26]

c. τάχα γὰρ διὰ τοῦτο ἐχωρίσθη πρὸς ὥραν

The sense of the aorist passive verb ἐχωρίσθη in Phlm. 15 is also seen by both sides as beneficial to their cases. Of all the possible textual arguments for either side, this is the least persuasive. Paul uses neither the active voice, which would satisfy those who see this as a reference

Pilate, argues for a political motivation for Jesus' movements between the two rulers, not a merely legal one.

25. Nordling, 'Onesimus Fugitivus', p. 108.
26. Winter, 'Paul's Letter', p. 7.

to the flight of Onesimus,[27] nor a different verbal construction altogether, which would satisfy those who see this as a reference to God's
role in the volitional act on the part of Philemon in sending Onesimus
to Paul in prison.[28] However, Nordling's argument that the verb, in the
passive, may have been a technical term for running away does bear
some further investigation. Although he is certainly correct that LSJ
does record 'depart, go away' as a later meaning of the passive, of their
examples,[29] only a reference in Diodorus Siculus is clearly passive.
References from Heraclitus, Polybius and Ezekiel the Tragedian are all
examples of the present middle/passive, and none of the contexts helps
us to make definite decisions regarding their nature. It hardly seems
that one example from Diodorus Siculus is a good basis upon which to
build a case for the sense of 'depart/go away'.[30] However, the passive
voice of this verb *does* seem to have taken on a technical sense to do
with the act of divorce, as LSJ note, providing examples from Polybius
(31.26.6)[31] and Euripides (*Fragment* 1063.13). Interestingly, the
Pauline usage of this verb in the passive (excluding Phlm. 15) is also

27. Nevertheless, Nordling still manages to construe this verb as supporting his
case: 'By this oblique expression Paul comes as close as he dares to mentioning
Onesimus's illegal flight from his master. Paul may even have intended the deliberate ambiguity of ἐχωρίσθη to protect Onesimus yet also give his master a precise
hint of Onesimus's crime' ('Onesimus Fugitivus', p. 109). It is difficult to ascertain
exactly what it is Nordling means by this, however. What is it, about which Paul
must be careful not to make mention? Would Philemon not have been aware of the
exact nature of any alleged crime on the part of Onesimus? How would the use of a
passive voice verb protect Onesimus? Nordling offers no evidence for his position.
28. See Winter, 'Paul's Letter', pp. 10-11.
29. Heraclitus, *Incred.* 8; Diodorus Siculus 19.65.3 καὶ τότε μὲν εἰς
Συρακούσσας ἐχωρίσθη; Polybius 3.94.9 καὶ πολλὰ χωριζόμενος ἐνετείλατο μὴ
τοσαύτην ποιεῖσθαι σπουδὴν ὑπὲρ τοῦ βλάψαι τοὺς πολεμίους; and Ezekiel the
Tragedian, *Exodus* 76 βασιλικὸν δ' ἔδωκέ μοι διάδημα καὶ αὐτὸς ἐκ θρόνων
χωρίζεται.
30. Nordling's further argument 'that the stem of χωρίζω could be used in a
technical sense, meaning "to run away" appears likely in light of the compound
form of the verb (ἀνακεχώρηκεν, *UPZ* 121, ll. 3, 21), used to denote the flight
of...two runaways...' ('Onesimus Fugitivus', p. 109 n. 2) is hardly cogent—the
very prefixing of this form argues strongly for the fact that the stem, on its own, did
not carry the sense for which Nordling argues.
31. This example is problematic, as there is a variant reading, albeit retaining
the same verb and voice thereof.

limited to his discussion of divorce in 1 Cor. 7.10-11, 15.[32] It seems within the realm of possibility that this verb was particularly suitable in contexts where one party left another (or another place), and the language user wished the leaving to focus on the person/place being left, rather than toward which person/place the subject is moving. The passive occurrences of this verb in Acts (1.4; 18.1-2) may provide support for this hypothesis. If so, of course, this could provide support for the idea that this verb should be taken as active in meaning, and so be translated 'Perhaps for this reason he left you for a while...' However, this still begs the question as to how exactly 'leaving' can be construed as 'running away', and this case has not been convincingly made.

d. οὐκέτι ὡς δοῦλον ἀλλ᾽ ὑπὲρ δοῦλον, ἀδελφὸν ἀγαπητόν

What Paul means by οὐκέτι ὡς δοῦλον ἀλλ᾽ ὑπὲρ δοῦλον, ἀδελφὸν ἀγαπητόν in Phlm. 16 is anyone's guess, although the most popular solution is that he is making reference to the fact that Onesimus is now a Christian (to whom Paul had 'given birth' in prison, v. 10), and that his status as Philemon's brother demands some kind of change in his status as a slave. This is one place where both sides in this issue are seemingly willing to agree. Winter discusses this in some detail,[33] while Nordling does not, apparently, consider it worth discussion. In actual fact, the implications of the level of change in the relationship between Philemon and Onesimus, at which Paul hints both here and elsewhere in the letter (especially v. 21), do not affect either position regarding the actual situation which called forth this *communiqué*. Paul's attitudes toward and teaching about slavery are, of course, important for the discussion of Pauline theology, and deserve much more attention than they have received in recent debate.[34] However, the exact attitude which Paul displays in this particular letter is quite difficult to establish.

32. Although the two occurrences of the verb in 1 Cor. 7.15 are also examples of present middle/passive forms, the context of the discussion, which includes clear examples of the aorist passive of the same verb in very similar circumstances, argues for the passive being the correct parsing for the present tense-forms.
33. 'Paul's Letter', p. 10.
34. One wonders if the widely-held belief in the pseudonymity of the *Haustafel*-bearing letters has not clouded discussion of this issue overmuch.

e. εἰ οὖν με ἔχεις κοινωνόν, προσλαβοῦ αὐτὸν ὡς ἐμέ, εἰ δέ τι ἠδίκησέν σε ἢ ὀφείλει, τοῦτο ἐμοὶ ἐλλόγα

The nature and sense of the first-class conditionals εἰ οὖν με ἔχεις κοινωνόν, προσλαβοῦ αὐτὸν ὡς ἐμέ in Phlm. 17, and εἰ δέ τι ἠδίκησέν σε ἢ ὀφείλει, τοῦτο ἐμοὶ ἐλλόγα in v. 18, is very important to the discussion of any hypothesis regarding the background of Philemon. Nordling limits his discussion mostly to the lexical level, while Winter attempts a more grammatically based analysis. Nordling's analysis follows the general pattern of commentaries on this passage, but, as he is specifically concerned with the background to Philemon, he goes on to suggest that the 'use and mutual proximity of ἀδικέω and ὀφείλω, however, are at least suggestive of Onesimus's robbery'.[35] He appears to be assuming his conclusions. It is too much to say this at this point, because *it remains to be established that such an event has taken place.*

Dunn finds the shift of terminology in these verses to the commercial realm somewhat surprising.[36] In actual fact, however, both hypotheses for the background of the letter require that this area be addressed by Paul. On the one hand, we have a runaway thieving slave who has deprived his master not only of his services, but also of the property, whatever it may have been, which he stole. Paul, in wishing some sort of forgiveness to take place, perhaps even to the point of manumission, would have no other vocabulary with which to address this situation. On the other hand, if what we have here is a request concerned not with some kind of wrongdoing on Onesimus's part, but rather with some kind of actual benefit to be received on Paul's part, then we would also expect Paul to discuss this in terms of the commercial and financial ramifications that this would have for his owner. If the request amounted to manumission, then we should be even less surprised that Paul speaks in terms of accounts and debts.

We still need to establish the sense of these two connected conditional statements. Contrary to Dunn, the first-class conditional does not carry the sense of 'whatever' rather than 'if'.[37] In fact, of all the classes

35. 'Onesimus Fugitivus', p. 110.
36. Dunn, *Colossians and Philemon*, p. 336.
37. Dunn, *Colossians and Philemon*, p. 338, in reference to the conditional in v. 18 (oddly, he does not make the same argument for the preceding conditional): 'The "if" has, indeed, the force of "whatever", the rhetorical effect being to underline the comprehensiveness of Paul's guarantee'. It seems that Dunn is reading this

of conditional statement available to Hellenistic Greek users, first-class conditionals carry the least interpretative weight. Rather than the sense for which Dunn argues here, the first-class conditional simply posits something for the sake of argument. As Porter's discussion indicates,

> Use of 'since' in translating the protasis of a first class conditional cannot be made the rule... [It is] estimated that, of the [300] first class conditionals [in the New Testament], 37% are obviously true, 12% are obviously false, and 51% are undetermined. If [this] is correct, then well over half *do not* show that the first class conditional is asserted as true ('since').[38]

Although Dunn cites Clarice Martin's essay on the commercial language in these verses, he ignores her clear presentation of similar analysis of the conditional, based on grammars by Smyth,[39] Zerwick,[40] and Brooks and Winbery,[41] as well as Robertson and Davis.[42] She is hardly without support in her statement that 'one cannot deduce from the commercial terminology in the conditional protasis alone that a crime has occurred',[43] making Dunn's response to this quite puzzling. Speaking of Martin's and Callahan's questioning of the weight usually placed on this conditional, he suggests that 'the aorist (ἠδίκησεν) hardly indicates the possibility of Onesimus's *future* indebtedness (for travel and lodging), and the thesis hardly explains the vehemence of Paul's

first-class conditional as if it were a third class, which can indeed be read with the sense for which he argues. The grammar of the verse does not, however, support the idea that this is a third class conditional statement.

38. S.E. Porter, *Idioms of the Greek New Testament* (BLG, 2; Sheffield: JSOT Press, 2nd edn, 1994), p. 257.

39. H.W. Smyth, *Greek Grammar* (Cambridge, MA: Harvard University Press, 1980).

40. M. Zerwick, *Biblical Greek* (SPIB, 114; Rome: Biblical Institute Press, 1963).

41. J.A. Brooks and C.L. Winbery, *Syntax of New Testament Greek* (Washington, DC: University Press of America, 1979).

42. A.T. Robertson and W.H. Davis, *A New Short Grammar of the Greek Testament* (Grand Rapids: Baker Book House, 10th edn, 1979).

43. C.L. Martin, 'The Rhetorical Function of Commercial Language in Paul's Letter to Philemon (Verse 18)', in D.F. Watson (ed.), *Persuasive Artistry: Studies in Honor of George A. Kennedy* (JSNTSup, 50; Sheffield: JSOT Press, 1991), pp. 332-33. Martin is supported in this by A.D. Callahan, 'Paul's Epistle to Philemon: Toward an Alternative *Argumentum*', *HTR* 86 (1993), p. 374.

repeated assurance that he would repay whatever Onesimus owed'.[44] Two problems emerge from this statement: (1) the categories Dunn is using to understand the function of the Greek tense-forms seem to be time-based, and (2) the simple acknowledgment on the part of Martin and Callahan (and the present writer) that first-class conditionals do not necessarily assert anything except for the sake of argument is not a *thesis*, it is a recognition of *a grammatical rule*. It is dealing with this *rule* that gives trouble to the *thesis* that Onesimus was a thieving runaway. The antiquity of the runaway slave hypothesis should not lead to its being treated as if it were fact! The first problem, however, is just as telling as this last—the use of the aorist tense-form does not convey anything to do with time. As the work on verbal aspect in the Greek of the New Testament has shown, the Greek verb can no longer be understood either in terms of time, or in terms of the first rejection of time-based categories in an attempt to make better sense of the ways in which the Greek verb worked, *Aktionsart* theory.[45] Contrary to what must be a time-based approach in Dunn's criticism of Martin and Callahan's position, the aorist is, albeit infrequently, used in future-referring contexts—the so-called proleptic or futuristic aorist.[46] It is also used in omnitemporal settings—the so-called 'gnomic' aorist[47]— and in timeless settings.[48] There is nothing to say that this particular aorist, ἠδίκησεν, is not, indeed, being used like most of its compatriots in Greek, as the normal background narrative tense-form, conveying perfective verbal aspect. However, that it is conveying perfective aspect does not mean that it must be past-referring, and so we are unable to rest this much weight on one particular verb, no matter which tense-form it may take. Context and other deictic indicators will have to give us the temporal sense, and, as we are discovering for many of the instances where a single grammatical feature or lexical item is thought

44. Dunn, *Colossians and Philemon*, p. 338 n. 34.

45. See K.L. McKay, *Greek Grammar for Students: A Concise Grammar of Classical Attic with Special Reference to Aspect in the Verb* (Canberra: Australian National University, 1974); S.E. Porter, *Verbal Aspect in the Greek of the New Testament, with Reference to Tense and Mood* (SBG, 1; New York: Peter Lang, 1989); and even B.M. Fanning, *Verbal Aspect in New Testament Greek* (Oxford: Clarendon Press, 1990); as well as the handy summary of Porter's position in *Idioms*, pp. 20-61.

46. Porter, *Idioms*, pp. 37-38.

47. Porter, *Idioms*, pp. 38-39.

48. Porter, *Idioms*, p. 39.

to convey much weight for one or other hypothesis regarding the background of Philemon, there is precious little upon which to go.

As far as verbal aspect in these two verses is concerned, it is worth noting the shift in verbal aspect in the protases and apodoses of these two conditional statements. In the first protasis, we have a present (ἔχεις), followed by an aorist imperative (προσλαβοῦ) in the apodosis (which must similarily be an action taking place in the future). In the second conditional, we have both an aorist (ἠδίκησεν) and a present (ὀφείλει) in the protasis, and a present imperative (ἐλλόγα) in the apodosis (which also must be seen as an action in the future, at least from the time of writing). If, following Dunn, we were to view these verbs as primarily time-based, a great deal of confusion is unavoidable; looking at the verbs in terms of their verbal aspect avoids this confusion. In v. 18, ἠδίκησεν, as a complete action (or, in the context of the first-class conditional, an allegedly complete action), is apparently viewed by the author perfectively, thus the use of the aorist tense-form. The use of the present tense-form, ὀφείλει, which conveys imperfective verbal aspect, simply shows that this 'action' is viewed as a progressing situation—it is difficult to view 'owing' perfectively, as Paul seems to be speaking of something viewed as still in progress, or he would not be suggesting the option of τοῦτο ἐμοὶ ἐλλόγα. The continued use of the present tense-form with ἐλλόγα suggests that Paul is linking his emphasis in this conditional on 'owing' to the consequent result which he wishes, namely that the onus be shifted to him. This is highlighted even more in the previous verse, with the use of the present indicative in the protasis, and then a switch to the aorist imperative in the apodosis. Again, the emphasis is on the relationship that Paul has with Philemon, and *not* on the reception of Onesimus.

This is emphasized elsewhere in the letter as well. The entire section leading up to the request in vv. 10-19 focuses on Philemon and his role within the community of saints (vv. 5-9). This is the basis and content of Paul's thankfulness in prayer in v. 4: εὐχαριστῶ τῷ θεῷ μου πάντοτε μνείαν σου ποιούμενος ἐπὶ τῶν προσευχῶν μου. In this passage, Paul clearly reinforces several characteristics of his recipient: his love and faithfulness (both for the Lord and for all the saints), as well as the fact that Philemon has refreshed many of the saints by his love. The ὅπως subjunctive clause in v. 6 is, however, somewhat obscure. Whether it depends on v. 4, or is to be seen as a parenthetical comment, is difficult to tell, but the likelihood is that vv. 5 and 6 are to be seen as

individually dependent on v. 4. Whatever its relationship to the surrounding verses, and whatever its exact meaning, v. 6 gives evidence of
at least one other reinforcement: Philemon's κοινωνία is either commended, or Philemon is commended to κοινωνία, and, either way, its
result (translated rather loosely) is a knowledge of 'every good [thing]
which is yours [or 'ours']⁴⁹ in Christ Jesus'.⁵⁰ Verse 7 goes on to give a
reason, or perhaps an explanation, for Paul's wish for Philemon: χαρὰν
γὰρ πολλὴν ἔσχον καὶ παράκλησιν ἐπὶ τῇ ἀγάπῃ σου, ὅτι τὰ σπλάγχνα τῶν ἁγίων ἀναπέπαυται διὰ σοῦ, ἀδελφέ. Here we meet for the
second time a word which will be repeated in the request which follows: σπλάγχνα. No matter which perspective one adopts concerning
the exact background of this letter, this must be recognized as a classic
set-up. Paul is indeed 'buttering up' Philemon. There is no need to see
this as a negative action on the part of Paul (although this is not ruled
out), but there is no getting around the fact that Paul is at least making
an attempt at being extremely persuasive. What is interesting and
notable when it comes to discussion of the significance of this set-up is
what seems to be its emphasis. The picture Paul paints of Philemon
here is that of a benefactor of the Christian community:

> I give thanks to my God always, remembering you in my prayers, having
> heard of your love and faith which you have toward the Lord Jesus and
> toward all the saints, [and, I give thanks] that the fellowship/sharing of
> your faith might be effective in [the] knowledge of all the good [which

49. There is a variant here which must be taken into consideration: in 𝔓⁶¹ and
ℵ, as well as several later majuscules, minuscules and versions, the reading is ἐν
ὑμῖν. The reading given here, ἐν ἡμῖν, adopted by the Nestle–Aland²⁷, is supported
by A, C, D, Ψ, as well as a fifth-century majuscule and the Majority text.
P.T. O'Brien (*Colossians, Philemon* [WBC, 44; Waco, TX: Word Books, 1982], p.
275) suggests that the variant should be accepted. See B.M. Metzger, *A Textual
Commentary on the Greek New Testament* (London: United Bible Societies, 2nd
edn, 1994), p. 588, for a discussion—'The Committee preferred ἐν ἡμῖν, which is
perhaps slightly less well supported…, because it is more expressive and because,
standing among other pronouns of the second person singular and plural, ἡμῖν was
more likely to be changed by copyists to ὑμῖν than vice versa'. By the same token,
however, it seems that the first plural could have been changed to be in keeping
with the second person nature of the letter, as there are three individual recipients
named, along with the church. Certainty based on internal factors seems impossible
on this point.
50. For a recent discussion of the various obscurities of this verse, see O'Brien,
Colossians, Philemon, pp. 279-81.

is] ours/yours in Christ.[51] For I have much joy and comfort at ['from'?]
your love, because the hearts of the saints are in a state of refreshment
through you, brother.

From here, Paul sets out to establish the basis of his request, and the
reason for the manner in which he puts it to Philemon:

> Therefore, [though] having much confidence in Christ to command you
> [concerning] what is fit/proper/pertinent, on account of love rather I
> ask...

Two things must be pointed out with reference to this build-up:
(1) Philemon's κοινωνία and ἀγάπην are commended and/or praised
by Paul, as well as their results in the refreshment of the saints' σπλάγχνα. Later, Paul appeals to Philemon, rather than commands him,
because of ἀγάπην. What is not clear is whose ἀγάπην, exactly, is in
view—Philemon's for the saints, Paul's for Philemon, Philemon's for
Paul, or even a mutual love. What seems most natural, given that it has
been emphasized in the preceding verses, is that it is *Philemon's* love
which is meant in this particular instance. On this reading, then, Paul is
not commanding Philemon out of some sense of delicacy, but because
he is trying to get Philemon to see that what Paul asks of him is similar
(both in content and results) to the previous love he had shown. The
circumstances of Paul also figure into the request—he refers to himself
as an aged prisoner for Christ Jesus, and simply 'Paul', with whatever
connotations that may have had for Philemon (or, by extension, for
Paul!). Onesimus has not yet been mentioned, and, no matter what the
background one assumes, at this point of the letter it is impossible to
deny that Paul is making an appeal for something which would fit in
with the picture he has drawn of Philemon in vv. 4-7. (2) The κοινωνία
Paul commends in v. 6 also figures later in the letter: the first
conditional clause discussing conditions which may have affected
Philemon's acceptance of Paul's request puts κοινωνία in the protasis.
The *translation* of this occurrence with a different word than that of the
occurrence in v. 6 (as in the CEV, JB, NASB, NIV, NKJV, etc.) obscures
the relation that these two verses and parts of the letter derive from
Paul's repetition of the word. While the first-class conditional, as

---

51. Although many exegetical issues upon which this translation of v. 6 rests
are left undiscussed, space dictates that they remain so. In the interest of clarity and
in the light of my conclusions below concerning the translation of Philemon, this
reading has been adopted simply to facilitate discussion.

discussed above, does nothing more than make a statement for the sake of argument, the previous discussion of Philemon's κοινωνία makes the use of the first-class conditional somewhat ironic—Philemon is now asked by Paul, in a very direct way, to *decide* whether he has a similar attitude to Paul as he does to others. The result of this decision, if positive, will, as the apodosis of the conditional suggests, result in the reception of Onesimus as if he were Paul.

f. *Why* προσλαβοῦ αὐτὸν *[Onesimus]* ὡς *Paul?*

Of course, the simple *recognition* that Onesimus is supposed to be received as Paul is only the beginning of the discussion. If, as we have seen above, the grammatical emphasis in these verses is *not* on this ultimate phrase, we are still left to explain what exactly Paul means, and for what reason it is that this request is made.

The usual explanation, of course, is that Paul makes this request, based on the 'guilt-trip' of the protasis in v. 17, because Onesimus was in deep trouble with his master as the result of both his running away and the act of theft that accompanied it. As we have seen, however, neither of these alleged acts is substantiated on the basis of the text itself, but is rather read out of what is an arguably unclear text. To read these inferences back into this verse, as this interpretation requires, is exegetically less than precise. The opposite to this, however, is *not* to simply repeat the process using an alternative hypothesis. The opposite action would be to determine what the text *does* say, and then see how that fits with the rest of the letter. Winter's hypothesis is that Onesimus is here being recommended to Philemon and, by extension, the church which meets at his house,[52] on the basis of a *societas* relationship[53] as

---

52. That Winter, following Knox, thinks that this letter is actually addressed to Archippus, who was both Onesimus's master and the owner of the house in which the addressed church met, makes little difference to the alternative hypothesis, but must be mentioned for the sake of accuracy. That this position is untenable is demonstrable in the examination of the evidence adduced by Knox (*Philemon*, pp. 51-61, whose reasoning is repeated without addition in Winter, 'Paul's Letter', pp. 1-2) that a letter with more than one recipient was not necessarily addressed to the first-named recipient. He cites *P. Giss.* 1.54 as an example where a letter is clearly sent to two individuals, to the second of whom the letter is largely addressed (pp. 53-54). Unfortunately, Knox's argument breaks down at several points, first and foremost of which is the very clarity with which the author of this papyrus letter switches from a plural pronoun to the singular, but also uses the name of the person to whom he is now addressing his comments. The further switch back to the

an equal partner. It is this equality that is in view here, not grace for a runaway. Although the parallel to the *societas* relationship is perhaps not as strong as Winter suggests, it is not necessary to read this alternative hypothesis into the material at hand (as she does) to find support for her argument. Two things about this request are telling: (1) It explains the idea of an equal reception being given to Paul much better than the runaway slave hypothesis—if Onesimus was a runaway, however repentant, why would Paul phrase the conditional the way he does? In this case, it seems rather odd that he would not simply appeal to Philemon's love for the saints again, and remind him concerning Onesimus's status as one of these, or, indeed, that he would not have been more explicit about this duty of charity, rather than appeal to the κοινωνία between Paul and Philemon. If Paul was appealing to Philemon to treat Onesimus gently, this is a rather strange way to couch it. As Winter suggests concerning the often quoted 'parallel' letter from Pliny to Sabinianus regarding Sabinianus's freedman (often mistaken for a slave in the literature) who had come to Pliny as an *amicus domine* ('master's friend', in the hope that this friend would intercede for him with the disgruntled master, as Pliny did indeed do),

> comparison of this letter with Paul's only shows how inadequate Paul's letter is as a request on behalf of a runaway slave. Even a short passage from Pliny's letter shows how he makes an explicit request:
> 'I know you are angry with him, and I know, too, it is not without reason; but clemency can never exert itself more laudably than when there is most cause for resentment. You once had an affection for this man, and, I hope, will have again; meanwhile, let me only prevail with you to forgive him. If he should incur your displeasure hereafter, you

first-named recipient is also accomplished by the use of that recipient's name, and the switch, right after that brief comment, is, presumably (were it not in actual fact slightly confusing to the recipients), an addendum to the list of instructions that were being given in the main part of the letter to the second named recipient. In the Corinthian correspondence, at least, Paul has a pattern of more than one listed recipient, the first of whom *must* be the primary intended recipients (although it must be admitted that these examples are dissimilar to Philemon in terms of the way in which they are structured): 1 Cor. 1.2 τῇ ἐκκλησίᾳ τοῦ θεοῦ τῇ οὔσῃ ἐν Κορίνθῳ, ἡγιασμένοις ἐν Χριστῷ Ἰησοῦ, κλητοῖς ἁγίοις, σὺν πᾶσιν τοῖς ἐπικαλουμένοις τὸ ὄνομα τοῦ κυρίου ἡμῶν Ἰησοῦ Χριστοῦ ἐν παντὶ τόπῳ; 2 Cor. 1.1 τῇ ἐκκλησίᾳ τοῦ θεοῦ τῇ οὔσῃ ἐν Κορίνθῳ σὺν τοῖς ἁγίοις πᾶσιν τοῖς οὖσιν ἐν ὅλῃ τῇ Ἀχαΐᾳ.

53. Following J.P. Sampley, *Pauline Partnership in Christ* (Philadelphia: Fortress Press, 1981).

will have so much the stronger plea in excuse of your anger as you show yourself more merciful to him now.'[54]

Paul's language, in comparison, does little to address the relationship between Onesimus and his master, but rather, perhaps, addresses a shift in that relationship *on the basis of Paul's needs*. This may have had to do with a shift in Onesimus's role within the Church. Either he was to be seen as a new Christian whom Paul hoped would be allowed by his master to function directly in the service of the Church, or as a Christian (perhaps in name only as the result of a household conversion?) now vitalized and marked out by Paul for his direct apostolic supervision in the service of the gospel.

It is also worth considering Winter's argument that the use of the verb διακονέω in v. 13 to refer to that for which Paul wanted to retain Onesimus in the first place must be a reference to religious service. She points out that διακονέω and its cognate noun form, διάκονος, are always used in Paul with a sense of religious service.[55] It is indeed true that, in the 28 Pauline uses of these words (including those in the 'deutero'-Pauline letters) outside Philemon, not one is found outside a religious context.[56] On this basis, it seems reasonable to suggest that Paul, in his request to Philemon to receive Onesimus as if he were Paul,

---

54. Pliny, *Ep.* 9.21-24; Winter, 'Paul's Letter', pp. 6-7, following Knox, *Philemon*, pp. 16-18. Note, also, Harrill's (*The Manumission of Slaves*, p. 164 n. 22) assessment: 'Note…the servility of Sabinianus's groveling freedman in Pliny, *Ep.* 9.21 (which is often cited, erroneously, as a parallel to Philemon; it deals with a freedman and not a slave, and Pliny's tone is entirely different from Paul's in Philemon)'.

55. Winter, 'Paul's Letter', p. 9.

56. Rom. 13.4; 15.8, 25; 16.1; 1 Cor. 3.5; 2 Cor. 3.3, 6; 6.4; 8.19, 20; 11.15, 23; Gal. 2.17; Eph. 3.7; 6.21; Phil. 1.1; Col. 1.7, 23, 25; 4.7; 1 Tim. 3.8, 10, 12, 13; 4.6; 2 Tim. 1.18. Dunn's argument that 'Winter…ignores the μοι' (*Colossians and Philemon*, p. 331) is aimed at a reading where Onesimus must be understood as Paul's personal servant. However, the simple presence of a pronoun does nothing of the kind. While Dunn does support the translation 'as a helper in the work of the mission' or 'as servant in the gospel', there is no reason to assume that the content of such service was 'not having a regular ministry in church worship or evangelism apart from Paul' (p. 331). Working *for* Paul may not mean that he was always working with Paul present! In fact, if we are to assume that Paul's bonds in v. 9 are real and not figurative, then we must likewise assume that, were Onesimus's function one of helping in the mission, that ministry must have taken place, in part, *away* from Paul.

wishes Philemon to accept Onesimus's new role as a minister in the gospel under Paul's command and/or tutelage.

g. ἐγὼ Παῦλος ἔγραψα τῇ ἐμῇ χειρί, ἐγὼ ἀποτίσω
The final point of textual contention in this debate is the meaning of Paul's assertion in Phlm. 19, written in his own hand, that he will pay whatever Onesimus may owe. Does Paul here affirm that Onesimus did indeed owe something to Philemon? Or is this instead a way for Paul to segue into the rather pointed comments in the rest of the verse and the following verses? Since, contrary to the received opinion, the preceding verses do not provide us with a definite answer to the question of Onesimus's possible debt, it is fallacious to assume that this 'autograph' on Paul's part makes the situation any clearer. In fact, the following statement, ἵνα μὴ λέγω σοι ὅτι καὶ σεαυτόν μοι προσοφείλεις, argues for a sense in which this statement of repayment or restitution must be seen as a statement of *personal* debt to Philemon, which is then being countered, rather unsubtly, by a reminder of the deep debt owed by Philemon himself to Paul. ἀποτίνω is a *hapax legomenon* in the New Testament, but its sense is seemingly quite easy to construe on the basis of both LXX and extra-biblical usage. Its sense of 'repay/make restitution/compensate' is well attested in the LXX,[57] and in legal formulations in the papyri (e.g. *P. Oxy.* 2.275[58]). However, it is this last usage which may be the most telling regarding how this verb is to be understood in Philemon.

P. Oxy. 2.275 is a contract for the service of an apprentice, given by the apprentice's father, concerning the conditions of his son's service. Interestingly, this example, used by Lohse to support the argument that Onesimus had injured Philemon in some way, seems rather to point to exactly the kind of situation for which the alternative hypothesis argues concerning the background of Philemon. In the papyrus, for every missed day of service, the father promises either to produce an equal amount of days service for the master (whether on the son's part, or on the father's is not clear), or to pay the equivalent in a silver drachma

---

57. Cf. LXX Exod. 21–22, throughout the legal codes of payment, compensation, and restitution (e.g. 21.19, 34, 36; 22.11-13).

58. ὅσας δ' ἐὰν ἐν τούτῳ ἀτακτήσῃ ἡμέρας ἐπὶ τὰς ἴσας αὐτὸν παρέξεται [με]τὰ τὸν χρόνον ἢ ἀ[πο]τεισάτω ἑκάσ[τ]ης ἡμέρας ἀργυρίου [δρ]αχμὴ μίαν (quoted in E. Lohse, *Colossians and Philemon* [trans. W.R. Poehlmann and R.J. Karris; Hermeneia; Philadelphia: Fortress Press, 1971], p. 204 n. 72).

per day of missed labour. Surely this situation recalls the alternative hypothesis much more clearly than the runaway slave hypothesis. The entry in Moulton and Milligan would seem to confirm this: speaking directly about *P. Oxy.* 2.275, they say that the 'verb is much stronger than ἀποδίδωμι, and carries with it the idea of repayment by way of punishment or fine..., a fact which lends emphasis to its use in Phlm. 19'.[59] Of course, Moulton and Milligan most likely assume the traditional background to Philemon, but their comment achieves its full weight in the light of the alternative hypothesis. Paul's language, which is similar to the father's in this papyrus, may very well convey a similar meaning, that is, Paul is offering Philemon compensation for the loss of his slave, and any economic benefit which Onesimus may have brought Philemon, or, indeed, any debt which Onesimus may have incurred during his time as Philemon's slave. We simply do not know enough about the master–slave relationship between Philemon and Onesimus to determine the nature of Onesimus's indenture to him. In fact, it is possible that this vocabulary in Philemon sheds light on the relationship between Onesimus and Philemon in a way that no other element of the letter does. Of course, it is impossible to determine *anything* from just one vocabulary item, but, by the same token, if we are to appeal to the usual use of this word outside this one occurrence in the New Testament, it seems less likely that this word could be used to support the traditional hypothesis than the alternative.

3. *Translating Philemon*

In the above discussion, the text of a portion of Philemon has been examined in detail. In the end, however, it does no justice either to Paul or to those reading him to take the scanty evidence that is available to us and read *either* major alternative into either criticism or translation. It is the latter problem that is of most concern for the present volume, but, although the comments in this section of my article are much shorter than those which precede them, this is not to suggest that translations are of any less intrinsic value than works of criticism. However, because of the nature of translations, there is less available with which to interact. The criticism of past translations is probably not as helpful as is providing a discussion of some of the issues that the previous section highlighted, which may be of benefit for future translators and

---

59. M–M *s.v.* ἀποτίνω.

translations. Still, in the translation of Philemon, translators and editors have both followed the traditional hypothesis regarding the background of Philemon and contributed to the atmosphere in which such a hypothesis has become 'fact'. As a result, it is important that we note some of this translational practice, and likewise acknowledge those who have resisted the temptation to read a hypothetical background into the translation of this tiny scrap of communication.

a. *Onesimus in the Dock?*

Although not formally an aspect of translations, the modern practice of inserting sub-titles and headings has achieved an almost canonical status for many of the users of translated Bibles. Some are outrightly interpretative (e.g. NEB/REB 'A Runaway Slave', CEV 'Paul Asks Philemon to Forgive Onesimus' [before v. 8, and the introduction to the letter, part of the officially published volume, calls Onesimus a 'runaway slave']). Others, given the wide dissemination of the usual understanding of the background of the letter, are less overt (NRSV [breaking with the RSV in including headings at all] 'Paul's Plea for Onesimus' [although the introduction to the Pauline letters tells us that the letter 'is a plea for Philemon to forgive the runaway slave Onesimus...'], NKJV 'The Plea for Onesimus', NIV 'Paul's Plea for Onesimus'). There are, however, a couple of exceptions to this trend towards interpretative headings, most notably the JB/NJB 'The Request about Onesimus', the *GNB* 'A Request for Onesimus', and, with a smaller audience, Phillips's 'A Personal Appeal'. Of course, the trend toward more interpretative headings is not helped by the *UBSGNT*, a Greek text designed in large part for the use of translators, including 'Paul Pleads for Onesimus' as a heading in their text. With these headings, the translators/editors/publishers of standard English translations have already foreclosed for their readers the question as to the background of this letter, and have made the manner in which their translations deal with the several points raised above a moot point.

b. *How Do We Translate Philemon?*

The simple answer to the question of this heading is 'very carefully'. In another chapter in this volume, I argue that the atmosphere created by contemporary biblical translational theory creates an air of (over-) confidence in the trustworthiness of the translation, tantamount to the atmosphere that allowed, even needed, the fantastic version of the story concerning the translation of the LXX to come about, so as to answer the psychological uncertainty that anyone feels who is forced to rely on a translation as an authority. The findings of the present article delve somewhat deeper into the contemporary process of interpreting the Pauline letter of Philemon, and how assumptions concerning the background of the letter, patently a debatable point, colour both interpretation and translation. A letter such as Romans, a Gospel, the book of Acts, even a shorter Pauline letter such as Philippians, are all much larger bodies to translate than Philemon. If translators face difficulties with *these* writings, how much more will this almost context-less letter with an obscure subject matter give the translator difficulty! In the face of this difficulty, it seems reasonable to suggest that translators have two choices with regard to the background of Philemon: (1) they can translate the document according to an assumed background, and leave it at that, relying on exegetes to discuss the problem, or (2) they can try to make the translation as open and transparent as possible, and allow the debate concerning the background of this letter to continue not only in the academy, but also at the level of the lay person who is forced to rely on the translated version. Of course, there seems to be a need on the part of some translational theorists and, by extension, translators, to close the text for their readers. As a result, difficult, conceptually laden words are interpretatively translated so as to avoid the need for the reader to be educated before necessarily being able to understand them. The above examination of the text of Philemon and the scholarly resistance to openness concerning its background are grounds in and of themselves for future translations either trying to reflect *neither* background, or maybe even reflecting both, and resisting the trend to pre-decide questions by using a purposely interpretative translation. Certainly, interpretative headings and introductions which present the letter according to the traditional view are to be avoided, but, at a more fundamental level, it is important that translators also try to read the text of Philemon as if they know nothing certain about its background, because they do not.

ORIGINAL TEXT OR CANONICAL TEXT? QUESTIONING THE SHAPE OF THE NEW TESTAMENT TEXT WE TRANSLATE

Kent D. Clarke

1. *Introduction*

It should be stated at the outset that this essay does not deal specifically with the discipline of Bible translation. However, what this essay does attempt to do is address a question of primary importance to this task—a question that in many regards precedes translation, and without its consideration and resolution translation cannot theoretically or practically begin. The question can be phrased in the following manner: Which form of text do we translate—original or canonical? Before deciding upon what any of the words mean, a translator must first calculate *what words* he or she seeks to derive meaning out of. The determination of the translator's exemplar or source text, at least on the majority of occasions, precedes the determination of the target text. The question of an original and canonical text takes on even greater significance when we realize that the majority of Christians have access to the New Testament only in the form of a translation. Therefore, it is essential that our biblical translations be based upon a text that can be established on sound methodological procedures.

In the words of B.F. Westcott (1825–1901) and F.J.A. Hort (1828–1892), arguably seen as two of the most influential scholars in New Testament textual criticism, the classic goal of the discipline constitutes the 'attempt to present exactly the original words of the New Testament, so far as they can now be determined from surviving documents'.[1] Elaborating further, G.D. Fee states that textual criticism 'is

---

1. B.F. Westcott and F.J.A. Hort, *Introduction to the New Testament in the Original Greek* (Peabody: Hendrickson, 1988; reprint of New York: Harper and Bros., 1882), p. 1. Affirmation of Westcott and Hort's importance to New Testament textual criticism can be found in virtually all the handbooks dealing with the discipline. See, for example, F.G. Kenyon, *Handbook to the Textual Criticism of*

the science that compares all known manuscripts of a given work in an effort to trace the history of variations within the text so as to discover its original form'.[2] Whereas Westcott, Hort, and Fee are concerned with textual criticism as applied to the New Testament, the same consensus can be found in those who apply textual criticism to both ancient and modern non-biblical material. 'The business of textual criticism', states P. Maas, 'is to produce a text as close as possible to the original (*constitutio textus*)', while J.J. McGann nuances the discussion by claiming that:

> All current textual critics, whether they work on Homer, Langland, Shakespeare, or a Romantic poet like Byron, agree that to produce a critical edition entails an assessment of the history of the text's transmission with the purpose of exposing and eliminating errors. Ultimately, the object in view is the same in each case: to establish a text which, in the now universally accepted formation, most nearly represents the author's original (or final) intentions.[3]

the New Testament (London: Macmillan, 2nd edn, 1912), pp. 294-95, 306-307; *idem, Recent Developments in the Textual Criticism of the Greek Bible* (Schweich Lectures 1932; London: British Academy, 1933), p. 1; K. Lake, *The Text of the New Testament* (rev. S. New; London: Rivingtons, 6th edn, 1928), pp. 66-67; K. Aland and B. Aland, *The Text of the New Testament* (trans. E.F. Rhodes; Grand Rapids: Eerdmans; Leiden: E.J. Brill, 2nd edn, 1989 [1981]), p. 18 and n. 38; L. Vaganay and C.-B. Amphoux, *An Introduction to New Testament Textual Criticism* (trans. J. Heimerdinger; Cambridge: Cambridge University Press, 2nd edn, 1991 [1986]), p. 151; B.M. Metzger, *The Text of the New Testament* (Oxford: Oxford University Press, 3rd edn, 1992), pp. 129, 137; E.J. Epp, 'Decision Points in Past, Present, and Future New Testament Textual Criticism', in E.J. Epp and G.D. Fee, *Studies in the Theory and Method of New Testament Textual Criticism* (SD, 45; Grand Rapids: Eerdmans, 1993), p. 22; J.H. Greenlee, *Introduction to New Testament Textual Criticism* (Peabody: Hendrickson, rev. edn, 1995), pp. 70-72. For concise introductions to the life and work of Westcott and Hort, see the above citations as well as A.H. McNeile, *An Introduction to the Study of the New Testament* (rev. C.S.C. Williams; Oxford: Oxford University Press, 2nd edn, 1953), pp. 419-30; S. Neill and T. Wright, *The Interpretation of the New Testament 1861–1986* (Oxford: Oxford University Press, 2nd edn, 1988), *ad loc.*; and K.D. Clarke, *Textual Optimism: A Critique of the United Bible Societies' Greek New Testament* (JSNTSup, 138; Sheffield: Sheffield Academic Press, 1997), pp. 17-56.

2.   G.D. Fee, 'Textual Criticism of the New Testament', in Epp and Fee, *Studies in the Theory and Method of New Testament Textual Criticism*, p. 3.

3.   See, respectively, P. Maas, *Textual Criticism* (trans. B. Flower; Oxford: Clarendon Press, 1958 [1927]), p. 1; and J.J. McGann, *A Critique of Modern Textual Criticism* (Chicago: University of Chicago Press, 1983), p. 15 and n. 13. For

However, the recent advent and continual growth of hermeneutical methodologies emphasizing the literary shape and final form of a text has instigated a re-questioning of this 'universally accepted formation'.[4] This essay will concern itself primarily with the state of affairs

the conviction that New Testament textual criticism's quest is for the 'original' text, see C.E. Hammond, *Outlines of Textual Criticism Applied to the New Testament* (Oxford: Clarendon Press, 3rd edn, 1880), p. 1; F.H.A. Scrivener, *A Plain Introduction to the Criticism of the New Testament*, I (ed. E. Miller; London: George Bell and Sons, 4th edn, 1894), p. 5; E. Nestle, *Introduction to the Textual Criticism of the Greek New Testament* (trans. W. Edie; London: Williams & Norgate, 1901), p. 156; C.R. Gregory, *Canon and Text of the New Testament* (Edinburgh: T. & T. Clark, 1907), pp. 483-85; Kenyon, *Handbook*, p. 1; Lake, *Text of the New Testament*, p. 1; B.H. Streeter, *The Four Gospels: A Study of Origins* (London: Macmillan, 1951), p. 22; A. Souter, *The Text and Canon of the New Testament* (ed. C.S.C. Williams; London: Gerald Duckworth, 2nd edn, 1954), p. 3; G. Zuntz, *The Text of the Epistles: A Disquisition upon the Corpus Paulinum* (Schweich Lectures 1946; London: British Academy, 1953), p. 1; V. Taylor, *The Text of the New Testament: A Short Introduction* (London: Macmillan, 1961), p. 1; Aland and Aland, *Text of the New Testament*, pp. 280-81; Metzger, *Text of the New Testament*, p. 5; *idem*, *A Textual Commentary on the Greek New Testament* (Stuttgart: Deutsche Bibelgesellschaft, 2nd edn, 1994), p. 1*; Vaganay and Amphoux, *Introduction to New Testament Textual Criticism*, p. 1; Greenlee, *Introduction to New Testament Textual Criticism*, p. 1. It should also be noted that even textual critics who advocate the later Byzantine (Syrian/Koine) or Majority text tradition still see this text-type as the closest representative of the 'original' text. See here J.W. Burgon, *The Traditional Text of the Holy Gospels Vindicated and Established* (ed. E. Miller; London: George Bell and Sons, 1896), p. 27; W.N. Pickering, *The Identity of the New Testament Text* (Nashville: Thomas Nelson, 1977), pp. 15-19, 129-30; H.A. Sturz, *The Byzantine Text-Type and New Testament Textual Criticism* (Nashville: Thomas Nelson, 1984), pp. 95-97; Z.C. Hodges and A.L. Farstad (eds.), *The Greek New Testament According to the Majority Text* (Nashville: Thomas Nelson, 1982), pp. ix-xiii. Although Old Testament textual critics also use the term 'original text', this is generally understood in a nuanced manner. Given the lack of knowledge concerning Old Testament ur-texts and the complex process of literary shaping, as well as the extensive time span between the original writings (some would question if there were original writings) and the extant manuscripts we now possess, most if not all Old Testament textual critics would pursue a form of text that is far removed from these so called original texts.

4. For the purposes of this essay, see especially M.M. Parvis, 'The Nature and Tasks of New Testament Textual Criticism: An Appraisal', *JR* 32 (1952), pp. 165-74; *idem*, 'The Goals of New Testament Textual Studies', *StudEv* 6 (1973), pp. 393-407; B.S. Childs, 'The Hermeneutical Problem of New Testament Textual Criticism', in his *The New Testament as Canon: An Introduction* (Valley Forge,

as found within New Testament textual criticism, seeking to address this reappraisal of the discipline in relation to the New Testament text and canon, and more briefly with matters of its translation. As already noted, one might formulate the central question concerning this essay in the following manner: *Which form of text—original or canonical—should act as the basis of biblical translation?* Necessary correlatives to this first question include: *Which form of text is canonical?* and *What is canonical—text or canon?*[5]

PA: Trinity Press International, 1994 [1984]), pp. 518-30. In fact, this re-questioning is not only based upon issues related to a text's literary shape and final form, but goes much deeper into the difficult hermeneutical battles concerning authorial intention, textual reference (i.e. what a text *meant* at its source or origin, what it *has meant* throughout its history, and what it *means* in its contemporary setting), and reader-oriented considerations. For pertinent discussion of these hermeneutical issues as specifically related to biblical studies, see such works as A.C. Thiselton, *The Two Horizons: New Testament Hermeneutics and Philosophical Description* (Grand Rapids: Eerdmans, 1980); *idem*, *New Horizons in Hermeneutics* (Grand Rapids: Zondervan, 1992); P. Ricoeur, *Essays on Biblical Interpretation* (ed. L.S. Mudge; Philadelphia: Fortress Press, 1980); G.R. Osborne, *The Hermeneutical Spiral: A Comprehensive Introduction to Biblical Interpretation* (Downers Grove, IL: InterVarsity Press, 1991); G. Maier, *Biblical Hermeneutics* (trans. R.W. Yarbrough; Wheaton: Crossway Books, 1994 [1990]); and W. Jeanrond, *Theological Hermeneutics: Development and Significance* (London: SCM Press, 1994).

5.   The issue of text and canon has been taken up to a greater or lesser extent by a number of biblical scholars. In relation to the New Testament, see again Parvis, 'Nature and Tasks', pp. 165-74; *idem*, 'Goals of New Testament Textual Studies' , pp. 393-407; Childs, 'Hermeneutical Problem', pp. 518-30; and others such as G.M. Burge, 'A Specific Problem in the New Testament Text and Canon: The Woman Caught in Adultery (John 7.53–8.11)', *JETS* 27 (1984), pp. 141-48. In relation to the Old Testament, see H.P. Scanlin, 'What is the Canonical Shape of the Old Testament Text We Translate?', in P.C. Stine (ed.), *Issues in Bible Translation* (UBS Monograph Series, 3; London: United Bible Societies, 1988), pp. 207-20; B.S. Childs, 'Text and Canon', in his *Introduction to the Old Testament as Scripture* (London: SCM Press, 1979), pp. 84-106; P.R. Ackroyd, 'Original Text and Canonical Text', *USQR* 32 (1977), pp. 166-73; *idem*, 'The Open Canon', in his *Studies in the Religious Tradition of the Old Testament* (London: SCM Press, 1987), pp. 209-24; J.A. Sanders, 'Cave 11 Surprises and the Question of Canon', *McCQ* 21 (1968), pp. 284-98; and *idem*, 'Text and Canon: Concepts and Method', *JBL* 98 (1979), pp. 5-29. Finally, for discussions of text and canon in relation to both Testaments, see J.A. Sanders, 'Text and Canon: Old Testament and New', in P. Casetti, O. Keel, and A. Schenker (eds.), *Mélanges Dominique Barthélemy: Etudes bibliques offertes à l'occasion de son 60e anniversaire* (OBO, 38; Fribourg: Editions Universitaires; Göttingen: Vandenhoeck & Ruprecht, 1981), pp. 374-94;

2. *Arguments against the Pursuit of an Original Text*

Individuals advocating a reappraisal of text-critical methodology do so on the basis of a number of premises. For the sake of clarity these have been divided into three foundational arguments which seek to place authority upon a later ecclesiastical or canonical text as opposed to the original. These three assertions include (a) methodological difficulties in retrieving an original text, (b) problems with the theory of authorial intent and authority, and (c) the absence of ecclesiastical endorsement for a reconstructed text.

a. *Difficulties in Retrieving an Original Text*

It has been argued that the concept of an original text is a 'retreating mirage' and that to achieve this goal is 'well-nigh impossible'.[6] During this century the work of textual scholars has suggested that there was a degree of acceptable fluidity involved in the early transmission process of the biblical text. F.G. Kenyon states that:

> [I]n the third century, and therefore presumably for some time back into the second, the text was in detail very far from being settled. Instead of a state of orderly decent, though with an ever-widening genealogical pedigree, from the original autographs to the extant copies of the fourth century, we seem to see a period of increasing disorder, from which a state of comparative order was ultimately produced when the church reached more settled conditions.[7]

In support of Kenyon, E.C. Colwell has more recently pointed out that the reproduction of New Testament manuscripts progressed from a relatively uncontrolled tradition to a tradition that was rigorously controlled. Using the early patristic biblical quotations as one example to support this assertion, Colwell states that the earliest citations are so

---

and T. Fornberg, 'Textual Criticism and Canon: Some Problems', *StudPat* 40 (1986), pp. 45-53. The issue may be considerably more difficult in regards to the Old Testament where the ur-text and original text would obviously far pre-date that of the New Testament and where textual fluidity appears to have been much more common. Cf. Fornberg, 'Some Problems', pp. 47-48.

6. See respectively K.W. Clark, 'The Theological Relevance of Textual Criticism in Current Criticism of the Greek New Testament', *JBL* 85 (1966), p. 15; and R.M. Grant, *A Historical Introduction to the New Testament* (London: Collins, 1971), p. 51.

7. F.G. Kenyon, *The Text of the Greek Bible* (London: Gerald Duckworth, 1949), p. 244. See also Aland and Aland, *Text of the New Testament*, pp. 69-70.

free that it becomes difficult to demonstrate an acquaintance with the biblical text. He then highlights the fact that Origen quotes the New Testament first from one strain of the tradition and then from another. Indeed, it is not uncommon to find an early Church Father who cites the same text on more than one occasion yet never twice in the same wording.[8] Colwell even goes so far as to claim that 'In the early centuries of the New Testament period accurate copying was not a common concept'.[9] Sanders summarizes this viewpoint when he claims:

> A new rule in method in text criticism, common to work on both Old Testament and New Testament texts, seems now to be emerging: the older the texts or versions the less likely they were copied accurately. The period of fluidity in text transmission obtains for the early period of extant texts for both testaments: it lasted longer for the New Testament a) because the New Testament was a late starter and b) because the crisis periods for Early Christianity, comparable to the Roman conquest in the first century BCE and the destruction of Jerusalem in 70 CE, did not effect stabilization of text form until later. The earlier the date of a biblical manuscript the further back into a period of belief in fluid living words and traditions ever adaptable to new contexts; the later the date the more likely the need in the several believing communities for some stability in text transmission. This new rule needs continued testing, but it is emerging with remarkable clarity in both disciplines, Old Testament and New Testament, without collusion between them.[10]

The obvious consequence of this situation, it is asserted, is that we are stopped short of the original writings and fall at best upon a text more representative of the late second or third century. And even here, instead of being left with 'one outstanding and dominant type of text there are five or six leading types'.[11] Furthermore, any notions of a 'neutral' text or a genealogical stemma of manuscripts and readings are said to be seriously brought into question given the extent of textual

---

8. See M.J. Suggs, 'The Use of Patristic Evidence in the Search for the Primitive New Testament Text', *NTS* 4 (1958), pp. 139-47, esp. pp. 141-42.

9. E.C. Colwell, *Studies in Methodology in Textual Criticism of the New Testament* (NTTS, 9; Leiden: E.J. Brill, 1969), p. 165.

10. Sanders, 'Old Testament and New', p. 379. See also Sanders, 'Concepts and Methods', pp. 13-14; and Childs, 'Hermeneutical Problem', p. 526. However, Sanders' 'new rule' is, at least for the New Testament, as old as 1949 if one takes into account Kenyon's similar assertion.

11. F.C. Grant, 'Where Form Criticism and Textual Criticism Overlap', *JBL* 59 (1940), p. 11; and see also Childs, 'Hermeneutical Problem', p. 525.

mixture and conflation at such an early date.[12]

In the light of recent literary work on the New Testament, some scholars have maintained that there is convincing evidence in support of not an original text or autograph, but rather an intermingling of written and oral tradition within the early Church.[13] Parvis, highlighting G.D. Kilpatrick's argument that the book of Matthew is actually a revised lectionary, questions if its composition could not have been the result of a prolonged process that gradually took shape in the life of the Church as opposed to a single act which came forth from the hand of the author. 'Is it not possible', asks Parvis, 'that there may have been a whole series of Matthews, a whole series of gradually approximating collections of the lectionary materials of the Church?' He then proposes the possibility that 'there never was any one point in time which marked the composition of the book as a book, that there never was any one autograph from which all of the later tradition descends'.[14] F.F. Bruce notes that the same questions concerning the issue of an original text might also be applied if one gives credence to Papias's statement that the author of Matthew composed his 'oracles' in the Hebrew language (cf. Eusebius, *H.E.* 3.39.16). Was Papias using the term 'oracles' in reference to a sayings source that preceded the actual Gospel we now have? Was he asserting that Matthew first appeared in Hebrew rather than Greek?[15] And, questions Parvis again, what of the Acts of the Apostles, where our earliest witnesses indicate that the work circulated in two differing forms, the Western text being nearly one-tenth longer

---

12. Childs, 'Hermeneutical Problem', p. 525.

13. See N.A. Dahl, 'The Passion Narrative in Matthew', in his *Jesus in the Memory of the Early Church* (Minneapolis: Augsburg, 1976), pp. 37-51. For reference to this same issue but applied more to the Old Testament, see Fornberg, 'Some Problems', p. 48.

14. Parvis, 'Goals of New Testament Textual Studies', p. 398. See also G.D. Kilpatrick, *The Origins of the Gospel According to St Matthew* (Oxford: Clarendon Press, 1946), p. 59.

15. See F.F. Bruce, *The Canon of Scripture* (Glasgow: Chapter House, 1988), p. 288. See also C.F.D. Moule, *The Birth of the New Testament* (London: A. & C. Black, 3rd edn, 1981), pp. 105, 126-27 for discussion of Papias and support for a pre-Matthean sayings source. Contra W.G. Kümmel, *Introduction to the New Testament* (NTL; trans. H.C. Kee; London: SCM Press, rev. edn, 1975 [1973]), pp. 53-55 who claims that there can be no serious doubt that Papias was referring to the canonical Matthew. For text and translation of Papias, see J.B. Lightfoot, *The Apostolic Fathers* (ed. J.R. Harmer; London: Macmillan, 1907), pp. 517, 529.

than the Alexandrian. Do both forms of the tradition come from the hand of a single author; or is one form of text a later edition composed after the original author's death? Despite the assertion by a majority of scholars that the Alexandrian text is to be preferred as the original, there is by no means consensus.[16] Regardless of how one answers these questions, potential problems are posed for those in pursuit of an original Matthean Gospel or an autographal book of Acts.

The problem of an original text likewise extends to the earliest writings found in the New Testament—the Pauline letter corpus. In 1946, Zuntz contended that our extant manuscripts of the Pauline Epistles attest to their collected form of about 100 CE rather than to an earlier period when the letters circulated independently. 'We shall indeed meet with some, though very few, textual features which may, just possibly, point back beyond this basic collection', states Zuntz, later adding that in the fifty years between the letters first being written by Paul and their collection 'important things could have happened... Faults which beset our whole tradition may have arisen then'.[17] Similarly, a number of individuals have noted that any acknowledgment of a composite document theory for Pauline letters such as 1 Corinthians and Philippians poses problems for those attempting to recover the original text.[18]

b. *Problematic Issues with Authorial Intent and Authority*
Within the textual criticism of both classical and modern literary works, a number of individuals have questioned whether or not the author's

16. See Parvis, 'Goals of New Testament Textual Studies', pp. 398-99. For a helpful introduction to the textual problems found in the book of Acts, see Metzger, *Commentary*, pp. 222-36. For the dilemma in dating the Alexandrian and Western texts, see E.J. Epp, 'The Twentieth-Century Interlude in New Testament Textual Criticism', in Epp and Fee, *Studies in the Theory and Method of New Testament Textual Criticism*, pp. 87-96.

17. Zuntz, *Text of the Epistles*, pp. 14 and 278 respectively.

18. See once more Parvis, 'Goals of New Testament Textual Studies', p. 399. A number of other New Testament issues that have been used to call into question textual criticism's goal of establishing an original text include the relationship between 2 Peter and Jude, the multiple accounts in Acts of Paul's Damascus road experience, the Q source hypothesis, the question of a Secret Mark or ur-Markus, and longer additions to books such as John (cf. ch. 21) and Romans (cf. ch. 16). On a number of these, see W.L. Petersen, 'What Text Can New Testament Textual Criticism Ultimately Reach?', in B. Aland and J. Delobel (eds.), *New Testament Textual Criticism, Exegesis and Church History: A Discussion of Methods* (Kampen: Kok, 1994), pp. 136-52.

original autograph should be regarded as the 'best' or most authoritative document. Although there is a tendency to associate 'original' with 'authoritative', it is advanced by some that this premise is not always the case and that the two terms are by no means equivalent.[19] The obvious application to modern literary works involves the questions of authority and intent in relation to the author's original pre-published manuscripts, published manuscripts, and successive later editions sanctioned or not sanctioned by that author. On the one hand, where various editions are produced, particularly with the author's direction and involvement, it is not uncommon for initial intentions as found in pre-published drafts and earlier editions to further develop or even change. The earlier manuscripts may preserve an outdated text which the author no longer wishes the reader to see. Therefore, original manuscripts and earlier editions may contain the author's *discarded* rather than *final* intentions, and so the general inclination would be the adoption of the latest text. As McGann explains:

> [T]he production of books, in the later modern periods especially, sometimes involves a close working relationship between the author and various editorial and publishing professionals associated with the institutions which serve to transmit literary works to the public. To regard the work done by such institutions as a contamination of authorized material is to equate the editorial work done by an author's original publishing institutions and the (historically belated) editorial work done by scribes of ancient texts.[20]

On the other hand, one can perceive the difficulties that are presented when the same process occurs without the author's involvement, as is the case in the publication of unfinished manuscripts, translations, and later editions produced after the writer's death. In this context, later manuscripts could contain a text that the author never wished the reader to see and, therefore, one is more inclined to adopt the earlier text. To quote McGann again:

> [An author's] early publisher, his editors, his printers are...entirely comparable to those older scribes who sought to preserve and transmit the classical texts, but who introduced, in the process, various contaminations. The business of the classical critic is to find and remove those corruptions, and the business of the critic of [a modern text] is seen in

---

19. See here the interesting discussion in McGann, *A Critique*, pp. 15-36.
20. McGann, *A Critique*, pp. 34-35.

the same way: to find and remove the corruptions and, by critical sub-traction, to restore the sincerity of the authoritative text.[21]

To be sure, there is sharp disagreement over which form of text is to be regarded as authoritative in any one of these given situations. And although these considerations are in need of some modifications before being transferred over to the biblical texts, it is difficult to deny that there are certainly more than a few possible correlatives as is seen in the case of those who would support the existence of sayings sources or ur-texts; the secretarial role of an amanuensis; multiple or successive literary editions; editorial redaction of single works by later individuals, believing communities or 'schools'; the collection of a particular cor-pus of material; or perhaps even the production of pseudonymous liter-ature—all theories often posited by biblical scholars. E. Best provides a good example of this issue of authority in relation to the biblical text when he asks,

> Why should the understanding of Christian faith which we find in Paul be assumed to be superior to that which we find in Anselm or Bultmann? To answer that the interpretation of Anselm or Bultmann depends upon the interpretation which is found in Paul is not wholly satisfactory for, while depending on Paul, Anselm or Bultmann may have seen more deeply than Paul. The understanding of life which we find in Shake-speare is almost always more profound than that in the chronicles which he used as sources for many of his plots'.[22]

Similarly, it has been proposed that editorial or even scribal interven-tion that takes place between the production of the author's original work and subsequent editions, copies, or translations may have 'stan-dardized', 'modernized', or improved upon the autograph in matters of style, orthography, diction and so on. What then is to be seen as the

21. McGann, *A Critique*, p. 21.

22. E. Best, 'Scripture, Tradition and the Canon of the New Testament', *BJRL* 61 (1979), p. 281. Although some Shakespearean scholars may question Best's statement, his calling into question the assertion that older texts or sources be deemed as superior to or more profound than later literary works is justified. Best also cites J.II. Newman who states, 'It is indeed sometimes said that the stream is clearest near the spring. Whatever use may fairly be made of this image, it does not apply to the history of a philosophy or sect, which, on the contrary, is more equable, and purer, and stronger, when its bed has become deep, and broad, and full.' See Newman's highly regarded work, *An Essay on the Development of Chris-tian Doctrine* (Harmondsworth: Penguin Books, 1974), p. 100.

'best' text—the exemplar or the standardization? Furthermore, examples such as Catholicism's favoring of the Latin Vulgate, traditional Judaism's proclivity for the Masoretic text, and Protestantism's championing of the *Textus Receptus*, all indicate that the issue of authority often has little connection to the question of originality and more to do with theological considerations. It is also apparent that these issues above fall not just within the realm of textual criticism, but also lie firmly at the heart of hermeneutical inquiry. Yet, despite the fact that a majority of New Testament textual critics would still claim that the preferred text is that which most nearly represents what the original author first wrote, one cannot help but recognize some of the perplexities involved in the discussion of these matters.

c. *Absence of Ecclesiastical Endorsement for a Reconstructed Original Text*

The absence of a reconstructed text's endorsement by an ecclesiastical body or community has been deemed problematic by various scholars. For example, in 1926 J.H. Ropes, upon writing one of the standard volumes still in use today for studying the text of Acts, explains why the time for constructing a new critical text of the book had not yet, in his opinion, arrived and why he did not himself undertake such a task: 'In the nature of the case a new text could not at present lay claim to finality, and the only certainty about it would seem to be that it never existed until its author, the critic, created it'.[23] Perhaps one of the more resolute opponents of textual criticism's pursuit of an original text is Parvis, himself a textual critic, who strongly asserts that in the effort expended upon attaining such an objective, we often end up being guilty of doing what Ropes cautiously warned against—creating a text which has never before existed at any place or time, that has never been endorsed by an ecclesiastical body, and which satisfies no one but the editor alone.[24] Clearly for Parvis there is a theological component operative in the choosing of a particular text as is seen in the necessity of that text being sanctioned by the Church and its tradition. Parvis draws attention to the fact that the New Testament is the Church's book. From this ecclesiastical context it was produced, guarded, and invested with

23. J.H. Ropes, 'The Text of Acts', in F.J. Foakes Jackson and K. Lake (eds.), *The Beginnings of Christianity: Part I, The Acts of the Apostles*, III (5 vols.; London: Macmillan, 1926), p. x.
24. Parvis, 'Goals of New Testament Texual Studies', pp. 397, 400, and 401.

authority. '[I]t is the tradition of the Church and not the vagaries of our own scholarship which must determine the contents of that book', states Parvis, who later concludes:

> We must always be ready to accept a particular reading as a part of the New Testament not because it is an 'original' reading, but because it comes to us in the tradition of the Church Catholic. Our goal must be to give to our contemporaries not only an 'original' text but also many readings which have been examined and criticized in the light of that tradition. The readings and the texts which we single out need not be the oldest possible texts and readings. If they proclaim the faith of the Church Catholic, they are Scripture.[25]

Parvis's concept of an ecclesiastical text, although differing in a number of particulars, has some notable affinities with Childs's proposal for constructing a canonical rather than original text. Childs states:

> [T]he process of seeking to discern the truest witness to the gospel from within the church's multiple traditions functions to remind the interpreter of the canonical corpus that the element of theological interpretation is not only constitutive of the church's scriptures in general, but has also entered in to the textual dimension of the tradition as well. This observation is not a defense of irrational subjectivity, but a further confirmation that the discipline of text criticism is not a strictly objective, or non-theological activity, but is an integral part of the same interpretive enterprise which comprises the church's life with its scriptures.[26]

In the attempt to combat the various methodological difficulties in retrieving an original text, the problematic issues concerning authorial intent, and concerns regarding ecclesiastical endorsement, scholars have tended to do one of two things. Either they have fallen back upon what is called 'eclecticism', or, as we have briefly seen, they have advanced an approach that places authority upon a later canonical (viz. Childs) or ecclesiastical (viz. Parvis) text.[27]

25. Parvis, 'Goals of New Testament Texual Studies', pp. 403 and 407 respectively.

26. Childs, 'Hermeneutical Problem', p. 529.

27. In using the term 'eclectic' or 'eclecticism', and by adhering to the eclectic method, one generally takes on the premise that because no single manuscript or text-type preserves a completely neutral (or error-free) text, the original New Testament text is to be chosen variant by variant from all our extant manuscripts. On the use and application of this term in textual criticism, including both reasoned and rigorous eclecticism, see E.J. Epp, 'The Eclectic Method in New Testament Texual

Before discussing the rationale of this latter choice, perhaps a few points might be made in response to a number of the above hurdles placed before those in pursuit of an original New Testament text. First of all, to admit, in the words of Clark, that 'textual bifurcations occurred in the earliest stage of transmission', one need not go so far as saying that 'the older the texts or versions the less likely they were copied accurately'.[28] In fact, predominant textual trajectories can be clearly traced from at least the late second and third centuries, and with the aid of citations from the sub-Apostolic Fathers perhaps this date can be pushed back even further. As Epp shows, although one cannot view the situation of the early text as static but rather as dynamic, it appears that there were also parameters governing the extent of acceptable textual fluidity:

> To argue as we have in terms of recognizable textual streams or trajectories which can be plotted from known points and also point backwards from them, may not in any way *prove* that text-types (as we commonly define the term) existed in the period of 200 to 300 or so, but the perspective which is provided by these extended trajectories (and the lack of them) is a valuable aid to sorting out the wide range of texts in the earliest documented period and in determining (albeit by hindsight) the extent to which these various early texts were utilized and the relative degree of influence which they brought to bear on the developing lines of NT textual transmission. Is it mere accident that our spectrum of the earliest texts, comprised of some forty papyri and uncials from around AD 300 and earlier, issues in *only two* distinct lines of development [i.e. the Alexandrian and Western texts], each at one extreme of that spectrum? Some will say 'yes', but I would suggest, rather, that the sorting process, of which only a portion remains open to our view, functioned as though it were under some centrifugal force and resulted in the concentration and consolidation of textual masses at the outer—and opposite—

Criticism: Solution or Symptom?', in Epp and Fee, *Studies in the Theory and Method of New Testament Textual Criticism*, pp. 141-73; G.D. Fee, 'Rigorous or Reasoned Eclecticism—Which?', in Epp and Fee, *Studies in the Theory and Method of New Testament Textual Criticism*, pp. 124-40; and J.H. Petzer, 'Eclecticism and the Text of the New Testament', in P.J. Hartin and J.H. Petzer (eds.), *Text and Interpretation: New Approaches in the Criticism of the New Testament* (NTTS, 15; Leiden: E.J. Brill, 1991), pp. 47-62.

28. See K.W. Clark, 'Today's Problems with the Critical Text of the New Testament', in J.C. Rylaarsdam (ed.), *Transitions in Biblical Scholarship* (Chicago: University of Chicago Press, 1968), p. 162; and again Sanders, 'Old Testament and New', p. 379.

edges of the textual spectrum. The reasons for this may be obscure, but the phenomenon itself is visible enough.[29]

Nor does the probability that oral tradition existed alongside the early written documents necessitate the conclusion that these apostolic texts were composed over a long period of time or that this written tradition was completely fluid. Again, although it is clear that there was a considerable degree of textual fluidity, this appears to have been encompassed by a significant amount of stability as well—as can be shown even in the case of the preservation of oral tradition itself.

Secondly, despite the assertion that we can only establish a text of the second or third century, and although our decisions must be based upon a textual situation that was to some degree variegated, is it not overly pessimistic to think that the earliest text has not survived, at least in most cases, somewhere amongst that later variation?[30] If penetration beyond the second-century barrier is not possible (and not all textual critics would assent to this belief) a text of this date still stands closer to the original apostolic written tradition than a later ecclesiastical or canonical text. One should not casually dismiss the obvious problems encountered in reconstructing the earliest textual history; however, it would appear that textual fluidity was not as pronounced as some would now claim.

Thirdly, in regard to authorial intentions, it should be pointed out that even if a textual critic is in danger of choosing discarded rather than final intentions in the pursuit of the original text, at least this will capture the author's, rather than another's—such as a later scribe's—purpose even if in a pre-developed form.[31]

Fourthly, by falling back upon a later ecclesiastical or canonical text one does not eliminate the majority of these problems. For example, if the Gospel of Matthew circulated in more than one edition, or if a number of Pauline epistles are composite in nature, these facets of the

---

29. Epp, 'Twentieth-Century Interlude', pp. 93-94.

30. See J.K. Elliott, 'Keeping Up with Recent Studies. XV. New Testament Textual Criticism', *ExpTim* 99 (1987), p. 43 who claims that it is unlikely that the original text has not survived *somewhere* in our known manuscripts, albeit perhaps in a later witness. See also Metzger, *Text of the New Testament*, p. 185 who explains that due to the amount of evidence for the text of the New Testament the need to resort to conjectural emendation is reduced to the smallest of dimensions.

31. This same point is made in McGann, *A Critique*, pp. 34-35.

Bible's textual history are still transferred over to a later ecclesiastical or canonical text. These later texts are still based upon one of the Matthean editions or the composite structure of a Pauline writing. If we cannot penetrate beyond a second-century text, it is still this text that all later texts must in some shape or form be influenced by. The difference is that the problems are now endorsed (and ignored?) because they have received the ecclesia's or the community of faith's sanctioning. In addition, Parvis's assertion that 'There are no spurious readings; all are the product of the tradition of the Church, whether they originated in the twelfth century or in the first', is simply untenable.[32] To turn Childs's argument against an original text back upon his own proposal, his desire to use the Byzantine (Koine) text as an 'outer parameter', from which the New Testament textual critic works backwards in the attempt to remove uncritical readings, likewise runs the risk of constructing a text never before witnessed to in an ecclesiastical context, a text that similarly has the potential of being promoted and received as a *textus receptus*, or a type of eclectic edition based upon the 'best received' texts.[33] And while textual criticism's eclectic approach may only be a temporary solution to the ongoing problem of the original New Testament text, in the current state of affairs, it is the best we can do.[34]

32. Parvis, 'Nature and Tasks', p. 172. For evidence against Parvis's point, see the fine work by B.D. Ehrman, *The Orthodox Corruption of Scripture: The Effect of Early Christological Controversies on the Text of the New Testament* (Oxford: Oxford University Press, 1993) who clearly shows that there were corruptions of the text resulting in spurious readings even if by orthodox contingencies.

33. For Childs's proposals, see his 'Hermeneutical Problem', pp. 529-30. Whereas Parvis appears to be more sympathetic to the Byzantine (Koine) text simply on the grounds of its long ecclesiastical standing, one should not make the mistake of assuming that Childs uncritically adopts this same position. Childs recognizes the difficulty inherent to the discussion and his finely nuanced arguments, developed to deal with these various problems, are at times thought-provoking and convincing.

34. For support of this point, see K.W. Clark, 'The Effect of Recent Textual Criticism upon New Testament Studies', in W.D. Davies and D. Daube (eds.), *The Background of the New Testament and its Eschatology* (Cambridge: Cambridge University Press, 1964), pp. 37-38; J.N. Birdsall, 'The Text of the Fourth Gospel: Some Current Questions', *EvQ* 29 (1957), p. 199; and Epp, 'Eclectic Method', pp. 172-73.

3. *Arguments against the Pursuit of a Canonical Text*

Whereas the previous section of this essay examined a number of the problems associated with the traditional goal of New Testament textual criticism—that is, its pursuit of an original text—the following section will discuss the assertion, usually endorsed by biblical scholars who advocate some type of literary-theological stance, that authority should be placed upon a later ecclesiastical or canonical text. Three considerations will be dealt with, including (a) the relationship between text and canon, (b) the diversity of *the* canonical text, and (c) the canonical status of textual accretions.

a. *The Relationship between Text and Canon*

The subject of the text and canon of the New Testament has traditionally been termed 'general introduction', while the title 'special introduction' has more often been reserved for the criticism of the contents found within the books themselves. Whether text and canon have served as the opening chapter of biblical studies (as in more recent times) or as the conclusion (as was prominent in the 1800s), the two disciplines have been commonly seen as going hand in hand.[35] This may be the reason why, at least of late, the common mistake is made of too closely associating these two quite distinct and specialized areas of critical inquiry. This is not to say that text and canon should be completely isolated, for as Childs makes clear, 'the issue of establishing a normative text cannot be separated from how the text was received, which involves the subject of canon'. However, to later conclude as Childs does that the goal of textual criticism is 'commensurate with its canonical role' may be an oversimplification that leads to a blurring of the processes integral to each discipline.[36] A similar mistake is made by McNeile, who rightly affirms that the recognized custom of the Church with regard to a group of books would naturally have caused those books which conformed to it to be written in a list; however, his overstatement comes when he adds, 'And thus the Canon of the Scripture

---

35. See Gregory, *Canon and Text*, p. 1; See also B.F. Westcott, *A General Survey of the History of the Canon of the New Testament* (London: Macmillan, 6th edn, 1889), p. 1.

36. Childs, 'Hermeneutical Problem', pp. 522 and 527 respectively.

became equivalent to the contents of Scripture contained in an authorative list'.[37] The point to be made here is that the two terms, 'text' and 'canon', are not synonymous and, therefore, one must be very cautious in directly equating the content of the canonical books with the process of canonization. W.R. Farmer appears to recognize this point when he states that, 'The task of discussing the topic "The Development of the New Testament Canon" must be distinguished from the task of discussing the topic "The Composition of the New Testament Books"'.[38] Whereas textual criticism is concerned with the verse-by-verse reconstruction of the original text, the study of canonization proper seeks to explain how, out of a much broader corpus of written material, the Church eventually came to accept as authoritative and normative a closed collection of New Testament books to which nothing could be added and from which nothing could be taken away.[39]

The watershed of the argument lies in the fact that we cannot equate the canonizing process with the endeavor to stabilize the *textual form* of the New Testament. One should not assume that those involved in the process of canonization saw as part of their task the *firm establishment*

---

37. McNeile, *Study of the New Testament*; p. 311.

38. W.R. Farmer and D.M. Farkasfalvy, *The Formation of the New Testament Canon: An Ecumenical Approach* (New York: Paulist Press, 1983), p. 7. Farmer does go on to add that one can *begin* discussing the development of the New Testament canon by starting with a treatment of the composition of some particular New Testament book; however, this would appear to be a precursor to the discussion of canonization proper. H. von Campenhausen, although asserting that the contents of Scripture cannot be rigorously separated from canon, refrains from any concerted dealing with the former in the context of the latter. See H. von Campenhausen, *The Formation of the Christian Bible* (trans. J.A. Baker; Philadelphia: Fortress Press, 1972 [1968]), p. x.

39. For definitions of canonization, canon, etc., consult the standard works such as Westcott, *A General Survey*, pp. 1, 504-11; Gregory, *Canon and Text*, pp. 1-2; E.J. Goodspeed, *The Formation of the New Testament* (Chicago: University of Chicago Press, 1926), pp. vii-viii; Souter, *Text and Canon*, pp. 154-59; R.M. Grant, *The Formation of the New Testament* (London: Hutchinson and Co., 1965), pp. 7-12, 181; von Campenhausen, *Christian Bible*, pp. x-xi; H.Y. Gamble, *The New Testament Canon: Its Making and Meaning* (GBS; Philadelphia: Fortress Press, 1985), pp. 11-19; B.M. Metzger, *The Canon of the New Testament: Its Origin, Development, and Significance* (Oxford: Clarendon Press, 1987), pp. 1, 289-93; Bruce, *Canon of Scripture*, pp. 17-24; and L.M. McDonald, *The Formation of the Christian Biblical Canon* (Peabody, MA: Hendrickson, 2nd edn, 1995), pp. 13-21.

of the *specific* New Testament text in terms of the aims of textual criticism. That the text or content of any given New Testament book played
a role in the ascription of that particular book's canonical status is clear.
For example, it was Marcion's expunging of a considerable number of
passages in the book of Luke that acted as at least one impetus, if not
the primary impetus, for the initial New Testament canonizing process.[40] Furthermore, a work that lacked the proper textual content, particularly doctrinal, would certainly not find its way into the canon.
Therefore, broadly speaking the two processes are not wholly separable. However, the growth of the canon is not commensurate with, as is
so often assumed, the stabilization of the biblical text.[41] Although it
cannot be denied that the broader textual form of the New Testament—

40. Whereas the majority of scholars would maintain that Marcion played at
least some role in the development of the New Testament canon, more recent work
has tended to marginalize the centrality of A. von Harnack's picture of Marcion as
the chief impetus for canonization. For the traditional view of Marcion's influence
upon canon, see A. von Harnack, *Marcion: Das Evangelium vom fremden Gott*
(TU, 45; Leipzig: J.C. Hinrichs, 2nd edn, 1924), pp. 151, 441*-444*; *idem, The
Origin of the New Testament* (trans. J.R. Wilkinson; New York: Macmillan; London: Williams and Norgate, 1925), pp. 30-33; J. Knox, *Marcion and the New Tes-
tament: An Essay in the Early History of the Canon* (Chicago: University of
Chicago Press, 1942), pp. 19-38; and von Campenhausen, *Christian Bible*, pp. 148,
153, 163. Fore more modern appraisals limiting Marcion's influence, see D.L.
Balás, 'Marcion Revisited: The "Post-Harnack" Perspective', in W.E. March (ed.),
Texts and Testaments: Critical Essays on the Bible and Early Church Fathers (San
Antonio, TX: Trinity University Press, 1980), pp. 102-105; McDonald, *Biblical
Canon*, pp. 154-61; Kümmel, *Introduction to the New Testament*, pp. 487-88;
W. Schneemelcher, 'History of the New Testament Canon', in W. Schneemelcher
(ed.), *New Testament Apocrypha*, I (2 vols.; trans. R.McL. Wilson; Philadelphia:
Westminster Press; London: Lutterworth, 1963 [1959]), pp. 33-36; Grant, *Histori-
cal Introduction*, pp. 27-28.

41. For support of this view, see G.W. Anderson, 'Canonical and Non-Canonical', in P.R. Ackroyd and C.F. Evans (eds.), *The Cambridge History of the Bible:
From the Beginnings to Jerome*, I (3 vols.; Cambridge: Cambridge University
Press, 1970), p. 117 who states, 'The Growth of the Canon is not identical with the
growth of the literature, even if the two processes are not wholly separable'. Anderson later adds, although now referring specifically to the Old Testament, '[I]t is
clear that at least a generation earlier the contents of the prophetic part of the Canon
had substantially been assembled, and that it had taken its place alongside the Pentateuch as a collection of sacred scriptures whose limits had been defined though its
text had not yet been finally fixed'. See also pp. 128 and 148. It is this same point
that is now being made for the New Testament.

understood at a more contextual, literary and theological level—served some role and had some prerogative in the minds of the biblical canonizers, the detailed task defined by the tenets of New Testament textual criticism—being the establishment of the original text—was apparently not of primary importance to those involved in this process at this time. Instead, this latter task continued *after* the formalization of the New Testament canon and still continues even to this day. The fact that those involved in the canonical process did not attempt to sanction or endorse one 'standard text', but instead continued to allow some degree of textual diversity is strong support for the above point. Whereas the process of canonization established which group of biblical books were to be authoritative for the life and teaching of the Church, textual criticism establishes the specific text of those individual books deemed to be closest to the originals. In agreement with this point is J.K. Elliott whose words are worth quoting at length:

> [T]he *text* of the New Testament that was found in the manuscripts was not of importance to those who pronounced on the canon. Jerome, Origen and others recognized certain books as approved, canonical scripture, but they did not try to specify a particular or precise form of the text to be found in the manuscripts even though these Fathers were alert to textual variation in manuscripts. As we know, the surviving manuscripts exhibit a marked difference between themselves—and this is especially true of the earliest manuscripts (precisely in the centuries before the canon was fixed). So what was fixed as canonical was 'Mark' without further qualification. The question was not raised whether Mark is to include 16.9-20 or not. 'John' was approved without a word being said about the inclusion or exclusion of the passage about the adulteress (Jn 7.53–8.11). In effect, the manuscript an individual church possessed was canonical; a neighboring church may have had radically different forms of the same books and these would be its canonical scriptures.[42]

Elliott goes on to point out that from the fourth century onwards the New Testament canon was essentially agreed, with a few exceptions in the Syriac or Ethiopic churches. Therefore, one could generally expect that the complete New Testament corpus consisted of the same 27 books, and a Pauline manuscript would contain the same 14 books (including Hebrews), or a manuscript of the Catholic Epistles would contain the same 7 letters. Elliott further states that since the invention

---

42. J.K. Elliott, 'Manuscripts, the Codex and the Canon', *JSNT* 63 (1996), pp. 112-13.

of the printing press an edition of the New Testament always contains the same 27 books; however, he goes on to add that:

> Obviously the same text is not always to be found: the Textus Receptus and Westcott and Hort's Greek testament do not agree throughout. In English the text in the AV (KJV) on one side and modern editions like RV, RSV, NIV, GNB on the other side differ in their textual base and textual decisions. But the titles of the works included in the New Testament are the same on the contents pages of all these editions.[43]

Metzger provides further support of this view when, after pointing out the textual diversity and various text-types found among the New Testament manuscripts, he asks what attitude with respect to the canon should be taken toward these several types of texts. 'Is one type of text to be regarded as the canonical text', asks Metzger, 'and if so, what authority should be accorded variant readings which differ from that text?'[44] He then goes on to consider the Church Fathers' attitude to this question and explains that, on the one hand, as far as certain readings involve sensitive points of doctrine, the Fathers often alleged that heretics had tampered with the accurate text. On the other hand, the question of the canonicity of a document apparently did not arise in connection with discussion of such variant readings even though they might involve considerable portions of text. Using Mk 16.9-20 as an example, Metzger explains that the pericope is not found in the oldest Greek, Latin, Syriac, Coptic or Armenian witnesses, and when it does appear in a manuscript it is often marked with asterisks or obeli indicating its spurious status. Eusebius and Jerome, points out Metzger, both well aware of the manuscript variation for this passage, discuss which form of text was to be preferred. However, neither Father suggested that one form was canonical and the other non-canonical. Furthermore, adds Metzger, the perception that the canon was basically closed did not lead to a slavish fixing of the text of the canonical books.[45] Metzger later concludes:

---

43. Elliott, 'Codex and the Canon', p. 113.

44. Metzger, *Canon of the New Testament*, p. 267.

45. Metzger, *Canon of the New Testament*, pp. 267-69. See also Hahneman who, drawing attention to Eusebius's *Ecclesiastical History*, asserts that Eusebius was more concerned with 'higher' rather than 'lower' criticism. For Eusebius, the issues of authorship and authenticity of the New Testament books, rather than the comparison of variant readings, were of greater concern. The determining factor for

In short, it appears that the question of canonicity pertains to the document *qua* document, and not to one particular form or version of that document. Translated into modern terms, Churches today accept a wide variety of contemporary versions as the canonical New Testament, though the versions differ not only as to rendering but also with respect to the presence or absence of certain verses in several of the books.[46]

R.E. Murphy takes a similar stance when he asks what is canonical—the book or the text? He answers by stating that

> Personally, I think canonicity refers to a book, whatever be the form of text (which can be determined only by textual criticism)... Writing for the New Testament is the tradition of the Word of God which occurred in Law and Promise—a tradition that was not exactly determined either in its text or in its extent.[47]

In similar fashion, Gregory points out in his classic work on the New Testament text and canon that the criticism of the canon delineates the extent of the writings with which we have to deal. Study of the canon affords one with the needed insights into the circumstances which accompanied the origin of these writings and examines not only the favorable judgment passed upon them, but also the adverse judgment that fell to the lot of other, in a certain measure similar, writings. However, with the criticism of the canon settled upon large lines, and with a circle drawn around the object of study, one next turns to the consideration of the text. Gregory then explains that, 'The criticism of the text, if we may play upon the words, must do intensively that which the criticism of the canon does extensively; the canon touches the exterior, the text the interior'.[48]

---

his attitude toward 'canonicity' lay almost exclusively in a book's use by the churches or other Christian writers. See G.M. Hahneman, *The Muratorian Fragment and the Development of the Canon* (OTM; Oxford: Clarendon Press, 1992), pp. 137-38. See also R.M. Grant and D. Tracy, *A Short History of the Interpretation of the Bible* (London: SCM Press, 2nd edn, 1984), p. 138 where they claim that textual criticism was rarely done well in the ancient Church, perhaps indirectly legitimating the statement that this was not likely a foundational concern in canonization.

46. Metzger, *Canon of the New Testament*, p. 270.

47. R.E. Murphy, 'A Symposium on the Canon of Scripture. I. The Old Testament Canon in the Catholic Church', *CBQ* 28 (1966), pp. 189-93 (191).

48. Gregory, *Canon and Text*, pp. 1-2. See also R.H. Bainton, 'The Bible in the Reformation: "Sola Scriptura"', in S.L. Greenslade (ed.), *The Cambridge History of the Bible: The West from the Reformation to the Present Day*, III (3 vols.;

In contrast to this view, Sanders indicates that for the Old Testament, but perhaps with implications for the New, 'Stabilization of the Old Testament text and canon had parallel developments, each informing the other'.[49] For the New Testament, text and canon may have had parallel developments, perhaps the occasions and reasons for the induced stabilization of the one being the same for the other; however, after the final fixing of the canon, although a growing emphasis was placed upon textual stability there was still a significant toleration of fluidity as is evidenced by the various New Testament text-types. As Vaganay and Amphoux contend:

> [I]t can be seen that the diversification of texts continued from the fourth to the ninth centuries in spite of all efforts to prevent it. The great recensions channeled, as it were, the streams of the manuscript tradition but they were far from obtaining the unification of the text; and to make things worse, they widened the gap between the texts in use and the original.[50]

Cambridge: Cambridge University Press, 1963), p. 10 who appears to take a similar stance.

49. Sanders, 'Old Testament and New', p. 381; see also J.A. Sanders, 'Canon, Hebrew Bible', *ABD* 1 (1992), p. 843. It may be helpful to point out for the Old Testament that despite clear indications of any major departure from the canonical corpus accepted by Palestinian Jewry, Qumran's biblical *text* and the Palestinian biblical *text* lack consensus at a period of decisive importance for the final definition of the Old Testament canon, and may be problematic for Sanders's declaration. For example, the stories of Bel and the Dragon and of Susanna, and the Song of the Three Holy Children appear not to have been included in manuscripts of Daniel found at Qumran. Similarly, several manuscripts containing canonical psalms (2QPs[a] and 4QPs[f]) also included apocryphal psalms and other extra-canonical material. However, although these textual discrepancies may dispel the idea of a standardization in the Old Testament text at the height of canonizing activity, the fact that the community at Qumran was an apocalyptic Jewish sect may also attest to this lack of textual congruity. With the sect's withdrawal from the main body of Judaism in the latter half of the second century BCE one might assert that these textual distinctions simply constitute one more of the various features that marked Qumran off from the rest of Judaism. See Anderson, 'Canonical and Non-canonical', pp. 149-53; and Scanlin, 'Canonical Shape of the Old Testament', p. 209.

50. Vaganay and Amphoux, *Introduction to New Testament Textual Criticism*, p. 16. In fact, Vaganay and Amphoux divide their work on the history of the written text into three separate sections including: (1) the period of relative freedom (to 313 CE); (2) the period of limited control (313 CE–around 850 CE); and (3) the period of standardization (850 CE–the sixteenth century).

The conclusion of the canonizing process far from marks the beginning of a monolithic New Testament text. With its differing textual strands and myriad of readings, not even the Byzantine text can be seen as such.[51] In fact, rather than directly linking the stabilization of the New Testament text to canonization, several scholars claim that the text's standardization and the development of text-types *began* instead as a result of the Diocletian edict in 303 CE ordering all sacred Christian books to be destroyed by fire. When peace was at last restored under Constantine the need for a mass-production of new manuscripts within the newly developed church scriptoria resulted in some degree of standardization.[52]

Once again, the question of a document's canonical status did not arise in direct connection with discussion of that document's specific textual form. Though the stabilization of the New Testament text may well have begun alongside the final fourth-century process of canonization, in many ways it still acted independently of that process. It seems more likely, however, that for both the Old and New Testaments the completion of their respective canonization processes marked the beginning of a renewed effort to address matters of textual discrepancy on a more thorough basis and to seek more earnestly some degree of standardization between the various textual traditions. Because the evidence seems to point more to the idea that these two processes—the finalization of the canon and the standardization of the text—occurred

51. See Metzger's remarks regarding von Soden and the various differing texts of the Byzantine family, yet all considered authoritative, in Metzger, *Canon of the New Testament*, pp. 267-68. See also Aland and Aland, *Text of the New Testament*, pp. 55-56.

52. See Aland and Aland, *Text of the New Testament*, pp. 70-71; and Vaganay and Amphoux, *Introduction to New Testament Textual Criticism*, p. 111. Interestingly enough, a number of scholars contend that it was this same historical circumstance that marked the *last* step in the finalization of the canon. For example, see W.R. Farmer, *Jesus and the Gospel: Tradition, Scripture, and Canon* (Philadelphia: Fortress Press, 1982), pp. 177-96; B.M. Metzger, 'Canon of the New Testament', in F.C. Grant and H.H. Rowley (eds.), *Hastings Dictionary of the Bible* (Edinburgh: T. & T. Clark, 2nd edn, 1963), p. 125; A.C. Sundberg, 'Canon of the New Testament', in K. Crim (ed.), *IDBSup* (Nashville: Abingdon Press, 1976), pp. 139-40; R.W. Hoover, 'How the Books of the New Testament Were Chosen', *BibRev* 9 (1993), p. 47; and McDonald, *Biblical Canon*, pp. 178-90; contra G.A. Robbins, '"Fifty Copies of the Sacred Writings" (*VC* 4.36): Entire Bibles or Gospel Books?', *StudPat* 19 (1989), pp. 97-98.

consecutively rather than simultaneously, with the former possibly acting as the impetus for the latter, there is an inherent freedom within the concept of canon for judgments to be made concerning textual matters. The original textual form or the exact textual form of the New Testament was not a priority for the finalization of the canon. No one text or text-type was given canonical status, rather, it was the larger literary units—the biblical books—to which canonicity was attributed. In the light of these points, one might justifiably posit that the canonical text can be that very same text which is sensitive to text-critical concerns. The concept of an original text need not be undermined by those individuals who invest authority in a later ecclesiastical or canonical text. When one understands that canonization did not authorize or sanction one specific text or text-type, even an early or reconstructed text can be equally regarded as canonical. Indeed, few would question the canonical status of critical editions such as the United Bible Societies' *Greek New Testament* or Nestle–Aland's *Novum Testamentum Graece*. The New Testament canon allows a degree of flexibility wherein questions concerning the nature of the text can be openly raised and satisfied. This is the same notion that the early Church Fathers had as well. When the New Testament canon was closed, regardless of the final dating of this process (for it was no single event), it did not mean that the issues concerning the text of the New Testament became irrelevant or were suddenly jettisoned. To question the text of the New Testament does not necessarily imply a questioning of the New Testament canon; conversely, to question the canon of the New Testament need not imply a questioning of the New Testament text.

Before moving on to the next area of discussion, it might be appropriate to briefly deal with, and perhaps circumvent, a number of difficulties that might be seen as problematic for the previous affirmations. First, one finds within a number of the canonical lists a system of stichometry (cf. the Clermont Canon found in Codex Claromontanus D^P [c. 303–67]; the African Cheltenham or Mommsen Canon [c. 365–90]; the Syriac Canon [c. 400]; the Roman Canon [c. 400]; and the Stichometric Canon of Nicephorus [c. 850]).[53] These

---

53. στίχοι were a standard unit of measure used to determine the length of a literary work. One στίχος was equivalent to approximately sixteen syllables or about thirty-six letters. See B.M. Metzger, *Manuscripts of the Greek Bible: An Introduction to Paleography* (Oxford: Oxford University Press, 1981), pp. 38-40;

stichometrical notations or numbers served several purposes including (a) indicating the length of a discourse or book, (b) establishing a standard of payment for scribes, (c) determining the price of a book, (d) aiding one to find the general location of a particular passage, and (e) guarding against later interpolations and excisions.[54] Despite the fact that stichometry was used as a means to guard against the possibility of later additions and omissions of text, there are a number of difficulties in using stichometry to closely associate the text and canon of the New Testament: (1) stichometrical notation may vary between differing geographical locations and scribal centers; (2) comparison of the various stichometric canon lists themselves reveals variation, which is at times significant; (3) the stichoi are not infrequently at fault;[55] (4) a number of the stichometric lists are of later provenance than what is generally considered to be the latter stages of the New Testament canonization process; and (5) the stichometric lists may point out the canonical status of larger textual accretions such as Mk 16.9-20 and Jn 7.53–8.11 but reveal nothing about variations found in smaller textual portions such as individual words or sentences.[56]

A second problem that may call into question the distinction that has been drawn between text and canon is raised by Fornberg in his discussion of Justin Martyr's *Dialogue*. In this dialogue with Trypho, Justin accuses the Jews of (a) rejecting the LXX and attempting 'to frame another' type of text in its place, and (b) deleting from Scripture several passages due to their christological importance. Justin states:

> But I am far from putting reliance in your teachers, who refuse to admit that the interpretation made by the seventy elders who were with Ptolemy [king] of the Egyptians is a correct one; and they attempt to frame another. And I wish you to observe, that they have altogether taken away many Scriptures from the translations effected by those seventy elders who were with Ptolemy, and by which this very man who

H.B. Swete, *An Introduction to the Old Testament in Greek* (Cambridge: Cambridge University Press, 2nd edn, 1914), pp. 344-66; Lake, *Text of the New Testament*, pp. 60-61; and Kenyon, *Handbook*, p. 98 and n. 1.

54. See Metzger, *Manuscripts*, p. 39.

55. For these first three points, see individuals such as Souter, *Text and Canon*, p. 225; Hahneman, *Muratorian Fragment*, p. 141; Metzger, *Manuscripts*, p. 39; Lake, *Text of the New Testament*, p. 61; and H.K. McArthur, 'The Earliest Divisions of the Gospels', *StudEv* 3 (1964), p. 272.

56. See Metzger, *Manuscripts*, p. 39; and Lake, *Text of the New Testament*, p. 61.

was crucified is proved to have been set forth expressly as God, and
man, and as being crucified, and as dying; but since I am aware that this
is denied by all of your nation, I do not address myself to these points,
but I proceed to carry on my discussions by means of those passages
which are still admitted by you (*Dial.* 71).[57]

Fornberg concludes from this excerpt that,

Thus, for Justin it is not enough to state which books he considered
canonical; he emphasized that he meant the LXX... Thus, in the second
century, the exact wording of the inspired text became important... We
soon got a collection of inspired texts, the wording of which was fixed
once and for all. The next step was the establishing of a canon corresponding to the Jewish one.[58]

Unfortunately, there are a number of problems with Fornberg's conclusion that Justin regarded the question of the Old Testament canon to be
clearly tied to the question of one single text (i.e. the LXX). First, the
specific issue of canon or canonization comes nowhere into the context
of Justin's statements but can only be assumed by his endorsement of
the LXX over another unspecified canon. In fact, by placing the discussion into the context of canon, Fornberg seems to take it out of its
original setting since Justin moves quickly away from the excised
Scriptures and turns to those that he and Trypho both admit. Secondly,
Fornberg's assertion that the 'exact wording of the inspired text became
important' is an overstatement since Justin is commenting upon what
appears to be only a few christological references. In these few cases
the wording was no doubt vital for Justin's apologetical arguments.
However, it is a mistake to assume that he had in mind a monolithic
Septuagint text, or that he was making a concerted effort to deal with
matters of textual criticism on a wider scale. Fornberg's allegation that
we soon arrived at a collection of inspired texts whose wording was
fixed once and for all is likewise untenable since we have ample proof
to the contrary.[59] And thirdly, though it is clear that the Septuagint

---

57. Origen presents a similar argument regarding the distinction between the
Septuagint and the Jewish Scriptures, as well as excised passages, in *Ep.* 1, *ad
africanum*.

58. Fornberg, 'Some Problems', p. 49.

59. See here K. Aland, *The Problem of the New Testament Canon* (London:
A.R. Mowbray, 1962), pp. 5-7 who clearly points out that in the second century not
only did the Septuagint contain various forms of text, but even its canonical contents could be at variance. Thus, Fornberg's insinuation that Justin had one static

endeared itself to the early Church, the Jewish canon also enjoyed considerable repute as well. Some time later Augustine, finding it difficult to dismiss the Jewish canon's claim to authenticity, posited the view that both the Septuagint and the Jewish Scriptures were inspired (*Civ.* 18.42-43).

In summary of the previous considerations, Parvis asks, 'If we could reconstruct an "original" text, a text which had never been read in the Church, would we still have the text of the canonical Scripture?'[60] The answer to Parvis's question is affirmative. First, as the above argument endorses, the term 'canonical scripture' or any such phrase refers to the placement of authority upon certain biblical books regardless of their exact form of text. Secondly, there is clear evidence showing some degree of flexibility and freedom in the exact form of the New Testament text before, during and after the canonizing process, thus relativizing Parvis's question.

b. *The Diversity of the Canonical Text*

Another issue that occasionally arises in discussions of text and canon, which admittedly appears to occur more at the level of assumptions rather than outright statements, is the mistaken notion of *the* canonical text (definite) as opposed to *a* canonical text (indefinite).[61] Because the concept of canon had relatively little to do with the exact form of a book's text, but instead sought to address whether or not that book— understood at more contextual, literary and theological levels—could rightfully be included in a larger authoritative collection, it is more accurate to speak of *various* canonical texts rather than *one* canonical text. In fact, there is not *one* text which is canonical, but a multitude of canonical texts; nor is there one final form of text, but many final forms (one could perhaps even contend that the term 'canonical text' is an oxymoron which should be replaced by some other term such as 'canonical book' thereby further distancing the textual element from the notion of canon). The fixation of the canon did not presuppose the standardization of that canon's exact textual form. Instead, as the manuscript evidence from antiquity attests, both preceding and following the process of canonization, there were various text-types, not to

text or canon in mind during his dialogue with Trypho may be a mistaken notion.

60. Parvis, 'Goals of New Testament Textual Studies', p. 402.

61. For more general statements to this effect, see among others Aland and Aland, *Text of the New Testament*, pp. 51, 69.

mention a plethora of individual textual discrepancies and variants. Furthermore, though separate Christian communities used the same authoritative canon (and in some Christian communities, both anti- quated and contemporary, not even this can be asserted),[62] the particular text of the various communities found in the one authoritative canon could be at some variance. Although Origen and Jerome could conceiv- ably use the same canon of books, the particular text of those books need not be in the same language for both to be considered equally canonical (the text of one being in Greek and the other in Latin). There- fore, one cannot even claim that the canonization process resulted in the determination of what language a text must be written in to be deemed authoritative. The conclusion of the canonical process gave no precedence to the specific dialect of the text of that canon. Taking this into account, one may conclude that the concept of canon transcends both the textual form and the textual language. To go even further, two texts of varying accuracy can still be considered equally canonical since, as we have already explained, the particular text of the various communities found in the one authoritative canon could and did vary considerably. Ackroyd draws attention to this situation when he states,

> The relation of text to community of use is here clearly relevant; but already the question of 'true' text and 'deviant' text is an issue of some difficulty. One may observe that the text-form authoritative for a particu- lar community at a particular moment does not necessarily prove accept- able to another community either at that moment or subsequently.[63]

The dilemma that this plurality of texts poses for advocates of a later ecclesiastical or canonical text is clear. Which canonical text (should we even use this phrase?) is to be considered most authoritative? To add further confusion to the issue, with the incomplete knowledge we possess regarding the actual outworking of canonical criteria, the can- onization process and dates of the canon's formation, emphasizing the biblical text's final canonical shape becomes even more arduous. Does the canonical form constitute a second- or a fourth-century text? And what community's canon should act as the authoritative standard for the Church? But even more problematic is the question of whether terms such as 'canonical shape' or 'canonical form' are valid when

62. See here Elliott, 'Codex and the Canon', pp. 111-12 regarding differing Coptic, Ethiopic and Syriac canons.

63. Ackroyd, 'Original Text', p. 170.

referring directly to the biblical text and canonization, since text and canon are not commensurate. After explaining that 'the Christian church did not develop an official, ecclesiastical position regarding one particular text', Childs later seeks to sidestep the resultant plurality of later texts by further clarifying that the canonical text is the 'best-received text'.[64] However, as Metzger points out, 'Unfortunately Childs provides no analysis of a specific textual problem, nor does he define what he understands to be "the best received text?"'.[65] McDonald notes a similar problem in Childs's proposals when he states:

> The biggest problem that emerges in the application of Childs' canonical emphasis is finding the final acceptable form of the 'canonical' text of Scripture. What and where is that text?... Childs also has difficulty in identifying precisely what canonical community he has in mind in his work. Since the biblical canon emerged over a long period of time and since it took the church centuries to recognize our current NT canon, which is still not universally accepted by all Christians, we must ask again which canonical community he has in mind as the authoritative community for the church.[66]

The discipline of textual criticism can answer the problematic question of 'Which canon?' It plays a vital role in ascertaining which of the various forms is the most authoritative canonical text. The assumption that this text is the one that conforms most closely to the ancient autographs or earliest written apostolic witness is a given in this line of reasoning. And though it may be argued that a critical or eclectic text reconstructed to this end has never been endorsed by a past community of faith, it can be equally stressed that a critical or eclectic reconstruction of the original text may well be that text which most closely conforms to the original witnesses. This same point appears to be conceded by Childs who states:

> For the Christian church canonization was a derivative of christology. The New Testament scriptures gained their unique authority in their role as the apostolic and prophetic witness to Christ's death and resurrection

---

64. Childs, 'Hermeneutical Problem', pp. 526, 528.

65. Metzger, *Canon of the New Testament*, pp. 268-69.

66. McDonald, *Biblical Canon*, p. 307. This may be the most criticized aspect of Childs's canonical approach. For further criticism, see C. Tuckett, *Reading the New Testament: Methods of Interpretation* (London: SPCK, 1987), p. 182 n. 11; and J. Barr, 'Childs' Introduction to the Old Testament as Scripture', *JSOT* 16 (1980), p. 22.

which was also uniquely tied to the one specific period of his earthly life. The effect of the canonization of the Gospels [*sic.*, but even prior to their canonization] was that the growth of church tradition always was tested as to its conformity with the normative apostolic witness. Because the post-apostolic church struggled to maintain this apostolic witness in a pure form, the concern for a true text of the pristine testimony was constitutive for the Christian understanding of canon... Theoretically, the goal of text criticism, which is commensurate with its canonical role, is to recover that New Testament text which best reflects the true apostolic witness found in the church's scripture.[67]

Most textual critics, after applauding Childs's assertion, would conclude that a critical or eclectic text, despite never being used in a confessional setting, comes closest to approximating the early apostolic authority and written witness—certainly giving credence to its validity since apostolic authority preceded and gave birth to ecclesiastical authority. And although elements of eclecticism are problematic, the simple fact is that for the moment it is the best we can do in our attempt to restore the most authoritative biblical text for all communities of faith—that first given by the Apostles—and surely this endeavor should receive priority of pursuit. Similarly, an eclectic text—which can arguably still be considered canonical—is as valid as any one of the myriad other forms of canonical texts used throughout the Church's history (again, emphasis being laid on the point that there is not *one* canonical text and that canon is not constitutive of text). It might also be noted that the eclectic text embodied within the United Bible Societies' *Greek New Testament* as well as Nestle–Aland's *Novum Testamentum Graece* is not only endorsed by a wide ecumenical community, but also serves as the standard source text for Bible translation the world over. Accordingly, one might ask when a text becomes ecclesiastical.

Although the textual accretions added to a particular community's canon may be an accurate reflection of the beliefs of that community, it may not be an accurate reflection of the beliefs of the original author and community that gave rise to that text. Without the discipline of

---

67. Childs, 'Hermeneutical Problem', pp. 526-27. Although we have already pointed out the problem with Childs's view that 'text is commensurate with canon' by emphasizing the plurality of texts equally regarded as canonical, it is interesting to note that Childs's admission of the Church's concern for an 'original' pristine text at least somewhat calls into question proposals for a later canonical or ecclesiastical text.

textual criticism, it is possible that a text used by later communities of faith could conceivably be historically inaccurate, at least in terms of apostolic historicity. In response to why the understanding of Christian faith which we find in Paul is assumed to be superior to that which we find in later Christians, Best lucidly answers:

> It is for this reason that, though later understandings may seem to be more profound, and we cannot deny this possibility while we believe the Spirit guides the church and is still active in it, yet we must prefer the earlier understanding. Later understandings are necessary because every understanding is related to a context; our context is not the same as that of the first-century church. We have through the history of the church a succession of understandings; each of these represents a freezing of the tradition in a particular situation and context... Each later interpretation depends on, though in varying degrees, all the earlier interpretations; thus it is important to retain the earliest as the correction to the later. Without the existence of earlier interpretation to act as corrections on those which follow there is a danger of a continuous deviation from a true or original understanding into a later false one; this can take place imperceptibly.[68]

It goes without saying that the earliest interpretation commends the need for the earliest text. New Testament textual criticism, therefore, serves to preserve the scriptural foundation upon which was built early Church tradition and doctrine. As a discipline it allows for continuity between the early communities who first produced and used the biblical writings and our own present faith community. It is the textual level which should act as the point of continuity between all Christian communities for all time. Let flexibility and diversity lie at the level of interpretation and contemporization (both of which are in obvious need, as Best makes clear, of being in harmony with what has 'gone before'), rather than at the historically foundational level of the text. It is the text that acts as the standard, guideline or restrainer—whatever one chooses to call it—against interpretational and exegetical excess. That flexibility and diversity should be invested in the realm of interpretation and reappropriation is supported by the praxis of the early Christian communities where one sees such diversity in action. It is the text, and prior to this oral tradition, that acts as the 'hedge' surrounding biblical interpretation and the contemporization of meaning. As Bruce explains:

---

68. Best, 'Tradition and the Canon', p. 284.

It may be argued that the final canonical form is that which should be acknowledged as the valid standard of authority in the church. But the textual or historical critic will not be deterred from working back to the form in which the document first appeared, or as nearly as it is possible to get to that form. And it may equally be argued that, if apostolic authority is the chief criterion of canonicity in the New Testament, the form of the letter to the Romans (say) as Paul dictated it and Tertius wrote it down must be its most authoritative form. To be sure, where the Pauline letters are concerned, textual critics would be happy if they could establish the wording of the first edition of the Pauline corpus but even that (if attainable) would be pre-canonical.[69]

This type of reasoning need not provide prescriptive answers to the complicated hermeneutical issue of what the text *meant* versus what it now *means* since the question of 'what text' precludes the question of that text's meaning. In other words, the issue of what the text meant and what it now means lies more firmly within the latter discipline of hermeneutics rather than within the former discipline of textual criticism.

c. *The Canonical Status of Textual Accretions*
Few passages in the New Testament provide interpreters with such a bewildering array of difficulties as the longer Markan ending (Mk 16.9-20) and the Johannine pericope of the woman caught in adultery (Jn 7.53–8.11). The individual attempting to deal with these passages is faced with a range of problems including text, canon, and interpretation. Should textual accretions such as these—passages generally found in no primary early manuscript—form part of the Church's canon and confession as some scholars—particularly canonical critics—would assert?[70]

Those advocating the retention of these accretions within the biblical text have often based their arguments upon the rubric that such passages were considered canonical in the early Church. 'The practice of concluding the gospel of Mark at 16.8', explain the Alands, 'continued to be observed in some Greek manuscripts as well as in versional manuscripts for centuries, although the "longer ending" of Mark 16.9-20 was recognized as canonical and its contents must have made it

---

69. Bruce, *Canon of Scripture*, p. 287.

70. See other textual accretions such as Mt. 6.13; 16.2-3; Lk. 22.43-44; Jn 5.3-4; Acts 8.37; and 1 Jn 5.7-8.

extremely attractive'.[71] Contending that larger textual accretions should be included in the biblical text, Parvis asks:

> Should we excise from our New Testaments and from our liturgies the doxology of the Lord's Prayer because it is not part of the original text of St. Matthew's Gospel? I think not. The usage of the Church since ancient times has made a place for these words; it has canonized them. It would be the work of an overzealous critic to cavil at their use now. What about the long ending of the Gospel according to Saint Mark? Justin, Tatian, and Irenaeus all knew this ending. There is no reason to assume that it was not found in some copies of Mark when that Gospel was first accepted as canonical. If the Church could canonize the Gospel as a whole, why could she not canonize this part of it as well? The long ending is not, presumably, original, but neither, we may surmise, are certain Pauline glosses which have been accepted as an unquestioned part of our canonical Scriptures. Why cannot the *Pericope Adulterae* be said to be a part of our canonical Scripture? Why in critical texts and in English translations made from those critical texts does it have to be consigned to a footnote? It was canonized by the Church even though it had no place in the text of Saint John's Gospel.[72]

As has been argued throughout this essay, however, it cannot be maintained that these textual accretions were regarded as canonical by the early Church since the issue of their inclusion or exclusion into the biblical canon was not of primary significance to the discussion of canonization itself, but more specifically fell into the area of textual criticism. Elliott's earlier affirmation that what was fixed as canonical was 'Mark' without further qualifications still rings true. The question was not raised whether Mark was to include 16.9-20. 'John' was approved without a word being said about the inclusion or exclusion of the passage about the adulteress.[73] Those in the early Church involved in the process of canonization did not specifically rule upon these textual accretions. Consequently, there is freedom within the demarcations of the New Testament canon to allow for the text-critical consideration of these passages.

It is certainly true, as Parvis points out, that various Church Fathers cited a number of these textual additions in their writings.[74] However,

---

71. Aland and Aland, *Text of the New Testament*, p. 69.

72. Parvis, 'Goals of New Testament Textual Studies', p. 402.

73. See again n. 42 and its corresponding citation.

74. Irenaeus (c. 185; *Haer.* 3.10.6 = Mk 16.19) and Tatian (c. 170; in his Diatessaron) are the earliest witnesses to make clear use of the longer ending of

at the same time, other Fathers make no mention of them—even in contexts where it would be especially befitting to do so.[75] Parvis fails to

Mark. Tatian's teacher Justin Martyr (†c. 165; *1 Apol.* 1.45 = Mk 16.20) may also have been acquainted with the longer ending. However, one makes several mistakes in assuming that these writers saw the longer ending of Mark as canonical. First, all three wrote, if not prior to the canonization process, only at its beginning. Secondly, for a Father to cite a particular passage as Scripture (meaning writings which are held to be authoritative) far from proves that he regarded it as canonical (meaning a defined collection of Scripture to which nothing could be added and from which nothing could be removed). Usage does not indicate canonicity since many texts cited as Scripture were never canonized. On this last point, see the excellent work by A.C. Sundberg in articles such as, 'The "Old Testament": A Christian Canon', *CBQ* 30 (1968), pp. 147-48; *idem*, 'The Bible Canon and the Christian Doctrine of Inspiration', *Int* 29 (1975), p. 356; and *idem*, 'Towards a Revised History of the New Testament Canon', *StudEv* 4 (1968), pp. 453-54. Furthermore, the fact that Tatian felt free enough to harmonize the four individual Gospels in his Diatessaron indicates that they were treated more as sources rather than as canonical Scripture. Jerome (†419; *Pelag.* 2.17) not only included Jn 7.53–8.11 in his Vulgate (c. 383) but also states that the passage is found in the Gospel of John in many Greek and Latin codices. Other Fathers such as Pacian (†430; *De Conj. adult.* 2.6; *Faust.* 22.25 and 33.1) also refer to the passage.

75. Clement of Alexandria (†c. 215) and Origin (†254) show no knowledge of these verses in their extant writings; however, this evidence from silence is causal rather than special. Westcott and Hort, *Introduction to the New Testament*, p. 37 of appendix, point out that there is no trace of vv. 9-20 found in the voluminous works of other Fathers such as Athanasius (†373), Basil (†379), Gregory of Nazianzus (†c. 390), Gregory of Nyssa (†394), Cyril of Alexandria (†444) or Theodoret (†c. 466). They add that the silence of some of these authors may well be accidental, especially Theodoret, but hardly with all. Other individuals who refrain from citing portions of Mark's longer ending in contexts perfectly suited to their inclusion are Cyril of Jerusalem (†386; cf. *Catech.* 14.27-30 where, if known, Mk 16.19 would almost assuredly have been included) and Cyprian (†258; where the absence of Mk 16.16 in his baptismal discussions concerning heretics found in *Ep.* 58, 69, and 73 likely points to its unfamiliarity). Lucifer (†c. 371) and Hilary (†367), who have purer texts than any of the later fifth-century Latin Fathers, leave vv. 9-20 unnoticed—a silence that may be due to the absence of sufficient motives for quotation. The original form of the Eusebian canons as well as the Ammonian canons make no provision for numbering sections of the text after Mk 16.8. Although Tertullian (†c. 220) may allude to a number of verses in the longer ending (*Apol.* 21 = Mk 16.8, 20; *Praescrip.* 30 = Mk 16.16, 17, cf. 20; and *Prax.* 2.1 = Mk 16.19), it seems more likely that he used parallel passages for his sources (cf. *Test. anim.* 25 = Lk. 8.2 not Mk 16.9; and *Res.* 51 = Mk 12.36 not Mk 16.19). For the first thousand years of Christianity no Greek commentator, including

see that a book's attainment of canonical status had little to do with its specific text as such and was not necessarily a direct endorsement of one specific textual form. Although a large number of manuscripts include the longer Markan ending and the Pericope of the Adulteress, it is clear that other witnesses exclude both passages. Therefore, Parvis's argument can be turned against him by declaring that these later textual accretions should be excluded from the New Testament canon since they are absent in some manuscripts. In fact, the picture appears to correspond to our earlier assertion that, although separate Christian communities may have used the same authoritative canon, the particular text of the various communities found in that canon could vary. Once again, the process of canonization was not primarily concerned with the exact textual form of a book and this consideration should, therefore, be left in the realm of textual criticism. As Parvis notes, the Church canonized the Gospel of Mark 'as a whole', but we do not know if this 'whole' actually included Mk 16.9-20 because the issue was not of primary importance and was, therefore, not specifically addressed. The Church did not directly canonize the specific text or form of the text of the book, but the whole of the book itself. Therefore, all additions and glosses, including Pauline glosses, should be evaluated under text-critical criteria rather than canonical criteria. Although Parvis and others claim that particular texts were canonized, why do we not see these texts in a greater number of our most important New Testament manuscripts? And when the particular reading does appear, why is it often marked by asterisks or obeli? Apparently a considerable number

Origen (†254; *Joh.*), Chrysostom (†407; *Hom. in Joh.*) and Nonnus (†c. 400; *Par. Joannis*)—all of whom deal with the Gospel of John verse by verse—discusses Jn 7.53–8.11. Likewise, Tatian (c. 170) shows no knowledge of the passage in his Diatessaron. No mention of the passage is made by either Latin or Greek Fathers such as Tertullian (†c. 220; where, if known, it would likely appear in *Pudic.*), Cyprian (†258; where, if known, it would likely appear in *Ep.* 54), Irenaeus (†c. 185) and again Origen, although each discusses in detail the problems of discipline for adultery. Similarly, it does not appear to have been included as a part of the Gospel of Hilary (†367), Theodore of Mopsuestia (†428) or Cyril of Alexandria (†444). The earliest Greek writer to comment on the pericope, stating that it is not found in the most accurate copies of the Gospel, is Euthymius Zigabenus (c. 1118). It is, instead, the Latin and Western evidence that gives the passage any kind of support. The earliest primary witness to the pericope is the fifth-century Codex Bezae where it is found as a Western interpolation. Like Mk 16.9-20, Jn 7.53–8.11 is often marked with asterisks and obeli to show its doubtful authenticity.

of scribes, even after the process of canonization, held some reservations as to the canonical status of these various accretions. In addition, if one were to discontinue the attempt to reconstruct an original text and instead acknowledge the canonical status of later textual accretions, to what extent should we go and at what point do we stop accepting these later additions?

There are certainly no canonical lists that make explicit reference to the authoritative status of these larger textual accretions. And to the best of our knowledge, no early Father discusses these passages in direct relationship to the canon or the canonization process. In his article on Jn 7.53–8.11 and the problem of text and canon, Burge states:

> It would be helpful to know what Athanasius was thinking in his Easter Letter of 367. What copy of John was he reading? We know at least that when North Africa discussed the canon at the Third Council of Carthage (397) Augustine appreciated the text and suspected that anxious husbands had earlier removed it (so that it could not be abused by their wives!).[76]

If the reader is not careful, Burge's statement appears to provide exactly what we seek—a direct reference to a larger textual accretion in the context of canonical discussions. However, what Burge intends to say is that about the same time Augustine is involved in the Council of Carthage, in a completely separate context he writes 'Some of little faith, or rather enemies of the true faith, I suppose from a fear lest their wives should gain impunity in sin, removed from their MSS the Lord's act of indulgence to the adulteress' (*De Conjugiis adulterinis* 2.6). Unfortunately, Augustine's reference to Jn 7.53–8.11 has nothing at all to do with any council or canonical discussion. The aged words of Westcott still apply:

> Augustine's assertion as to the removal of the passage from the text of St. John, on prudential grounds, which has been maintained by the modern scholars who defend the genuineness of the passage, is wholly at variance with the cardinal facts of the history of the text of the New Testament. Willful corruptions of the apostolic writings, however recklessly they were imputed in controversy, are happily in fact all but unknown. Changes, and even such a change as the insertion of this passage, can be accounted for without recourse to the assumption of dishonesty.[77]

---

76. Burge, 'A Specific Problem', p. 148.
77. B.F. Westcott, *The Gospel According to St John* (London: John Murray,

Although we can find no early Father directly endorsing the canonical status of textual accretions such as Mk 16.9-20, Lk. 22.43-44 and
Jn 7.53–8.11, the situation appears to have changed at the much later
Council of Trent in 1545–1563. Here, apparently for the first time,
direct reference is made to the issue of text in the context of canon.[78]
During the fourth session (April, 1546) delegates firmly declared its list
of books 'as sacred and canonical in their entirety, *with all their parts*,
according to the text usually read in the Catholic Church and as they
are in the ancient Latin Vulgate'.[79] The phrase 'with all their parts'
qualified such passages as Mk 16.9-20, Lk. 22.43-44 and Jn 7.53–
8.11.[80] Commenting on this specific Tridentine decree, R.E. Brown and

1903), p. 142. See also Westcott and Hort, *Introduction to the New Testament*, p. 86
of the appendix, who claim that, 'The transcriptional evidence leads to the same
conclusion. Supposing the Section to have been an original part of St John's
Gospel, it is impossible to account reasonably for its omission. The hypothesis
taken for granted by Aug[ustine] and Nicon, that the Section was omitted as liable
to be understood in a sense too indulgent to adultery, finds no support either in the
practice of the scribes elsewhere or in Church History. The utmost license of the
boldest transcribers never makes even a remote approach to the excision of a complete narrative from the Gospels; and such rash omissions as do occur are all but
confined to the Western texts; while here the authorities for omission include all the
early Non-Western texts. Few in ancient times, there is reason to think, would have
found the Section a stumbling-block except Montanists and Novatians.' This latter
book is still one of the most detailed and extensive works dealing with the patristic
citations of Mk 16.9-20 and Jn 7.53–8.11.

78. Bruce, *Canon of Scripture*, p. 104 states that, 'This was probably the first
occasion on which a ruling on the canon of scripture was given by a general (or
ecumenical) council of the church, as opposed to a local or provincial council'.
However, it is well documented that this council was not in the true sense
'ecumenical'. Although Protestant states sent delegates, most of their demands
were dismissed since the primary decrees of the council were specifically framed to
combat Protestant statements. For various works commenting on this aspect of
Trent, see O. Chadwick, *The Reformation* (Penguin History of the Church, 3; Harmondsworth: Penguin Books, 1972), pp. 273-81; R.H. Bainton, *The Reformation of
the Sixteenth Century* (London: Hodder & Stoughton, 1953), p. 153; and P. John-
son, *A History of Christianity* (Harmondsworth: Penguin Books, 1976), pp. 299-
300.

79. R.E. Brown and R.F. Collins, 'Canonicity', in R.E. Brown, J.A. Fitzmyer,
and R.E. Murphy (eds.), *The New Jerome Biblical Commentary* (London: Geoffrey
Chapman, 1989), p. 1052.

80. See H. Jedin, *History of the Council of Trent* (vol. 2; London: Thomas Nelson, 1957–61), p. 81; P.G. Duncker, 'The Canon of the Old Testament at the

R.F. Collins explain that although the council Fathers and the authorities in Rome used the Vulgate as a yardstick, they were aware that the
translation contained errors and that not all copies of the Vulgate
agreed. They further point out that even the official Sixto-Clementine
Vulgate of 1592, produced in answer to Trent's request for a carefully
edited Vulgate, leaves much to be desired by modern standards; and in
many places it is not faithful to Jerome's original Vulgate. A further
difficulty is pointed out by Brown and Collins who ask: which Vulgate
is to serve as a guide when we raise the question of whether certain
passages or verses are canonical Scripture?[81] They explain:

> Both Jerome's Vg and the Sixto-Clementine Vg contained the long
> ending of Mark and the pericope of the adulteress, and Roman Catholic
> scholars have no real problem in accepting these passages as Scrip-
> ture...But in other instances, where the Sixto-Clementine Vg has pas-
> sages that Jerome's Vg did not have [Jn 5.4, and 1 Jn 5.7-8], the problem
> of acceptance should be settled on the grounds of scholarship rather than
> by any mechanical application of the principle of Trent, which was not
> meant to solve all difficulties or to end scholarly discussion. Roman
> Catholics must solve textual problems as others do, viz., by the laws of
> criticism—a principle that holds for other questions too (authorship,
> dating, history). The church's guidance covers primarily the meaning of
> Scripture for faith and morals.[82]

Brown and Collins provide a number of sound warnings; however, to
accept without question textual accretions because they are found in
both Jerome's Vulgate and the Sixto-Clementine Vulgate appears com-
parable to a 'mechanical application of the principle of Trent'. If
textual criticism is to be performed at all, should one not consider all
passages? Is it not somewhat subjective for modern criticism to declare
that only certain larger accretions be exempt from text-critical investigation and at the same time be deemed canonical, while other less
significant passages undergo text-critical inquiry? In addition, there is
probably little need to point out—whether for right or for wrong—that
few Protestant Christians would endorse the decrees of Trent. Regardless, to accept the longer accretions because Jerome included them in
his Vulgate—although various other Fathers did not—should this not

---

Council of Trent', *CBQ* 15 (1953), pp. 280-81, 292; and Brown and Collins,
'Canonicity', p. 1052.
    81. Brown and Collins, 'Canonicity', p. 1052.
    82. Brown and Collins, 'Canonicity', p. 1052.

mean the canonical acceptance of the Latin translation itself? Despite this being the actual position adopted at Trent (and later promulgated at the first Vatican Council of 1869–70) few Catholic or Protestant scholars would accede to this—particularly when the quality of text is considered in the light of our oldest extant Greek and Hebrew manuscripts.[83]

John 7.53–8.11 poses further problems for scholars where the consensus appears to be that this pericope is a genuine *agraphon* of Jesus that floated alongside the early written tradition until it was later included into the text.[84] Given the antiquity and importance of this text, a number of individuals have deemed it worthy of canonical status.[85] However, the task of textual criticism is not to authenticate the oral traditions or early sayings that existed prior to the original apostolic text, but to authenticate the text itself. In addition, various other non-canonical writings may well contain or record early Jesus material, yet few would give credence to their inclusion in the canon. If, in the light of this text's antiquity, we were to include it into the New Testament, could the same criteria be applied to numerous other works presently excluded from the canon? Decisions of this nature need to be grounded more firmly on the basis of text-critical concerns rather than on canonical concerns since most would adjudicate that the canonizing process has been completed as well as closed. If text-critical inquiry can affirm the inclusion of this passage into the New Testament text, then sobeit, thus vindicating its antiquity, authenticity and edificatory value. If not, the passage should remain excluded (or, at least identified as a secondary, even if early, tradition) although it may well be a genuine Jesus *agraphon* or oral tradition—that is, unless we are willing to re-open the

83. For affirmation of this point, see E.F. Sutcliffe, 'The Council of Trent on the *Authentia* of the Vulgate', *JTS* 49 (1948), pp. 35-42; and Bruce, *Canon of Scripture*, pp. 247-48.

84. For this view, see C.K. Barrett, *The Gospel According to St John* (London: SPCK, 1962), p. 491; J.H. Bernard, *A Critical and Exegetical Commentary on the Gospel According to St John* (ICC; 2 vols.; Edinburgh: T. & T. Clark, 1928), p. 719; E.C. Hoskyns and F.N. Davey, *The Fourth Gospel* (London: Faber and Faber, 1948), pp. 565-66; J. Marsh, *Saint John* (Harmondsworth: Penguin Books, 1968), p. 684; Bruce, *Canon of Scripture*, p. 289; Metzger, *Commentary*, p. 188; Westcott and Hort, *Introduction to the New Testament*, p. 87 of appendix; and Burge, 'A Specific Problem', p. 148.

85. See Bruce, *Canon of Scripture*, p. 289; and Burge, 'A Specific Problem', p. 148.

New Testament canon. Burge pinpoints the primary issue in his statement concerning Jn 7.53–8.11:

> If our notion of canonical authority rests in the books of the Bible themselves—that is, in those literary units called gospels and epistles penned by inspired authoritative authors (so Irenaeus)—then our passage cannot be a part of the canon. The textual evidence conforms to what a literary study only suggests: The Passage is an insertion.[86]

All this is not to say that these textual accretions play no part in the study of the biblical text or that they should be, as Burge facetiously states, 'relegated to the graveyard of quietly dismissed passages'.[87] On the contrary, they play an essential role in our understanding of Church history, doctrinal development and the unfolding textual tradition. Whereas disciplines such as source- and form-criticism, although beginning from a critically reconstructed text, put exegetical energies into the 'pre-autographal' form of that text by emphasizing oral tradition, ur-texts and early sources, one would do well to endeavor to provide insights into a 'post-autographal' form of text as well. In support of this view, Fee states,

> A knowledge of the history of textual variation will also help the interpreter to see how a passage was understood during the early history of the Church. In many instances variant readings are a reflection of a scribe's or a church's theological interests, and sometimes such changes put one in direct contact with historical exegesis.[88]

In similar fashion Ropes adds:

> Without an adequate history of the text the determination of that text remains insecure. But textual history also has intrinsic value, for it is a true, though minor, branch of Church history. As an account of the development of one phase of the life and activity of the Church it is significant for its own sake, and not unworthy to take a place beside the history of liturgies or creeds or vestments. Not only does it abundantly illustrate the history of biblical exegesis, but in it many characteristic traits of the thought and aspiration of successive ages may be studied from original sources.[89]

86. Burge, 'A Specific Problem', p. 148.
87. Burge, 'A Specific Problem', p. 145.
88. Fee, 'Textual Criticism of New Testament', p. 3.
89. Ropes, 'The Text of Acts', p. vii.

In the light of these points, a critical edition with apparatus becomes the best vehicle to record these important accretions and from this platform the text's historical development could provide the biblical scholar and theologian alike with further material to carry out their investigations. Furthermore, in making a moderate shift in methodology, a more text-critically sensitive canonical approach could become an even greater asset to New Testament studies by emphasizing not just a text's canonical history/shape and post-canonical history/shape, but its pre-canonical history/shape as well. In other words, Childs's canonical approach could provide further insight into a text's history and development, already one important endeavor of New Testament textual criticism, by explaining how and why later accretions such as Mk 16.9-20 and Jn 7.53–8.11 arose and the impact these additions had upon that community's faith, development of doctrine, and praxis. Literary or canonical shaping as envisaged by individuals like Childs (i.e. that process whereby the literature developed beyond its original shape and early stages to reflect a different canonical shape that had new theological significance for later communities) could be explained in this light. Both textual and canonical criticism could work in unison in seeking to answer questions regarding the text's history and development. If we understand that no manuscript—regardless of its supposed 'accuracy'—is without some type of editorial revision which was intended to contemporize the message of the text so as to speak to the later faith community, the discipline of textual criticism and the insights it provides into a text's history take on a new importance. Nothing is lost to the canonical approach, and, in fact, the traditional emphasis upon the relatedness of text and canon found in many early biblical introductions is refurbished and reaffirmed, albeit in somewhat of a new guise.

4. *Conclusion*

This essay has sought to defend the legitimacy of textual criticism's traditional pursuit of an 'original' text. Despite recognized problems associated with this endeavor, this essay has attempted to show that alternative approaches—primarily the pursuit of a later ecclesiastical or canonical text—are equally prone to misgivings. The foundational premises of those advocating an ecclesiastical or canonical text are open to serious question. First, one must cautiously recognize that canon is not prescriptive for text; nor is canonization directly commensurate with textual stabilization. Therefore, the former allows a degree of freedom wherein the latter can operate. Secondly, there is not *one* single canonical text but a diversity of canonical texts; nor is there one final ecclesiastical form of text. Therefore, textual criticism as traditionally defined seeks to adjudicate to some measure on this resulting plurality of texts and allows for continuity between past and present faith communities. Thirdly, the appropriation of accretions into the New Testament text cannot be legitimated on the grounds that they are 'canonical' or were 'canonized'. One would do better to base such decisions on the more objective findings of textual criticism. McDonald aptly summarizes these various considerations when he states:

> Childs' focus on the biblical text at the end of the canonical process, which includes the redactional material added to the writer's original message and intentions, is at variance with the perspective of the very canonical community he is anxious to preserve. Why should the second through the fourth-century additions to the biblical text be added to the canon base of the church or be given equal weight to those of the apostolic community? Has the authoritative base of the church shifted from Jesus and those who first knew him to include equally the redactors of later generations? Does that not fly in the face of all that the earliest Christian community believed they were recognizing in the first place? What else does the criterion of apostolicity suggest if not that? Why should the text of a later generation of Christians, which admittedly has been corrupted by mistakes, glosses, and deliberate changes, be given priority over the earliest recoverable text? Childs does not answer this question satisfactorily. His work, in practice, if not in principle, denies the valuable work of the textual critics as well as the historical critics who have made great strides in recovering the historical context, date, authorship, and provenance of many of the biblical writings, all of which have aided significantly in our ability to understand the meaning of the text.[90]

90. McDonald, *Biblical Canon*, p. 307.

INDEXES

INDEX OF REFERENCES

OLD TESTAMENT

NEW TESTAMENT

OTHER ANCIENT REFERENCES

INDEX OF AUTHORS